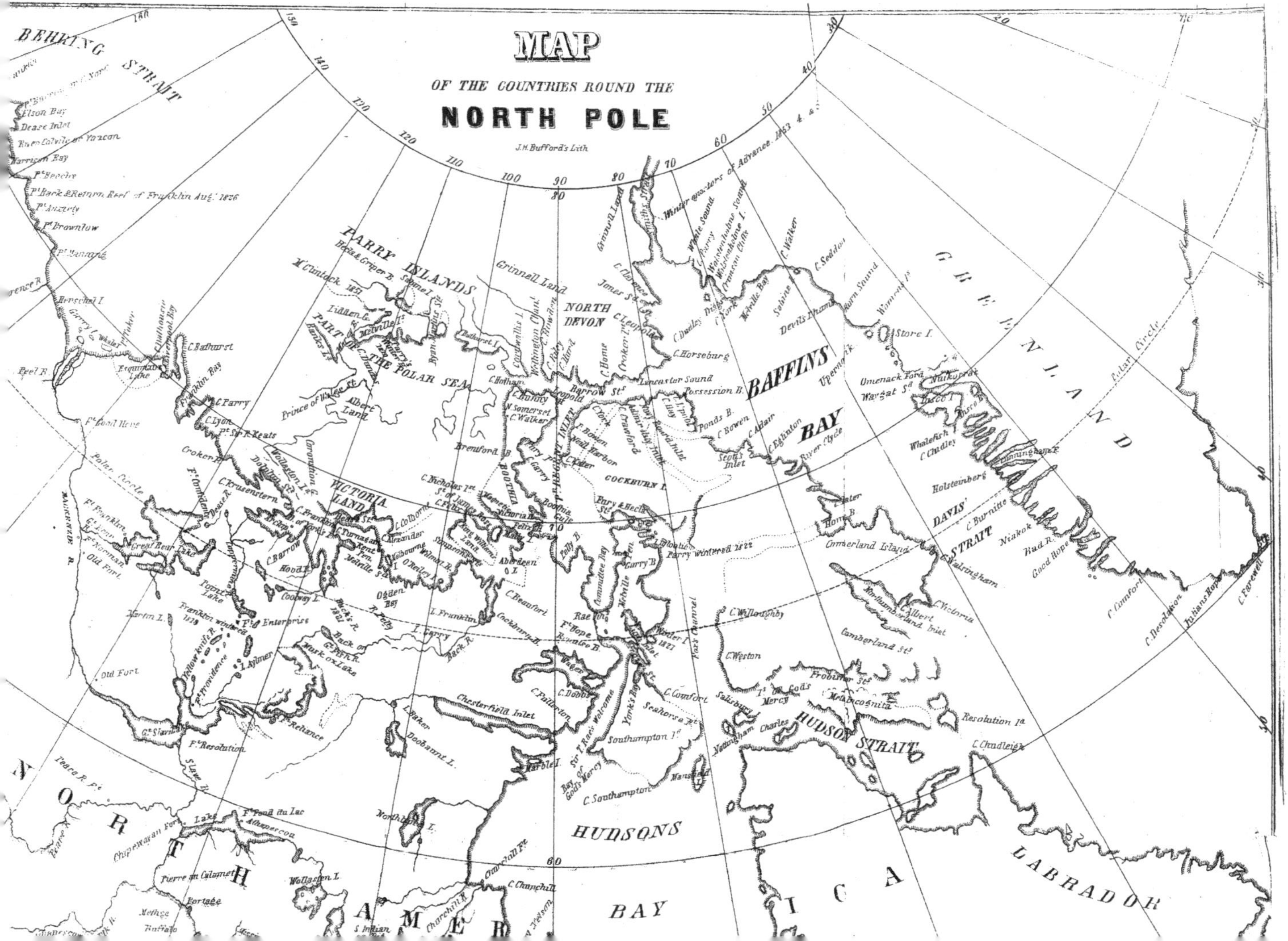

MAP OF THE COUNTRIES ROUND THE NORTH POLE

J. H. Bufford's Lith.

ARCTIC ADVENTURE

BY SEA AND LAND.

ELISHA KENT KANE.
The American Arctic Discoverer

ARCTIC ADVENTURE

BY SEA AND LAND

FROM

The Earliest Date to the Last Expeditions

IN SEARCH OF

SIR JOHN FRANKLIN.

EDITED BY

EPES SARGENT.

WITH MAPS AND ILLUSTRATIONS.

BOSTON:
PHILLIPS, SAMPSON & COMPANY.
LONDON: SAMPSON LOW, SON & CO.
M DCCC LVII.

Stereotyped by
HOBART & ROBBINS,
NEW ENGLAND TYPE AND STEREOTYPE FOUNDERY,
BOSTON.

PREFACE.

The interest in the history of Arctic adventure created by the various expeditions in search of Sir John Franklin, has been wonderfully increased, of late, by the deeply interesting narrative of Dr. Kane. Presented to the public in two elegant volumes, and embellished with some three hundred engravings and wood-cuts, conveying new and striking illustrations of the characteristics of Arctic scenery, this work is at once an honor to the American press and to the much-lamented author, who exhibited the rare union of those Cæsar-like gifts which make both the successful man of action and the skilful historian. To Messrs. Childs & Peterson, of Philadelphia, the liberal publishers, we are indebted for the wood-cuts which illustrate that chapter in the present work devoted to Kane's expedition.

No one, we believe, can lay down Dr. Kane's book, after perusal, without a strong desire to know something more of Arctic adventure — something of the preliminary parts of a history, of which his volumes form the fascinating sequel. It has certainly been our fortune to hear this desire expressed by many, and we have prepared the present work to meet an actual demand. To the narratives of Ross, Parry, Franklin, Beechey, Back, and other explorers — to Sir John Barrow's abstract of Arctic voyages — to the different publications on Arctic subjects of the Messrs. Chambers, of Edinburgh, and of Nelson & Sons, of London — to the British quarterly reviews, magazines, and journals — we have been largely indebted; in many instances adopting, without alteration, the language in which events are narrated. Still, with all our obligations, no small amount of original labor and research has been found necessary, in order to render our narrative clear and complete.

It would be unjust if we did not mention, in this connection, our indebtedness to Lieutenant Sherard Osborn, the latest Arctic historian, who, in his account of M'Clure's expedition, and of the discovery of a north-west passage, has given us the record of achievements the magnitude of which has been hardly appreciated as yet. The world looked for the dénouement of a personal tragedy; and turns, with comparative indifference, from the solution of the great geographical problem of the last three centuries.

TABLE OF CONTENTS.

NORTH POLE
West 180 East
KAMTSCHATKA
N. AMERICA
ASIA
SIBERIA
EUROPE
Behrings St
Kotzebue Sd
Colville R.
Mackenzie R.
Coppermine R.
Kolyma R.
C. Chelagskoi
Siberian Is
Lena R.
Yenisei R.
Obi R.
Waigats St
NOVA ZEMBLA
Melville I.
Mag. Pole
Boothia
Regent Inlt
Barrow St
Repulse B.
Southampton I.
HUDSONS BAY
Hudsons St
BAFFINS BAY
DAVIS St
GREENLAND
C. Farewell
ICELAND
Shetland Is
Spitzbergen
N. Cape
LAPLAND
White Sea
Archangel
Bothnia G.
Bergen

TECHNICAL TERMS

PECULIAR TO THE NAVIGATION AMONG ICE.

BAY-ICE. — Ice newly formed upon the surface of the sea. The expression is, however, applied also to ice a foot or two in thickness.

BESET. — The situation of a ship when closely surrounded by ice.

BIGHT. — An indentation in a floe of ice, like a bay, by which name it is sometimes called.

BLINK. — A peculiar brightness in the atmosphere, often assuming an arch-like form, which is generally perceptible over ice or land covered with snow. The blink of land, as well as that over *large* quantities of ice, is usually of a yellowish cast.

BORE. — The operation of "boring" through loose ice consists in entering it under a press of sail, and forcing the ship through by separating the masses.

BRASH. — Ice broken up into small fragments.

CACHE. — Literally a hiding-place. The places of deposit of provision in Arctic travel are so called.

CALF. — A mass of ice lying under a floe near its margin, and, when disengaged from that position, rising with violence to the surface of the water. — See TONGUE.

CROW'S NEST. — A small circular house, like a cask, fixed at the masthead, in which the look-out man sits, either to guide the ship through the ice, or to give notice of whales.

DOCK. — In a floe may be natural or artificial: the former being simply a small "bight," in which a ship is placed to secure her from the danger of external pressure; and the latter, a square space cut out with saws for a similar purpose.

FIELD. — A sheet of ice generally of great thickness, and of too great extent to be seen over from a ship's masthead.

FIORD. — An abrupt opening in the coast-line admitting the sea.

FLOE. — The same as a field, except that its extent can be distinguished from a ship's masthead. A "bay-floe" is a floe of ice newly formed.

FLOE-PIECE. — An expression generally applied to small pieces of floes, not more than a furlong square.

GLACIER. — A mass of ice derived from the atmosphere, sometimes abutting on the sea.

HUMMOCK. — A mass of ice rising to a considerable height above the general level of a floe, and forming a part of it. Hummocks are originally raised by the pressure of floes against each other.

ICE-ANCHOR. — A hook or grapnel adapted to take hold upon ice.

ICE-BELT. — A continued margin of ice, which, in high northern latitudes, adheres to the coast above the ordinary level of the sea.

ICEBERG. — A large floating mass of ice detached from a glacier.

ICE-FOOT. — The Danish name of the limited ice-belt of the more southern coast.

LAND-ICE. — Ice attached to the land, either in floes or in heavy grounded masses lying near the shore.

LANE OF WATER. — A narrow channel among the masses of ice, through which a boat or ship may pass.

LEAD. — A channel through the ice. A ship is said to "take the right lead" when she follows a channel conducting her into a more navigable sea, and *vice versâ*.

NIPPED. — The situation of a ship when forcibly pressed by ice on both sides.

PACK. — A large body of ice, consisting of separate masses, lying close together, and whose extent cannot be seen.

PANCAKE-ICE. — Newly-formed ice, assuming the peculiar conformation of numberless patches of "sludge," and giving the surface of the sea the appearance of a handsome pavement.

PATCH OF ICE. — The same as a pack, but of small dimensions.

PEMMICAN. — Meat cured, pulverized, and mixed with fat, containing much nutriment in a small compass.

SAILING-ICE. — Ice of which the masses are so much separated as to allow a ship to sail among them.

SLUDGE. — Ice of the consistence of thick honey, offering little impediment to a ship while in this state, but greatly favoring the formation of a "bay-floe."

STREAM. — A long and narrow, but generally continuous, collection of loose ice.

TONGUE. — A mass of ice projecting under water from an iceberg or floe, and generally distinguishable at a considerable depth of smooth water. It differs from a "calf" in being fixed to, or a part of, the larger body.

TRACKING. — Towing along a margin of ice.

WATER-SKY. — A dark appearance in the sky, indicating "clear water" in that direction, and forming a striking contrast with the "blink" over land or ice.

YOUNG-ICE. — Nearly the same as "bay-ice," but generally applied to ice more recently formed than the latter.

ARCTIC ADVENTURE.

CHAPTER I.

ASPECTS OF THE ARCTIC REGIONS. — PHENOMENA. — THE ARCTIC OCEAN. — EARLIEST EXPLORERS. — THE NORTHMEN. — THE CABOTS. — THE CORTEREALS. — SIR HUGH WILLOUGHBY. — FROBISHER. — SIR HUMPHREY GILBERT. — DAVIS. — BARENTZ. — HUDSON. — BAFFIN.

The varied physical aspect of the globe offers as much to charm or awe the eye of man as to minister to his comfort and well-being. From the glowing heat and gorgeous vegetation of the torrid zone, we move through all gradations of climate and feature, to the frigid regions of either pole, where perpetual ice and a depressed temperature present an extraordinary contrast to the lands of the sun: from intensest heat we pass to intensest cold; from the sandy deserts of the south to the icy deserts of the north. Yet there is as much in the frozen zone to impress and elevate the mind of the beholder as in the countries where nature displays herself in rich and exuberant loveliness.

Beyond the seventieth degree of latitude not a tree meets the eye, wearied with the white waste of snow; forests, woods, even shrubs, have disappeared, and given place to a few lichens and creeping woody plants, which scantily clothe the indurated soil. Still, in the furthest north, nature claims her birthright of beauty; and in the brief and rapid summer she brings forth numerous flowers and grasses to bloom for a few days, until again blasted by the swiftly-recurring winter.

In these regions certain mysterious phenomena exhibit their most powerful effects. Here is the point of attraction of the compass needle; and here the dipping needle, which lies horizontal at the equator, points straight downwards. Slowly, in its cycle of nearly two thousand years, this centre or pole of magnetic attraction revolves in obedience to laws as yet unknown. Two degrees further toward the north is situated the pole of cold — a mystery like the former to science, but equally inciting to curiosity. If induction may be trusted, the pole of the earth is less cold than the latitudes fifteen degrees below it.

Round the shores and seas of the arctic regions ice ever accumulates: a circle of two thousand miles' diameter is occupied by frozen fields and floes of vast extent, or piled high with hugest forms, awful yet fantastic as a dreamer's fancy. Mountain masses —

> "Whose blocks of sapphire seem to mortal eye
> Hewn from cerulean quarries in the sky,
> With glacier battlements that crowd the spheres,
> The slow creation of six thousand years,
> Amidst immensity they tower sublime,
> Winter's eternal palace, built by Time."

Here the months are divided into long periods of daylight and darkness: for many weeks the sun sinks not below the horizon; for three dreary months he appears not above it —

> "And morning comes, but comes not clad in light;
> Uprisen day is but a paler night."

But, in the absence of the great luminary, the vivid coruscations of the aurora borealis illuminate the wintry landscape, streaming across the skies in broad sheets of light, flashing in multi-colored rays, or quivering in faint and feathery scintillations — a light that takes away the irksomeness of gloom, and makes the long night wondrous.

The desolate grandeur of the scene is in many parts increased by the entire absence of animated nature; in others the dearth of vegetation is compensated by superabundance of animal life. Wrangell tells us that "countless herds of reindeer, elks, black bears, foxes, sables, and gray squirrels, fill the upland forests; stone foxes and wolves roam over the low grounds. Enormous flights of swans, geese, and ducks, arrive in spring, and seek deserts where they may moult and build their nests in safety. Eagles, owls, and gulls, pursue their prey along the sea-coast; ptarmigan run in troops among the bushes; little snipes are busy along the brooks and in the morasses; the social crows seek the neighborhood of men's habitations; and when the sun shines in spring, one may even sometimes hear the cheerful note of the finch, and in autumn that of the thrush."

"There is," as observed by Lieutenant-Colonel Sabine, "a striking resemblance in the configuration of the northern coasts of the continents of Asia and America for several hundred miles on either side of Behring's Strait; the general direction of the coast is the same in both continents, the latitude is nearly the same, and each has its attendant group of islands to the north: the Asiatic continent, those usually known as the New Siberian Islands; and the American, those called by Sir Edward Parry the North Georgian Group, and since fitly named, from their discoverer, the Parry Islands. The resemblance includes the islands also, both in general character and latitude."

With respect to the Arctic Ocean, a late writer explains: "We may view this great polar sea as enclosed within a circle whose diameter is 40°, or two thousand four hundred geographical miles, and circumference seven thousand two hundred miles. On the Asiatic side of this sea are Nova Zembla and the New Siberian Islands, each extending to about the 76th degree of latitude. On the European and American sides are Spitzbergen, extending to about 80°, and a part of Old Greenland, whose northern extremity is yet unknown. Facing America is the large island washed by Regent's Inlet, Parry's or Melville's Islands, with some others, in latitude 70° to 76°, and beyond these nothing is known of any other land or islands; and if we may form an opinion, by inspecting the general chart of the earth, it would be that no islands exist which could in any shape obstruct navigation." It is to these regions, and the labors of which they have been the scene, that we have for a short period to direct our attention.

The history of Arctic explorations properly begins at a period earlier by several centuries than is generally believed. Careful researches promoted and carried on of late years by the Society of Northern Antiquaries of Copenhagen, and others interested in the subject, have established the fact, that Newfoundland, Greenland, and several parts of the American coast, were visited by the Scandinavians — the Northmen and Sea-Kings of old — in the ninth and tenth centuries. While Alfred was engaged in expelling the Danes from England, and bestowing the rudiments of civilization on his country, and Charles the Bald was defending his kingdom against a host of competitors, the daring sea-rovers were forming settlements in Iceland.

One hundred and twenty-five years later, A. D. 1000, Leif Erickson, as many antiquarians believe, led the way to the westward, and landed on the shores of Massachusetts, naming the country Vinland, from the wild vines which grew in the woods. These adventurers made their way also to a high northern latitude, and set up stones, carved with Runic inscriptions, with the date 1135, on Women's Islands — in latitude 72° 55′ — Baffin's Bay, where they were discovered in 1824. The colonists on the eastern coast of this great bay made regular trips to Lancaster Sound and part of Barrow's Strait, in pursuit of fish "more than six centuries before the adventurous voyage of Parry," and carried on a trade with the settlers in Markland, as Nova Scotia was then called. Their numbers must have been considerable, for in Greenland there were three hundred homesteads or villages, and twenty churches and convents. They kept up intercourse with Europe until 1406, when it was interrupted by extraordinary accumulations of ice upon their coasts; and though the Danish government has made repeated attempts to ascertain their fate, it still remains in doubt; the supposition is, that all have perished from privation or violence of the natives. Spitzbergen, too, contained numerous colonists: graves are frequently met with on its shores; in one place Captain Buchan saw several thousands, the corpses of some of them as fresh as when first interred, preserved by the rigor of the climate.

These early explorers were unable to take full advantage of their American discoveries; this was reserved for a later period. "Intervening," observes Humboldt, "between two different stages of cultivation, the fifteenth century forms a transition epoch, belonging at once to the middle ages and to the commencement of modern times. It is the epoch of the greatest discoveries in geographical space, comprising almost all degrees of latitude, and almost every gradation of elevation of the earth's surface. To the inhabitants of Europe it doubled the works of creation, while at the same time it offered to the intellect new and powerful incitements to the improvement of the natural sciences in their physical and mathematical departments."

As we approach the period here referred to, we find a new spirit at work ; no longer the boisterous adventurousness of the Northmen, but an earnest spirit of enterprise. In 1380, the Zeni, two Venetian navigators, voyaged into the north, ignorant of the fact that the Scandinavians had preceded them by three centuries, and brought home accounts of the countries they had seen. In 1497, during the reign of Henry VII., British enterprise was first directed to a region in which it has been subsequently developed to a degree without example ; and Cabot, or Cabota, the younger, landed at Labrador eighteen months before Columbus saw the mainland of tropical America. He contemplated also a voyage to the pole, and sailed up to 67½° of north latitude. It was thought scarcely possible that the newly-discovered continent stretched so far from north to south without a single opening to the westward, and the search for this became the prime object with mercantile adventurers, who hoped to find a way to the rich and gorgeous countries lying beyond.

In the year 1500, Gaspar Cortereal, a Portuguese, animated with the desire to emulate Columbus in making discoveries in the western world, set sail for that part of the globe, and reached the latitude of 50° north, whence he appears to have run as far as 60°. The account given of his voyage is very vague. After entrapping on board no less that fifty-seven of the natives of the western continent, there can be very little doubt for the purpose of making them slaves, he returned to Portugal, carrying them away with him. He arrived at Lisbon on the 8th of October, 1501. He sailed again the next season with two vessels, when, in entering a strait, supposed to be that known since as Hudson's, the ships were separated by a storm. One of them returned home in safety, but, as if it were a retribution for his kidnapping the unfortunate aborigines of the country on his previous voyage, neither Gaspar Cortereal nor his crew returned again, nor could the slightest trace of their fate ever be discovered. Gaspar Cortereal had a brother named Miguel, who was much attached to him, and full of the same spirit of enterprise; — he determined to set out in search of Gaspar.

In the early part of the spring of 1502, Miguel sailed from Lisbon with three vessels. On reaching the numerous straits and islets about Hudson's Bay, the ships separated with the intention of exploring each of them a particular inlet. This was an impolitic measure, as their union would have enabled them to give each other aid in case of distress, or to bring off the crew, should either of them chance to be shipwrecked on any of the numerous islands, either rock or ice, which abound in that dangerous navigation. The result was an unfortunate one. Two of the ships met at the point of rendezvous, and returned home in safety. The third, with Miguel Cortereal on board, shared the melancholy fate of the navigators of whom it had gone from Portugal expressly to get tidings, — it never returned. The place where it perished, whether by storm, rock, ice, or famine, was never known. The two vessels which were so fortunate as to reach Lisbon reported the disaster, in addition to that which had been previously known. There yet remained a third brother, Vasco, who endeavored to obtain leave of the king to set out and try to discover his two absent brothers. The king refused him permission, upon the ground that the loss of two out of such an adventurous family was much greater than he could afford to sustain, in servants so enthusiastic and noble-minded. Thus died the brothers Cortereal; and this is all that is known of their fate to the present hour.

Sir Hugh Willoughby was sent out by the Muscovy Company with two ships to find a north-east passage "to Kathay and India;" and pushed his way as far as Nova Zembla, from whence, being stopped by ice, he returned to a lower latitude, and in September, 1553, put in at the mouth of the river Arzina, in Lapland. A melancholy interest attended this event, little anticipated by the unfortunate leader when he wrote in his journal — "Thus remaining in this haven the space of a weeke, seeing the yeare farre spent, and also very evill wether — as frost, snowe, and haile, as though it had beene the deepe of winter, wee thought it best to winter there." The dreary season passed away, and in the following year some Russian fishermen found Sir Hugh and his crew all frozen to death. The other vessel, commanded by Richard Chancelor, reached Archangel, and opened the way for commercial intercourse with Russia.

Next in importance are the three voyages by Frobisher, in 1576–78. He discovered the entrance to Hudson's Strait, and explored that still known as Frobisher's, but failed in penetrating to the westward. Great hopes were excited by some lumps of yellow glistening ore which he brought home, and in his later voyages gold-mines were not less to be searched for than the north-west passage. The study of natural phenomena was not, however, altogether lost sight of, as appears by a passage from the instructions issued under the authority of Elizabeth for the gallant seaman's guidance. "Yf yt be possible," so runs the official document, "you shall leave some persons to winter in the straight, giving them instructions how they may observe the nature of the ayre and state of the countrie, and what tyme of the yeare the straight is most free from yce; with who you shall leave a sufficient preparation of victualls and weapons, and also a pynnas, with a carpenter, and thyngs necessarie, so well as may be."

Sir Humphrey Gilbert's expedition to colonize Newfoundland soon followed. This naval commander was distinguished for his intellectual acquirements, his courage, and bold actions. He was nearly related to Sir Walter Raleigh. In 1578, he obtained full power from Queen Elizabeth to undertake a voyage of discovery on the continent of America, and to settle such parts as no Christian prince or his subjects could claim from previous possession. A discourse, written by him, and creditable to his talents, upon the practicability of a north-west passage, is extant in Hakluyt.

In 1583, Sir Humphrey left England, on his second voyage, with five ships, sailing out of Plymouth Sound on the 11th of June. On the 30th, four vessels were in sight of Newfoundland; one of the ships, commanded by Captain Butler, and the property of Sir Walter, then Mr. Raleigh, having returned home on account of a contagious disorder breaking out on board. On the 3d of August they landed in Newfoundland, and took possession of the harbor of St. John's, in the name of the Queen of England. A discovery was made at the same time of a supposed silver-mine, by a Saxon miner, brought out on purpose in the squadron. The vessels remaining with Sir Humphrey at this time were the Delight, Golden Hinde, Swallow, and Squirrel. The largest vessel was but one hundred and twenty tons, while the smallest was only ten. The Swallow was sent home with the sick. Sir Humphrey then embarked in the Squirrel, of ten tons.

Sir Humphrey left the harbor of St. John's on the 20th of August. On the 27th, he was in latitude 44°, with fair weather. On the 29th, a storm arose, and the Delight, the largest vessel of the squadron, was lost. Sixteen only made their escape in the boat. The first appearance of change was a dense fog, which enveloped the ships, followed by a gale of wind, south by east. They could not see beyond the head of the vessel. The Golden Hinde, all of a sudden, got entangled among rocks and shoals. The Delight beat still further in among them. Finding the soundings constantly varied, a signal was made to the Delight, by the Golden Hinde, to stand out, but it remained unnoticed. She soon afterwards struck on a shoal, and her stern was quickly beat to pieces. This was a fatal blow to the prospects of Sir Humphrey.

The Golden Hinde and Squirrel, all now left of the five ships which originally set sail from Plymouth, stood east by south. The water shoaled, and then deepened from four to seven fathoms, and then shoaled to four or five again, with a very high sea. At the time the Delight went on the rocks, her boat was afloat at the stern, it having fortunately been hoisted out the day before, when the weather was fine, to pick up some birds which had been shot. Into this boat a part of the crew were, by great exertion, enabled to get, and to pick up others. The captain and a hundred of the crew perished with the ship ; and besides the Saxon before mentioned, who said he had discovered the silver ore, a learned man from Buda, in Hungary, called Budæus on board, but whose name was Stephen Parmenius, who had written a Latin poem in praise of Sir Humphrey, and had gone out to write an account of the voyage, and what he saw, in the Latin tongue, was among the sufferers.

The bearing of Captain Browne, who had been transferred from the Swallow into the Delight, was, upon this occasion, of the most heroic character. When the fate of the vessel was seen to be inevitable, he was advised to save himself by the boat, or, at least, to make the attempt. He spurned the counsel, refusing to set the example of deserting the ship and abandoning the larger portion of the crew, who could have no hope of escape. He continued to the last to exhort those on board not to give way to despair; and firmly upon the deck of his vessel he awaited, with magnanimous resignation, the termination of the catastrophe. He could not endure the apprehension of a reproach for leaving his ship, even when hope was extinguished. The master, named Richard Clarke, was one of those preserved in the boat.

During two days, in this destitute situation, and without provisions of any kind, they drifted before the tempest. It was feared the boat could not live much longer in such a sea unless lightened, and one of the party, by name Headley, proposed that lots should be drawn, and those who drew the four shortest of the number should be thrown overboard. Thus a better chance would be afforded to the survivors of keeping afloat and reaching land. The master nobly answered, "No, we will all live or die in company!" The conduct both of the captain and master of this vessel exhibited that striking heroism to which bravery in the field of battle is but secondary.

The third and fourth day passed over the heads of these unfortunate men without sustenance. They picked up the weed borne on the surface of the foaming waves around them, and eagerly devoured it, drinking the sea-water. Their strength was rapidly leaving them, and death, in its most fearful form, was before them. The man called Headley, and another, died on the fifth day. All wished it would please God to take them out of their misery. Since they had left the ship, the sun had been but once visible. All the nights but one had been starless, so that the darkness augmented their sufferings. They were all, except the master, Richard Clarke, praying for death. On the sixth day after the wreck, Clarke, calm and collected, still endeavored to comfort them with the hope of soon making the land. They expressed their doubts that they should ever again cast their eyes on the welcome shore. He told them to throw him overboard if they did not make land on the seventh day; and this rallied their spirits, for they seem to have reposed great trust in his skill and knowledge.

The seventh day broke, and one hour before noon they got a sight of the shore. In the afternoon they landed, but were so weak that it was with difficulty they could assist each other out of the boat. They fell on their knees and thanked God for their deliverance. The stronger then helped the more feeble to a brook, where they refreshed themselves with the water, and quenched their intolerable thirst. They gathered and ate of some berries they found growing wild near the spot.

The next day, Clarke divided them into parties of three, to search for food; being to rendezvous together at noon, with what they could collect, for the common stock. They were fortunate enough to find a great quantity of peas growing wild. For three days they lived on these peas and on berries, and at night sheltered themselves in a hut, rudely constructed of the boughs of trees.

They had preserved their boat, and, being a little recovered from their former feeble state, they rowed along the shore, with the design of making the Great Bay of Newfoundland, which was then annually frequented by Spaniards engaged in the whale fishery. When hungry, they landed to eat berries and peas.

They had not proceeded far in this way, when a Spanish ship fell in with them, the captain of which proved a kind friend. He took them to St. Jean de Luz, in the Bay of Biscay; and when the Spaniards came on board, told them they were poor fishermen cast away at Newfoundland. He set them on shore in the night, only ten miles from the French frontiers, which they reached before day broke, and, thus having escaped, travelled to England through France, where they safely arrived about the end of the year 1583.

Their history having thus terminated, it will be proper to go back to the Golden Hinde and Squirrel. The crews of these ships, dispirited at the loss of the best vessel of the squadron, still continued to beat about in those thick fogs which are so common on the shores of Newfoundland. The crew of the Squirrel, already on short allowance, besought Sir Humphrey Gilbert to return to England. The crew of the Golden Hinde joined in the same request. Sir Humphrey Gilbert, whose enthusiasm did not seem abated by his disasters, engaged them to accompany him again in the following spring. On the 31st of August they altered their course, during a fresh breeze and high sea, and directed it for their native land.

Sir Humphrey had hurt his foot, and, on the 2d of September, went on board the Golden Hinde to get it dressed by the surgeon of that ship. He repeated the visit to partake of an entertainment with the captain, master, and crew. He spoke of his disappointment on losing his papers and some ore which the Saxon refiner had procured in Newfoundland, which had been lost in the Delight. The Squirrel was overloaded, having heavy artillery on board, and things on deck so much above her tonnage, that her situation at that season of the year was considered dangerous by those on board the Hinde. They advised Sir Humphrey to shift into the larger vessel. He generously replied in the negative. "I will not," said he, "now desert my little vessel and crew, after we have encountered so many perils and storms together."

The Golden Hinde supplied the boat of the Squirrel with what provisions were necessary, and Sir Humphrey returned in it to that ship. They were then about three hundred leagues on their voyage to England. A vessel of ten tons, laden like the Squirrel, was too small to resist the waves in the Atlantic. On the 9th of September she foundered, and Sir Humphrey perished, when they were in the latitude of England. The Squirrel was near foundering in the afternoon of the same day she went down; at which time, and when they were in imminent danger, Sir Humphrey was seen from the Hinde, sitting in the stern of the ship with a book in his hand, and was heard to call out, "Courage, my lads! we are as near heaven at sea as on land!" It was about twelve o'clock at night when the ship went down.

The three voyages by Davis, in 1585–88, enlarged the limits of research. By the discovery of the strait which still bears his name, he opened the way to Baffin's Bay and the Polar Sea; he also surveyed a considerable extent of the Greenland coast. Various attempts to find a passage were also made during this century by Spaniards, French, Danes, and Dutch, those of the last-mentioned nation being the most memorable. To avoid the risk of a voyage to India across the ocean, over which Spain claimed the supremacy, they sought for a shorter passage by the north-east.

The three voyages by William Barentz, 1594–96, afford striking examples of dangers encountered, and manful perseverance in struggling against them. He made his way to the sea between Spitzbergen and Nova Zembla, until, to quote the narrative of the third voyage, "we came to so great a heape of ice that we could not sayle through it." In August of the last-mentioned year, the vessel was embayed by an unusual drifting of the ice, which, crushing around them with a violence that "made all the haire of our heads to rise upright with feare," forced them "in great cold, povertie, miserie, and griefe, to stay all that winter." They exerted themselves to the utmost to avoid so terrible an alternative; but on the 11th of September, as is related, "we saw that we could not get out of the ice, but rather became faster, and could not loose our ship, as at other times we had done, as also that it began to be winter, we tooke counsell together what we were best to doe, according to the time, that we might winter there, and attend such adventure as God would send us; and after we had debated upon the matter (to keepe and defend ourselves both from the colde and wilde beastes), we determined to build a house upon the land, to keepe us therein as well as wee could, and so to commit ourselves unto the tuition of God." While casting about for material for the edifice, to their great joy they discovered a quantity of drift timber, which they regarded as a special interposition of Providence in their behalf, and "were much comforted, being in good hope that God would show us some further favour; for that wood served us not onely to build our house, but also to burne, and serve us all the winter long; otherwise, without all doubt, we had died there miserably with extreme cold."

Parties were thereupon set to work to build the house, and drag their stores from the ship on hand-sleds, in which labors they were grievously interrupted by bears and severity of the weather. If any one held a nail between his lips, the skin came off with as much pain, on taking it out again, as though the iron had been red-not; yet, notwithstanding the cold, there was open sea for many weeks an "arrow-shot" beyond their ship. The dwelling, slow in progress, was finished by the end of October, and thatched with sea-wrack, the more effectually to close the chinks in the roof and walls, and "we set up our dyall, and made the clocke strike." On the 4th of November "wee saw the sunne no more, for it was no longer above the horison; then our chirurgion made a bath (to bathe us in) of a wine-pipe, wherein wee entred one after the other, and it did us much good, and was a great meanes of our health." All the spare clothing was distributed, regulations established with regard to diet, and duties apportioned; the master and pilot being exempted from cleaving wood, and other rude labors. Traps were set to catch foxes for food, and cheerfulness was as much as possible promoted; but at times they were snowed up, and could not open their door for many days, and had no light but that of their fire; they were tormented with smoke, while ice two inches thick formed in their sleeping-berths. The clock stopped with the cold, after which they could only reckon time by "the twelve-hour glass."

The misery they endured may be judged of by the tone of some of the entries in their journal; such suffering was but too frequent: "It was foule weather againe, with an easterly wind and extreame cold, almost not to bee indured; whereupon wee lookt pittifully one upon the other, being in great feare that if the extreamitie of the cold grew to bee more and more, wee should all dye there with cold; for that what fire soever wee made it would not warme us; yea, and our sacke, which is so hot, was frozen very hard, so that when we were every man to have his part, we were forced to melt it in the fire, which we shared every second day about halfe a pint for a man, wherewith we were forced to sustayne ourselves ; and at other times we dranke water, which agreed not well with the cold, and we needed not to coole it with snow or ice ; but we were forced to melt it out of the snow."

Linen froze in an instant taken out of warm water. The closeness of the hut nearly suffocated them from the smoke, and if the fire became low the walls were soon covered with thick ice, — even the beds were lined with it. Except when employed in cooking, they lay constantly in their beds. Oftentimes they heard tremendous noises like thunder break the fearful stillness of the unbounded frozen waste around them ; it seemed like the bursting asunder of mountains, and the dashing them into atoms. This sound was probably caused by the fracture of the ice at sea. They knew not day from night, the moon shining brightly. On the 7th of December they went on board their ship for some coals, and made up a good fire in the evening, which gave them much comfort. They had a narrow escape, however, from the vapor ; for, closing every aperture of the hut to keep in the heat as much as possible, a seaman, who was indisposed, first complained of not being able to bear it, and then they were all attacked with vertigo, and could scarcely stand, until the door was opened, when the first who reached it fell down faint on the snow. Gerard de Veer recovered the fallen man by sprinkling his face with vinegar, and the fresh air rushing in restored them again. A glass of wine was then served out to each man to recover him completely.

On the 19th of December they comforted themselves that half the time of the sun's absence was over. The seamen's shoes were now frozen so hard that they could not be worn, and they made themselves slippers of skins, and put on several pairs of socks together, to keep their feet in heat. The ice was an inch thick on the sides of their hut, and when they went out in clear weather their clothes became white with frost and ice. They increased the size of their fire, but from their recent warning kept an opening for the smoke. They had used all the wood laid up in their hut by the middle of January, and they were obliged to shovel away the snow on the outside to get at a fresh stock. This they found a task of great difficulty, from the excessive rigor of the climate. A party also proceeded to the ship, but found her frozen up as before, and the ice accumulated within. They caught a fox in the cabin, which they took to their hut and ate.

They had been economical of their wine, but they kept Twelfth night with savings from their scanty allowance, thus making as merry as their dismal situation would permit. They fancied themselves at home in Holland. They made pancakes with meal and oil, and, soaking biscuit in their wine, drank to the three kings of Cologne, and comforted themselves as if they had been at a "great feast." They drew lots who should be king of Nova Zembla, and it fell to the gunner to be the monarch of that domain of cold and desolation. In short, they made themselves as happy as if they had been in their own houses among the dykes of Holland. Thus does enjoyment, even in the most adverse times, come to the very portal of misery at the mind's bidding.

They had stormy weather for several succeeding days, till about the 15th of January, during which they confined themselves to their hut. They heard the foxes running over their heads, but could not catch them, which they regretted, as their provisions were beginning to run short. The intense cold absorbed every other sensation. They applied hot stones to their feet and bodies to keep them warm: comforting themselves, that now the sun was about returning to them, with a little patience he would warm and gladden them again with his beams. Even sitting before their fire, their backs would become white with frost, while their stockings would be burned before they could feel the heat to their feet.

They visited their ship a second time, and found traces of bears; and, going below, discovered the ice a foot higher in the hold than it had been originally. They had little hope now that their vessel would ever float again.

Gerard de Veer and Jacob Heemskirk, going with a third person to the sea-side towards the south, on the 24th of January, the day being clear, saw the edge of the sun above the horizon. They imparted the welcome news to their friends, but Barentz was incredulous, as the return was thought too early by fourteen days. For two days afterwards they had no opportunity of verifying the fact, owing to the weather being thick and cloudy.

They lost one of their number on the 26th; he had long been ill; they dug a grave seven feet in the snow; and then, as is mournfully recorded, "after that we had read certaine chapters and sung some psalmes, we all went out and buried the man." As the days lengthened, the light enabled them to take exercise, though the weather still remained as severe as before. A slight relaxation of cold in February was followed in the next month by cold of increased rigor. They were totally blocked up in their hut by snow on the 24th of March.

On the 6th of April they attempted to shoot a bear which approached close to their dwelling; but their guns missed fire, and the animal came down the steps they had cut in the snow directly against their door. The captain, frightened and confused, could not fix the bar of wood which usually constituted the fastening, but they contrived to hold the door home so fast that the animal could not enter, and it then walked away. The creature soon returned again, roaring around the hut, to the great terror of the inmates ; at last it got on the roof, which they feared it would have broken, being quite furious. A sail hoisted on the outside of the hut the bear tore to pieces in his anger. No other injury ensued.

The sea began to open, as early as the middle of March, to within seventy-five paces of the ship ; though a new frost came on, and increased the distance to five hundred on the 4th of May. They did not wait to see whether their vessel might again be serviceable. They preferred the chance of going in their boats, and of venturing in them to cross a sea three or four hundred leagues rather than to trust an uncertain event.

They now set about preparations for departure. They repaired their two boats, and had good hope "to get out of that wilde, desart, irkesome, fearfull, and cold countrey." On the 13th of June the survivors, twelve in number, left the desolate shore, after a stay of ten months. Their privations and exposures in small boats, in an ice-encumbered sea, may be imagined. Three of them perished, worn out with disease. The indefatigable Barentz himself at last succumbed. They had passed Icy Cape two days before. This cape is a headland in Russian America, in the Arctic Ocean, in lat. 70°. 20′. N. ; lon. 161°. 46′. W. ; it is the furthest land attained by Cook in 1778.

As they were approaching this cape, Barentz asked if they had yet reached it ; and, on being told it was in sight, requested he might be lifted up to see it once more, the ruling passion of this adventurous seaman being strong in death. About nine o'clock on the morning of the 20th, it was communicated to those who were in the launch that Claes Andriz was near his end, he being in the other boat. Barentz then told his companions he should not long survive Andriz. He was at the moment examining a chart of all the countries and objects they had seen on their voyage, made by Gerard de Veer. No one suspected that what he said was so immediately to be fulfilled. Putting the chart on one side, he asked De Veer to give him something to drink. Barentz swallowed what was given him, and found himself worse immediately; his eyes moved rapidly about for a moment, and he died so suddenly, they had not time to call the captain, who was in the other boat. Andriz expired at nearly the same moment. The death of Barentz was a severe blow to his companions. Upon his experience and knowledge in navigation they relied for their safety in the future conduct of their navigation during a perilous voyage in boats, they hardly knew whither.

They struggled on, however, manfully overcoming the perils that beset them; and in September reached the coast of Lapland, where "wee saw some trees on the river side, which comforted us and made us glad, as if wee had then come into a new world; for, in all the time that wee had been out, wee had not seene any trees." On the eleventh of the same month, after a voyage of eleven hundred and forty-three miles, these brave-hearted men set up their boats in the "Merchants' house," at Coola, as "a sign and token of their deliverance;" and, embarking on board a Dutch ship, in the course of a few weeks once more set foot in their native country.

The survivors appeared before the people of Amsterdam in the dress they wore at Nova Zembla. Curiosity was awakened everywhere respecting them. They were taken to the ministers of foreign states, at the Hague, to relate their perils and give an account of the frigid land, which none of the southern natives had visited before. Their treatment on their arrival home must, in those days, have been an ample compensation to the survivors for their past sufferings.

One of the boldest of early navigators, and one of the most successful, was Henry Hudson, the discoverer of the immense bay which will carry his name and unfortunate end to the latest times. This intrepid mariner first distinguished himself in 1607, being sent out by the Muscovy Company on a voyage, with instructions to penetrate directly to the pole. He succeeded in pushing north as far as latitude 81½°, and returned home, after coasting Spitzbergen, with the conviction, which modern experience has not impugned, that a passage to the pole was completely barred out by the ice in that direction. In 1608, he again set sail, to decide the practicability of a north-east passage, then a favorite subject of debate in the maritime countries of Europe. He saw North Cape on the 3d of June, and reached latitude 75°, when he got among the ice. He now pushed on in the parallels of 74° and 75° to the eastward, and made the coast of Nova Zembla, in latitude 72° 25′; but, finding a further course impracticable, he returned, with the conviction that there was no hope of a north-east passage ; and here again time has proved his judgment to have been correct.

The Dutch sent him, in 1609, to try this passage again ; but he gave it up, after passing Wardhuys, and, returning past North Cape, crossed to the coast of America, where he searched for a passage, and discovered the bay on which New York now stands, and the magnificent river named after him, the Hudson. On the 17th of April, 1610, Hudson set sail in a vessel called the Discovery, of fifty-five tons' burthen, fitted out in the Thames, at the expense of Sir John Wolstenholme, Sir Dudley Digges, and other distinguished persons, and victualled for six months. The ship touched at the Orkney and Faro Islands, and, on the 11th of May, the crew descried the south-eastern part of Iceland; but hearing breakers, and a fog coming on, they cast anchor. They now found themselves embayed. Weighing anchor, they next proceeded northward along the western coast, taking a quantity of fine fish during a day's calm, which overtook them. A south-east wind then arose, and they reached the Vestmanna Isles, where the Danes had a fort, and passed the grand and awful mountain called Snow Fell, which towers to a vast height over those inhospitable and desert shores. They saw Mount Hecla in the blaze of an eruption, surrounded by eternal snows; and fell in soon afterwards with a mass of ice, stretching far to the westward from the northern part of the island. Here Hudson entered a port in the north-west side, where they killed a quantity of wild fowl. They sailed, but were again obliged to put back, without being able to make the harbor, but fortunately fell in with another haven, where they found some hot springs, and bathed. The water of this spring was so hot it would boil a fowl.

On the first of June they set sail for Greenland, and soon fancied they saw land to the westward, but it proved to be fog. It was not until the fourth that Greenland appeared in sight. The coast was lined with a vast barrier of ice. "This day," says Hudson, "we saw Greenland perfectly, over the ice; and this night the sun went down due north, and rose north-north-east; so, plying the fifth day, we were in 65°."

Their course lay mostly west and north-west, till Cape Desolation appeared on the western side. Here they saw a great number of whales. They now made their course north-west, the wind preventing them from sailing more to the north, and here they first fell in with the icebergs. At the end of June they saw an island, perhaps Resolution Island. Hudson would still have sailed more to the north, but the wind would not permit; so he went south of the island, and found the current setting to the west. They entered the stream, and were carried north-west, until they fell in with ice, which was attached to the shore. Hudson then kept to the south and west again, through floating ice, upon which they found numerous seals. They now had a clear sea, and sailed until they again encountered icebergs, and floating pieces of ice, keeping north-west. They saw an iceberg overturn, and took warning from it not to approach too near them in future; yet they were soon obliged to take shelter between two masses, owing to a storm, and there lie snug.

On the cessation of the storm, they stood on, as they found it clear enough of ice around them to venture. Their course lay with the ice, and whenever it permitted them to make a passage they moved with it, though still enclosed. Hudson, trying to get clear of it by steering south, found the more he tried the worse they were off, until he could go no further. Here the navigator himself was in despair, thinking they should never get out of it. He, therefore, brought out his chart, and showed the crew that they had sailed a hundred leagues further than any of their countrymen had gone before, and left it to them to say whether they should proceed further or not. Some seem to have replied one way and some another, but there was evidently much growling and discontent among them. After much labor they got clear, and shaped their course north and north-west It is most probable that the commander, seeing the discontent of a part of his crew, ended the conference and took his own course. He still seems to have relied upon his own resources and courage, and to have continued to pursue the object of his voyage, sometimes environed by the ice, yet often in a clear sea. He found a harbor among some islands, which he named the "Isles of God's Mercy." Here some of the crew went on shore. They saw a bay to the north, with a large iceberg aground, which afterwards floated away. They took in drift-wood, which they found cast up on the shore.

After a good deal of sailing to the south and northwest, and west, and then south, as the intricate navigation required, they stood to the westward in a clear, open sea, and saw three headlands, which Hudson named Prince Henry's Cape, King James's, and Queen Anne's. They now proceeded north to double the headlands, until they saw the north shore, on which Hudson put about until he made the south land again, but very much to the west of what he expected, owing to a strong current, which arose, no doubt, from the set-in of the tide to the great bay which bears his name. They now saw a hill on the south shore, which they named Mount Charles; and soon after a cape, which was called Cape Salisbury. Still proceeding along the south shore, they came to an island, distant from the mainland about two leagues, one point of which they named Deepe's Cape, the other Wolstenholme's. At this island the boat was sent on shore to make discoveries. Those in it were overtaken by a storm, but they succeeded in landing and climbing up the rocks, when they came to some level ground, in which they found a herd of deer, but could not get within musket-shot of them. On this island they found plenty of fowl, and some excellent herbage, also sorrel and scurvy grass. They saw some hollow cells of stone, in which they found a quantity of fowls hung up by the necks. The ship now fired a gun to call off the people who had landed, for a fog had come on. Upon returning on board, Hudson would not stay to refresh on the island, as some of the crew recommended, but proceeded, his mind, no doubt, contemplating the discovery of the great sea on which he was about to enter.

At this time it was that the discontent, which had no doubt been increasing on board, was visited by an exercise of the commander's authority. Some discussion, it appears, took place about entering a bay, and going out of it. On this occasion, Hudson is said to have revived some old grudge, and to have displaced one Juet from the situation of mate, and degraded the boatswain for words which had been spoken some time before, making Billet, or Bylot, his mate, and William Wilson his boatswain. The crew thought it harsh in Hudson to revive this old affair. They were obedient, however, and sailed again in a northerly direction until they saw land, and then to the south, and so on from land to land, on the opposite side the straits. On Michaelmas day they entered a bay, which Hudson named Michaelmas Bay. They afterwards stood to the north until they came into shoal water, with thick, foggy weather. They were now obliged to anchor, and so remained for eight days, when, the wind dropping, Hudson insisted on heaving the anchor up, against the opinions of those on board. While the crew were lifting the anchor, a sea struck the ship, and knocked all hands from the capstan, several of whom were much hurt. They lost an anchor, and would have lost all their cable, had not the carpenter fortunately been by with an axe and cut it.

They now stood to the south and south-west, through a sea clear of obstructions, but changing in soundings and in color. After sailing further, they came into shallow water, — so shallow that their boat could not reach the shore, which they saw at some distance, and to which they were obliged to wade. There they discovered the marks of a man's foot in the snow, and plenty of wood, of which they shipped a good stock, and returned on board. Soon after, they saw a ledge of rocks, upon which they ran, and remained fast for twelve hours, but at length got off, not wholly uninjured.

They now began to look out for a place where they might winter. The nights were become long and cold, while the snow covered all the country. The party sent to explore were at first unsuccessful, but on the 1st of November they found a place where they might haul their vessel aground. By the tenth day they were frozen in, and began to look at their stock of provisions, when they found they must be fed upon such an allowance as would hardly keep in life, or last them to the headlands, where fowls might be captured for their supply. Hudson regulated the present allowances in the best way he could, and offered a reward to those who added to the general stock, by killing or capturing anything serviceable for food. In this they must have had success, or their subsistence from April, the 17th, even as far as Christmas, is a miracle, upon six months' victualling.

It appears that, on taking up their winter quarters, it had been proposed to Hudson to erect a house on shore, which he would not hear of being done while it was practicable. The severe northern winter had set in, when he altered his mind, and desired the carpenter to put it in hand. The latter said he neither could nor would set about it. Hudson pursued to strike him, calling him names, and threatened to hang him. The carpenter made his rejoinder by telling Hudson he knew his duty, — that he was no house-carpenter. Such, at least, is the story of Pricket, one of those who came home in the vessel; but the subsequent noble conduct of the carpenter, in refusing to desert Hudson, shows that the latter must have stood high in his esteem and affection, notwithstanding this altercation. The house was ultimately built, but proved to be of no use.

The winter was intensely cold, and the ship's company ill provided with necessaries. Their sufferings were great, and most of them were lamed, or some way injured. They eked out their provisions by wild fowl of several kinds, having taken more than a hundred dozen of "white partridges," as they styled them. When these birds left in the spring, they had swans, geese, ducks, and teal. When these had gone away, they devoured moss, frogs, and buds. One of the crew having brought the buds of a tree full of some substance like turpentine, a decoction of it was made by the surgeon for drink, and much ease was experienced by applying it hot to their frozen limbs. While the spring lasted, about the time the ice was breaking up, the savages visited them, and they trafficked with them, and gave the crew furs in exchange for knives, looking-glasses, and buttons.

Hudson now prepared to return home. He delivered out the last pound of bread to each man, just as they were preparing for a long and perilous voyage, without provisions for the entire crew for more than ten days; and also gave what Pricket calls a "bill of returne," that if ever they got home they might show it, — and he wept as he gave it to them. Fourscore small fish, taken just afterwards, were a seasonable relief to them, though but little towards satisfying their hunger beyond the moment.

They now set sail, and came to anchor in the sea of that immense bay, in which the discoverer, having undergone so much suffering and danger, was to find his grave. They were without bread; five cheeses only were left, and these were equally divided by Hudson among his men.

But a report calumnious of Hudson, for secreting bread, was now spread among the crew. The discontent which had been for some time excited by one Green, a worthless fellow, whom Hudson had befriended, broke out into open mutiny on the 21st of June. The ship's company, both sick and well, were in berths, dispersed generally two and two about the ship. King, one of the crew who was supposed to be friendly to Hudson, was up, and in the morning they secured him in the hold by fastening down the hatches. Green then went and held the carpenter in conversation to amuse him, while two of the crew, keeping just before Hudson, and one, named Wilson, behind him, bound his hands. He asked what they were about, and they told him he should know when he was in the shallop. Another mutineer, Juet, went down to King in the hold, who kept him at bay, being armed with his sword. He came upon deck to Hudson, whom he found with his hands tied. Hudson was heard to call to the carpenter, and tell him he was bound. Two of the devoted party, who were sick, told the mutineers their knavery would be punished. They paid no attention; the shallop was hauled up to the side of the vessel, and the sick and lame were made to get into it.

The carpenter, whom they had agreed to retain in the vessel, asked them if they would not be hanged when they reached England, and boldly refused to remain with them, preferring to share the fate of Hudson and the sick men. He demanded his chest, which was given him, and put into the boat. The names of the persons put out of the ship were Henry Hudson, John Hudson, Arnold Lodlo, Sydrack Faner, Phillip Staffe, Thomas Wodehouse, Adam Moore, Henry King, and Michael Bate. The carpenter contrived to get a musket, powder and shot, some pikes, an iron pot, some meal, and a few other necessaries. The crew then cast the boat off the ship, loosened the topsails, and stood out to sea, steering to the eastward. The boat in which were Hudson and his companions was seen no more, nor was it ever heard of again.

The mutineers now stood to the north-east, contrary to Juet's opinion, who was for steering north-west. The next day they had a storm, and ran into ice, where they remained fourteen days, locked up. In that storm the intrepid commander and his forlorn party in the boat may have perished. It is probable they either died of hunger at sea, or got out of their course, and perished in the storm. They might, indeed, have been starved on the shore, or killed by the aborigines. The end of Hudson is a melancholy and affecting incident. His talents, courage, and perseverance, rank him among the first navigators of any age. In the comparative infancy of discovery in the northern regions, he deserves to take the lead. Left in the great bay which he brought to light, the victim of treachery, he has not been forgotten by posterity, like many of his contemporaries. The mystery of his fate causes his name to be pronounced, even now, with pity, while his skill and courage make the man an object of our admiration, even in these times, when a northern navigation and wintering are not considered such extraordinary perils by the navigator.

The ship continued her navigation homeward. Steering north-east, the mutineers shaped their course for the capes or headlands where, as they supposed, the wild fowl frequented. Landing on one of these, in search of fowl, they fell in with a party of natives, who behaved so peaceably that the Englishmen soon began to traffic with them. For this purpose, they ran the ship in as near to the land as was practicable, and sent a boat ashore laden with goods. Leaving Pricket in charge of the boat, the rest of her crew, one of whom was Green, landed and mixed among the natives, showing them looking-glasses and other articles. Suddenly, one of the savages came into the boat and attacked Pricket with a knife. He defended himself, and a deadly struggle ensued, in which the savage was at last killed. In the mean while, those of the crew on shore were attacked. Thomas and Wilson were stabbed in the bowels; Perse and Green, both dreadfully wounded, fell together into the boat; Moter jumped from the rocks into the sea, and swam to the boat, where, holding the stern, he begged to be taken in; Perse beat off the savages with a hatchet, and Green with a fragment of a pike. The savages then took their bows and arrows. Green was killed on the spot; Perse received many other wounds, as did all the others, but he pushed off the boat, having taken in Moter. Perse and Moter then rowed away, while Pricket received a bad wound in his back from an arrow, as the boat came round. The savages ran to their canoes, but did not pursue the crew. They regained the ship, but three died of their wounds. There were now scarcely hands enough left to work the ship through the entrance of the strait; and the same men who worked the ship were obliged to go in the boat and kill fowls for subsistence on the passage home. With great labor, they killed three hundred, which they salted. They then sailed to the

Cape of God's Mercies, and thence bent their course for Cape Desolation, in Greenland. But, the wind coming on adverse, they shaped their course for Ireland. They suffered, during the passage, the most dreadful extremities of famine, allowing only half a fowl a day to each man, and considering it a luxury to have it fried with candles, of which a weekly distribution was made for that purpose. Ivet, now the sole survivor of the ringleaders in the atrocious conspiracy, sank under these privations. The last fowl was in the steep-tub, and the men were become nearly desperate, when suddenly it pleased God to give them sight of land, which proved to be the north of Ireland. They complain that, on going ashore at Berehaven, they did not receive the sympathy and kindness which they so much needed; nor was it until they had mortgaged their vessel that they obtained the means of proceeding to Plymouth.

Strange to relate, no attempt was made to bring the mutineers to trial; some of them, indeed, were afterwards employed in making further explorations.

Great hopes were entertained that the much-desired passage would be found leading out of Hudson's Bay; and a good deal of controversy on the question arose, from time to time, among contending voyagers and their abettors. Between this period and 1616, those arms of the sea known as Sir Thomas Rowe's Welcome and Fox Channel were discovered; and in the year just mentioned Baffin sailed into and explored the vast bay, eight hundred miles long, and three hundred wide, named after him. For a long time his report of its great length was disbelieved, but later researches have confirmed the accuracy of his statements; even the latitudes laid down by him are almost identical with those recently determined, with all the advantage of superior instruments. Among other openings, Baffin saw Lancaster Sound, and, had he explored it, Parry's discoveries would have been anticipated by two hundred years, as they had been to some extent by the long-forgotten Northmen. The opinion, however, at that time, and, indeed, until within the past fifty years, was, that no practicable opening to the Polar Sea existed, except that at Behring's Strait. From this period to about the middle of last century, the outlets to the west of Hudson's Bay were the points to which effort was directed; and truly may it be said, that these earlier navigators left very little for those who came later. In small vessels, varying from ten to fifty tons' burthen, they accomplished more than has since been effected by lavishly-equipped expeditions.

THE WALRUS.

CHAPTER II.

RUSSIAN EXPLORATIONS. — DESHNEFF. — EXPEDITIONS OF 1711. — FRUITLESS EFFORTS. — LAPTEFF. — BEHRING. — HIS SHIPWRECK AND DEATH. — FATE OF THE SURVIVORS. — SCHALAROFF. — SLEDGE EXPEDITION. — ADMIRAL VON WRANGELL'S EXPEDITIONS.

Hitherto we have been chiefly occupied with the explorations on and around Northern America, and we now come to the history of those along the continent of Asia, the northern limit of which extends over a space of 145° of longitude. The discovery and survey of this vast region is due entirely to the Russians; for, although other nations attempted the passage, they penetrated no further than the Karskoie Sea and Cape North on the east. The first knowledge of the countries which here bound the polar basin was, as in the case of the other continent, derived from private adventurers, who undertook journeys into those desolate regions in hopes of a profitable trade in furs, skins, and ivory. Russian traders, sailing from the White Sea and mouth of the Petchora, voyaged as far as Obi and the Iennissei; their vessels, similar to those of early British navigators, were little better than shallops, and it is impossible not to be struck with the labors of those whose chief resource was indomitable perseverance.

The first endeavors under government authority were made about the year 1600; and trading-stations were established at the mouths of most of the larger rivers, with the double view of exploration and of subjecting the natives to Russian authority. The Lena, Iana, Indigirka, Alaseia, and Kolyma, were discovered before 1640, by parties sent under Cossack leaders to collect tribute, who at the same time fell in with the Tchuktches, and heard their reports of islands lying off the coast. The earliest attempt to sail to eastward of the Kolyma was made in 1646, and repeated in the two following years, with several small vessels, all of which were wrecked, except one commanded by Deshneff, a government functionary, whose name stands high among the early explorers. His grand object was to get round to the mouth of the Anadyr, on the eastern coast, to trade for sable-skins ; and the summer of 1648 proving favorable to navigation among the ice, he sailed along the shore, and through the strait explored by Behring nearly a century later, and founded a settlement at the place to which he was bound — the Anadyr river. This is the only occasion on which such a voyage has been made ; and to Deshneff and his companions belongs the honor of having been the first and sole navigators from the Arctic Sea to the Pacific, and of having proved, at a period much earlier than is commonly supposed, that the American and Asiatic continents are not united.

Other expeditions followed ; the Bear Islands were seen ; and, to obtain accurate particulars concerning them, the government of Siberia sent out two parties, in 1711, who crossed the ice to the Likahoff Islands, and saw others yet further to the north. On their return to the mainland, the leaders were murdered by the crews, who feared the hardships of further explorations. Thus the work went on with varying fortune, the positions mostly ill-defined, as must be the case in the absence of accurate instruments, until 1734, the reign of the

Empress Anne, when the Russian admiralty fitted out three expeditions "to obtain a correct knowledge of the northern coast of Siberia from the White Sea to Behring's Strait;" "one, consisting of two vessels, was to sail from Archangel eastward to the mouth of the Obi; another, from the Obi to the Iennissei. The third was to sail from the Lena, and consisted of two vessels, one of which was to sail westward to the Iennissei, and the other eastward, past the Kolyma, to Behring's Strait."

Insurmountable impediments to navigation, recall of commanders, wintering in the rivers, overland journeys to St. Petersburg, renewed attempts, scurvy, and shipwreck, comprise the history of these expeditions. One of the mates, in observations on the compass, makes the remark, "The variation of the needle was so great, and it was so unsteady, that I am inclined to believe the magnet ceases to act in these high latitudes." This fact is worthy of record, as bearing on phenomena which have subsequently been regarded with much attention. But, on the main question, the Russian admiralty refused to receive the reports of impossible navigation; and, in 1739, sent out another expedition, under Lieut. Lapteff, who, by dint of perseverance in four successive voyages, did at last pass to the eastward of the Kolyma; but here fields of ice, extending far to the north, barred his further progress.

Next in order come the voyages by Behring, the explorer of the strait which bears his name. In the year 1741 this celebrated navigator set sail from the harbor of St. Peter and St. Paul, in Kamtschatka, in two vessels, from which he had named the port. It was the 4th of June when they weighed anchor, and on the 12th they had reached latitude 46° without seeing land. They proceeded as high as 50° of latitude with little success. They now determined to steer eastward, towards the American continent. On the 20th the two ships were separated by a storm, followed by hazy weather.

On the 18th of July, Behring, while waiting for the other vessel, discovered the American continent, in latitude 58° 28′, and in 50° longitude, from Awatska. Three days before, Captain Tschirikov, who commanded the second vessel, had fallen in with the same coast, at 56° latitude, and 50° longitude, from Awatska. He sent on shore his long-boat and shallop with seventeen men, to observe the coast, but neither the one nor the other ever returned. Upon a consultation, in consequence, held on board, it was resolved to return to Kamtschatka. Behring, in the mean time, endeavored to explore the coast he first saw, and to take in water. He set sail on the 21st of July, determined to run as high as 60° north. He found it impossible to advance direct, the coast constantly running out to the south-west. He found himself in a labyrinth of islands which bordered the continent, so that often, when he thought himself clear, he discovered land on the larboard and starboard bow. He was then obliged to drop astern, and find a passage that way, encountering great difficulties from calms and currents.

On the 3d of September, while still among those islands, they discovered some of the inhabitants, by whom they were well received. The natives presented whale's flesh to the Russians, — the only provision they had with them, — and seemed to desire they would regale themselves. They had been on a fishing expedition, as their canoes were drawn up on the shore ; but no females or habitations were seen, their dwellings probably being on the mainland. They were unarmed. After some other communications with the natives, and encountering contrary winds, the Russians were overtaken by a violent storm, which lasted for seventeen days. They found, though they had not kept up their sails, that they had been driven back to 48° 18′ of latitude. The scurvy now began to appear among them; hardly a day passed without the death of one of the crew, and hands enough, in health, were scarcely left to manœuvre the vessel.

A return to Kamtschatka was resolved upon. After discovering and naming several capes and islands, they saw two which, by an unfortunate mistake, they took for the two first of the Kourile Isles. By this they erred in their reckoning. They in vain took their course to the west; the shore of Kamtschatka remained invisible, and there was soon no hope, so late in the season, of making a port in that country. The crew, notwithstanding their sufferings from cold and continued rain, attended to their duty. The scurvy had already so far advanced that the steersman was conducted to the helm by two other invalids, who happened still to have the use of their legs, by supporting him under the arms. When he could no longer steer, from suffering, he was succeeded by another no better able to execute the labor than himself. Thus did the miserable crew waste away into death. They were obliged to carry few sails, for they had not hands to reef them, if at any time it should be required; and such as they had were nearly worn out, so that the slightest storm was sufficient to shiver them into threads; in this case they could not be replaced from the stores, for want of sailors able to bend new ones. The rain was soon succeeded by snow. The nights now grew longer and darker, and they had now, in addition to their former precautions, to guard against shipwreck. The fresh water on board was rapidly diminishing. The labor of the ship became too hard for the few who were still able to be about.

For some days the ship had remained impassive in the water, lying as the wind and waves drove her. On the 4th of November they again endeavored to sail to the westward, without knowing in what latitude they were, or at what distance from Kamtschatka; but it was the only point on which a single hope of their deliverance remained. The joy of the crew, when they came in sight of land, may be conceived; it was about eight o'clock in the morning. They attempted to approach, but they were still at a great distance, and could only see the tops of mountains covered with snow. As they drew nearer, night came upon them. It was judged best, therefore, to keep out to sea until day appeared, that they might not be exposed to shipwreck in the dark. In the morning they found the cordage on the starboard side of the vessel had given way. They could not, therefore, manage the ship much longer. A consultation was held. It was agreed that the ship was no longer manageable, that the water was much diminished, and the sickness on board increased. The humidity had been succeeded by intense cold, of which the increase was now, from the season, to be expected, and life must soon become insupportable. It was, therefore, decided, at all risks, to make for the land, to save their lives, and, perhaps, their ship.

The small sails were alone set, from the weakness of the mast, after the failure of the cordage. The wind was north; the depth of water thirty-six fathoms, with a bottom of sand; two hours after, they found twelve fathoms. They now contrived to get overboard an anchor, and run it out three quarters of a cable's length. At six the cable parted, and tremendous waves bore the ship upon a rock, where she struck twice, yet, in a

5

moment after, they had five fathoms of water. A second anchor was thrown out, and the cable again parted. They had no third anchor ready. While they were preparing to let go another, a huge wave lifted the vessel over the reef. In an instant she lay in calm water. The anchor was put out, and she was safely moored in four fathoms and a half, with a sandy bottom, and only about three hundred fathoms from the shore. The next morning they discovered that, by a good providence, they had been led to the only spot where it was possible they could have been carried over the ridge of rocks, and that twenty fathoms' distance right or left of the place high rocks rose out of the sea, against which they must have perished during the darkness of the night.

Winter was now come. The crew, worn down with fatigue, reposed until mid-day, and then the boat was lowered. On the 6th of November, the second in command, Mr. Waxall, landed. They found the country barren, and covered with snow. A clear stream of excellent water, not yet frozen, ran down from the mountains to the shore. No trees, or even shrubs, were visible. Firewood might be obtained from what the sea had drifted on the land, but it must be collected from under the snow. Hut or shelter there was none; but they discovered near the banks of a torrent some deep hollows in the sand, which they prepared to clear out, and cover over with the ship's sails, so as to make a shelter, until they could construct cabins of wood. It was accordingly resolved to take the sick on shore the next day, as soon as places were prepared for them.

On the 8th of November they were landed. Some died on being brought up into the air from below, others in the boat, and some upon getting ashore. The bodies of the dead were instantly attacked by foxes, which came to their prey without fear, as if they had never before seen man. They were obliged to drive these animals away from the corpses, the feet and hands of which were mangled before they could be interred. On the 9th of November the captain was landed, well secured from the atmosphere, and placed in a hollow by himself. The sick were all brought to the land in a day or two more; but it was remarked that, of all who took to their beds in the ship, not one survived. These were principally such as were indifferent to existence, or feared the disease, and succumbed to it. Their disorder commenced with extreme lassitude, which made the person attacked spiritless, and indifferent to everything. A sort of asthma then came on, which was felt on the smallest movement of the body. The person attacked preferred inactivity, and would rather lie down and die than move about. Soon after, the limbs were struck with severe pains, the legs became inflamed, the skin yellow, the body covered with livid marks, the teeth loose, and the mouth and gums bloody. Some of those attacked were nervous, and terrified at the slightest sound they heard. Others seemed to eat heartily, and did not think themselves in danger. They quitted their hammocks when they heard the order for going on shore, dressed themselves, and believed they should quickly be well. On leaving the interior of the ship, and the close, corrupted air of the hold, and coming into the keen atmosphere, they speedily expired.

Those survived who resisted the complaint so much as not to take to their beds, — who kept in motion on their feet as much as possible, especially if they succeeded, by natural lightness of temper, in driving away melancholy thoughts. The instances of successful resistance to the disorder were most observed in the officers of the ship, who were obliged to be on deck to look into everything. The captain, alone, of all the officers, died. His age and temperament inclined him to inactivity. He took his friends, at last, for his enemies, and some could not come into his sight, on that account, towards the close of his illness. Two of the officers took the disease by remaining on board in the bad air of the hold, after the crew had quitted the ship, but they both recovered.

Behring died on the 8th of December, 1741, on the island which now bears his name. He had a great passion for voyages and travels in his youth, and had seen many parts of the world, and a great deal of service. In a previous voyage he had sailed through the strait that bears his name. He had served under Peter the Great; was made lieutenant in 1707, and captain-lieutenant in 1710. He was thus a seaman from his cradle, and was chosen to command the expedition from Kamtschatka on account of his previous services. He left his name a record to the end of time in the straits that separate Asia and America. His death was singular. He was almost buried before he breathed his last sigh. His men placed him in the most commodious spot, the day after the disembarkation of the sick commenced. He was borne with great care into a sort of tent, upon or rather in the sand, and as well secured as possible. Every day he detached the loose sand from the sides of the place where he lay, so that he soon covered his feet with it. Those who attended him cleared it away, but at last he would not suffer them to do it any more. He showed anger if it were attempted, and by degrees had so accumulated it about him that when he died he was half covered. They buried him near the spot; and the island is his monument, bearing his name in the charts of all nations.

Not long after the death of the captain, the Russians saw their vessel wrecked before their eyes. It was their only means of escape from the dreary spot in which they were wintering. A storm arose on the 29th of December, the cable snapped, and the ship came ashore almost close to where the Russians were living. In the morning she was found buried eight or ten feet in sand, and completely shattered. The sea had spoiled a great proportion of their remaining provisions. This was a fearful loss to them.

They had now two important objects to attain. The first was to discover on what part of the world they had been cast. The second, to find the means of subsistence. Parties were sent out to explore. After an absence of three days, one returned, and stated that they had not perceived the least trace of men, but they had seen a great number of what were called in Kamtschatka sea-beavers. They had also seen a great number of blue and white foxes, which showed no signs of fear upon observing them. Hence they concluded that the country on which they had landed was not inhabited. They set out again more in the interior of the island, with the design to cross the country to the opposite side from that where they had come on shore. They found a high hill three or four leagues from the sea, and, ascending it, could see the sea both to the eastward and westward of them, from which observation they had no doubt they were upon an island. They found no trees, except a few willows on the sides of a rivulet.

Having thus satisfied themselves they were upon an island, they proceeded to examine what stores and provisions had been left them that they could use. They first made a reserve of eight hundred-weight of flour, which was to serve as sea stock in their voyage to

Kamtschatka, after which they regulated the daily allowance of each person. Although thirty of the crew had died, there would not have been sufficient for their subsistence, had there not been wild animals on the island to eke out their stores.

The flesh of the beavers was hard and stringy. They killed a great number for their skins, of which they collected nine hundred. The surgeon had three hundred to his own share when they embarked from the island to return to Siberia.

In the month of March no more beavers were seen, and in their places seals made their appearance. The flesh of these animals they found disagreeable. They were relieved from the necessity of feeding upon them by killing sea-lions, the flesh of which they found excellent. The walrus, or sea-horse, was also taken, and served them for food. One of these, of eight hundredweight, was sufficient for fifteen days' consumption. The flesh was like beef, and that of the young ones not inferior to the best veal. The fat, which lined the flesh to the depth of three or four inches, very much resembled lard; and the Russians used it as a substitute for butter. They filled several hogsheads with the flesh, which they salted, as part of their provisions for their future voyage.

A whale came on shore during the winter near their habitation, and, being short of other food at the time, they cut out the blubber in square masses, and boiled it to separate the oil, which they ate. On the commencement of spring, a second whale was cast on shore in the same way, and then, rejecting the stale meat, they supplied themselves with that which was more fresh.

When the snow melted in the month of March, 1742, these unfortunate men began to think of some means of return. They were forty-five in number. The chief officer, Mr. Waxall, proposed that the old vessel should be pulled to pieces, and a new one constructed, of a size to carry them all. This plan was unanimously adopted. It was now the beginning of April, a favorable time to commence operations. All took their share in the work, and the entire month was employed in breaking up the wreck to obtain materials for the new vessel.

Three Russian carpenters had died since their arrival on the island, and there was not one left. A Cossack of Siberia, named Sawa Slaradoubzov, who had worked in the yard at Okhotsk, offered to construct the vessel if the proportions were given to him. He succeeded in laying down the new ship, a service considered of such importance, as well as ingenuity, that he was rewarded, on his return, by being elevated to the rank of Sinboiarskoy, the lowest degree of nobility in Russia.

On the 6th of May they began to construct their new ship. It was forty feet long by thirteen broad. At the beginning of June it was ready for planking up, the frame being complete. It had but one mast and deck, a cabin was built on the poop, and a cooking place in the forepart of the vessel; it had four places for oars on each side. Many things were still wanting, but they nevertheless proceeded to calk the planks, that the ship might be got ready for sea. They took care to construct a boat to accompany their vessel, capable of holding nine or ten persons.

They launched their vessel on the 10th of August, and called it the St. Peter, after the ship out of which she had been built. The shot and iron-work of the old vessel they employed for ballast in the new. The weather was fortunately calm for six days, during which time they got in the mast and rudder, bent the sails, and took in their provisions. Their vessel drew five feet water. All having embarked, they set sail on the 16th.

They cleared the rocks by the aid of their oars, and continued to row until they were about three leagues at sea, when they hoisted their sails with a slight breeze from the north. They found that their ship sailed and worked as well as if she had been built by able workmen. On the 18th, they had a strong gale against them from the south-west. The fear of a storm made them fling a part of their ballast overboard. On the 25th, they came in sight of Kamtschatka, entered the Bay of Awatska the next day, and on the 27th anchored in the port of Petropalauski.

In 1760, Schalaroff, a merchant of Yakutsk, whose name is venerated throughout Siberia, determined on trying whether the passage attempted by Behring could or could not be accomplished. He persevered during three seasons, in defiance of mutiny and hardships innumerable. He, too, was wrecked on the desolate coast seventy miles east of Cape Chelagskoi, and, with all his crew, died of starvation. Three years later, Sergeant Andrejeff conducted a sledge expedition across the ice to the Bear Islands ; his reports, which were much exaggerated, led shortly afterwards to the accurate survey of this and the adjacent country. Cook's exploration, of which we shall hereafter speak, led to another expedition on the part of the Russians, which sailed from the Kolyma in 1787, under Captain Billings ; but the attempts made to navigate either to the east or the west were both defeated. Further efforts were made at intervals during the first quarter of the present century, some of them mainly to search for the northern continent, whose existence, far in the Polar Sea, had so often been the subject of rumor.

Last we come to the expeditions commanded by Lieutenant Anjou and Admiral von Wrangell, carried on also by means of dogs and sledges, from the year

1820 to 1823; the latter taking the mouth of the Kolyma for his starting-point, the former the river Iana. These undertakings were especially promoted by the Emperor Alexander, and were conducted with all the care and skill warranted by an advanced state of science and philosophy. They failed but in one particular — the discovery of the northern continent. How diligently and perseveringly this was searched for, is best proved by the narrative of perils endured, even to the risk of life, in the arduous enterprise. Three times was the frozen surface of the sea traversed without leading to any definite result; on the fourth journey, in March, 1823, Von Wrangell reached the latitude of 70° 51′, longitude 175° 27′ west — one hundred and five wersts in a direct line from the mainland. Soundings gave a depth of twenty-two and a half fathoms; the ice here was thin and weak. More than once the party had only been saved from breaking through by the speed at which the dogs travelled over it. In the distance a screen of dense blue vapor — a certain indication of open water — was visible, on which the admiral remarks:

"Notwithstanding this sure token of the impossibility of proceeding much further, we continued to go due north for about nine wersts, when we arrived at the edge of an immense break in the ice, extending east and west further than the eye could reach, and which at the narrowest part was more than a hundred and fifty fathoms across. * * * * We climbed one of the loftiest ice-hills, where we obtained an extensive view towards the north, and whence we beheld the wide, immeasurable ocean spread before our gaze. It was a fearful and magnificent, but to us a melancholy spectacle. Fragments of ice of enormous size floated on the surface of the agitated ocean, and were thrown by the waves with awful violence against the edge of the ice-field on the further side of the channel before us. The collisions were so tremendous, that large masses were every instant broken away; and it was evident that the portion of ice which still divided the channel from the open ocean would soon be completely destroyed. Had we attempted to have ferried ourselves across upon one of the floating pieces of ice, we should not have found firm footing upon our arrival. Even on our own side, fresh lanes of water were continually forming, and extending in every direction in the field of ice behind us. With a painful feeling of the impossibility of overcoming the obstacles which nature opposed to us, our last hope vanished of discovering the land, which we yet believed to exist."

On returning from this extreme limit of their adventurous journey, the party were placed in a situation of extreme risk. "We had hardly proceeded one werst," writes M. von Wrangell, "when we found ourselves in a fresh labyrinth of lanes of water, which hemmed us in on every side. As all the floating pieces around us were smaller than the one on which we stood, which was seventy-five fathoms across, and as we saw many certain indications of an approaching storm, I thought it better to remain on the larger mass, which offered us somewhat more security; and thus we waited quietly whatever Providence should decree. Dark clouds now rose from the west, and the whole atmosphere became filled with a damp vapor. A strong breeze suddenly sprang up from the west, and increased in less than half an hour to a storm. Every moment huge masses of ice around us were dashed against each other, and broken into a thousand fragments. Our little party remained fast on our ice-island, which was tossed to and fro by the waves. We gazed in most painful inactivity on the wild conflict of the elements, expecting every moment to be swallowed up. We had been three long hours in this position, and still the mass of ice beneath us held together, when suddenly it was caught by the storm, and hurled against a large field of ice. The crash was terrific, and the mass beneath us was shattered into fragments. At that dreadful moment, when escape seemed impossible, the impulse of self-preservation implanted in every living being saved us. Instinctively we all sprang at once on the sledges, and urged the dogs to their full speed. They flew across the yielding fragments to the field on which we had been stranded, and safely reached a part of it of firmer character, on which were several hummocks, and where the dogs immediately ceased running, conscious, apparently, that the danger was past. We were saved: we joyfully embraced each other, and united in thanks to God for our preservation from such imminent peril."

More than once during this trip the party heard from the Tchuktches that land could be seen far away in the northern seas. The part of the coast alluded to was Cape Jakan, which the explorers afterwards visited; but, although "they gazed long and earnestly on the horizon, in hopes, as the atmosphere was clear, of discerning some appearance of the northern land," they "could see nothing of it."

ICE-RAFT.

CHAPTER III.

OFFER OF PARLIAMENT. — HEARNE'S JOURNEY. — PHIPPS. — NELSON. — COOK. — MACKENZIE. — SIR JOHN ROSS'S FIRST VOYAGE. — BUCHAN AND FRANKLIN. — DANGEROUS SITUATION OF THE TRENT AND DOROTHEA.

In 1743 the British Parliament offered a reward of twenty thousand pounds to any one who should sail to the north-west by way of Hudson's Strait, which passage, it was declared, would be "of great benefit and advantage to the kingdom." Between 1769–72 Mr. Hearne undertook three overland journeys across the territories of the Hudson's Bay Company, to the shores of the Polar Sea. He failed in the first two attempts; in the third he succeeded in reaching a large and rapid river, — the Coppermine, — and followed it down nearly to its mouth; but, as there is reason to believe, without actually viewing the sea. The proof of the existence of the river was the most important result of Mr. Hearne's labors; for such scientific observations as he attempted are loose and unsatisfactory.

In the following year (1773), in consequence of communications made to the Royal Society on the possibility of reaching the North Pole, Captain Phipps (afterwards Lord Mulgrave) was sent out with two vessels to effect this interesting object. He coasted the eastern shore of Spitzbergen to 80° 48′ of latitude, and was there stopped by the ice. With Phipps on this expedition was Nelson, the future naval hero of England, then a mere boy. Young as he was, he was on one occasion appointed to command a boat, sent out to explore a passage into the open water. It was the means of saving another boat from imminent danger. One of the officers had wounded a walrus. As no other animal has so human-like an expression of countenance, so also is there no one that seems to possess more of the passions of humanity. The wounded animal dived immediately, and brought up a number of its companions; and they all joined in an attack on the boat. They wrested an oar from one of the men, and it was with the utmost difficulty that the crew could prevent them from staving or upsetting her, till Nelson came up: and the walruses, finding their enemies thus reinforced, dispersed. Young Nelson exposed himself in a most daring manner.

For a time Captain Phipps was so surrounded by ice,

that he made preparations to abandon his ships. On the 7th of August the men began to haul the boats over the ice. But on the 9th the ships were moved a little through some small openings; and in the course of the day they got past the boats, and took them on board again. On the morrow a favorable wind sprang up; all sail was set, and, after forcing their way through much heavy ice, the ships cleared it, and gained the open sea. The season was now so far advanced that nothing more could be attempted, and the expedition returned to England.

In 1776 Cook sailed on the fatal expedition which cost England her famous navigator, with instructions to attempt the passage of the Icy Sea from Behring's Strait to Baffin's Bay. The clause of the act above referred to, wherein Hudson's Strait was exclusively specified, was altered to include "any northern passage" for ships; and five thousand pounds was further voted to any one who should get within one degree of the pole. Cook, with all his perseverance, could not penetrate beyond Icy Cape, latitude 70° 45′, where he found the ice stretching in a compact mass across to the opposite continent, which he also visited, sailing as far as Cape North, on the coast of Asia. It would appear that expectations prevailed of the enterprising mariner's success; for a vessel was sent to Baffin's Bay to wait for him, in 1777, in charge of Lieutenant Pickersgill.

One other journey within this century remains to be noticed—that by Mackenzie, under sanction of the Hudson's Bay Company, with objects similar to those of Hearne. In 1789 he left Fort Chipewyan, crossed Slave Lake, and descended the Mackenzie River, a stream of much greater magnitude than the Coppermine, to an island where the tide rose and fell. But, as in the case of his predecessor, we have no certainty that he reached the ocean. Rivers, however, play an important part in Arctic discovery; and it was something gained to know that the sea could be reached by their means. We may here observe, once for all, that these land expeditions, whose prime object has been to determine the northern coast-line of America, are not to be confounded with the attempts to discover the north-west passage.

The result of these discouragements was a cessation of naval researches, which continued for many years; but at length a change took place, as sudden and inexplicable as the accumulation of ice from centuries before which cut off the Danish colonies in Greenland from communication with the mother country. In 1816–17, the Greenland whalers reported the sea to be clearer of ice than at any former time within their knowledge. This fact engaged the attention of the British Admiralty; and the Council of the Royal Society were consulted as to the prospects of renewed operations in the Arctic regions. Their reply was favorable; and in 1818 two expeditions were fitted out — the one to discover the north-west passage, the other to reach the pole. Captain (soon Sir John) Ross and Lieut. (soon Sir Edward) Parry, in the vessels Isabella and Alexander, were intrusted with the former of these objects. They were especially charged to examine the great openings described by Baffin as existing at the head of the vast bay which he so diligently explored; and, in carrying out these instructions, the commanders found full reason to applaud the care and perseverance of the able navigator, who had preceded them by two hundred years. It must be remembered that we are now treating of a period when science put forward its imperative claims, and when, as at present, something more was required than a meagre chart of a previously-unexplored coast, and graphic accounts of new countries and their inhabitants. Astronomy, geology, meteorology, magnetism, natural history, were all clamorous for new facts, or for satisfactory tests of those already known; and not only men of science, but the public at large, looked with deep interest to the results.

The open state of the sea greatly facilitated the purposes of the expedition. On the 18th of April the navigators sailed down the Thames, and by the end of the month were off the Shetland Islands. On the 27th of May they came in view of Cape Farewell, round which, as usual, were floating numerous and lofty icebergs of the most varied forms and tints. On the 14th of June they reached the Whale Islands, where they were informed by the governor of the Danish settlement that the past winter had been uncommonly severe; that the neighboring bays and straits had been all frozen two months earlier than usual; and that some of the channels northward of his station were still inaccessible, owing to the ice. On the 17th of June, in the neighborhood of Waygat Island, an impenetrable barrier obliged the discoverers to stop their course, making themselves fast to an iceberg, and having forty-five whale-ships in company. Observations made ashore proved this island to be misplaced on the maps by no less than five degrees of longitude. On the 7th of August, in the same latitude, a heavy gale sprang up, which, driving the ice against the vessels, made a display of its terrible power. Providentially, when instant destruction was expected, the mass receded, and the ships, owing to the extraordinary strength of their construction, escaped without material injury.

Proceeding along a high mountainous coast, the expedition came to a tribe of Esquimaux, who, of all human beings, seemed to live in a state of the deepest seclusion. They had never before seen men belonging to the civilized world, or to a race different from their own. The first party whom the navigators approached showed every sign of alarm, dreading, as was afterwards understood, a fatal influence from the mere touch of beings whom they regarded as members of an unknown species. They soon, however, acquired greater confidence, and gave the usual proof of it by making free with whatever they could carry away. Following the general usage, they have sledges drawn by large and powerful teams of dogs; their chase is chiefly confined to hares, foxes of various colors, the seal, and the narwal. They rejected with horror the proffered luxuries of biscuit, sweetmeats, or spirits; train-oil, as it streamed from various species of fish, alone gratified their palate. Captain Ross, swayed by national impressions, gave to this district the name of the Arctic Highlands.

In the northern part of this coast the navigators observed a remarkable phenomenon — a range of cliffs, the snowy covering of which had exchanged its native white for a tint of deep crimson. The latest observations on this red snow have established the vegetable origin of the color.

Having now passed Cape Dudley Digges, the commodore found himself among those spacious sounds which Baffin had named, but so imperfectly described. They all appeared to him, however, to be either bays enclosed by land, or obstructed by impenetrable barriers of ice. He sailed past Wolstenholme and Whale Sounds very quickly, without approaching even their entrance, concluding them to be blocked up with ice, and to afford no hope of a passage. As these openings stretched towards the north, it must be admitted that they could not, in this high latitude, be considered very favorable as to the object he had in view. He came next to Sir Thomas Smith's Sound, which Baffin described as the most spacious in the whole circuit of these coasts. This was regarded with greater attention;

but Captain Ross satisfied himself that he had distinctly seen it, at the distance of eighteen leagues, completely enclosed by land. He soon arrived at an extensive bay, which had hitherto been unobserved; afterwards to that which Baffin called Alderman Jones's Sound; but in respect to both, the ice at their entrance, and the apparent boundary of high land in the interior, led, as in the other instances, to an unfavorable conclusion.

The season was now somewhat advanced, the end of August approached, the sun set after an uninterrupted day of two months and a half, and a thick fog rendered the lengthening nights more gloomy. The land, seen at some distance, consisted of very high and steep hills, presenting, however, some spots fit for human habitation. An opening forty-five miles wide, to the southward of a promontory which was named Cape Charlotte, was decided against on the usual grounds. On the 30th of August the expedition came to a most magnificent inlet, bordered by lofty mountains of peculiar grandeur, while the water, being clear, and free from ice, presented so tempting an appearance, that it was impossible to refrain from entering. This channel, which soon proved to be Lancaster Sound, was ascended for thirty miles, during which run officers and men crowded the topmast, filled with enthusiastic hope, and judging that it afforded a much fairer prospect of success than any of those so hastily passed. Captain Ross, however, soon thought that he discovered a high ridge stretching directly across the inlet; and though a great part of it was deeply involved in mist, a passage in this direction was by him judged to be hopeless. The sea being open, however, the commander proceeded; but about twelve o'clock, Mr. Beverley, the assistant-surgeon, came down from the crow's nest, and stated that he had seen the land extending very nearly across the entire bay. Hereupon, it is said, all hopes were renounced, even by the most sanguine, and Captain Ross sailed onward merely for the purpose of making some magnetical observations.

At three o'clock, the sky having cleared, the commander himself went on deck, when he states that he distinctly saw across the bottom of the bay a chain of mountains, continuous, and connected with those which formed its opposite shores. The weather then becoming unsettled, he made the signal to steer the vessels out of Lancaster Sound.

On regaining the entrance of this great channel, Captain Ross continued to steer southward along the western shore, without seeing any entrance which afforded equal promise. Cumberland Strait alone was similar in magnitude ; but, as it could lead only into the higher latitudes of Hudson's Bay, it afforded little chance of a passage into the Arctic Sea. After surveying, therefore, some of these shores, he returned home early in October. The captain arrived in England under the most decided conviction that Baffin's observations had been perfectly correct, and that Lancaster Sound was a bay, affording no entrance into any western sea. If even any strait existed between the mountains, it must, he conceived, be forever innavigable, on account of the ice with which it is filled.

The Dorothea and Trent, commanded by Captain Buchan and Lieut. (afterwards Sir John) Franklin, comprised the expedition destined for the pole. Franklin, in regard to whose fate so much public interest was in subsequent years excited, entered the navy in early life as midshipman of the Porpoise, one of the ships employed by Captain Flinders on the survey of the coasts of Australia, and was wrecked in her. Next in the Polyphemus, as midshipman and master's mate, from

1801 to 1808, he was in the fleet with Nelson at the battle of Copenhagen. He was next appointed acting-lieutenant in the Bedford; and was lieutenant of the Bellerophon in the battle of Trafalgar, in 1805, and also in the Bedford in the attack on New Orleans, in 1815, where he commanded in the boats, was wounded, gazetted, and highly spoken of. He was considered a good nautical surveyor, well versed in the use of instruments, and a thorough seaman.

Captain Beechey, to whom we are indebted for an interesting account of the present voyage, observes: "The peculiarity of the proposed route afforded opportunities of making some useful experiments on the elliptical figure of the earth; on magnetic phenomena; on the refraction of the atmosphere in high latitudes in ordinary circumstances, and over extensive masses of ice; and on the temperature and specific gravity of the sea at the surface, and at various depths; and on meteorological and other interesting phenomena." The vessels sailed in April, 1818; Magdalena Bay, in Spitzbergen, having been appointed as a place of rendezvous, in case of separation.

Though this expedition, like that of Ross, was a failure in its main object, yet, unlike the other, it was not owing to any want of exertion, zeal, or intelligence, in the two commanders or officers; on the contrary, the two ships were supplied with some of those who, in future voyages, so greatly distinguished themselves as to obtain the highest steps of promotion, and to receive honorary rewards. The instructions directed that they were to make the best of their way into the Spitzbergen seas, where they should endeavor to pass to the northward, between Spitzbergen and Greenland, without stopping on either of their coasts, and use their best endeavors to reach the North Pole; with a suggestion, that where the sea is deepest and least connected with the land, it will be found most clear of ice.

On the 18th of May the ships encountered a severe gale, and under even storm staysails were buried gunwale deep in the waves. On the 24th they sighted Cherie Island, situated in lat. 74° 33′ N., and long. 17° 40′ E., formerly so noted for its fishery, being much frequented by walruses. For many years the Muscovy Company carried on a lucrative trade by sending ships to the island for oil; as many as a thousand animals being often captured by the crew of a single ship in the course of six or seven hours.

The discovery ships passed slowly through the small floes and huge masses of ice which floated by in succession. The progress through such a labyrinth of frozen masses was a most interesting sight. The officers and crew did not tire of watching the scene. Captain Beechey thus describes the general impression created: "Very few of us had ever seen the sun at midnight; and this night happening to be particularly clear, his broad red disc, curiously distorted by refraction, and sweeping majestically along the northern horizon, was an object of imposing grandeur, which riveted to the deck some of our crew, who would perhaps have beheld with indifference the less imposing effect of the icebergs. The rays were too oblique to illuminate more than the inequalities of the floes, and, falling thus partially on the grotesque shapes, either really assumed by the ice or distorted by the unequal refraction of the atmosphere, so betrayed the imagination that it required no great exertion of fancy to trace in various directions architectural edifices, grottos, and caves, here and there, glittering as if with precious metals."

At Cherie Island the walruses were found very numerous. Of the habits and character of the walrus

Lieut. Beechey gives, after frequent intercourse with them, a very interesting account. Their affection for their young, and their unflinching courage in defending them, are remarkable; not more so their compassionate conduct toward a wounded companion, whom they will never leave till carried off to a place of safety; and even the young ones on such occasions will turn fiercely against the boats of the pursuers. A single instance will suffice to show the care and affection bestowed on their young.

"We were greatly amused by the singular and affectionate conduct of a walrus towards its young. In the vast sheet of ice that surrounded the ships there were occasionally many pools; and, when the weather was clear and warm, animals of various kinds would frequently rise and sport about in them, or crawl from thence upon the ice to bask in the warmth of the sun. A walrus rose in one of these pools close to the ship, and, finding everything quiet, dived down and brought up its young, which it held by its breast by pressing it with its flipper. In this manner it moved about the pool, keeping in an erect posture, and always directing the face of the young toward the vessel. On the slightest movement on board, the mother released her flipper and pushed the young one under water; but, when everything was again quiet, brought it up as before, and for a length of time continued to play about in the pool, to the great amusement of the seamen, who gave her credit for abilities in tuition which, though possessed of considerable sagacity, she hardly merited."

On one occasion, some of the crew of the Trent, having wounded a walrus, took to their boat, when they were assailed by a large number of walruses. These animals rose, snorting with rage, and rushed at the boat; and it was with the utmost difficulty they were prevented from upsetting or staving it. They would place their tusks on the gunwale, or rush at it with their heads. The herd was so numerous, and their attacks so incessant, that there was not time to load a musket. The purser fortunately had his gun loaded, and the men now being nearly exhausted with chopping and sticking at their assailants, he snatched it up, and, thrusting the muzzle down the throat of a large and formidable walrus, who seemed to be the leader of the herd, fired into his bowels. The wound proved mortal, and the animal

ATTACK BY WALRUSES.

fell back among his companions, who immediately desisted from the attack, assembled round him, and in a moment quitted the boat, swimming away as hard as they could with their leader, whom they actually bore up with their tusks, and assiduously preserved from sinking.

Many similar acts of compassion, on the part of these animals towards their wounded companions, were observed. On one occasion, when several walruses were attacked upon a beach, near Magdalena Bay, the first discharge of muskets drove all those who could crawl into the sea; but, immediately upon their panic subsiding, they returned to the shore and dragged their wounded companions into the water, either by main force, or by rolling them over with their tusks.

On the 28th of May, the weather being foggy and severe, with heavy falls of snow, the ships separated, and the Trent stood to the northward toward Magdalena Bay, the place of rendezvous, along the edge of the main body of ice: they met here, and, seeing it impossible to penetrate the marginal line of the ice, and the season being very early, the commander determined on passing a few days in that bay, in which they anchored on the 3d of June. The ice was in the cove and upper part of the harbor, but was in a rapidly decaying state, and, on revisiting their anchorage here in the beginning of August, it had entirely disappeared. Magdalena Bay is rendered conspicuous by four glaciers, the smallest two hundred feet above the sea, on the slope of a mountain. It is called the Hanging Iceberg, and seems, so Beechey says, as if a very slight matter would detach it from the mountain, and precipitate it into the sea. The largest of the four extends two or three miles inland: owing to the great rents in the surface, it has been named the Wagon-way, from the resemblance of the fissures to ruts made by wheels. Several glaciers similar to those were observed near Dane's Gut, the largest about ten thousand feet in length by two or three hundred feet in perpendicular height. In the vicinity of these icebergs a strict observance of silence is necessary; the explosion of a gun scarcely ever fails to bring down one of these masses. Mr. Beechey says that on two occasions they witnessed avalanches on the most magnificent scale.

"The first was occasioned by the discharge of a musket at about half a mile's distance from the glacier. Immediately after the report of the gun, a noise resembling thunder was heard in the direction of the iceberg (glacier), and in a few seconds more an immense piece broke away, and fell headlong into the sea. The crew of the launch, supposing themselves beyond the reach of its influence, quietly looked upon the scene, when presently a sea arose and rolled toward the shore with such rapidity, that the crew had not time to take any precautions, and the boat was in consequence washed upon the beach, and completely filled by the succeeding wave. As soon as their astonishment had subsided, they examined the boat, and found her so badly stove that it became necessary to repair her in order to return to the ship. They had also the curiosity to measure the distance the boat had been carried by the wave, and found it to be ninety-six feet."

In viewing the same glacier from a boat at a distance, a second avalanche took place, which afforded them the gratification of witnessing the creation, as it were, of a sea iceberg; an opportunity which has occurred to few, though it is generally understood that such monsters can only be generated on shore.

"This occurred on a remarkably fine day, when the quietness of the bay was first interrupted by the noise of the falling body. Lieutenant Franklin and myself had approached one of these stupendous walls of ice, and were endeavoring to search into the innermost recess of a deep cavern that was near the foot of the glacier, when we heard a report as if of a cannon, and, turning to the quarter whence it proceeded, we perceived an immense piece of the front of the berg sliding down from the height of two hundred feet at least into the sea, and dispersing the water in every direction, accompanied by a loud, grinding noise, and followed by a quantity of water, which, being previously lodged in the fissures, now made its escape in numberless small cataracts over the front of the glacier."

After describing the disturbance occasioned by the plunge of this enormous fragment, and the rollers which swept over the surface of the bay, and obliged the Dorothea, then careening at the distance of four miles, to aright, by releasing the tackles, he thus proceeds:

"The piece that had been disengaged at first wholly disappeared under water, and nothing was seen but a violent boiling of the sea, and a shooting up of clouds of spray, like that which occurs at the foot of a great cataract. After a short time it reäppeared, raising its head full a hundred feet above the surface, with water pouring down from all parts of it; and then, laboring as if doubtful which way it should fall, it rolled over, and, after rocking about some minutes, at length became settled. We now approached it, and found it nearly a quarter of a mile in circumference, and sixty feet out of the water. Knowing its specific gravity, and making a fair allowance for its inequalities, we computed its weight at 421,660 tons. A stream of salt water was still pouring down its sides, and there was a continual cracking noise, as loud as that of a cart-whip, occasioned, I suppose, by the escape of fixed (confined) air."

Mr. Beechey confirms what has frequently been found and noticed — the mildness of the temperature on the western coast of Spitzbergen, there being little or no sensation of cold, though the thermometer might be only a few degrees above the freezing point. The brilliant and lively effect of a clear day, when the sun shines forth, with a pure sky, whose azure hue is so intense as to find no parallel even in the boasted Italian sky, affords, in Mr. Beechey's opinion, a full compensation for the cloudy and misty weather, when the hills are clothed with new-fallen snow, and all appears dreary and desolate. The radiation of the sun, he observes, in some sheltered situations, is so powerful, during two hours on either side of noon, that they frequently observed the thermometer upon the ice in the offing at 58°, 62°, 67° ; and once at *midnight* it rose to 73°, although in the shade at the same time it was only 36°. Hence are found varieties of Alpine plants, grasses, and lichens, such as in the more southern aspects flourish in great luxuriance ; they are here found ascending to a considerable height, "so that," says Beechey, "we have frequently seen the reindeer browsing at an elevation of fifteen hundred feet."

On account of the mildness of the temperature, the shores of Spitzbergen are frequented by multitudes of animals of various descriptions. "From an early hour in the morning until the period of rest returned, the shores around us reverberated with the merry cry of the little auk, willocks, divers, cormorants, gulls, and other aquatic birds; and, wherever we went, groups of walruses, basking in the sun, mingled their playful roar with the husky bark of the seal." The little auks or rotges (the *Alca alle*) are stated to be so numerous, that "we have frequently seen an uninterrupted line of them extending full half-way over the bay, or to a distance of more than three miles, and so close together that thirty have fallen at one shot. This living column might be about six yards broad and as many deep ; so that, allowing sixteen birds to a cubic yard, there would be four millions of these creatures on the wing at one time." This number, he adds, appears very large ; yet, when it is told that the little rotges rise in such multitudes as to darken the air, and that their chorus is distinctly audible at a distance of four miles, the estimate will not appear to be exaggerated.

At Vogel Sang and Cloven Cliff, between which is Fair Haven, wherein the ships anchored, the surrounding islands are described as clothed with lichens and other rich pasturage for reindeer, which creatures are here so abundant (upon Vogel Sang in particular), that this island alone supplied the expedition with forty carcasses in high condition, the fat on the loins being from four to six inches thick, and a carcass prepared for dressing weighing two hundred and eighty-five pounds. These fine creatures showed evident marks of affection for each other. "They were at this time in pairs, and when one was shot the other would hang over it, and occasionally lick it, apparently bemoaning its fate ; and, if not immediately killed, would stand three or four shots rather than desert its fallen companion." "This compassionate conduct," continues Beechey, "it is needless to say, doubled our chance of success, though I must confess it was obtained in violation of our better feelings." These animals are said to take to the water freely, and swim from one island to another. The boats of the Trent took four, which they wished to retain alive ; but they were so wild that they broke their slender limbs, and inflicted other serious wounds, so that it became necessary to put an end to their sufferings by killing them.

At one of the islets near Vogel Sang were also the King Eider-ducks, in such numbers that it was impossible, almost, to walk without treading on their nests, which they defended with determined resolution. If driven off by foxes, or other large animals, they hastily draw the down of the nest over the eggs, and glue it with a yellow fluid, not only to preserve the warmth of the eggs, but that, being of so offensive a nature, the foxes would not touch the eggs tainted with it. Foxes and bears are everywhere found on the shore and on the ice ; and the sea about Spitzbergen is as much alive as the land, from the multitude of burgomasters, strontjaggers, malmouks, kittiwakes, and the rest of the gull tribe, while the amphibious animals and the fish enliven both the ice and the water, from the huge whale to the minute clio on which it feeds, swallowing perhaps a million at a mouthful. In this respect of animal life, the Arctic regions of the globe essentially differ from those within the Antarctic Circle, where all appears to be stillness, silence, and solitude.

On the 7th of June the ships left Magdalena Bay, and were hampered with fragments of ice, usually called *brash-ice,* which, as they proceeded, became thicker and more solid, and, indeed, impenetrable ; but a breeze opened and dispersed it, and carried the ships into clear water. In going westerly they fell in with several whale-ships, by which they learned that the ice in that quarter was quite compact, and that fifteen vessels were beset in it. Buchan, therefore, stood to the northward. They passed Cloven Cliff, — a remarkable isolated rock, which marks the north-western boundary of Spitzbergen, — and also Red Bay, when they were stopped by the ice closing the channel between it and the shore, and became firmly fixed. By great exertions, however, they got into the floe of ice, where they remained thirteen days, when the field began to separate, and to set to the southward, at the rate of three miles an hour, and the ships got into an open sea, where, however, they were not long permitted to remain, and took shelter in Fair Haven.

Finding, from the view afforded by the hills, that the ice was driving to the northward, they again put to sea on the 6th of July, and sailed as far as 80° 15′ N., where the same impenetrable barrier obstructed their further progress. On the following day, however, so rapid had been the motion of the ice during the night, that channels of water were observed in every quarter, and the wind was favorable for proceeding along one of the open channels. Captain Buchan lost not a moment in pushing his ship into one of these openings, spreading every sail his masts would bear, and was cheerfully followed by his enterprising consort, to the great joy of all on board. In the evening, however, the channels began to close again, and the vessels were soon beset and pressed close by the packed ice. This was the end of their voyage northward, and the latitude gained was 80° 34′ N. In vain they labored two days in dragging the vessels with ropes and ice-anchors ; for, though they had left the ice behind them, the current had carried them back to the southward three miles, and it was clear that all attempts to get one mile further to the northward would be vain.

Captain Buchan being now satisfied that he had given the ice a fair trial in the vicinity of Spitzbergen, resolved on standing over toward the coast of Greenland. Having succeeded in getting the ships to the edge of the pack, and sailing along it, a violent gale of wind came on so suddenly that they were at once reduced to storm staysails. The ice was setting fast upon them, and the Dorothea being nearest to it, in order to escape immediate shipwreck, it was deemed necessary to take refuge among it. The Trent followed her example, and dashed into the "unbroken line of furious breakers, in which immense pieces of ice were heaving and subsiding with the waves, and dashing together with a violence which nothing, apparently, but a solid body, could withstand, occasioning such a noise that it was with the greatest difficulty we could make our orders heard by the crew."

"No language," he says, "I am convinced, can convey an adequate idea of the terrific grandeur of the effect now produced by the collision of the ice and the tempestuous ocean."

But when the moment arrived that the strength of the little bark was to be placed in competition with that of the great icy continent, and doubts might reasonably have arisen of her surviving the unequal conflict, the crew preserved the greatest calmness and resolution.

Captain Beechey says :

"If ever the fortitude of seamen was fairly tried, it was assuredly not less so on this occasion ; and I will not conceal the pride I felt in witnessing the bold and decisive tone in which the orders were issued by the commander of our little vessel (Franklin), and the promptitude and steadiness with which they were executed by the crew. Each person instinctively secured his own hold, and, with his eyes fixed upon the masts, awaited in breathless anxiety the moment of concussion. It soon arrived ; the brig, cutting her way through the light ice, came in violent contact with the main body. In an instant we all lost our footing, the masts bent with the impetus, and the cracking timbers from below bespoke a pressure which was calculated to awaken our serious apprehensions."

Captain Beechey proceeds to give a vivid and graphic account of the state of the ship, accompanied by a spirited and well-executed print, descriptive of her situation. "Her motion," he says, "was so great, that the ship's bell, which in the heaviest gale of wind had never struck of itself, now tolled so continually that it was ordered to be muffled for the purpose of escaping the unpleasant association it was calculated to produce." After a few hours the gale ceased, and the pack broke up sufficiently to release the ships, which were so disabled that the

Dorothea was in a foundering condition. They made the best of their way to Fair Haven in a sinking state, where they repaired their damages as well as they could ; it was obvious, however, there was an end to any further attempt as regarded the main object of the expedition. The Trent being the less damaged of the two, Lieutenant Franklin requested that he might be allowed to proceed alone in the execution of the service. This could not be acceded to, as, in the event which had occurred, Captain Buchan was directed by his instructions to take command of the Trent, provided her consort was rendered unserviceable ; had he done so, the Dorothea, unaccompanied in her way home, might have risked the lives of her crew in a ship so shattered and unsafe. It was therefore decided that both should return home ; and on the 30th of August they put to sea, and on the 22d of October arrived at Deptford.

SITUATION OF THE TRENT.

CHAPTER IV.

PARRY'S FIRST VOYAGE. — ICEBERGS. — PASSAGE THROUGH LANCASTER SOUND. — PRINCE REGENT'S INLET. — WELLINGTON CHANNEL. — MELVILLE ISLAND. — WINTER QUARTERS. — SCURVY. — SNOW BLINDNESS. — THEATRICALS. — BREAKING UP OF THE ICE. — RETURN OF THE EXPEDITION.

MUCH dissatisfaction was felt in England at the result of Ross's expedition, described in the last chapter. The grounds, in particular, on which Lancaster Sound, an opening so spacious, and in a position so favorable in respect to western discovery, had been so abruptly quitted, appeared inadmissible. The "Croker Mountains," which had barred the progress of Sir John Ross, were affirmed by some who had borne part in the abortive voyage to be an ocular illusion. This opinion was very decidedly espoused by Lieut. Parry, the second in command. It was determined, therefore, that a fresh expedition should be equipped and intrusted to him, that he might fulfil, if possible, his own sanguine hopes, and those of the government.

He was furnished with the Hecla, of 375 tons, and a crew of fifty-eight men; and with the Griper gun-brig, of 180 tons, and thirty-six men, commanded by Lieut. Liddon. These ships were made as strong as possible for the navigation of the Arctic seas; and were stored with ample provisions for two years, a copious supply of anti-scorbutics, and everything which could enable the crews to endure the most extreme rigors of a polar winter.

Lieut. Parry, destined to outstrip all his predecessors in the career of northern discovery, weighed anchor at the Nore on the 11th May, 1819, and on the 20th rounded the remotest point of the Orkneys. He endeavored to cross the Atlantic about the parallel of 58°, and, though impeded during the first fortnight of June by a course of unfavorable weather, obtained, on the 15th, from the distance apparently of not less than forty leagues, a view of the lofty cliffs composing Cape Farewell. On the 18th the ships first fell in with icebergs, the air being also filled with petrels, kittiwakes, terns, and other winged inhabitants of the northern sky. He now made an effort to push north and west, through the icy masses, in the direction of Lancaster Sound; but these suddenly closed upon him; and on the 25th both vessels were so immovably beset, that no power could turn their heads a single point of the compass. They remained thus fixed, but safe, when, on the morning of the second day, a heavy roll of the sea loosened the ice, and drove it against them with such violence, that only their very strong construction saved them from severe injury. The discoverers, therefore, were fain to extricate themselves as soon as possible; and, resigning the idea of reaching Lancaster Sound by the most direct course, resolved to steer northward along the border of this great icy field till they should find open water. In this progress they verified the observation of Davis, that in the narrowest part of the great sea, misnamed his Strait, the shores on each side could be seen at the same moment. Thus they proceeded till they reached the Women's Islands and Hope Sanderson, in about latitude 73°. As every step was now likely to carry them further from their destination, Parry determined upon a desperate push to the westward. Favored with a moderate breeze, the ships were run into the detached pieces and floes of ice, through which they were heaved with hawsers ; but, the obstacles becoming always more insuperable, they were at length completely beset, and a heavy fog coming on, made them little able to take advantage of any favorable change. Yet, in the course of a week, though repeatedly and sometimes dangerously surrounded, they warped their way from lane to lane of open water, till only one lengthened floe separated them from an open sea. By laboriously sawing through this obstruction, they finally penetrated the great barrier, and saw the shore, clear of ice, extending before them.

The navigators now bore directly for Lancaster Sound, and on the 30th July found themselves at its entrance. They felt an extraordinary emotion as they recognized this magnificent channel, with the lofty cliffs by which it was guarded, aware that a very short time would decide the fate of their grand undertaking. They were tantalized, however, by a fresh breeze coming directly down the sound, which did not suffer them to make more than a very slow progress. Still, there was no appearance of obstruction either from ice or land, and even the heavy swell which they had to encounter, driving the water repeatedly in at the stern windows, was hailed as an indication of open sea to the westward.

The Hecla left the Griper behind, but still without making any great way herself, till the 3d August, when an easterly breeze sprang up, carrying both vessels rapidly forward. A crowd of sail was set, and they proceeded triumphantly in their course. The minds of all were filled with anxious hope and suspense. The mastheads were crowded with officers and men, and the successive reports brought down from the highest pinnacle called the crow's nest, were eagerly listened to on deck. Their path was still unobstructed. They passed various headlands, with several wide openings towards the north and south, to which they hastily gave the names of Croker Bay, Navy Board Inlet, and similar designations; but these it was not their present object to explore. The wind, freshening more and more, carried them happily forward, till at midnight they found themselves in longitude 83° 12′, nearly a hundred and fifty miles from the mouth of the sound, which still retained a breadth of fifty miles. The success of the expedition, they fondly hoped, was now, to a great extent, decided.

The Hecla at this time slackened her course, to allow her companion to come up, which she did in longitude 85°. They proceeded together to longitude 86° 30′, and found two other inlets, which they named Burnet and Stratton; then a bold cape, named Fellfoot, forming, apparently, the termination of this long line of coast. The lengthened swell, which still rolled in from the north and west, with the oceanic color of the waters, inspired the flattering persuasion that they had already passed the region of straits and inlets, and were now wafted along the wide expanse of the polar basin. Nothing, in short, it was hoped, would henceforth obstruct their progress to Icy Cape, the western boundary of America. An alarm of land was given, but it proved to arise only from an island of no great extent. However, more land was soon discovered, beyond Cape Fellfoot, which was ascertained to be the entrance to a noble recess, extending on their right, which they named Maxwell Bay. An uninterrupted range of sea still stretched out before them, though they were somewhat discomposed by seeing, on the south, a line of continuous ice; but it left an open passage, and they hoped to find it merely a detached stream.

A little space onwards, however, they discovered, with deep dismay, that this ice was joined to a compact and impenetrable body of floes, which completely crossed the channel, and joined the western point of Maxwell Bay. It behoved them, therefore, immediately to draw back, to avoid being embayed in the ice, along the edges of which a violent surf was then beating. The officers began to amuse themselves with fruitless attempts to catch white whales, when the weather cleared, and they saw, to the south, an open sea, with a dark water-sky. Parry, hoping that this might lead to an unencumbered passage in a lower latitude, steered in this direction, and found himself at the mouth of a great inlet, ten leagues broad, with no visible termination; and to the two capes at its entrance he gave the names of Clarence and Seppings.

The mariners, finding the western shore of this inlet greatly obstructed with ice, moved across to the eastern, where they entered a broad and open channel. The coast was the most dreary and desolate they had ever beheld, even in the Arctic world, presenting scarcely a semblance either of animal or vegetable life. Navigation was rendered more arduous, from the entire irregularity of the compass, now evidently approaching to the magnetic pole, and showing an excess of variation which they vainly attempted to measure, so that the binnacles were laid aside as useless lumber.

They sailed a hundred and twenty miles up this inlet, and its augmenting width inspired them with corresponding hopes; when, with extreme consternation, they suddenly perceived the ice to diverge from its parallel course, running close in with a point of land which appeared to form the southern extremity of the eastern shore. To this foreland they gave the name of Cape Kater. The western horizon also appeared covered with heavy and extensive floes, a bright and dazzling ice-blink extending from right to left. The name of the Prince Regent was given to this spacious inlet, which Parry strongly suspected must have a communication with Hudson's Bay. He now determined to return to the old station, and watch the opportunity when the relenting ice would allow the ships to proceed westward. That point was reached, not without some difficulty, amid ice and fog.

At Prince Leopold's Islands, on the 15th, the barrier was as impenetrable as ever, with a bright blink; and from the top of a high hill there was no water to be seen; luckily, also, there was no land. On the 18th, on getting once more close to the northern shore, the navigators began to make a little way, and some showers of rain and snow, accompanied with heavy wind, produced such an effect, that on the 21st the whole ice had disappeared, and they could scarcely believe it to be the same sea which had just before been covered with floes upon floes, as far as the eye could reach.

Parry now crowded all sail to the westward, and, though detained by want of wind, he passed Radstock Bay, Capes Hurd and Hotham, and Beechey Island; after which he discovered a fine and broad inlet leading to the north, which he called Wellington. The sea at the mouth being perfectly open, he would not have hesitated to ascend it, had there not been before him, along the southern side of an island named Cornwallis, an open channel leading due west. Wellington Inlet was now considered by the officers, so high were their hopes, as forming the western boundary of the land stretching from Baffin's Bay to the Polar Sea, into which they had little doubt they were entering. For this reason, Lieutenant Parry did not hesitate to give to the great channel, which was understood to effect so desirable a junction, the merited appellation of Barrow's Strait, after the much-esteemed promoter of the expedition. A favorable breeze now sprang up, and the adventurers passed gayly and triumphantly along the extensive shore of Cornwallis Island, then coasted a larger island, named Bathurst, and next a smaller one, called Byam Martin. At this last place they judged, by some experiments, that they had passed the magnetic meridian, situated, probably, in about 100° west longitude, and where the compass would have pointed due south instead of due north.

The navigation now became extremely difficult, in consequence of thick fogs, which not only froze on the shrouds, but, as the compass was also useless, took away all means of knowing the direction in which they sailed. They were obliged to trust that the land and ice would preserve the same line, and sometimes employed the oddest expedients for ascertaining the precise point. They encountered, also, a compact floe, through which they were obliged to bore their way by main force.

Notwithstanding all these obstacles, they reached the coast of an island larger than any before discovered, to which they gave the name of Melville. The wind now failed, and they moved slowly forward by towing and warping, till, on the 4th September, the lieutenant could announce to his joyful crew that, having reached the longitude of 110° west, they were become entitled to the reward of five thousand pounds promised by Parliament to the first ship's company who should attain that meridian. They still pushed forward with redoubled ardor, but soon found their course arrested by an impenetrable barrier of ice. They waited nearly a fortnight, in hopes of overcoming it, till, about the 20th, their situation became alarming. The young ice began rapidly to form on the surface of the waters, retarded only by winds and swells, so that the commanding officer was convinced that, in the event of a single hour's calm, he would be frozen up in the midst of the sea.

No option was therefore left but to return, and to choose between two apparently good harbors, which had been recently passed on Melville Island. Not without difficulty he reached this place on the 24th, and decided in favor of the more western haven, as affording the fullest security; but it was necessary to cut his way two miles through a large floe with which it was encumbered. To effect this arduous operation, the seamen marked with boarding-pikes two parallel lines, at the distance of somewhat more than the breadth of the larger ship. They sawed, in the first place, along the path tracked out, and then, by cross-sawings, detached large pieces, which were separated diagonally, in order to be floated out; and sometimes boat-sails were fastened to them, to take the advantage of a favorable breeze. On the 26th the ships were established in five fathoms water, at about a cable's length from the beach. For some time the ice was daily cleared round them; but this was soon found an endless and useless labor, and they were allowed to be regularly frozen in for the winter.

Parry then applied himself to name the varied group of islands along which he had passed. He called them, at first, New Georgia; but, recollecting that this appellation was preöccupied by one in the Pacific, he gave the title of the "North Georgian Islands," in honor of his majesty George III., whose reign had been so eminently distinguished by the extension of nautical and geographical knowledge.

SAWING A CHANNEL. P. 88.

Hunting parties occasionally went out and procured a few reindeer; but a migration of these animals took place before the close of October, leaving behind them only wolves and foxes to keep the party company during the long winter months. Even the polar hare, so common in the Arctic regions, never once showed itself on Melville Island in the course of the winter. The musk-ox, also very common during its proper season, arrived on Melville Island in the middle of May, by crossing the ice from the southward, and quitted it by the same way on its return towards the end of September. On the 15th the last covey of ptarmigan was met with; and on the same day were seen fifteen deer, all lying down, except one large one, probably a stag; this, after the rising of the rest, seemed to guard the animals in their flight, frequently going round the herd, sometimes striking them with his horns to make them go on, which they appeared not much inclined to do. Even seals were not found in this neighborhood; but whales of different kinds were commonly met with; gulls and ducks, however, so numerous in Davis's Strait and the Georgian Islands, condescended not to visit Melville Island, but "two or three specimens of a caterpillar were obtained, one of which was brought to England" — of course as an Arctic curiosity. One large white bear, having pursued Captain Sabine's servant to the ship, was shot at and wounded, but made his escape; it was the only one met with during the stay of the party, but described as being more purely white than any they had before seen. A feeble willow, a saxifrage, lichens, and stunted grasses, constitute pretty nearly the *flora* of Melville Island.

The total privation of game of any kind now afforded few excursions for the exercise and amusement of hunting. Parties, however, had occasionally been sent out shortly after the taking up of their winter quarters. One of these did not return on board before sunset, as strictly ordered, and the consequence is stated to have been as follows:

"John Pearson, a marine belonging to the Griper, who was the last that returned on board, had his hands severely frost-bitten, having imprudently gone away without mittens, and with a musket in his hand. A party of our people most providentially found him, although the night was very dark, just as he had fallen down a bank of snow, and was beginning to feel that degree of torpor and drowsiness which, if indulged, inevitably proves fatal. When he was brought on board, his fingers were quite stiff, and bent into the shape of that part of the musket which he had been carrying; and the frost had so far destroyed the animation in his fingers on one hand that it was necessary to amputate three of them a short time after, notwithstanding all the care and attention paid to him by the medical gentlemen. The effect which exposure to severe frost has in benumbing the mental as well as the corporeal faculties was very striking in this man, as well as in two of the young gentlemen, who returned after dark, and of whom we were anxious to make inquiries respecting Pearson. When I sent for them into my cabin they looked wild, spoke thick and indistinctly, and it was impossible to draw from them a rational answer to any of our questions. After being on board for a short time the mental faculties appeared gradually to return with the returning circulation; and it was not till then that a looker-on could easily persuade himself that they had not been drinking too freely."

So early as the 29th of October the thermometer was down to twenty-four degrees below zero. It was now distressing to touch any metallic substance with the naked hand in the open air; it produced a feeling of intense heat, and took off the skin. If the eye-piece of a telescope touched the face, it occasioned an intense burning pain; the remedy was to cover them and other instruments with soft leather. The officers, notwithstanding, indulged themselves in walking for an hour or two in the middle of the day, in the depth of winter, even when the thermometer was down to forty degrees or even fifty degrees below zero, without experiencing much inconvenience from this intense degree of cold, provided always that there was no wind; but the least breeze made the exposure to it intolerable.

The commander, finding himself and his ships shut in for a long and dreary winter, devoted his attention, with a mixture of firmness and kindness, to mitigate those evils which, even in lower latitudes, had often rendered an abode in the Arctic regions so fatal, and to economize both the fresh provisions and fuel.

From the first, Parry was aware that nothing acted more strongly as an antiscorbutic than to keep the men's minds in a lively and cheerful state. Arrangements were accordingly made for the occasional performance of a play, in circumstances certainly very remote from any to which the drama appeared congenial. Lieutenant Beechey was nominated stage-manager, and the other gentlemen came forward as amateur performers. The very expectation thus raised among the sailors, and the bustle of preparing a room for the purpose, were extremely beneficial; and when the North Georgian Theatre opened with "Miss in her Teens," these hardy tars were convulsed with laughter. The Arctic management was extremely popular. The officers had another source of amusement in the North Georgian Gazette, of which Captain Sabine became editor, and all were invited to contribute to this chronicle of the frozen regions.

On the 1st and 2d of February the sun was looked for, but the sky was wrapped in mist; however, on the 3d he was perceived from the maintop of the Hecla.

Health was maintained on board the ships, by enforced exercise and other means, to a surprising degree. Early in January, however, Mr. Scallon, the gunner, felt symptoms, first in the legs, and then in the gums, that decidedly indicated the presence of scurvy, of which the immediate cause appeared to be the great collection of damp that had formed around his bed-place. At this alarm, all the antiscorbutics on board — lemon-juice, pickles, and spruce-beer — were put into requisition; a small quantity of mustard and cress was also raised from mould placed over the stove-pipe; and such was the success of these remedies, that in nine days the patient could walk without pain.

"Some of our men," says Parry; "having, in the course of their shooting excursions, been exposed for several hours to the glare of the sun and snow, returned at night much affected with that painful inflammation in the eyes occasioned by the reflection of intense light from the snow, aided by the warmth of the sun, and called in America 'snow blindness.' This complaint, of which the sensation exactly resembles that produced by large particles of sand or dust in the eyes, is cured by some tribes of American Indians by holding them over the steam of warm water; but we found a cooling wash, made by a small quantity of acetate of lead mixed with cold water, more efficacious in relieving the irritation, which was always done in three or four days, even in the most severe cases, provided the eyes were carefully guarded from the light. As a preventive of this complaint, a piece of black crape was given to each man, to be worn as a kind of short veil attached to the hat, which we found to be very serviceable. A still more convenient mode, adopted by some of the officers, was found equally efficacious; this consisted in taking the glasses out of a pair of spectacles, and substituting black or green crape, the glass having been found to heat the eyes and increase the irritation."

On the 16th of March the North Georgian Theatre was closed with an appropriate address, and the general attention was now turned to the means of extrication from the ice. By the 17th of May the seamen had so far cut it from around the ships as to allow them to float; but in the sea it was still immovable.

This interval of painful inaction was employed by Parry in an excursion across Melville Island. The ground was still mostly covered with softened snow, and even the cleared tracts were extremely desolate, though checkered by patches of fine verdure. Deer were seen traversing the plains in considerable numbers. Towards the north appeared another island, to which was given the name of Sabine. It was found that those parts of Melville Island which were clear of snow produced the dwarf willow, sorrel, and poppy, and that the moss was very luxuriant. On the second day they saw a pair of ducks, and killed seven ptarmigan; sorrel and saxifrage were abundant. The party found pieces of coal imbedded in sandstone; passed a very extensive, dreary, and uninteresting level plain, covered with snow; and this kind of ground, with occasional ravines and foggy weather, continued for three days, during which they saw not a living animal, except one or two flocks of geese.

Arrived at Bushman's Cove, in Liddon's Gulf, on the western side of Melville Island, the party found "one of the pleasantest and most habitable spots we had yet seen in the Arctic regions, the vegetation being more abundant and forward than in any other place, and the situation sheltered and favorable for game." They found here a good deal of moss, grass, dwarf-willow, and saxifrage, and Captain Sabine met with a ranunculus in full flower. Thus we see that even in this, the most desolate region of the earth, the superiority of the western coast predominates. The hunters saw and fired at a musk-ox, but did not kill him; they saw also several golden plovers. On the 15th of June they reached the ships, and were complimented by their shipmates on their good looks, and as appearing in more robust health than when they departed.

"Having observed," says Parry, "that the sorrel was now so far advanced in foliage as to be easily gathered in sufficient quantity for eating, I gave orders that two afternoons in each week should be occupied by all hands in collecting the leaves of this plant; each man being required to bring in, for the present, one ounce, to be served in lieu of lemon-juice, pickles, and dried herbs, which had been hitherto issued. The growth of the sorrel was from this time so quick, and the quantity of it so great on every part of the ground about the harbor, that we shortly after sent the men out every afternoon for an hour or two; in which time, besides the advantage of a healthy walk, they could, without difficulty, pick nearly a pound each of this valuable antiscorbutic, of which they were all extremely fond.

"By the 20th of June, the land in the immediate neighborhood of the ships, and especially in low and sheltered situations, was much covered with the handsome purple flower of the *saxifraga oppositifolia,* which was at this time in great perfection, and gave something like cheerfulness and animation to a scene hitherto indescribably dreary in its appearance.

"The suddenness with which the changes take place during the short season which may be called summer in this climate, must appear very striking when it is remembered that, for a part of the first week in June, we were under the necessity of thawing artificially the snow which we made use of for water during the early part of our journey to the northward; that, during the second week, the ground was in most parts so wet and swampy that we could with difficulty travel; and that, had we not returned before the end of the third week, we should probably have been prevented doing so for some time, by the impossibility of crossing the ravines without great danger of being carried away by the torrents,—an accident that happened to our hunting parties on one or two occasions in endeavoring to return with their game to the ships."

By the middle of June, pools were everywhere formed; the water flowed in streams, and even in torrents, which rendered hunting and travelling unsafe. There were also channels in which boats could pass; yet, throughout this month and the following, the great covering of ice in the surrounding sea remained entire, and kept the ships in harbor.

On the 2d of August, however, the whole mass, by one of those sudden movements to which it is liable, broke up, and floated out, and the explorers had now open water in which to prosecute their great object.

On the 15th they were enabled to make a certain advance, after which the frozen surface of the ocean assumed a more compact and impenetrable aspect than had ever before been witnessed. The officers ascended some of the lofty heights which bordered the coast; but, in a long reach of sea to the westward, no boundary was seen to these icy barriers. There appeared only the western extremity of Melville Island, named Cape

Dundas, and in the distance a bold coast, which they named Banks's Land. As even a brisk gale from the east did not produce the slightest movement on the glassy face of the deep, they were led to believe that on the other side there must be a large body of land, by which it was held in a fixed state. On considering all circumstances, there appeared no alternative but to make their way homeward while yet the season permitted. Some additional observations were made, as they returned, on the two coasts extending along Barrow's Strait.

Parry's arrival in Britain was hailed with the warmest exultation. To have sailed upwards of thirty degrees of longitude beyond the point reached by any former navigator; to have discovered so many new lands, islands, and bays; to have established the much-contested existence of a Polar Sea north of America; finally, after a wintering of eleven months, to have brought back his crew in a sound and vigorous state, were enough to raise his name above that of any other Arctic voyager.

ESQUIMAUX SNOW-HUT.

CHAPTER V.

FRANKLIN'S FIRST LAND EXPEDITION. — INCIDENTS. — BACK'S JOURNEY. — SEVERITY OF THE WEATHER. — AURORA BOREALIS. — ANECDOTES. — SURVEY OF THE COAST. — RETURN TRIP. — SUFFERINGS. — MURDER OF MR. HOOD. — DEATHS. — UNEXPECTED RELIEF. — ARRIVAL AT YORK FACTORY.

IN September of the same year that Parry sailed, an overland expedition started from York Factory, Hudson's Bay, under charge of Sir John Franklin, accompanied by Dr. (now Sir John) Richardson, two midshipmen, — Messrs. Back and Hood, — and Hepburn, a seaman, with the object of exploring the north coast of America to its eastern extremity from the mouth of the Coppermine. There was a chance that Parry might make for the coast in his ships ; and, if so, the two parties would have coöperated with mutual advantage.

On the 19th of January, 1820, Franklin set out in company with Mr. Back, and a seaman named Hepburn, with provisions for fifteen days stowed in two sledges, on their journey to Fort Chipewyan. Dr. Richardson, Mr. Hood, and Mr. Connolly, accompanied them a short distance. After touching at different posts of the company, they reached their destination safely on the 26th of March, after a winter's journey of eight hundred and fifty-seven miles. The greatest difficulty experienced by the travellers was the labor of walking in snow-shoes, a weight of between two and three pounds being constantly attached to galled feet and swelled ankles.

Of the state of the temperature during this journey

there is no record, for a reason explained by Franklin, who says that "this evening (18th of January) we found the mercury of our thermometer had sunk into the bulb, and was frozen."

On the 15th of April the first shower of rain fell; and on the 17th the thermometer rose to 77° in the shade. The return of the swans, geese, and ducks, now gave certain indications of spring. The warm weather, by the sudden melting of the snow and ice, deluged the face of the country. Mr. Hood says: "The noise made by the frogs which this inundation produced is almost incredible. There is strong reason to believe that they outlive the severity of winter. They have often been found frozen, and revived by warmth; nor is it possible that the multitude which incessantly filled our ears with their discordant notes could have been matured in two or three days."

Captain Franklin also notices the resuscitation of fishes after being frozen: "It may be worthy of notice here, that the fish froze as they were taken out of the nets, and in a short time became a solid mass of ice, and by a blow or two of the hatchet were easily split open, when the intestines might be removed in one lump. If, in this completely frozen state, they were thawed before the fire, they recovered their animation. This was particularly the case with the carp; and we had occasion to observe it repeatedly, as Dr. Richardson occupied himself in examining the structure of the different species of fish, and was always, in the winter, under the necessity of thawing them before he could cut them. We have seen a carp recover so far as to leap about with much vigor after it had been frozen for thirty-six hours." It may be stated that the same effect is produced on the insect tribe.

Franklin and his party, increased by the addition of

sixteen Canadian voyageurs, interpreters, &c., left Fort Chipewyan in July, 1820, for Fort Enterprise, on Winter Lake, more than five hundred miles distant. Here, after walking eighty miles to get a look at the Coppermine, they wintered, while Mr. (now Sir George) Back returned on foot to Fort Chipewyan, to expedite the transit of stores required for the next year's operations. At the end of five months he rejoined his companions, after a journey which put his powers of endurance to a severe test.

Some interesting instances of Indian generosity are recorded in the report of Back's long and perilous journey. "One of the women caught a fine pike, by making a hole in the ice, which she gave to us; the Indians positively refused to partake of it, from the idea (as we afterwards learned) that we should not have sufficient for ourselves. 'We are accustomed to starvation,' said they, 'but you are not.'"

Back, in this dreadful journey, was not only exposed to starvation and the extremity of cold, but also to the danger of perishing in some of the lakes which they had to cross on foot. On a narrow branch of the Slave Lake he fell through the ice, but escaped without injury; on another occasion the ice bent so that it required the utmost speed to avoid falling through where it gave way, as it seems to have done at every step he took. In short, it was little less than miraculous, considering the season and the severity of the winter, that he ever returned safe; which, however, he had the good fortune to do on the 17th of March, when he arrived at Fort Enterprise, where, he says, "I had the pleasure of meeting my friends all in good health, after an absence of nearly five months, during which time I had travelled eleven hundred and four miles on snow-shoes, and had no other covering, at night, in the woods, than a blanket and deer-skin, with the thermometer frequently at —40°, and once at —57°, and sometimes passing two or three days without tasting food."

Franklin gives the following statement in regard to the severity of the weather in December: "The weather during this month was the coldest we experienced during our residence in America. The thermometer sank on one occasion to 57° below zero, and never rose beyond 6° above it; the mean for the month was —29°–7. During these intense colds, however, the atmosphere was generally calm, and the wood-cutters and others went about their ordinary occupations without using any extraordinary precautions, yet without feeling any bad effects. The heat is abstracted most rapidly from the body during strong breezes; and most of those who have perished from cold in this country have fallen a sacrifice to their being overtaken on a lake, or other unsheltered place, by a storm of wind. The intense colds were, however, detrimental to us in another way. The trees froze to their very centres, and became as hard as stones, and more difficult to cut. Some of the axes were broken daily, and by the end of the month we had only one left that was fit for felling trees."

The aurora borealis made its appearance frequently, with more or less brilliancy, but was not particularly remarkable; in the month of December it was visible twenty-eight of the long nights.

The Indians, it appears, have nearly destroyed the fur-bearing animals; and so scarce is the beaver become, that in the whole journey to the shores of the Polar Sea and back, one single habitation, and one dam only, of that industrious and ingenious creature, were met with. Among the many interesting anecdotes that have been told of this animal, Dr. Richardson relates the following:

"One day a gentleman, long resident in this country, espied five young beavers sporting in the water, leaping upon the trunk of a tree, pushing one another off, and playing a thousand interesting tricks. He approached softly, under cover of the bushes, and prepared to fire on the unsuspecting creatures; but a nearer approach discovered to him such a similitude between their gestures and the infantile caresses of his own children, that he threw aside his gun. This gentleman's feelings are to be envied, but few traders in furs would have acted so feelingly."

On the last day of June, 1821, the whole party having dragged their canoes and baggage to the bank of the Coppermine, — a tedious and fatiguing service, — embarked on the rapid stream, and reached the sea on the 18th July. The main object of the expedition then commenced; and, with two birch-bark canoes, each manned by ten men, and fifteen days' provision, Franklin paddled to the eastward.

Proceeding along the coast on the inside of a crowded range of islands, they encamped on shore after a run of thirty-seven miles, in which they experienced little interruption. The coast was found of moderate height, easy of access, and covered with vegetation; but the islands were rocky and barren, presenting high cliffs, of a columnar structure. In continuing their voyage, the dangers which beset a navigator in these dreadful polar solitudes thickened gloomily around them. The coast became broken and sterile, and at length rose into a high and rugged promontory, against which some large masses of ice had drifted, threatening destruction to their slender canoes.

In attempting to round this cape the wind rose, an awful gloom involved the sky, and the thunder burst over their heads, compelling them to encamp till the storm subsided. They then, at the imminent risk of having the canoes crushed by the floating ice, doubled the dreary promontory, which they denominated Cape Barrow, and entered Detention Harbor, where they landed. Around them the land consisted of mountains of granite, rising abruptly from the water's edge, destitute of vegetation, and attaining an elevation of fourteen or fifteen hundred feet; seals and small deer were the only animals seen, and the former were so shy that all attempts to approach within shot were unsuccessful.

With the deer the hunters were more fortunate, but these were not numerous; and, while the ice closed gradually around them, and their little stock of provisions every day diminished, it was impossible not to regard their situation with uneasiness. Rounding Cape Kater, they entered Arctic Sound, and sent a party to explore a river upon the banks of which they expected to find an Esquimaux encampment. All, however, was silent, desolate, and deserted; even these hardy natives, bred amidst the polar ices, had removed from so barren a spot, and the hunters returned with two small deer and a brown bear, the latter animal so lean and sickly-looking that the men declined eating it; but the officers boiled its paws, and found them excellent.

Proceeding along the eastern shore of Arctic Sound, to which they gave the name of Banks's Peninsula, the expedition made its painful way along a coast indented by bays, and in many places studded with islands, till, on the 10th of August, they reached the open sea; and sailing, as they imagined, between the continent and a large island, found, to their deep disappointment, that, instead of an open channel, they were in the centre of a vast bay.

The state of the expedition now called for the most serious consideration upon the part of their commander.

So much time had already been spent in exploring the sounds and inlets, that all hope of reaching Repulse Bay was vain; both canoes had sustained material injury; the fuel was expended; their provisions were sufficient only for three days; the appearances of the setting in of the Arctic winter were too unequivocal to be mistaken; the deer, which had hitherto supplied them with fresh meat, would, it was well known, soon disappear; the geese and other aquatic birds were already seen winging their way to the southward; while the men, who had up to this moment displayed the utmost courage, began to look disheartened, and to entertain serious apprehensions for their safety. Under these circumstances, the leaders resolved to return. After spending four days in a careful survey of the bay, they terminated their exploration at a spot which, with literal truth, was named Point Turnagain, a distance, reckoning the indentations of the shore, of five hundred and fifty-five geographical miles. To attempt to reach the Coppermine so late in the season would have been fatal to the whole of the party; they, therefore, made for Hood's River, discovered by them a few days previously, up which they had ascended to the first rapid by the 26th of August. Two small portable canoes were then constructed from the two larger ones, for the purpose of crossing rivers on the journey now before them; and, on the 1st of September, they set off on a straight course for Fort Enterprise, one hundred and fifty miles distant.

The fatigues and privations endured on this route are scarcely to be paralleled; short of food, ill supplied with clothing, and exposed to the howling severity of the climate, the escape of any one of the number appears almost a miracle. Some days, when there was nothing to eat, and no means of making a fire, they passed entirely in bed; on others, after a weary and exhausting travel, their only nourishment on halting for the night was *tripe de roche,* or rock-tripe, a species of lichen, a plant of most nauseous taste, and the cause of cruel bowel complaints to the whole party. Daily they became weaker, and less capable of exertion; one of the canoes was so much broken by a fall, that it was burned to cook a supper; the resource of fishing, too, was denied them, for some of the men, in the recklessness of misery, threw away the nets. Rivers were to be crossed by wading, or in the canoe; on one of these occasions Franklin took his seat with two of the voyageurs in their frail bark, when they were driven by the force of the stream and the wind to the verge of a frightful rapid, in which the canoe upset, and, but for a rock on which they found footing, they would there have perished. On the 19th, "previous to setting out, the whole party ate the remains of their old shoes, and whatever scraps of leather they had, to strengthen their stomachs for the fatigue of the day's journey. These," adds Franklin, "would have satisfied us in ordinary times, but we were now almost exhausted by slender fare and travel, and our appetites had become ravenous. We looked, however, with humble confidence to the great Author and Giver of all good for a continuance of the support which had hitherto been always supplied to us at our greatest need."

A day or two afterwards the remaining canoe was left behind; no entreaties could prevail on the men to carry it further. Dr. Richardson, too, was obliged to abandon his collection of plants and minerals, from inability to endure the burthen. The killing of five small deer at this time, however, enabled them to rest for a couple of days to recruit their exhausted strength. On the 26th they came to the Coppermine, the crossing of which, owing to their weak condition, the loss of the canoe, and having to construct a raft of willow branches, detained them until the 4th of October. Dr. Richardson, actuated by the noble desire of making a last effort for the safety of the party, and of relieving his suffering companions from a state of misery, which could only terminate, and that speedily, in death, volunteered to make the attempt to swim across the stream, carrying with him a line by which the raft might be hauled over.

"He launched into the stream," says Franklin, "with the line round his middle, but when he had got to a short distance from the opposite bank, his arms became benumbed with cold, and he lost the power of moving them; still he persevered, and, turning on his back, had nearly gained the opposite shore, when his legs also became powerless, and, to our infinite alarm, we beheld him sink. We instantly hauled upon the line, and he came again on the surface, and was gradually drawn ashore in an almost lifeless state. Being rolled up in blankets, he was placed before a good fire of willows, and, fortunately, was just able to speak sufficiently to give some slight directions respecting the manner of treating him. He recovered strength gradually, and, through the blessing of God, was enabled, in the course of a few hours, to converse, and by the evening was sufficiently recovered to remove into the tent. We then regretted to learn that the skin of his whole left side was deprived of feeling, in consequence of exposure to too great heat. He did not perfectly recover the sensation of that side until the following summer. I cannot describe what every one felt at beholding the skeleton which the doctor's debilitated frame exhibited. When he stripped, the Canadians simultaneously exclaimed, '*Ah! que nous sommes maigres!*'" They were now almost in the last stage of starvation; and, had it not been for the exertions of Hepburn in collecting *tripe de roche*, not one of them would have survived.

On the 7th, when at twenty-four miles from Fort Enterprise, a division of the party took place: Franklin, with eight of the men, went on, while Richardson stayed behind at the encampment to tend on Hood, who was scarcely able to move. Hepburn remained with them. Franklin was most unwilling to part with any of his comrades, but saw the necessity of doing so. "And, after," he says, "we had united in thanksgiving and prayers to almighty God, I separated from my companions, deeply afflicted that a train of melancholy circumstances should have demanded of me the severe trial of parting, in such a condition, from friends who had become endeared to me by their constant kindness and coöperation, and a participation of numerous sufferings."

Three of the voyageurs, unable to proceed with Franklin, and Michel, an Iroquois, were permitted to return to the halting-place, where they would be at least certain of fire and rock-tripe; but, with the exception of the Indian, they perished by the way — not one of them was ever seen again. Franklin, with his five survivors, reached Fort Enterprise on the 11th. What a disappointment awaited them! Instead of a cordial welcome from friendly hunters, and abundance of provisions, as had been promised, all was a blank; the building was tenantless.

A note was found from Mr. Back, who had journeyed on in advance, stating that he had gone in search of the Indians, and, if need were, to Fort Providence. This was but poor comfort for the famished travellers, who were obliged to take up their quarters in the dilapidated edifice. The rubbish-heaps concealed beneath the snow were searched for old skins, bones, or any kind of offal that might serve as food when stewed with rock-tripe.

A good fire was a luxury seldom enjoyed, for they had scarcely strength to collect wood.

Eighteen weary days were passed in these painful privations, when the monotony was interrupted by the arrival of Dr. Richardson and Hepburn. Their emaciated countenances gave evidence of their debilitated state. "The doctor particularly remarked the sepulchral tones of our voices, which he requested of us to make more cheerful, if possible, unconscious that his own partook of the same key." A partridge which Hepburn had shot was held to the fire, and then divided into six portions. "I and my three companions," says Franklin, "ravenously devoured our shares, as it was the first morsel of flesh any of us had tasted for *thirty-one days*, unless, indeed, the small, gristly particles which we found occasionally adhering to the pounded bones may be called flesh." Richardson brought the melancholy intelligence that Mr. Hood and the Iroquois were both dead. Michel, in a fit of sullen spite, to which uncivilized natures are liable, had shot the young and talented officer at the encampment where they had last parted; and his demeanor towards the two survivors becoming more and more threatening, the doctor, under the imperious instinct of self-preservation, took upon himself the responsibility of putting the Indian to death by a pistol-shot. As afterwards appeared, there was reason to believe that two of the missing voyageurs had also been murdered by the Iroquois.

Two others of the wretched party died on the second day after Richardson's arrival at the fort. At last, on the 7th of November, relief came, borne by three Indians sent by Mr. Back. The messengers proved themselves most kind, assiduous attendants, "evincing humanity that would have done honor to the most civilized people." And, with good fires and sufficient food, the sufferers began to recover strength. A week later, they were able to set out for Fort Chipewyan, where they remained until June of the following year. In July they reached York Factory, from whence they had started three years before; and thus terminated a journey of five thousand five hundred and fifty miles, during which human courage and patience were exposed to trials such as few can bear with fortitude, unless, as is seen in Franklin's interesting narrative, it arises out of reliance on the ever-sustaining care of an Almighty Providence.

SIR JOHN FRANKLIN.

CHAPTER VI.

PARRY'S SECOND VOYAGE. — ARRIVAL AT HUDSON'S STRAIT. — REPULSE BAY. — BAFFLING NAVIGATION. — ESQUIMAUX FRIENDS. — ARCTIC CLIMATE. — FROZEN UP. — AMUSEMENTS. — ILIGLIUK. — LYON'S JOURNEY. — SNOW HUTS. — LAND EXCURSIONS. — HARBOR AT IGLOOIK. — ANOTHER WINTER. — PARHELIA. — RETURN HOME. — PARRY'S THIRD VOYAGE.

THE possibility of entering the Polar Sea having been proved by Parry's first voyage, it was considered that the north-west passage might probably be effected in a lower latitude than that of Melville Island, where the icy barrier had proved impassable. Parry accordingly was sent out a second time with the Hecla and Fury, in May, 1821, with instructions to make for Repulse Bay by way of Hudson's Strait. The former never having been fully examined, it was supposed that some opening would be found leading from it to the ocean beyond.

Parry, now promoted to the rank of captain, hoisted his flag on board the Fury, while Captain Lyon, already distinguished by his services in Africa, received the command of the Hecla. The equipment, the victualling, and the heating of the vessels, were all accomplished with the greatest care, and with various improvements suggested by experience.

The adventurers quitted the Nore on the 8th of May, 1821, passed through the Pentland Frith and by Cape Farewell, and on the 2d of July were at the mouth of Hudson's Strait. Parry, accustomed as he was to views of polar desolation, was struck with the exceedingly dreary aspect which these shores presented. The naked rocks, the snow still covering the valleys, and the thick fogs that hung over them, rendered the scene indescribably gloomy. The ships were soon surrounded by icebergs, amounting to the number of fifty-four, one of which rose at least two hundred and fifty-eight feet above the sea. They were attended by large floes, and rendered very formidable by their rotatory motion.

In spite of every obstruction, Parry, early in August, reached the entrance of Fox's Channel, and came in view of Southampton Island. It was now the question whether to sail directly up this inlet, and reach, by a comparatively short route, Repulse Bay and the higher latitudes, or to make the south-western circuit of Southampton Island, and ascend the beaten track of the Welcome. Parry judiciously preferred the former, notwithstanding its uncertainties, on account of the great time which would be saved should the course be found practicable. On the 15th he came to an opening stretching westward, and apparently separating the island from other land on the north. Hoping to find this the Frozen Strait of Middleton, he entered it; but it soon proved a spacious and beautiful basin, enclosed by land on every side. He named it the Duke of York's Bay, and considered it one of the finest harbors in the world; but, after admiring a large floe covered entirely with minerals, shells, and plants, he moved out of it, and pursued the voyage.

On the 21st the navigators found themselves in another strait, not much encumbered with ice, but darkened by thick fogs; and before they knew distinctly where they were, a heavy swell from the southward showed that they had already passed through the Frozen Strait, and were in the broad channel of the

Welcome. They speedily entered Repulse Bay, in which modern speculation had cherished the hope of a passage; but a short investigation made by boats in every direction proved that it was really, as Middleton had described it, completely enclosed. A good deal of time had thus been lost through the scepticism so unjustly attached to the narrative of that eminent seaman.

The appearance of the shores of Repulse Bay was far from uninviting. "The surrounding land rose from six or seven hundred to a thousand feet, and there was no want of vegetation usually found in this part of the Arctic regions, and in many parts it was extremely luxuriant." Reindeer and hares were plentiful; so were ducks, dovekies, and snow-buntings. Several black whales also were observed in the bay. In one spot the remains of no less than sixty Esquimaux habitations were found, consisting of stones laid one over the other, in very regular circles, eight or nine feet in diameter; besides about a hundred artificial structures, fireplaces, store-houses, and other walled enclosures four or five feet high, used for keeping their skin canoes from being gnawed by the dogs. In various parts of the shore were found numbers of circles of stones, which were supposed to have been burying-places, a human skull being found near one of them.

Leaving Repulse Bay, Parry began the career of discovery along a coast hitherto unknown. An inlet was soon observed, and called by the name of Gore; but was not found to extend far into the interior. At the mouth of this opening, the valleys were richly clad with grass and moss, the birds singing, butterflies and other insects displaying the most gaudy tints, so that the sailors might have fancied themselves in some happier climate, had not the mighty piles of ice in the Frozen Strait told a different tale.

Having passed Gore Inlet, the discoverers found themselves among those numerous isles described by Middleton, which formed a complete labyrinth of various shapes and sizes, while strong currents setting between them in various directions, amid fogs and drifting ice, rendered the navigation truly perilous. However, one channel was observed, by which the mariners at last made their way through this perilous maze. No sooner had they reached the open sea, than, being obliged to run before a strong northerly breeze, they were much disheartened to find themselves, on the 3d of September, at the very point which they had left on the 6th of August. All the interval had been employed in the merely negative discovery, that there was nothing to discover.

The commander soon reached the northern coast, and resumed his task, which was rendered very tedious by the necessity of examining every opening and channel, in the hope that each might prove the desired passage into the Polar Ocean. He first explored a large inlet, the name of which he gave to Captain Lyon ; then a smaller one, which was named from Lieutenant Hoppner ; and by connecting these with Gore Inlet, he completed his delineation of the coast.

The seamen had the pleasure of opening a traffic with a party of Esquimaux, whose first timidity was soon overcome by the hope of being supplied with some iron tools. In the course of this transaction, the surprise of the crew was roused by the conduct of a lady, who had sold one boot, but obstinately retained the other, in disregard of the strongest remonstrances as to the ridiculous figure she in consequence made. At length suspicion rose to such a pitch, that, all courtesy being set aside, her person was seized, and the buskin pulled off. Then, indeed, it proved a complete depository of stolen treasure, there being no less than two spoons and a pewter plate secreted within its capacious cavity.

The end of September now approached, and Parry found himself suddenly in the depth of winter. An alarming symptom appeared in the rapid formation of the soft or pancake ice on the surface of the deep. The obstacle thereby occasioned was at first so slight as to be scarcely felt by a ship before a brisk gale; but it continually increased, till at length the vessel, rolling from side to side, became like Gulliver bound by the feeble hands of Lilliputians. At the same time the various pieces of drift-ice, which were tossing in the sea without, had been cemented into one great field called "the ice," that threatened every moment to bear down upon the brigs and dash them in pieces. Under these circumstances, the navigators could no longer even attempt to reach the land, but determined to saw into the heart of an adjoining floe, and there take up their winter quarters. There was about half a mile to penetrate, which, in the soft state of the pancake ice, was not very laborious. It was, however, far from pleasant, as it bended like leather beneath their feet, and caused them sometimes to sink into the water, whence it was impossible they could escape without a very cold bath.

An observation of Parry shows that the Arctic climate, equally with our own, is influenced by a change of the wind. Thus, on the 20th of October, when the wind was N. N. W., the thermometer fell to —10°; but, veering to the S. E. on the 24th and 25th, it rose to +23°. "I may possibly," he says, "incur the charge of affectation in stating that this temperature was much too high to be agreeable to us; but it is, nevertheless, the fact, that everybody felt and complained of the change. This is explained by their clothing, bedding, fires, and other precautions against the severity of the climate, having been once adapted to a low degree of cold, an increase of temperature renders them oppressive and inconvenient." Another circumstance is mentioned, which may serve to confirm a conjecture which has long been maintained by some, that an open sea, free of ice, exists at or near the pole. "On the 2d of November," says Parry, "the wind, freshened up to a gale from N. by W., lowered the thermometer before midnight to —5°, whereas a rise of wind at Melville Island was generally accompanied by a simultaneous rise in the thermometer at low temperatures. May not this," he asks, "be occasioned by the wind blowing over an open sea in the quarter from which the wind blows, and tend to confirm the opinion that at or near the pole an open sea, free of ice, exists?"

Parry was now frozen up for another winter in the midst of the Northern Sea, and he forthwith applied himself to make the necessary arrangements, with that judicious foresight which had been already so conspicuous in the same trying circumstances. As the result of experience, not less than of several ingenious contrivances, the ships were much more thoroughly heated than in the former voyage; the provisioning, too, was more ample, and antidotes against scurvy still more copiously supplied. The Polar Theatre opened, on the 9th of February, with "The Rivals." The two captains appeared as Sir Anthony and Captain Absolute; while those who personated the ladies had very generously removed an ample growth of beard, disregarding the comfortable warmth which it afforded in an Arctic climate. The company were well received, and went through their performances with unabated spirit. But the discomfort of a stage, the exhibitions of which were attended with a cold thirty degrees under the freezing-point, became rather severe.

The sailors found for themselves a more sober and useful, as well as efficacious remedy against *ennui.* They established a school, in which the better instructed undertook to revive the knowledge of letters among those who had almost entirely lost the slight tincture that they had once imbibed. These hardy tars applied themselves to their book with ardent and laudable zeal, and showed a pride in their new attainments like that of little boys in their first class. At Christmas, sixteen well-written copies were produced by those who, two months before, could scarcely form a letter. Amid these varied and pleasing occupations, the shortest day passed over their heads almost unobserved, especially as the sun did not entirely leave them. Captain Lyon never saw a merrier festival than was celebrated on board.

The first day of the new year is described as being a very severe one in the open air, the thermometer down to —22°, and the wind blowing strong from the N. W., on which it may be observed, that the effect of a strong breeze on the feelings, even in temperate climates, is well known, but at low temperatures it becomes painful, and almost insupportable. "Thus," says Parry, "with the thermometer at —55°, and no wind stirring, the hands may remain uncovered for ten minutes or a quarter of an hour without inconvenience; while, with a fresh breeze, and the thermometer nearly as high as zero, few people can keep their hands exposed so long without considerable pain."

The monotony of the scene was now greatly relieved by a friendly visit from the natives, and an invitation was given to the Esquimaux to repair to the ships, when fifty accepted it with alacrity. Partly walking, and partly skipping, they speedily reached the vessels, where a striking congeniality of spirit was soon found to exist between them and the sailors ; boisterous fun forming to each the chief source of enjoyment. A fiddle and drum being produced, the natives struck up a dance, or rather a succession of vehement leaps, accompanied with loud shouts and yells. Seeing the Kabloonas, or Whites, as they called our countrymen, engaged in the game of leap-frog, they attempted to join ; but not duly understanding how to measure their movements, they made such over-leaps as sometimes to pitch on the crown of their heads ; however, they sprang up quite unconcerned. Their attention was specially attracted to the effects of a winch, by which one sailor drew towards him a party of ten or twelve of their number, though grinning and straining every nerve in resistance ; but, finding all in vain, they joined in the burst of good-humored laughter till tears streamed from their eyes.

One intelligent old man followed Captain Lyon to the cabin, and viewed, with rational surprise, various objects which were presented. The performance of a hand-organ and a musical snuff-box struck him with breathless admiration ; and, on seeing drawings of the Esquimaux in Hudson's Strait, he soon understood them, and pointed out the difference between their dress and appearance and that of his own tribe. On viewing the sketch of a bear, he raised a loud cry, drew up his sleeves, and showed the scars of three deep wounds recived in encounters with that terrible animal.

As spring advanced, the attention of the officers was almost wholly engrossed by the prospects of discovery during the approaching summer. The Esquimaux, by no means destitute of intelligence, and accustomed to shift continually from place to place, were found to have acquired a very extensive knowledge of the seas and coasts of this part of America. One female, in particular, named Iligliuk, who bore even among her countrymen the character of "a wise woman," was, after a little instruction, enabled to convey to the strangers the outlines of her geographical knowledge in the form of a rude map. A pencil being put into her hand, she traced the shore from Repulse Bay with such a degree of accuracy as inspired great confidence in what she might further delineate. She then began to exhibit a coast reaching far to the north, being, in fact, the eastern limits of Melville Peninsula. Next her pencil took a western direction, when her further progress was watched with the deepest interest; in the course of which she represented a strait between two opposite lands, that extended westward till it opened on each side, and spread into an ocean apparently unbounded. This sketch, which promised to fulfil their most sanguine hopes, gratified the officers beyond measure, and they loaded Iligliuk with attentions.

Parry gives an interesting account of the sudden appearance of an Esquimaux snow village near the ships. "If the first view," he says, "of the exterior of this little village was such as to create astonishment, that feeling was in no small degree heightened on accepting the invitation soon given us to enter these extraordinary houses, in the construction of which we observed that not a single material was used but snow and ice. After creeping through two low passages, having each its arched doorway, we came to a small circular apartment, of which the roof was a perfect arched dome. From this three doorways, also arched, and of larger dimensions than the outer ones, led into as many inhabited apartments, one on each side, and the other facing us as we entered. The interior of these presented a scene no less novel than interesting. The women were seated on the beds at the sides of the huts, each having her little fireplace, or lamp, with all her domestic utensils about her; the children crept behind their mothers, and the dogs, except the female ones, which were indulged with a part of the beds, slunk out past us in dismay. The construction of this inhabited part of the huts was similar to that of the outer apartment, being a dome formed by separate blocks of snow, laid with great regularity and no small art, each being cut into the shape requisite to form a substantial arch, from seven to eight feet high in the centre, and having no support whatever but what this principle of building supplied."

These Esquimaux display much skill in fitting and sewing their dresses, and in the manufacture of canoes, weapons, and domestic implements. They eat little else than animal food, and, whenever they can get it, will devour from ten to twelve pounds of flesh or blubber in a day. Their only domestic animal is the dog; deprived of this useful creature, their existence would be extremely precarious. On the long journeys which they take in search of food, six of these dogs will draw a sledge with a load of half a ton from seven to eight miles an hour during a whole day.

Captain Lyon, in the middle of March, undertook a journey across a piece of land lying between the station of the ships and the continent, which had been named Winter Island. The party were scarcely gone, when they encountered a heavy gale, bringing with it clouds of drift, and a cold so intense that they could not stop for a moment without having their faces covered with frost-bites; and their escape with their lives during the night and following day was nearly miraculous. Their sledge was lost in the snow. Some began to sink into that dreadful insensibility which is the prelude to death by cold, and to reel about like drunken men. In fact, they had resigned almost every hope of escape, when, providentially, there appeared a newly-beaten track, which they determined to follow, and in ten minutes it led them to the ships. Their arrival there caused indescribable joy, as they had been nearly given up for lost; while no one could be sent in search of them without imminent risk of sharing their fate.

After various incidents, and unsuccessful attempts to free the vessels from the ice, they at length, on the 2d July, resumed their voyage of discovery. They had a favorable run through the entrance, which formed a continuation of Fox's Channel; but a strong current from the north was still bringing down the ice with great force. The Hecla underwent some severe pressures, and, within five or six hundred yards of the Fury, two large floes dashed against each other with such a tremendous concussion, that numberless huge masses were thrown fifty or sixty feet into the air. The vessel, had she come for a second within the sphere of these movements, must have been crushed to pieces — happily she escaped. This current, however, was highly promising, since it could not be traced to the mouth of Hudson's Strait, and must therefore, they concluded, have come from the Western Ocean, which they were so anxious to reach.

The ice passed by, and the ships proceeded with a favoring wind and tide. The shores began now to put on their summer aspect; the snow had nearly disappeared, and the ground was covered with the richest bloom of Arctic vegetation. The navigators came to a fine river named Barrow, which formed a most picturesque fall down rocks richly fringed with very brilliant plants. Here the reindeer sporting, the eider-duck, the golden plover, and the snow bunting spreading their wings, produced a gay and delightful scene. On the 14th they reached the island of Amitioke, which had been described as situated near the strait they were then endeavoring to attain.

The discoverers now proceeded northwards, and saw before them a bold and high range of coast, apparently separated from that along which they were sailing. This feature, agreeing with the indications of Iligliuk, flattered them that they were approaching the strait exhibited by her as forming the entrance into the Polar Basin. They pushed on, full of hope and animation, and were further cheered by reaching the small island of Igloolik, which she had described as situated at the very commencement of the passage. Accordingly, they soon saw the strait stretching westward before them in long perspective; but, alas! they discovered at the same moment an unbroken sheet of ice from shore to shore, crossing and blocking up the passage; and this not a loose accidental floe, but the field of the preceding winter, on which the midsummer sun had not produced the slightest change. Unable to advance, they amused themselves with land excursions in different directions; and Parry at length determined, on the 14th August, with a party of six, to undertake an expedition along the frozen surface of the strait.

The journey was very laborious, the ice being sometimes thrown up in rugged hummocks, and occasionally leaving large spaces of open water, which it was necessary to cross on a plank, or on pieces of ice, instead of boats. In four days they came in view of a peninsula terminated by a bold cape, the approach to which was guarded by successive ranges of strata, resembling the tiers or galleries of a commanding fortification. The party, however, scrambled to the summit, whence they enjoyed a most gratifying spectacle. They were at the narrowest part of the strait, here about two miles across, with a tide or current running through it at the rate of two miles an hour. Westward, the shores on each side receded, till, for three points of the compass, and amid a clear horizon, no land was visible. Parry doubted not that from this position he beheld the Polar Sea, into which, notwithstanding the formidable barriers of ice which intervened, he cherished the most sanguine hopes of forcing his way. He named this the Strait of the Fury and Hecla.

He now lost no time in returning to the ships, where his arrival was very seasonable ; for the opposing barrier, which had been gradually softening and breaking into various rents and fissures, at once almost entirely disappeared, and the vessels next morning were in open water. On the 21st they got under weigh, and, though retarded by fogs and other obstructions, had arrived on the 26th at that central and narrowest channel which the commander had formerly reached. A brisk breeze now sprang up, the sky cleared, they dashed across a current of three or four knots an hour, and sanguinely hoped for an entire success, which would compensate so many delays and disappointments.

Suddenly, it was announced from the crow's nest that ice, in a continuous field, unmoved from its winter station, occupied the whole breadth of the channel. In an hour they reached this barrier, which they found soft, porous, and what is termed rotten. Spreading all their canvas, they bore down upon it, and actually forced their way through a space of three or four hundred yards ; but there they stuck, and found their progress arrested by an impenetrable mass. From this point, during the whole season, the ships were unable to advance a single yard; nor had the crews any means of exerting their activity except in land journeys.

Captain Lyon undertook an expedition southward, to ascertain if any inlet or passage from sea to sea in this direction had escaped notice. The country, however, was so filled with rugged and rocky hills, some a thousand feet high, and with chains of lakes in which much ice was floating, that he could not proceed above seven miles. Though it was the beginning of September, the season was only that of early spring; and the buds of the poppy and saxifrage were just unfolding, to be prematurely nipped by the fast-approaching winter.

More satisfactory information was derived from another excursion made by Messrs. Reid and Bushman, who penetrated sixty miles westward along the southern coast of Cockburn Island, till they reached a pinnacle, whence they saw, beyond all doubt, the Polar Ocean spreading its vast expanse before them; but tremendous barriers of ice filled the strait, and precluded all approach towards that great and desired object.

It was now the middle of September, and the usual symptoms of deer trooping in herds southward, floating pieces of ice consolidated into masses, and the thin pancake crust forming on the surface of the waters, reminded the mariners not only that they could hope for no further removal of the obstacles which arrested their progress, but that they must lose no time in providing winter quarters. The middle of the strait, at the spot where they had been first stopped, occurred as the station whence they would be most likely to push future discovery; but prudence suggested a doubt, whether the ships, enclosed in this icy prison, with such strong barriers on each side, might ever be able to effect their extrication. The chance of being shut up here for eleven months, amid the privations of an Arctic winter, appeared, at all events, a serious consideration. By returning to Igloolik, they would be ready to catch the earliest opening, which was expected to take place on the eastern side, from whence a few days would bring them back to their present station.

On the 30th of October, by the usual operation of sawing, the ships were established in a harbor at Igloolik. The ensuing season was passed with the most careful attention to the health and comfort of the crews; but, though their spirits did not sink, there appears to have been, on the whole, less of gayety and lightness of heart than in the two former years. We hear nothing of the drama, or even of the school. In this position, north of Winter Island, they were deprived for about seven weeks of the sun's cheering beams. On the 2d of December refraction still showed, from the deck of the Fury, about the sixteenth part of his disk. At the New Year, *Arcturus* and *Capella*, stars of the first magnitude, were visible half an hour before and after mid-day. On the 5th of January, 1823, the horizon was so brightly suffused with red, that they hoped ere long to see the sun's orb burst forth; but a fortnight of thick fog occasioned a disappointment. On the 19th, the sky having cleared, they saw him rise, attended by two parhelia,

PARHELIA.

and both crews turned out to enjoy the novelty and splendor of this cheering spectacle. One of these parhelia was very bright and prismatic, being thrown upon a thick cloud ; the other scarcely perceptible, having a blue sky as its back-ground. To each of these mock suns bright yellow bands of light were attached, as shown in the diagram.

The sailors found at Igloolik a colony of Esquimaux, who received them at first with surprise and some degree of alarm ; but, on learning they were from Winter Island, and intimate with its tenants of last season, they welcomed them as familiar acquaintances. The crews spent the winter with them on a friendly footing, and rendered important services to many individuals during a period of severe sickness.

The spring proved unfavorable. Captain Lyon attempted to penetrate across Melville Peninsula, but found the road so barred by steep chains of mountains, that he was obliged to return in nineteen days, without any discovery, except of two rapid rivers falling into the sea near Igloolik. Lieut. Hoppner accompanied a party of Esquimaux to Cockburn Island, but could not make his way to any distance inland. It was the 7th of August before they were able, by severe sawing, to reach the open sea ; by which time Parry had renounced the hope of effecting anything important during the short remnant of this season. He formed, however, a very bold plan, which was to bring all the stores of the other vessel on board the Fury, and with it alone to brave a third winter in the polar regions, hoping that the succeeding summer might be more propitious. But, as he was preparing to carry this too daring project into effect, a report was made that symptoms of scurvy had broken out on several of the crew, whose physical strength appeared to be generally impaired by the two hard winters through which they had passed. This left no choice ; and, in compliance with the general opinion of his officers, he forthwith began his voyage homewards.

The ships were drifted about in a stormy sea, covered with ice, for twenty-four days ; but, being at last favored with a westerly breeze, they crossed the Atlantic, and on the 10th of October, 1823, arrived in Brassa Sound, Shetland.

Two attempts had thus been made, each to a certain point successful, but both arrested much short of the completion of the grand enterprise. The government at home, however, were not willing to stop short in their spirited career. The western extremity of Melville Island, and the Strait of the Fury and Hecla, appeared to be both so blocked up as to afford little hope ; but Prince Regent's Inlet seemed more likely to lead to a prosperous issue. A passage through this channel would bring the ships to the great sea bounding the northern coast of America, that had been seen from the strait mentioned above, and by which there was the fairest prospect of reaching, by the most direct route, the waters of the great Pacific. To follow up these views, Parry was again fitted out in the Hecla ; while, in the accidental absence of Captain Lyon, the Fury was intrusted to Lieutenant, now Captain, Hoppner, who had taken an active part in the operations of the preceding voyage.

The expedition set sail from Northfleet on the 19th of May, 1824, and was in Davis's Strait by the middle of June. As the season, however, chanced to be peculiarly rigorous, it was not till the 10th of September that, after repeated repulses and severe straining, they caught a view of the bold and magnificent shores of Lancaster Sound, in which a few solitary icebergs were floating. After this they thought themselves fortunate when, by pushing their way through many miles of newly-formed ice, they reached Port Bowen, in time to make it their winter quarters.

Here they remained until the 20th of July, 1825, when the voyage was resumed, but under very discouraging circumstances. Great accumulations of ice rendered it almost impossible to advance; the Fury was driven on shore, and abandoned, though most of her stores were saved and piled on the beach; and the Hecla returned to England with a double complement of men and officers. This was the least successful of Parry's voyages, but there is a fact connected with it which deserves to be recorded: it proved that the anxiety and difficulty consequent on the loss of power in the compasses need no longer exist. The placing of a small circular plate of iron in the line of no direction of the ship, and near to the needle, effects a compensation which keeps the latter in working condition. This contrivance is due to Mr. Peter Barlow, of Woolwich, and Parry says, "Never had an invention a more complete and satisfactory triumph; for to the last moment of our operations at sea did the compass indicate the true magnetic direction."

CHAPTER VII.

LYON'S VOYAGE. — BEECHEY'S EXPEDITION. — FRANKLIN'S SECOND LAND EXPEDITION. — FORT FRANKLIN. — WINTER AT GREAT BEAR LAKE. — EMBARKATION. — SEPARATION OF THE PARTY. — PROGRESS OF FRANKLIN'S DIVISION. — ATTACK BY ESQUIMAUX. — RETURN TO FORT FRANKLIN. — RICHARDSON'S DIVISION. — SECOND WINTER AT THE FORT.

CONCURRENTLY with Parry's third voyage, three other expeditions were undertaken, with the two-fold object of making the north-west passage and of completing the survey of the North American coast. The first, by Captain Lyon, in the Griper, was to proceed by Hudson's Strait and Sir Thomas Rowe's Welcome to Repulse Bay; then to cross over Melville Isthmus, and survey the coast of America as far as where Franklin left off, at Point Turnagain. The vessel sailed in June, 1824, but, being totally unfit for the service, except in the quality of strength, she was nearly wrecked on two occasions in the Welcome, and all on board placed in imminent peril of their lives; and at last, Repulse Bay being eighty miles distant, the enterprise was abandoned.

The second expedition, in the Blossom, under the command of Captain Beechey, was despatched in 1825, to sail round Cape Horn, and enter the Polar Sea by Behring's Strait, so as to arrive at Chamisso Island, in Kotzebue Sound, by the 10th of July, 1826, there to wait for the third expedition, under Franklin, of which more presently.

On the 2d of June, having left the Sandwich Islands, he shaped his course for Kamtschatka, and on the 27th was becalmed within six miles of Petropalauski. The best guides to this harbor are a range of high mountains, on one of which, upwards of eleven thousand feet in height, a volcano is in constant action. It was a serene and beautiful evening when they approached this remote quarter of the world, and all were struck with the magnificence of the mountains capped with perennial snow, and rising in solemn grandeur one above the other. At intervals the volcano emitted dark columns of smoke; and, from a sprinkling of black spots upon the snow to the leeward, it was conjectured there had been a recent eruption.

From Petropalauski, Beechey sailed, on the 1st of July, for Kotzebue's Sound. "We approached," says he, "the strait which separates the two great continents of Asia and America, on one of those beautiful still nights well known to all who have visited the Arctic regions, when the sky is without a cloud, and when the midnight sun, scarcely his own diameter below the horizon, tinges with a bright hue all the northern circle. Our ship, propelled by an increasing breeze, glided rapidly along a smooth sea, startling from her path flocks of aquatic birds, whose flight, in the deep silence of the scene, could be traced by the ear to a great distance." Having closed in with the American shore some miles northward of Cape Prince of Wales, they were visited by a little Esquimaux squadron belonging to a village situated on a low sandy island.

The natives readily sold everything they possessed, and were cheerful and good-humored, though exceedingly noisy and energetic. Their bows were more slender than those of the islanders to the southward, but made on the same principle, with drift-pine, assisted with thongs of hide, or pieces of whalebone placed at the back, and neatly bound with small cord. The points of their arrows were of bone, flint, or iron, and their spears headed with the same materials. Their dress was similar to that of the other tribes on the coast. It consisted of a shirt, which reached half-way down the thigh, with long sleeves, and a hood of rein-deer-skin, and edged with gray or white fox fur. Besides this they had a jacket of eider-drake skins sewed together, which, when engaged in war, they wore below their other dress, reckoning it a tolerably efficient protection against an arrow or a spear-thrust. In wet weather they threw over the fur dress a shirt made of the entrails of the whale, which, being well saturated with oil and grease, was water-tight; and they also used breeches of deer's hide, and seal-skin boots, to the upper end of which were fixed strings of sea-horse hide. It was their fashion to tie one of these strings round the waist, and attach to it a long tuft of hair, the wing of a bird, or, sometimes, a fox's tail, which, dangling behind as they walked, gave them a ridiculous appearance, and may probably have occasioned the report of the Tschuktschi recorded in Muller, that the people of this country have tails like dogs.

On the 22d of July the ship anchored in Kotzebue's Sound, and, after exploring a deep inlet on its northern shore, which they named Hotham Inlet, proceeded to Chamisso Island, where the Blossom was to await Franklin. A discretionary power had, however, been permitted to Beechey, of employing the period of his stay in surveying the coast, provided this could be done without the risk of missing Franklin. Having, accordingly, directed the barge to keep in-shore on the lookout for the land party, he sailed to the northward, and, doubling Cape Krusenstern, completed an examination of the coast by Cape Thomson, Point Hope, Cape Lisburn, Cape Beaufort, and Icy Cape. As there were here strong indications of the ice closing in, and his instructions were positive to keep in open water, if possible, he determined to return to Kotzebue's Sound, whilst he despatched the barge, under his lieutenants, to trace the coast to the north-eastward, as far as they could navigate.

On this service the barge set out, on the 17th of August. She proceeded along the coast, and surveyed one hundred and twenty-six miles of new shore, until stopped by a long, low, projecting tongue of land, to which the name of Point Barrow was given, but without meeting or hearing any tidings of the expected overland party; though it was afterwards ascertained that Point Barrow was distant only one hundred and forty-six miles from the extreme point reached by Franklin.

In the mean time Beechey returned with the Blossom to Kotzebue's Sound. There she remained at the anchorage till October, when it became necessary to depart, to prevent her being frozen in for the winter; and, after a cruise in the Pacific, she shaped her course once more for the rendezvous at Chamisso Island. During the voyage to that point, where they arrived August 27th, 1827, Beechey and his men had repeated interviews with the Esquimaux, whose habits and disposition were in no respect different from those of the natives already described. They found them uniformly friendly, sociable, devotedly fond of tobacco, eager to engage in traffic, and, upon the whole, honest, though disposed to drive a hard bargain. On some occasions they attempted to impose upon their customers, by skins artfully put together, so as to represent an entire fish; but it was difficult to determine whether they intended a serious fraud or only a piece of humor, for they laughed heartily when detected, and appeared to consider it a good joke. Their persons, houses, and cookery, were all exceedingly dirty, and their mode of salutation was by a mutual contact of noses ; sometimes licking their hands, and stroking first their own faces, and afterwards those of the strangers.

The weather proved unfavorable for further operations ; there was very little open sea ; and, in endeavoring to push along the shore, the barge was wrecked, and several of her crew drowned ; and on the 6th of October Beechey was obliged to abandon further exploration, grieved and disappointed that he had not the satisfaction of bearing with him the adventurous party whom he had been sent especially to meet. He arrived in England October 12, 1828, having been absent on his voyage three years and a half.

The party under Franklin comprised the third of the expeditions to which we have referred. In 1824, Franklin, undeterred by the recollection of the fearful hardships endured in his former overland journey, proposed a second, which, descending the Mackenzie River to the sea, should there divide its force ; and, while one party explored the coast easterly to the Coppermine, the other should make its way westerly to Icy Cape, or, if possible, Behring's Strait. The project was duly sanctioned, and every preparation made to insure success, by building boats, providing scientific instruments, and supplying abundant provisions. Besides three strong and light boats, better suited to navigation among ice than bark canoes, a smaller one, covered with Mackintosh's prepared canvas, weighing only eighty-five pounds, and named "The Walnut Shell," was constructed for the purpose of crossing rivers.

In the preparations nothing appears to have been omitted. Scientific instruments of all kinds, fowling-pieces and ammunition, marquees and tents, bedding, clothing, and water-proof dresses, flour, arrow-root, maccaroni, portable soup, chocolate, essence of coffee, sugar, and tea, not omitting an adequate supply of that essential article for all North American travellers, *pemmican*, — were supplied.

The officers under Franklin's orders were his old and tried companions and fellow-sufferers in the former journey, Dr. Richardson and Lieut. Back, with Mr. Kendall, a mate in the navy, and Mr. T. Drummond, a naturalist. Four boats, specially prepared for the purposes of the expedition, were sent out by the Hudson's Bay Company's ship. In July, 1825, the party arrived at Fort Chipewyan. They reached Great Bear Lake in safety, and erected a winter dwelling on its western shore, to which the name of Fort Franklin was given. To Back and Mr. Dease, an officer in the Hudson's Bay Company's service, were intrusted the arrangements for their winter quarters.

From here a small party set out with Franklin down the Mackenzie to examine the state of the Polar Sea. The sixth day after their departure they passed the last of the fir-trees, in latitude 68° 40′, these being succeeded by stunted willows, which became more dwarfish as they approached the sea. After the dissipation of a thick fog, the expanse of water to the northward was so great, that Franklin was inclined to think they had reached the sea; and in this he was almost confirmed on reaching the shore of Ellice Island, where they "were rejoiced at the sea-like appearance to the northward." "This point was observed to be in latitude 69° 14′, longitude 135° 57′, and forms the north-eastern entrance of the main channel of the Mackenzie River, which from Slave Lake to this point is one thousand and forty-five miles, according to our survey." On reaching Garry Island, they ascended the summit, and from it "the sea appeared in all its majesty, entirely free from ice, and without any visible obstruction to its navigation, and never was a prospect more gratifying than that which lay open to us."

Franklin had left England under affecting circumstances. His first wife, who was then lying at the point of death, with heroic fortitude urged his departure at the very day appointed, entreating him, as he valued her peace of mind and his own glory, not to delay a moment on her account; that she was fully aware that her days were numbered, and that his delay, even if she wished it, could only be to close her eyes. She died the day after he left her. His feelings may be inferred, but not described, when he had to elevate on Garry Island a silk flag which she had made and given him as a parting gift, with the instruction that he was to hoist it only on reaching the Polar Sea.

On the 8th of September, Franklin and his party got back to their companions on Great Bear Lake, and prepared to pass the long winter of seven or eight months. On 5th October the last swan had passed to the southward, and on the 11th the last brown duck was noticed. On 6th May the first swan was seen, and on the 8th the brown ducks reäppeared on the lake. The mosses began to sprout, and various singing-birds and orioles, along with some swifts and white geese, arrived soon after.

It is remarked by Dr. Richardson that the singing birds, which were silent on the banks of the Bear Lake during the day, serenaded their mates at midnight; at which time, however, it was quite light. On 20th May the little stream which flowed past the fort burst its icy chains, and the laughing geese arrived, to give renewed cheerfulness to the lake. Soon after this the winter-green began to push forth its flowers; and under the increasing warmth of the sun's rays the whole face of nature underwent a delightful change. The snow gradually melted, the ice broke up from the shores of the lake, the northern sky became red and luminous at midnight, the dwarf-birch and willows expanded their leaves, and by the 3d June the anemones, the tussilago, the Lapland rose, and other early plants, were in full flower.

On the 28th June they embarked upon the Mackenzie; on the 4th July they reached that part where the river divides into various channels, and the two parties were to pursue different directions. The western branch was the route to be pursued by the boats of Franklin's party, and the eastern branch by those of Richardson: the former to proceed along the northern coast westerly as far as Icy Cape, where it was expected to fall in with the Blossom; the latter to examine the coast-line between the mouth of the Mackenzie and that of the Coppermine.

The parties now separated. On reaching the mouth of the Mackenzie, the western expedition came in contact with the Esquimaux. Franklin proceeded to open a communication with them. At first everything proceeded in a friendly manner. Augustus, after delivering a present, informed them that if the English succeeded in finding a navigable channel for large ships, an advantageous trade would be opened. This intimation was received with a deafening shout; the boats were in a moment surrounded by nearly three hundred persons, offering for sale their bows, arrows, and spears, with a violence and perseverance which became at last troublesome, and Franklin directed the boats to be put to seaward.

At this moment a kayak was upset by one of the oars of the Lion, and its unhappy possessor was stuck by the accident with his head in the mud, and his heels in the air. He was instantly extricated, wrapt in a warm great-coat, and placed in the boat; where, though at first frightened and angry, he soon became reconciled to his situation, and, looking about, discovered many bales and other articles which had hitherto been carefully concealed. His first impulse was to ask for everything he saw; his next, to be indignant that his requests were not granted; and, on joining his companions, he proposed a plan for a general attack and pillage of both the boats. This scheme was immediately carried into execution; and, though the plunderers at first affected to be partly in sport, matters soon assumed a serious complexion.

Two of the most powerful men, leaping on board, seized Captain Franklin, forced him to sit between them; and when he shook them off, a third took his station in front to catch his arm whenever he attempted to raise his gun, or lay his hand on the broad dagger which hung by his side. During this assault the two boats were violently dragged to the shore, and a numerous party, stripping to the waist and brandishing their long sharp knives, ran to the Reliance, and commenced a regular pillage, handing the articles to the women, who, ranged in a row behind, quickly conveyed them out of sight. No sooner was the bow cleared of one set of marauders, than another party commenced their operations at the stern. The crew in the Lion were nearly overpowered, and their commander disarmed, when all at once the natives took to their heels, and concealed themselves behind the drift timber and canoes on the beach. This sudden panic was occasioned by Captain Back, whose boat at this time had been got afloat, commanding his crew to level their muskets. The Lion happily floated soon after; and as both boats pulled off, Franklin desired Augustus to inform the Esquimaux that he would shoot the first man who ventured to approach within musket-range.

An amicable leave was, however, afterwards taken of these people, and on the 13th of July Franklin put to sea. On the 27th he came to the mouth of a wide river, to which, as it proceeded from the British range of mountains, and was near the line of demarkation between Great Britain and Russia, Franklin gave the name of Clarence. They were now in lat. 70° 5′, long. 143° 55′. The further they advanced westerly the more dense became the fogs; the temperature descended to 35°, and the gales of wind became more constant; at night the water froze; and, the middle of August having arrived, the winter might here be said to have set in; the more early, probably, from the vicinity of the Rocky Mountains, and the extensive swampy plains between them and the sea. The men had suffered much, and on the 18th Franklin set out on his return to the Mackenzie, from the extreme point gained, named by him the Return Reef, in lat. 70° 24′ N., long. 149° 37′ W.

About this time, as it afterward appeared, the Blossom's boat, sent by Beechey from Behring's Strait, arrived on the coast, on which Franklin observes: "Could I have known, or by possibility imagined, that a party from the Blossom had been at the distance of only one hundred and sixty miles from me, no difficulties, dangers, or discouraging circumstances, should have prevailed on me to return; but, taking into account the uncertainty of all voyages in a sea obstructed by ice, I had no right to expect that the Blossom had advanced beyond Kotzebue Inlet, or that any party from her had doubled the Icy Cape."

Franklin states the distance traced westerly from the mouth of the Mackenzie River to have been three hundred and seventy-four miles, along one of the most dreary, miserable, and uninteresting portions of sea-coast that can perhaps be found in any part of the world; and in all that space not a harbor exists in which a ship could find shelter.

On the 21st of September the party reached Fort Franklin, after a voyage of two thousand and forty-eight miles. Here they had the happiness of meeting all their friends in safety; the eastern detachment had arrived on the 1st of September, after a most successful voyage.

Richardson's party had been generally favored with fine weather. On one occasion a storm compelled them to take shelter in Refuge Cove, in lat. 69° 29′, which they left the following day. At their halting-place on the 13th July, the doctor says: "Myriads of mosquitos, which reposed among the grass, rose in clouds when disturbed, and gave us much annoyance. Many snow-birds were hatching on the point; and we saw swans, Canada geese, eider, king, Arctic, and surf ducks; several glaucous, silvery, black-headed, and ivory gulls, together with terns and northern divers. Some laughing geese passed to the northward in the evening, which may be considered as a sure indication of land in that direction." On the 14th the party took shelter from the fog and a heavy gale in a cove called Browell Cove, in latitude 70°, longitude 130° 19′.

EIDER DUCK.

With some interruptions, their sail of five hundred

miles, or nine hundred and two by the coast-line, from one river to another, afforded a pleasant voyage, during which they added somewhat to the stores of natural history, botany, and geology.

A second winter passed at the fort. The cold was intense, the thermometer at one time standing at 58° below zero ; but such a temperature even as this may be defied, with a weather-tight dwelling, plenty of provisions, and congenial companions. A series of magnetic observations was commenced ; and, as the locality lay on the opposite side of the magnetic pole to that along which Parry had sailed in his voyages, some interesting results were arrived at. "It appears," says Franklin, "that for the same months, at the interval of only one year, Captain Parry and myself were making hourly observations on two needles, the north ends of which pointed almost directly towards each other, though our actual distance did not exceed eight hundred and fifty-five geographical miles ; and while the needle of Port Bowen was increasing its westerly direction, ours was increasing its easterly, and the contrary — the variation being west at Port Bowen, and east at Fort Franklin — a beautiful and satisfactory proof of the solar influence on the daily variation."

In addition to magnetism, observations of the aurora borealis were also recorded, and the fact established that no disturbance of the needle (in that locality, at least) takes place during the play of the phenomenon. A course of lectures, too, on practical geology, was delivered by Richardson — an eminently useful subject in a new district. And, as an instance of what a love for science may accomplish, when animated by a persevering and self-reliant spirit, we must not omit to mention Mr. Drummond, one of the party, who passed the winter alone at the foot of the Rocky Mountains, in a small hut erected by himself, where he collected fifteen hundred specimens of plants, and two hundred birds and quadrupeds, besides insects. These, though points of minor interest, when compared with the grand objects of the expeditions, serve, nevertheless to connect the individuals whose names they distinguish, by many links of sympathy and esteem, with unobtrusive thousands who can admire where they cannot imitate.

MUSK OX.

CHAPTER VIII.

SCORESBY'S DISCOVERIES. — CLAVERING. — PARRY'S POLAR VOYAGE. — THE REINDEER. — HECLA COVE. — BOAT AND SLEDGE EXPEDITION. — NIGHT TRAVELLING. — HUMMOCKS. — SOFTENING OF THE ICE. — DRIFTING OF THE FLOES. — HIGHEST POINT REACHED. — THE POLAR BEAR. — RETURN TO THE SHIP. — HOMEWARD BOUND.

WHILE Parry, under the auspices of the British government, was engaged in his second attempt to effect the north-west passage, a private adventurer, Mr. Scoresby, was making a voyage towards the north pole, which must not be passed without notice. As early as 1806, this gentleman, who was bred a practical whaleman, had, in the pursuit of his calling, penetrated to latitude 81° 30′, being a degree higher than Phipps had attained, and only five hundred geographical miles from the pole. In 1817 he also made an excursion on Jan Mayen's Island. He had, on both occasions, made observations and explorations with an intelligent and scientific eye, very unusual among those who pursue a calling so rough and dangerous as whaling.

At Mitre Cape he ascended to the summit of the singular cliff of which it consists, and which is estimated to be three thousand feet above the level of the ocean. The view is described as sublime: on the east were two finely-sheltered bays; the sea formed an immense unruffled expanse to the west, the icebergs rearing their fantastic forms, glittering in the sunshine; the valleys were enamelled with beds of snow and ice, and in the interior mountains rose beyond mountains, till they melted in the distant horizon. The beach of this cape was found nearly covered with the nests of terns, ducks, and other tenants of the Arctic air, in some of which were young, over whom the parents kept watch, and, by loud cries and quick, vehement movements, sought to defend them against the predatory tribes which hovered round.

WILD DUCK.

But the most important discoveries made by Scoresby were in 1822, when he sailed in the ship Baffin, of three hundred and twenty-one tons, and fifty men, for the whale fishery. In search of a better fishing-ground, he was led to the eastern coast of Greenland — a tract absolutely unknown, unless at a few points which the Dutch had approached ; and it formed a continuous line with the shore on which the colonies of old Greenland, the subject of much controversy, were supposed to have been situated.

On the 8th of June, in 74° 6′ north latitude, the coast was discovered, extending from north to south about ninety miles ; and of which the most northerly point was concluded to be that named on the charts Gale Hamkes's Land, while the most southerly appeared to be Hudson's Hold-with-Hope. Scoresby's ambition, however, to mount some of its crags, which no European foot had ever trodden, was defeated by an impassable barrier of ice; and a similar one having closed in behind him, he was obliged to sail back and forward several days through a narrow channel. During this interval he had a good opportunity of taking the bearings and directions of the principal objects on land. The latitude, as given in the maps, was tolerably correct, and was, indeed, his only guide in tracing the positions; for the longitude, after the most careful observation, was found to differ seven degrees from that in the best charts, and ten degrees from what is found in those usually supplied to the whale-fishers. The country was generally mountainous, rugged, and barren, bearing much resemblance to Spitzbergen, though less covered with snow.

Scoresby followed the usual system of naming the more prominent objects in the territory embraced by his discoveries. The two principal bays, or inlets, were designated Captain Kater and Sir Walter Scott; while two spacious forelands, or projecting peninsulas — the former supposed to be an island — were assigned to Dr. Wollaston and Sir Everard Home. Other bays and capes were bestowed on some of the author's personal friends. He now made a movement eastward, in search of whales, of which he found no traces in the vicinity of land.

On the 19th of July the navigators came in view of a range of coast of a very bold and peculiar character, extending about forty miles. It presented a mountain chain from three to four thousand feet high, rising at once from the beach in precipitous cliffs, which terminated in numberless peaks, cones, and pyramids. In one instance there appeared to rise six or seven tall parallel chimneys, one of which, crowned with two vertical towers, was called Church Mount. This coast received the name of Liverpool, while to the mountains was given that of Roscoe. The range of shore terminated at Cape Hodgson; beyond which, however, steering south-west, they descried three other promontories; to these were successively given the appellation of Cape Lister, Cape Swainson, and Cape Tobin.

Here Scoresby landed; when he found the beach much lower than that further to the north, and consisting, in a great measure, of loose, stony hills. After some examination, he came, near Cape Swainson, to an enclosure similar to those which the Esquimaux construct for their summer huts, and within which were hollow structures, like bee-hives, such as they use for stores.

Resuming his course at sea, and still holding south-westward, he now discovered a spacious inlet, to which, in looking upwards, no boundary could be seen. While penetrating this opening, he observed another sound branching to the northward behind the Liverpool coast, and supposed to form it into an island. The opposite shore of this entrance was named Jameson's Land, from the eminent professor of natural history in Edinburgh. Beyond Cape Hooker, the southern point of the coast just described, another large inlet stretched towards the north, to which was given the name of Basil Hall. It had every appearance of converting Jameson's Land into an island; and the coast to the westward of it received the name of Milne's Land. Between Cape Leslie, constituting the northern point of that coast, and Cape Stevenson, on the opposite shore, the original opening continued to stretch into the interior, without any appearance of a termination. There appeared a strong presumption that, instead of the continuous mass of land which our maps represent, Greenland composes only an immense archipelago of islands. To this great inlet, the entrance of which was bounded by Cape Tobin on the north, and Cape Brewster on the south, the navigator gave the name of his father, though posterity will probably be apt to associate with himself the name of "Scoresby's Sound."

These coasts, especially that of Jameson's Land, were found richer in plants and verdure than any others seen on this occasion within the Arctic circle, and almost meriting the distinction of Greenland. The grass rose in one place to a foot in height, and there were meadows of several acres, which appeared nearly equal to any in England. But nowhere could a human being be discovered, though there were everywhere traces of recent and even frequent inhabitation. At the foot of certain cliffs, named after Dr. Neill, were several hamlets of some extent. The huts appear to have been winter abodes, not constructed of snow-slabs, like the cells of the Esquimaux of Hudson's Bay, but resembling those of the Greenlanders, dug deep in the ground, entered by a long winding passage or funnel, and roofed with a wooden frame overlaid with moss and earth. The mansion had thus the appearance of a slight hillock. Near the hamlets were excavations in the earth, serving as graves, where implements of hunting, found along with the bones of the deceased, proved the prevalence here of the general belief of savage nations, that the employments of man in the future life will exactly resemble those of the present.

On emerging from this large sound, and proceeding southward, Scoresby discovered another continuous range of coast.

Disappointed as to any appearance of whales on this coast, he again steered to the northward, where icebergs surrounded him, amounting at one place to the number of five hundred. This course brought him in a

SCORESBY AMONG ICEBERGS P. 145.

few days within sight of lands stretching still higher than those recently surveyed, and connecting them with the others which he had first discovered. There appeared two large territories, seemingly insular, to which were given the names of Canning and Traill; and between them was a most spacious inlet, named Sir Humphrey Davy. He landed on Traill Island, and with incredible toil clambered to the top of a hill, where he hoped to have found a small plain containing a few specimens of Arctic vegetation; but this summit was steeper than the most narrowly-pitched roof of a house; and, had not the opposite side been a little smoother, he would have found much difficulty in sliding down. Beyond this island, and separated from it by a considerable inlet, named after Lord Mountnorris, was another coast, the pointed extremity of which received the name of Parry. This promontory being at no great distance from Cape Freycinct, which had been seen in the first survey, there was thus completed the observation of a range of four hundred miles of coast, formerly known only by the most imperfect notices, and which might, therefore, be strictly considered as a new discovery.

Scoresby afterwards approached more closely to Canning Island, and penetrated a sound between it and the main, connected apparently with Hurry's Inlet. He would have been happy to examine more of the Greenland coast, having on one occasion had a fair prospect of being able to run southward to Cape Farewell; but the ship was not his own, and his duty to his employers compelled him to turn in another direction. He had hitherto met with much disappointment; and, the season being far advanced, he was apprehensive of being obliged to return with a deficient cargo. But, on the 15th of August, numerous whales appeared round the ship; of these five were struck, and three taken, which at once rendered the ship *full-fished,* and placed him among the most successful adventurers of the year. He could, therefore, return with satisfactory feelings; and the pleasure of the voyage homeward was only alloyed by the occurrence of a violent storm off Lewis, in which Sam Chambers, one of the most esteemed and active of his crew, was washed overboard.

To these discoveries some additions were made next year by Captain Clavering, who was employed by the British Admiralty to convey Captain Sabine to different stations in the Arctic Sea, for the purpose of making observations on the comparative length of the pendulum, as affected by the principle of attraction.

Clavering sailed on the 3d of May, 1823, and on the 2d of June arrived at Hammerfest, in Norway, where he landed the philosopher with his tents and instruments. The observations being completed, he weighed anchor on the 23d, reached the northern coast of Spitzbergen, and fixed on a small island between Vogel Sang and Cloven Cliff for further operations.

He left this coast on the 22d of July, and steered for the eastern shores of Greenland, of which he came in view on the 5th of August. The scene appeared the most desolate he had ever beheld. The mountains rose to the height of several thousand feet, without a vestige of vegetation, or the appearance of any living creature on the earth or in the air. Even the dreary waste of Spitzbergen appeared a paradise to this. He landed his passenger and the scientific apparatus on two islands detached from the eastern shore of the continent, which he called the Pendulum Islands, and of which the outermost point is marked by a bold headland rising to the height of three thousand feet.

While Sabine was employed in his peculiar researches, the other surveyed a part of the coast which lay to the northward, being the first which Scoresby saw. It lay at some distance, with an icy barrier interposed ; but was found indented with deep and spacious bays, suspected even to penetrate so far as to convert all this range of coast into a cluster of islands. The inlet which the former navigator had assigned to Sir Walter Scott was believed by Clavering to be that discovered by the Dutch mariner, Gale Hamkes ; but we have not ventured to remove this last from the more northerly position preferred by the scientific whaler. Other openings, which occurred in proceeding towards the north, were named by the captain Foster's Bay, Ardincaple, and Roseneath Inlets ; and he saw bold and high land still stretching in this direction as far as the seventy-sixth degree of latitude.

In regard to the natives this commander was more fortunate than his predecessor, who saw only their deserted habitations. On landing at a point on the southern coast of Sir Walter Scott's Inlet, he received intelligence of Esquimaux having been seen at the distance of a mile, and hastened thither with one of his officers. The natives, on seeing them, immediately ran to the top of some rocks ; but the English advanced, made friendly signs, deposited a mirror and a pair of worsted mittens at the foot of the precipice, and then retired. The savages came down, took these articles, and carried them away to the place of their retreat ; but they soon allowed the strangers to approach them, though their hands, when shaken, were found to tremble violently. By degrees confidence was established, and they conducted the visitors to their tent, five feet high, and twelve in circumference, composed of wood and whalebone. Their aspect and conformation, their boats and implements, exactly corresponded to those observed by Parry and Lyon in Hudson's Bay. A child, after being diligently cleared of its thick coating of dirt and oil, was found to have a tawny, copper-colored skin. The natives were astonished and alarmed beyond measure by the effect of fire-arms. A seal being shot, one of them was sent to fetch it. He examined it all over till he found the hole made by the ball, when, thrusting his finger into it, he set up a shout of astonishment, dancing and capering in the most extravagant manner. Another was prevailed upon to fire a pistol; but instantly, on hearing the report, started and ran back into the tent.

The observations were not completed till the beginning of September, when the season was too late to allow Clavering to gratify his wish of making a run to the northward. Nor did he extricate himself from the ice without some severe shocks; but nevertheless, after spending six weeks at Drontheim, he entered the Thames about the middle of December.

After the abortive voyage of Buchan and Franklin, in 1818, no further attempt was made to reach the pole in *ships;* but a plan was devised to accomplish that object in vehicles drawn over the frozen surface of the ocean — a scheme first suggested by Scoresby, who endeavored to prove that such a journey was neither so visionary nor so very perilous as it might appear to those who were unacquainted with the Arctic regions.

His suggestions did not, for a considerable time, attract attention; but at length Captain Parry, after his three brilliant voyages to the north-west, finding reason to suspect that his further progress in that direction was hopeless, turned his thoughts to the probability of penetrating over the frozen sea to the pole. Combining Scoresby's ideas with his own observations, and with a series of reflections derived by Captain Franklin from his extensive experience, he submitted to the Lords of the Admiralty the plan of an expedition over the polar ice. Their lordships, having referred this proposal to the council and committee of the Royal Society, and received a favorable report as to the advantages which science might derive from such a journey, applied themselves with their usual alacrity to supply the captain with everything which could assist him in this bold undertaking.

The Hecla was employed to carry him to the northern coast of Spitzbergen, where she was to be secured in a safe harbor or cove; and with her were sent two boats, to be dragged or navigated, according to circumstances, from that island to the pole. These boats being framed of ash and hickory, covered with water-proof canvas, over which were successive planks of fir and oak, with a sheet of stout felt interposed, united the greatest possible degree of strength and elasticity. The interior was made capacious, and flat-floored, somewhat as in troop-boats; and a runner, attached to each side of the keel, fitted them to be drawn along the ice like a sledge. Wheels were also taken on board, in case their use should be found practicable.

The adventurers started on the 27th of March, 1827, and on the 19th of April entered the fine harbor of Hammerfest, in Norway, where they remained two or three weeks, and took on board eight reindeer, with a quantity of picked moss for their provender. Departing on the 11th of May, they soon found themselves among the ice, and met a number of whale-ships. On the 13th they were in view of Hakluyt's Headland, when the captain endeavored to push his way to the north-east, in the track of Phipps. The vessel, however, was soon completely beset, and even enclosed in a large floe, which carried her slowly along with it.

As every day was now an irretrievable loss, Parry

became impatient in the extreme, and formed a plan to push off northward, leaving the ship to find a harbor for herself, where he trusted, on his return, to trace her out. But the survey of the route in the proposed direction was most discouraging. In consequence of some violent agitation the preceding season, the ice had been piled up in innumerable hummocks, causing the sea to resemble a stone-mason's yard, except that it contained masses ten times larger. This state of the surface, which would have rendered it impossible to drag the boats more than a mile in the day, was found to prevail for a considerable space with little interruption.

The current, meantime, continued to carry the ship, with the floe to which she was fastened, slowly to the eastward, till it brought her into shoal water. Parry lowered a boat, and found some heavy masses of ice attached to the bottom in six fathoms; after which he felt it quite out of the question to leave her with a diminished crew, and exposed to so much danger, arising from the combined difficulty of unsurveyed ground and ice. The conclusion was therefore irresistibly forced upon his mind, that a secure harbor must be sought for the vessel before setting out with the boats. No choice was then left but to steer back for the coast of Spitzbergen, where he unexpectedly lighted on a very convenient recess, named by him Hecla Cove; and it proved to be part of the bay to which an old Dutch chart gives the name of Treurenberg.

The animals met with here during the Hecla's stay were principally reindeer, bears, foxes, kittiwakes, glaucous and ivory gulls, tern, eider-ducks, and a few grouse. Looms and rotges were numerous in the offing. Seventy reindeer were killed, chiefly very small, and, until the middle of August, not in good condition.

REINDEER.

They were usually met with in herds of from six or eight to twenty, and were most abundant on the west and north sides of the bay. Three bears were killed. The vegetation was tolerably abundant.

The neighborhood of this bay, like most of the northern shores of Spitzbergen, appears to have been much visited by the Dutch at a very early period. There are thirty graves on a point of land on the north side of the bay. The bodies are usually deposited in an oblong wooden coffin, which, on account of the difficulty of digging the ground, is not buried, but merely covered by large stones ; and a board is generally placed near the head, having, either cut or painted upon it, the name of the deceased, with those of his ship and commander, and the month and year of his burial. Several of these were fifty or sixty years old ; one bore the date of 1738 ; and another, which Parry found on the beach to the eastward of Hecla Cove, that of 1690; the inscription distinctly appearing in prominent relief, occasioned by the preservation of the wood by the paint, while the unpainted part had decayed around it.

It was now the 20th of June, and the best of the season had been spent in beating backwards and forwards on these ice-bound shores; he therefore resolved, without further delay, to prosecute the main object of his enterprise; and, though scarcely hoping to reach the pole, he determined, at all events, to push as far north as possible. He took with him seventy-one days' provision, consisting of pemmican, biscuit, cocoa, and rum. The spirit of wine, as the most portable and concentrated fuel, was alone used for that purpose. There were provided changes of warm clothing, thick fur dresses for sleeping in, and strong Esquimaux boots. The reindeer, and also the wheels, were given up at once, as altogether useless in the present rugged state of the ice; but four sledges, constructed out of the native snow-shoes, proved very convenient for dragging along the baggage.

On the 22d of June the expeditionary party quitted the ship, and betook themselves to the boats, amid the cheers of their associates. Although all the shores were still frozen, they had an open sea, calm and smooth as a mirror, through which, with their loaded vessels, they advanced slowly, but agreeably. After proceeding thus for about eighty miles, they reached, not, as they had hoped, the main body of the ice, but a surface intermediate between ice and water. This could neither be walked nor sailed over, but was to be passed by the two methods alternately; and it was on such a strange and perilous plain that they had to land, in order to commence their laborious journey toward the pole.

Parry describes in an interesting manner the singular

mode of travelling which they were compelled to adopt. The first step was to convert night into day — to begin their journey in the evening, and end it in the morning. Thus, while they had quite enough of light, they avoided the snow-glare, and the blindness which it usually produces ; besides, the ice was drier and harder beneath them ; and they enjoyed the greatest warmth when it was most wanted, during the period of sleep, though they were a little annoyed by dense and frequent fogs. Thus their notions of night and day became inverted. Several of the men declared that they never knew night from day, during the whole excursion. They rose in what they called the morning, but which was really late in the evening, and, having performed their devotions, breakfasted on warm cocoa and biscuit ; then, drawing on their boots, usually either wet or hard frozen, and which, though perfectly dried, would have been equally soaked in fifteen minutes, the party travelled five or six hours, and a little after midnight stopped to dine. They next accomplished an equal journey in what was called the afternoon ; and in the evening, that is, at an advanced hour in the morning, halted as for the night. After applying themselves to obtain rest and comfort, they put on dry stockings and fur boots, cooked something warm for supper, smoked their pipes, told over their exploits, and, forgetting the toils of the day, enjoyed an interval of ease and gayety ; then, well wrapped in their fur cloaks, they lay down in the boat, rather too close together, perhaps, but with very tolerable comfort ; and in due time the sound of a bugle roused them to their breakfast of cocoa, and to a repetition of the same arduous duties.

The progress for several days was most slow and laborious. The floes were small, exceedingly rough, and intersected by lanes of water, which could not be crossed without unloading the boats. It was commonly necessary to convey these and the stores by two stages; and the sailors, being obliged to return for the second portion, had to go three times over the same ground. Sometimes they were obliged to make three stages, and thus to pass over it five times.

There fell as much rain as they had experienced during the whole course of seven years in the lower latitude. A great deal of the ice over which they travelled was formed into numberless irregular needle-like crystals, standing upwards, and pointed at both ends. The horizontal surface of this part had sometimes the appearance of greenish velvet, while the vertical sections, when in a compact state, resembled the most beautiful satin spar, and asbestos when going to pieces. These peculiar wedges, it was supposed, were produced by the drops of rain piercing through the superficial ice. The needles at first afforded tolerably firm footing; but, becoming always more loose and movable as the summer advanced, they at last cut the boots and feet as if they had been pen-knives. Occasionally, too, there arose hummocks so elevated and rugged that the boats could only be borne over them, in a direction almost perpendicular, by those vigorous operations called "a standing pull and a bowline haul."

The result of all this was, that a severe exertion of five or six hours did not usually produce a progress of above a mile and a half or two miles, and that in a winding direction; so that, after having entered upon the ice on the 24th of June, in latitude 81° 13′, they found themselves on the 29th only in 81° 23′, having thus made only about eight miles of direct northing. Parry soon relinquished all hope of reaching the pole; however, it was resolved to push on as far as possible; and the party coming at length to somewhat smoother ice and larger floes, made rather better progress. While the boats were landing on one of these, the commander and Lieut. Ross usually pushed on to the other end, to ascertain the best course. On reaching the extremity, they commonly mounted the largest hummock, whence they beheld a sight of which nothing could exceed the dreariness. The eye rested solely upon ice, and a sky hid in dense and dismal fogs.

One warm day, two flies on the ice were regarded with a degree of attention that would have been ludicrous under other circumstances ; and equally important was the sight of an *aphis borealis,* in a languid state, a hundred miles away from land. Amid this scene of inanimate desolation, the view of a passing bird, or of ice in any peculiar shape, excited an intense interest, which they smiled to recollect ; but they were principally cheered by viewing the two boats in the distance, the moving figures of the men winding with their sledges among the hummocks, and by hearing the sound of human voices, which broke the silence of this frozen wilderness. The rain and the increasing warmth of the season, indeed, gradually softened the ice and snow, but this only caused the travellers to sink deeper at every step. At one place they sank repeatedly three feet, and required three hours to make a hundred yards. Having attained 82° 40′, they began to hold it as a fixed point that their efforts would be crowned with success so far as to reach the eighty-third parallel. This hope seemed converted into certainty when, on the 22d, they had travelled seventeen miles, the greater proportion of which was directly north. But there now occurred an unfavorable change, which baffled all their exertions.

Down to the 19th, the wind had blown steadily from the south, which, though without aiding them much, had at least checked the usual movement of the ice in that direction. On the last of these days, however, a breeze sprang up from the north, which opened, indeed, a few lanes of water; but this, it was feared, could not compensate for the manner in which it must cause the loosened masses of ice, with the travellers upon them, to drift to the southward. This effect was soon found to take place to an extent still more alarming than had been at first anticipated; for, instead of ten or twelve miles, which they reckoned themselves to have achieved northward on the 22d, they were found not to have made quite four. This most discouraging fact was at first concealed from the sailors, who only remarked that they were very long in getting to the eighty-third degree.

The expedition was now fast approaching the utmost limits of animal life. During their long journey of the 22d, they only saw two seals, a fish, and a bird. On the 24th only one solitary *rotge* was heard; and it might be presumed that, from thence to the pole, all would be a uniform scene of silence and solitude. The adventurers pushed on without hesitation beyond the realms of life; but now, after three days of bad travelling, when their reckoning gave them ten or eleven miles of progress, observation showed them to be four miles south of the position which they occupied on the evening of the 22d — the drifting of the snow-fields having in that time carried them fourteen miles backward.

This was too much; and to reach even the eighty-third degree, though only twenty miles distant, was now beyond all reasonable hope. To ask the men to undergo such unparalleled toil and hardship, with the danger of their means being exhausted, while an invisible power undid what their most strenuous labors accomplished, was contrary to the views of their considerate commander. In short, he determined that they should take a day of rest, and then set out on their return. This resolution was communicated to the crew, who, though deeply disappointed at having achieved so little, acquiesced in the necessity, and consoled themselves with the idea of having gone further north than any previous expedition of which there was a well-authenticated record.

The furthest point of latitude reached was on the 23d, and was, probably, to 82° 45′. "At the extreme point of our journey," says Parry, "our distance from the Hecla was only one hundred and seventy-two miles in a S. 8° W. direction. To accomplish this distance we had traversed, by our reckoning, two hundred and ninety-two miles, of which about one hundred were performed by water previously to our entering the ice. As we travelled by far the greater part of our distance on the ice three, and not unfrequently five, times over, we may safely multiply the length of the road by two and a half; so that our whole distance, on a very moderate calculation, amounted to five hundred and eighty geographical, or six hundred and sixty-eight statute miles, being nearly sufficient to have reached the pole in a direct line. Up to this period we had been particularly fortunate in the preservation of our health." Their day of rest (July 27th), before starting to return, was one of the pleasantest they had experienced upon the ice; the thermometer only from 31° to 36° in the shade, and 37° in the sun; no bottom with five hundred fathoms of line.

The return was equally laborious as the going out, and in some respects more unpleasant, from the increasing softness of the ice and snow — depriving them of confidence in any spot on which they placed their boats or persons, and often sinking two or three feet in an instant. On the 1st of August some recent bear-tracks were seen, and, soon after, Bruin himself appeared; but, though attempts were made to draw him within gunshot, he escaped unharmed. But, on the 4th, a fat bear

POLAR BEAR.

was shot by Lieut. Ross; and "the men were frying steaks, during the whole day, over a large fire made of the blubber." To some the consequence of their indulgence was an indigestion. On the 10th another bear was killed; "and our encampment," says Parry, "became so like an Esquimaux establishment that we were obliged to shift our place upon the floe in the course of the day, for the sake of cleanliness and comfort."

At length, on the 11th of August, Parry and his party heard the sound of the surge breaking against the exterior margin of the great icy field. They were soon launched on the open sea, and reached Table Island, where a supply of bread had been deposited; but Bruin had discovered it, and devoured the whole. They found, however, some accommodations, while the stores left at the Warden Island were still quite undisturbed. On the 21st the navigators arrived in Hecla Cove, from whence, soon afterwards, they sailed for England.

Such was the result of the first and only attempt to penetrate to the pole over the frozen surface of the deep. All the energy and hardihood of British seamen were exerted to the utmost, without making even an approach towards the fulfilment of their intention; yet there seems nothing in the details just given to deter from the enterprise, as impossible, or even to render it very unfeasible. The unfavorable issue was evidently owing to the advanced season of the year, when the thaw and consequent dissolution of the ice had made great progress, and all the materials of the great northern floor were broken up.

CHAPTER IX.

ROSS'S SECOND VOYAGE. — HOLSTEINBORG. — DISCO ISLAND. — LANCASTER SOUND. — BOOTHIA. — DISCOVERY OF THE FURY'S STORES. — DANGEROUS NAVIGATION. — PREPARATIONS FOR WINTERING. — VISIT FROM ESQUIMAUX. — EXCURSION. — SECOND WINTER IN THE ICE. — THE MAGNETIC POLE. — THIRD AND FOURTH WINTER. — ABANDONMENT OF THE VICTORY. — MEETING WITH A WHALER.

NEXT in chronological order is the expedition equipped at the cost of Sir Felix Booth, and conducted by Captain Ross, and his nephew, Commander (afterwards Sir James) Ross. They sailed in May, 1829, in the Victory, a vessel fitted with a steam-engine, in addition to her sails, so as to be able to navigate in calm weather, or in baffling winds. The object of the voyage was to search for the north-west passage, as Parry had done before, by some opening leading out of Regent's Inlet.

On the 22d of July they entered a bay which opened into two magnificent inlets, bordered by rocks of imposing form; and every spot, not absolutely a precipice, was covered with such bright verdure as to justify the appellation of Greenland. In sailing upwards, the unexpected appearance of a Danish flag surprised the crew, and they learned that they were now near a settlement belonging to that nation, called Holsteinborg. The governor had seen the masts above the rocks, and, apprehensive of their being those of a vessel in distress, kindly sent an offer of aid. The party were immediately conducted to the village, where they had a hospitable reception, with entertainment such as they little expected on those dreary shores.

They here found a disabled vessel, and from it replenished their stores and spars. The provisions were raised to their full complement. Some boots and gloves were obtained from the natives, and the governor made a useful present of six Esquimaux dogs.

On the 26th the discoverers sailed to the northward; and on the morning of the 28th the stupendous mountains of Disco Island, long enveloped in mist, burst on their view, only a few miles distant. The range nearest the shore was entirely free from snow, and the interior hills were but partially covered. Hare Island was almost equally clear; and, though forty icebergs were observed, yet, as the navigators approached the latitude of 74°, near to where the Hecla and Fury had been beset in 1824, not a vestige of ice was perceived. They might have fancied themselves sailing on the summer seas of England, or even of the Mediterranean; the men threw off their jackets, and worked in their shirts, without shoes or stockings. They had several times recourse to the engine, though, from practical defects, it never enabled them to sail above a mile and a half an hour; and it was subsequently thrown overboard, as a useless encumbrance.

On the 6th of August, a thick fog having dispersed, the coast was suddenly displayed, with all its highlands, among which Cape Byam Martin was conspicuous, covered with snow. On reaching the entrance of Lancaster Sound, and reverting to the blame imputed to him for not having explored it, the captain observes that, from the deceptive appearances presented by bays and inlets, similar mistakes had been made by Cook, and other navigators of the greatest skill. No opinion differing

14*

from his had been expressed by any one of his officers, who, if they entertained any such, were unquestionably bound to have stated it. The ice, moreover, lay then so thick that he could have penetrated but a few miles further.

Now, however, he sailed through the middle of the strait, perceiving scarcely any trace of ice or snow, unless on the tops of the lofty mountains. The thermometer stood at 40°, while the sensible heat was so much greater that they felt it agreeable to dine without a fire, and with half the skylight removed. For two days they made only a slow and laborious progress, by the aid of steam; but, on the 9th, a welcome breeze sprang up from the east, and, all sail being set, on the 10th they passed Cape York, after which the land begins to turn southward, and, with the opposite coast of North Somerset (Boothia), forms the broad opening of Prince Regent's Inlet. This being the channel by which Ross hoped to accomplish his passage, he immediately steered across, and reached the western shore on the afternoon of the 11th, between Cape Seppings and Elwin Bay.

In sailing southward along this coast, some heavy gales were encountered; and the ice having been broken off in the various forms of streams, packs, and bergs, the full difficulties of Arctic navigation began to be experienced. These were increased by the near approach to the magnetic pole, so that the compass ceased to traverse; and the bearings could be ascertained only by observations on the sun, which was often obscured by heavy fogs. The navigators made their way, however, and on the 12th descried the place of the Fury's wreck, with the poles of the tents standing. They hastened, with intense interest, to examine this spot. The hull of the ship, which was left on the beach, had disappeared, without even a vestige remaining. The moving masses of ice had either carried it out in a body, or broken it into fragments and scattered it as drift-wood over the surrounding sea. But it was an ample compensation to find that the canisters of preserved provisions, after being exposed during four years, were in as perfect condition as if they had been newly prepared. The tightness of these vessels had prevented the bear from smelling the rich feast they contained for him, and to which otherwise he would soon have forced his way. The wine, spirits, sugar, bread, flour, and cocoa, were, with little exception, equally good, and the sails were found in complete preservation. After taking in all the provisions they could conveniently stow, raising their stock to two years and three months' supply, the accumulated pile seemed scarcely diminished. Here, also, they procured a store of coal.

Crossing now the broad mouth of Cresswell Bay, they reached, on the 15th of August, a cape to which the name of Garry has been attached, the furthest point seen by Parry. The land trended in a south-south-west direction, which, with few variations, it continued to follow. Deprived of all aid from the compass, and often enveloped in fogs, they worked their way slowly, amid many difficulties and frequent dangers, being obliged to steer merely according to the direction which the wind, or even the floating ice, had, in the last clear interval, been observed to pursue. While mountains of ice were tossing around them on every side, they were often forced to seek safety by mooring themselves to these formidable masses, and drifting with them, sometimes forward, sometimes backward. In this manner, on one occasion, no less than nineteen miles were lost in a few hours ; at other times they underwent frequent and severe shocks, yet escaped any serious damage. Ross conceives that his little bark, merely by its moderate draught of water, was much better fitted for such a navigation than the larger vessels employed in previous expeditions, and that those of Parry would have been shattered to pieces by the rocks over which the Victory was carried in safety.

On several points of this coast they observed Esquimaux tents,—at one place twenty in number,—but none of the natives. Many whales appeared on the surface of the water close to them, without showing any apprehension of man.

Among the leading features of the coast was Brentford Bay, of considerable extent, with some fine harbors, thirty miles beyond Cape Garry. Here the captain landed, displayed his colors, and, drinking the king's health, took possession, in his majesty's name, of the land, to which he gave the name of Boothia.

Under all impediments, in the course of August and September, he worked his way along three hundred miles of undiscovered coast, and to within two hundred and eighty miles of the point which Franklin had reached. Here the land, taking a westerly direction, seemed to afford the fair promise of a passage between the country now surveyed and the continent of America. But, by the end of September, snow began to fall thick; the thermometer sank far below the freezing-point, while ice in large masses was closing around them. They therefore considered themselves fortunate when, in a spacious bay between a rocky island and two icebergs, they found a station in Felix Harbor, in which, after due arrangements, they could reckon on passing the dreary season in security.

On the 7th of October, by sawing through the ice, the vessel was placed in the position where it could be most advantageously lodged for the winter. On the

8th, there appeared no longer an atom of clear water; and, except some occasional points of rock, "nothing but one dazzling and monotonous, dull and wearisome, extent of snow was visible." The temperature, which had been ranging between 10° and 22°, rapidly fell, and, on the night of the 20th, descended as low as 9° under zero, or 41° below the freezing-point, and, before the end of the month, was at —16°.

In preparing for the gloom and rigor of this long winter, Ross made some improvements even upon the admirable arrangements of Parry. The upper deck having been covered two feet and a half deep with snow, it was trodden down to the consistence of solid ice, and sand spread over it, till it resembled a rolled gravel-walk. It was then roofed with canvas, which was conducted over the sides till it united with a bank of snow that had been formed around the vessel, thus completely fencing it in on every side. The vapor from the steam-kitchen and oven, instead of being allowed to spread through the cabins, was conveyed by apertures in the upper deck, over which were placed to receive it iron tanks, with the open side downwards, where it soon froze, and the ice was cleared out once a week. By this plan the apartments were preserved perfectly dry, and it was not necessary, as formerly, to keep them up to the temperature of 70°, in order to prevent the vapor from freezing on their sides; that of 45° was found quite sufficient for health and comfort, and a great saving of fuel was in consequence effected. Two small ante-chambers were formed, and in the outer one such of the men as had been exposed to the atmosphere were required to leave the clothes on which snow had fallen. The air necessary to produce combustion was introduced by a copper pipe direct to the fireplace, where it was immediately warmed, and, instead of chilling, served to heat and dry the room. The strength and spirits of the crew were supported by regular meals and constant occupation. Divine service was duly performed, and religious instruction dispensed at a school held every Sunday evening. On the other nights a school also was attended.

The stock of provisions, on examination, was found sufficient for two years and ten months at full allowance, a quantity which could easily be managed so as to last three years. Fuel was equally abundant. The only article deficient was spirits, of which there was only one year's full supply ; but this want the commander by no means regretted, being satisfied that *their habitual use impaired the strength of the seaman, diminished his power of enduring cold, and rendered him more liable to scurvy.* He was gratified, therefore, when the crew cheerfully consented to their being withheld, unless on special occasions ; and he considers this circumstance as having remarkably contributed to the preservation of their health.

Traces of Esquimaux had been observed on different parts of the coast, but none had been hitherto seen. At length, on the morning of the 9th of January, 1830, a party were discovered. Ross immediately proceeded to the spot, upon which they retreated, but soon returned with a body of their companions, ranged in a line of ten in front and three deep, one man being detached, who appeared to be sitting in a sledge. The captain, having sent for his nephew and some of the crew, desired them to remain behind, while he walked toward the Esquimaux, who were armed with spears and knives. He hailed them by the well-known national salutation, *Tima! tima!* which was shouted by them in return. The navigators then advanced, and, throwing away their guns, called out, *Aja, tima!* upon which the others tossed their knives and spears in the air, repeating the shout, *Aja!* and extending their hands to show that they had now no weapons. As they stood still, however, the discoverers approached, and embraced all those in the front line, stroking their dress, and receiving in their turn this customary greeting. Their gratification was testified by laughing, clamor, and strange gestures. Thus full confidence was at once established between the two parties.

Next day the discoverers visited this people at their own village, which consisted of twelve snow huts, constructed in the same manner as those observed by Parry. This tribe were thought, on the whole, to be cleaner and better dressed than those more to the northward ; besides, they kept a store of seal and reindeer buried in the snow — a precaution not before noticed among any Esquimaux.

While the British remained on these shores, they held frequent intercourse with this and other parties of natives. Some of the places about Repulse Bay being named and described, they showed an intimate acquaintance with them, stating that they had recently journeyed from that quarter. Two of them, Tulluahiu and Ikmallik, drew a sketch of the line of coast by which they had travelled, and this was amended by a learned lady, Tiriksiu. The general result proved to be, that between the present station and Repulse Bay there intervened a very extensive gulf, of which the limits were Melville Peninsula on the east, the American coast on the south, and the country in which they now were, on the west.

The grand question, whether there was any navigable opening further westward, could not be then ascertained, though they had reason to believe that, if there was, it must be very narrow. The strongest interest, however, was excited by the accounts given by another party of a great sea lying to the westward, and of a strait which it was hoped might lead into it. On the 5th of April, therefore, when the rigor of winter had somewhat abated, Commander Ross, with Mr. Blanky, the chief mate, and two native guides, undertook an expedition to explore it. The weather being still very inclement, they were frequently obliged to pause and seek refuge from the drift, when the Esquimaux in half an hour erected snow huts, which afforded tolerable shelter. Unluckily the fire necessary for heat and light, melting the walls of this frail tenement, enveloped them in moisture, to avoid which they were obliged to creep into their fur bags.

After a difficult journey of three days, they reached a bay facing the westward, and, on proceeding a short distance inland to the south and south-east, discovered a very extensive lake, called by the natives Nei-tyel-le, whence a broad river flowed into the bay. On their return to the coast, the guides pointed out a lofty cape, beyond which there was said to be a vast sea, the termination of which could not be descried. They declared, however, that a tract of land, or isthmus, connecting the territory on which they stood with the continent of America, would render it impossible for the vessel to reach the western sea in this direction, or otherwise than by a channel considerably *north* of her present station.

The journey so far had issued only in disappointment. They learned that, on the coast nearest them, facing the eastward, there was a place called Shagavoke, where the water rushed through a narrow strait with extraordinary rapidity. Hence arose hopes that this tide might come from the opposite sea, and afford a channel through which the ship could be worked. But, on examination, this idea proved fallacious, and every idea of a passage south of the ship's present station was renounced.

It was to the north that all hopes of finding the desired passage were now directed. So far, however, as they were personally able to examine the land, its aspect was unpromising, and the most intelligent natives intimated that the only channel was in a much more northerly quarter, supposed to be no other than Barrow's Strait, through which Parry had already navigated.

Before prosecuting further discoveries in this direction, another journey was resolved upon to the westward, beyond the isthmus, to trace the coast of America as it extended along the newly-discovered sea. They thus hoped to reach Cape Turnagain, and to connect their discoveries with those of Franklin. The younger Ross again set out on the 17th May, with three companions, eight dogs, and provisions for twenty-one days ; and on the 19th, having crossed the great middle lake of the isthmus, he reached his former station on the western sea. The first view of it was celebrated by three loud and even joyous cheers, though tempered with regret at the diminished prospect of ever being able to navigate it. Having to spend the night here, they contrived a more comfortable sleeping-place, by excavating a sort of burrow in the snow, roofing it with their skin boat, and placing a block of snow as a door.

After passing Cape Isabella, formed of gray granite five hundred feet high, the party travelled along the coast west and north for twenty miles. On the morning of the 21st of May they discovered, behind a lofty point, an inlet, which, from its breadth and the different character of its opposite coasts, afforded the hope that it might open into the Polar Ocean. They therefore made a complete circuit and a careful survey of its shores; but the only opening found was clearly ascertained to be the mouth of a river, named by them Garry. On ascending a high hill, they perceived several large lakes extending to the north-east, and forming, in fact, an almost continuous chain to Thom's Bay, near the Victory's station; with interruptions enough, however, to prevent a ship passing through. Next day they proceeded north-west along the coast; but, resolving to reach the opposite land some miles distant, they crossed the frozen surface of the strait, and came to a large island, which was named Matty. They pursued their fatiguing journey along its northern shore, over rough ice; and, passing another narrow strait, which they called Wellington, found themselves on the mainland of America.

The coast now stretched due west, and, the surface being level, they proceeded with comparative ease and rapidity. The direction changing to the north-west, they soon arrived at a spacious bay, which was named Parry. They then travelled onwards two days, but with difficulties continually increasing, and experiencing great embarrassment, as regarded both their advance and return, in distinguishing between land and sea. "When all is ice, and all one dazzling mass of white — when the surface of the sea itself is tossed up and fixed into rocks, while the land is, on the contrary, very often flat — it is not always so easy a problem as it might seem, on a superficial view, to determine a fact which appears in words to be extremely simple."

After experiencing great hardships from the exhausted state of their dogs, and the necessity of abandoning a great part of their provisions, their return was attended with a considerable increase of suffering. The dogs fell victims to successive calamities, till, of eight, only two remained alive. It was proposed to vary the scene by keeping south of Matty Island, along the coast of the continent; but, observing that it formed an extensive bay with winding shores, to follow the sinuosities of which would have consumed too much time, they pushed forward in a direct line over the frozen surface of the sea. On the 8th June they arrived in a very exhausted state in the neighborhood of Nei-tyel-le, where they met a party of natives, who received them hospitably, and supplied them so plentifully with fish, that they were able to take a day's rest, and proceed at leisure to the vessel, which they reached on the 13th.

Meantime, Captain Ross himself had made a journey, though of more limited extent, with the intention of surveying the isthmus of Boothia, when he made the partial discovery of another large lake, to which he gave the name of Lady Melville.

The nephew, upon his return, found that he had arrived just in time. The early spring, the only season when travelling is practicable in this region, was over. The thaw had set in with extraordinary rapidity; the country was under water; the streams impassable, and the surface of the ocean could not have been traversed without the greatest danger. Except a short excursion to procure fish, all their attention and efforts were directed to the extrication of the vessel with a view to her voyage northward, in which direction alone they could now hope to discover a passage to the western sea. But month after month rolled on, the height of summer passed, and the sea remained still bound in icy chains. In August its aspect began to present hopes, but these were followed by successive disappointments. Its close arrived, and they had the mortification to reflect that they had remained eleven months — a period in which they might have circumnavigated the globe — fixed to that dreary spot.

At last, on the 17th of September, with a transport of joy, they found themselves free, and the ship, so long immovable, again buoyant on the waves. They advanced about three miles, when, encountering a ridge of ice, they made fast to one of its extremities, in a tolerably secure position between two bergs. On the 23d they were completely frozen in, and by the 30th the sea exhibited one unbroken surface. The greater part of October was employed in laboriously sawing their way through the ice, the thickness of which was always increasing; and they were at length obliged to desist, after reaching a spot not exactly such as could be wished, but which, amid an ocean immovable on every side, afforded tolerable protection.

Another dreary winter having now set in, it became necessary to look narrowly into the stock of provisions. A certain reduction in the daily allowance was found requisite, leaving, at the same time, enough to maintain the crew in health and vigor, which they continued to preserve uninterruptedly during the season. They felt, however, the utter monotony of their situation pressing upon them with increasing severity; they began almost to envy the Esquimaux, to whom eating and sleeping constituted the whole of existence. In this manner passed 1830; nor was it till April of the following year that excursions of any extent could be undertaken over the frozen surface of land and sea.

The first adventure of this kind was conducted by Commander Ross. One interesting circumstance in his excursion was the discovery of the north magnetic pole; the situation of which on the land of Boothia is marked on the circular map attached to this volume. "The place of the observatory," he remarks, was as near to the magnetic pole as the limited means which I possessed enabled me to determine. The amount of the dip, as indicated by my dipping-needle, was 89° 59′, being thus within one minute of the vertical; while the proximity, at least, of this pole, if not its actual existence where we stood, was further confirmed by the action, or, rather, by the total inaction, of the several horizontal needles then in my possession." This was very nearly the position assigned to it by scientific men several years earlier, and arrived at by protracting the direction lines of compass-needles in various circumjacent latitudes, till they met in a central point. Parry's observations placed it eleven minutes distant only from the site determined by Ross.

"As soon," says the latter, "as I had satisfied my own mind on the subject, I made known to the party this gratifying result of all our joint labors; and it was then that, amidst mutual congratulations, we fixed the British flag on the spot, and took possession of the North Magnetic Pole and its adjoining territory in the name of Great Britain and King William IV. We had abundance of materials for building in the fragments of limestone that covered the beach, and we therefore erected a cairn of some magnitude, under which we buried a canister containing a record of the interesting fact, only regretting that we had not the means of constructing a pyramid of more importance, and of strength sufficient to withstand the assaults of time and of the Esquimaux. Had it been a pyramid as large as that of Cheops, I am not quite sure that it would have done more than satisfy our ambition, under the feelings of that exciting day. The latitude of this spot is 70° 5′ 17″, and its longitude 96° 46′ 45″ west."

Even if the pole were stationary, this determination could only be regarded as approximate; but when we know that the centre of magnetic intensity is a movable point, we shall readily understand that the cairn erected with so much enthusiasm can now only show where it *was*. According to Hansteen, the pole moves 11′ 4″ every year, and revolves within the frigid zone in 1890 years, so that it will not reach the same spot in Boothia until the year 3722 ! The precise determination of this point, however, is said to be comparatively unimportant, because its position can always be ascertained by observations of the compass and dipping-needles.

As soon as Commander Ross and his party returned, it was thought time, amid alternate hopes and fears, to watch the progress of the ice, and escape, if possible, from the prison of a third dreary winter. The season was not, on the whole, more favorable than that of 1830 ; yet, on the 28th August, a somewhat earlier period, they contrived to warp out into the open sea, and on the morning of the 29th were in full sail. But they were baffled by changes of wind and heavy gales. On the 14th of September they could again take exercise by skating on the newly-formed ice. On the 27th they found themselves completely fixed for a third winter. Their last year's navigation had been three miles — this season it was extended to four !

The spirits of the adventurers now began to droop in earnest. Their only means of escape seemed to be to proceed in the boats, or draw them over the ice to the wreck of the Fury, when, after supplying themselves with a fresh stock of provisions out of her stores, they might reach Davis's Straits, and be taken up by a whale-ship. In November the scurvy began to appear. The extraordinary exemption hitherto enjoyed from this dreadful malady, in the absence of the grand specific of vegetable food, Ross is inclined to ascribe to the abundance with which the men were supplied with water, notwithstanding the quantity of fuel requisite to melt the snow ; to their never having been too long at once exposed to cold, and to the care that was taken not to allow them to remain in their wet clothes.

It was now determined to abandon the Victory, and move away to Fury Beach, as early in the spring as travelling should be practicable. The beach was one hundred and eighty miles distant in a direct line, and three hundred by the necessary windings. They set out on the 23d of April, 1832, on the first part of their expedition. The loads being too heavy to be carried at once, made it necessary to go back and forward twice, and even oftener, the same day. They had to encounter dreadful tempests of snow and drift, and to make circuits, in order to avoid impassable barriers. The general result was, that by the 21st May they had travelled three hundred and twenty-nine miles to gain thirty in a direct line, having in this labor expended a month.

After this preliminary movement, they returned to the ship, of which they were soon to take a final leave. On the 29th of May they hoisted the colors, nailed them to the mast, and drank a parting glass to the Victory, which they considered worthy of a better fate. In a few days they reached their former deposit; and the men, extremely exhausted, were anxious to leave the boats and spare provisions, and push on to Fury Beach. The captain, however, considered it indispensable to carry these to the other side of Elizabeth Harbor, as the nearest spot to which there was full security of being able to return. The 9th of June arrived before everything was brought forward to that point. It was soon after arranged that his nephew and two others should set forward as a light party, with a fortnight's provisions, to ascertain the state of the supplies, and then return with their report to the main body, who were to proceed by slower marches, but more heavily loaded.

On this laborious journey Ross had an opportunity of examining the coast, and ascertaining that the large inlet in Brentford Bay was formed merely by a river, and could afford no passage to the western sea. On the 25th of June he met the advanced party, who reported that they had found three of the boats washed away, but enough still left for their purpose, and all the provisions in good condition. On the 1st of July the whole crew reached their destination. They immediately enjoyed a hearty meal, and soon reared a canvas mansion, which they named Somerset House.

The month of July was spent in fitting out the boats, which were ready by the 1st of August, when there appeared a considerable extent of open sea, cheering them with the hope of being able to penetrate through Barrow's Strait into Baffin's Bay. The voyage, however, proved very difficult; masses of ice, still tossing amid the waves, placed them sometimes in dangerous positions; and, when they sought shelter on the beach, it was mostly bordered by lofty, precipitous cliffs, from which, at this season of thaw, fragments were often detached, one of which might have crushed them to pieces. It was the 29th of August before they passed Cape Seppings, and arrived at the junction between Prince Regent's Inlet and Barrow's Strait. After several attempts to run along the latter, rendered fruitless by the ice, they were obliged to haul the boats on shore and pitch their tents. There was still time to have accomplished their object; but repeated surveys from the neighboring mountains convinced them that Barrow's Strait was now, and had been during the whole summer, an impenetrable mass.

By the 24th of September all were agreed that no

choice was left but to return to Fury Beach, and there spend their fourth Arctic winter. Proceeding, therefore, in the boats, on the 30th of September they reached Batty Bay, more than half the distance; but the ice rendering it impossible to sail further, they hauled them on shore, and left them above high-water mark. Then, carrying the provisions on sledges, and making a somewhat difficult journey, they arrived, on the 7th of October, at what they now accounted their home.

The party suffered, at first, a good deal from cold, against which their canvas covering afforded very imperfect shelter. They contrived, however, to envelop it in a wall of snow, and set up an additional stove, which was so effectual that the heat of 51° could be maintained within. It was necessary to make a reduction in the allowance of preserved meats; bread was somewhat deficient; and the stock of wine and spirits was entirely exhausted. However, as they had caught a few foxes, which were considered a delicacy, and there was plenty of flour, sugar, soups, and vegetables, a diet could be easily arranged sufficient to maintain the party in health and vigor.

The winter, as it advanced, proved one of great severity; and, when the cold reached its utmost rigor, their slight walls could no longer keep the mansion in a comfortable heat. The tempestuous weather made it impossible to take exercise in the open air; and at length their patience appears to have been wearied out by this long and dreary imprisonment within the Arctic wastes. On the 16th of February, 1833, Thomas, the carpenter, died of scurvy — an event deeply regretted in itself, and regarded as a warning of what was too likely to befall the rest. Several of the seamen, in fact, became affected with this cruel disease, of which Ross himself felt the sure approach, by the return of pain in his old wounds. Their situation was becoming truly awful; since, if they were not liberated in the ensuing summer, little prospect appeared of their surviving another year.

In April and May, as soon as it was possible to travel, while yet the ice remained firm, it was necessary to carry forward an ample stock of provisions to the position of the boats, and there await the opportunities of release. Though the distance was only thirty-two miles, their reduced numbers, and the weight of the loads, obliged them to go over the same ground eight times, raising the space actually traversed to two hundred and fifty-six miles; so that it afforded laborious employment for a whole month. They then returned to Somerset House, where they remained till the 8th of July, on which day the whole party quitted, without regret, this dreary home, and, though much encumbered by the transport of the sick, arrived, on the 12th, at their boat-station in Batty Bay.

The aspect of the sea was now watched with intense anxiety, not unmingled with dread; yet the very habit of observing and of speculating on their prospects — some daily mounting the neighboring hill, and others reviewing their report — kept their spirits in a state of salutary activity. The pursuit of feathered game, which always afforded the hope, and sometimes the reality, of a good supper, also enlivened their time. A month was passed in vain expectation; when, at length, on the evening of the 14th of August, a lane of water appeared, leading to the northward. Next morning the seamen were in movement at an early hour; and, having cleared the shore of the ice that obstructed it, they embarked the provisions and stores, and by eight o'clock were under way, with a favorable wind.

At midnight they passed Elwin's Bay, and on the

16th had come to the furthest point reached in the preceding year, a spot which excited some painful recollections. However, though all passage to the east was closed, there was still an open lane by which they could proceed northwards. In the evening of that day they were at the north-eastern point of America, and beheld the sea in that direction quite navigable, though encumbered with ice. At three in the morning of the 17th they were in motion, making their way through the loose pieces, till, favored by a southern breeze, they turned the point of the solid mass which obstructed the inlet, and saw the wide expanse of Barrow's Strait open before them. Wafted on as if by magic, they reached the opposite shore, which they sailed along to within twelve miles of Cape York, having made in this day seventy-two miles. In the two following they passed Admiralty Inlet, and came within six or seven miles of that called Navy Board; after which they were detained four days by contrary winds, and obliged to reduce their allowance of provisions. On the 25th, however, they could again use their oars, and reached the eastern side of Navy Board Inlet, where they found a good harbor for the night.

At four in the morning of the 26th they were roused from sleep by the look-out man announcing "a sail," which, viewed through a glass, proved evidently to be a ship. All were presently in motion, and their hopes and fears were variously expressed. But they were detained by calms and light shifting airs; and, a breeze springing up, the vessel made sail with a rapidity which left them hopelessly behind. About ten, however, they descried another, which seemed to be lying to; but she, also, soon bore up under all sail, and appeared to be fast leaving them. Happily, a calm succeeded; and, by hard rowing, they approached so near that their signals were perceived, when she was seen to heave to and lower a boat, which made directly towards them.

On its arrival, the mate in command asked if they were in distress and had lost their vessel, proffering his aid, stating, in answer to their inquiries, that he belonged to the Isabella, of Hull, once commanded by Captain Ross, now by Captain Humphreys. On being told that the former person stood before him, his brain was so puzzled that he declared the captain must be under a mistake, as he had certainly been dead two years. When satisfied, however, of the contrary, and that he was in the presence of the long-absent navigator, he offered his hearty congratulations.

Such was the effect of previous hardship, that few of Ross's men could sleep on a bed; and some time was necessary to enable them to enjoy this and other accommodations of ordinary life.

On the 30th of September, 1833, the Isabella left Davis's Straits, and on the 11th of October reached Stromness, in Orkney. On Ross's landing at Hull, on the 18th, such crowds were attracted that he could with difficulty reach the inn. He proceeded next day to London, and, having reported himself to the Admiralty, was presented, on the morrow, to his majesty at Windsor.

THE PTARMIGAN.

ROSS'S RESCUE.

P. 180.

CHAPTER X.

BACK'S LAND EXPEDITION. — ARRIVAL AT FORT WILLIAM. — ANECDOTE OF A CANOE PARTY. — FRANKLIN. — SCENERY. — ASCENT OF RIVERS. — AYLMER LAKE. — WINTER QUARTERS. — STARVING INDIANS. — INTENSE COLD. — NEWS OF ROSS'S SAFETY. — EXPERT CANOE-MAN. — ESQUIMAUX FRIENDS. — THE THLEW-EE-CHOH. — THE POLAR SEA. — RETURN TO ENGLAND. — BACK'S VOYAGE IN THE TERROR. — REMARKABLE PERILS AMONG THE ICE. — HOMEWARD BOUND. — DEASE AND SIMPSON'S DISCOVERIES.

Ross's protracted stay of four years in the inhospitable north induced the government to send out an expedition to look for the absent party. Back, who was then in Italy, hurried home to volunteer his services ; his offer was accepted ; and with Dr. King, surgeon and naturalist, he left England in February, 1833. At Montreal he engaged three artillery-men and some voyageurs, and embarked on the St. Lawrence in two canoes. At the Sault de Ste Mary, on the 11th of May, they purchased a third canoe, and commenced coasting along the northern shores of Lake Superior. On the 20th they arrived at the Hudson's Bay Company's establishment, Fort William.

Passing the height of land which separates the waters which flow into Lake Superior from those which enter Hudson's Bay, the three canoes proceeded rapidly on their ever-changing and romantic route, at times dashing down rapids, then crossing small lakes, or making slow progress along small and shallow rivers, so that portages were often necessary.

It is related by Back, that, not many years ago, a canoe was pursuing its way quietly down one of the streams through which the Arctic exploring party was now passing. It was approaching one of the many portages with which these streams abound, and the bowman and steersman were standing erect at stem and stern, casting quick glances ahead and on either side as they neared the waterfall which obstructed their progress. The approach to the landing-place was somewhat difficult, owing to a point of rocks which projected into the stream, in the direction of the fall, and round which point it was necessary to steer with some dexterity, in order to avoid being drawn into the strong current. The fearless guides, however, had often passed the place in former years in safety, and, accordingly, dashed at the point with reckless indifference, their paddles flinging a circle of spray over their heads, as they changed them from side to side, with graceful but vigorous rapidity. The swift stream carried them quickly round the point of danger, and they had almost reached the quiet eddy near the landing-place, when the stem of the canoe was caught by the stream, which in an instant whirled them out from the shore, and carried them downwards with fearful rapidity. Another moment, and the gushing waters dragged them, despite their most frantic efforts, to the verge of the waterfall, which thundered and foamed among frightful chasms and rocks many feet below. The stem of the canoe overhung the abyss, and now the *voyageurs* plied their paddles with the desperation of men who felt that their lives depended on the exertions of that terrible minute. For a second or two the canoe remained stationary, and seemed to tremble on the brink of destruction; and then, inch by inch, it began slowly to ascend the stream. The danger was past! A few more nervous strokes,

PERILOUS ESCAPE OF VOYAGEURS. P. 182.

and the trembling bark shot like an arrow out of the current, and floated in safety on the still water under the point. The whole thing, from beginning to end, was the work of a few seconds; yet who can describe or comprehend the tumultuous gush of feelings created, during these short seconds, in the bosoms of the careless *voyageurs?* The sudden, electric change from tranquil safety to the verge of almost certain destruction — and then — deliverance!

On the 6th of June the canoes arrived at Fort Alexander — situated at the southern extremity of Lake Winipeg. Here Back remained a few days, to await the arrival of Governor Simpson. During this period he and Mr. King made some observations on the dip of the needle, while the men busied themselves in unpacking and drying the provisions and packages.

The mosquitos here were very numerous and annoying. Of the sand-flies, near the lakes, Back says, that even the Indians do not contrive any way of escaping this tormenting insect. Their usual mode is to throw themselves on their faces to the ground, and to moan with pain. Back thought of killing them by smoke; upon which Maufelly, his interpreter, expressed surprise that he "should be so unlike the *old chief*, who would not destroy a single mosquito." By the "old chief" was meant Sir John Franklin, of whom Back says: "It was his custom never to kill a fly; and, though teased by them beyond expression, especially when engaged in taking observations, he would quietly desist from his work, and patiently blow the half-gorged intruders from his hands: 'the world was wide enough for both.'"

Leaving Fort Alexander on the 11th of June, Back coasted Lake Winipeg, toward Norway House, where he arrived on the 17th. Here he obtained the requisite number of voyageurs and attendants, amounting to eighteen in all; and, in high spirits, they started for their winter quarters on the eastern shore of Great Slave Lake.

On the 21st of July they arrived at Portage La Loche, the high ridge of land which divides the waters running into Hudson's Bay from those flowing into the Arctic Ocean. Here they had to carry their canoe and baggage over the ridge, a distance of fourteen miles — a tedious labor, which consumed eight days.

Of the scenery at this place Mr. King says: "Within a mile of the termination of the portage, a most extensive and magnificent scene burst upon our view, and we discovered ourselves, through an opening in the trees, to be on a hill upwards of a thousand feet high, and at the brink of a tremendous precipice. We were certainly prepared to expect an extensive prospect, but the beautiful landscape before us was far superior to anything that could be anticipated from the nature of the country we had hitherto seen. At a depth of two hundred fathoms below the summit on which we stood, the Clear Water River was to be seen winding its serpentine course in beautiful meanders for thirty miles, broken here and there, and interrupted by intervening woods; while

——'the tall pines dwindled as to shrubs,
In dizziness of distance!'

"The valley, at once refreshed and adorned by the smooth pellucid stream, was embanked by two parallel chains of hills extending towards the west, till it became lost in the purple hue of distance. The inclining heights, here and there covered with stately forests, and occasionally interspersed with barren spots or promontories of the most luxuriant verdure, were beautifully contrasted with the icinerated tinge which overspread vast tracts of country where once the dense forests had been consumed by fire."

The party arrived at Fort Chipewyan the 29th of July; at Fort Resolution, on Great Slave Lake, the 8th of August. Here, having obtained all possible information from the Indians relative to the course of the northern rivers of which he was in search, he divided his men into two parties, five being left as an escort for Mr. McLeod, and four being appointed to accompany himself in search of the Thlew-ee-choh or Great Fish River, since named after Back himself.

On the 19th of August, Back and his men began the ascent of the Hoar Frost River. Its course was a series of the most fearful cascades and rapids. Almost impervious woods of stunted firs, bogs, and swamps, occasioned great trouble to the party. They arrived, at length, in an open space, where the scene was one of barrenness and desolation: crag was piled upon crag to the height of two thousand feet from the base, and the course of the river here, in a state of contraction, was marked by an uninterrupted line of foam.

Rapid now succeeded rapid; scarcely had the party surmounted one fall than another presented itself, rising like an amphitheatre before them to the height of fifty feet. They, however, gained at length the ascent of this turbulent and unfriendly river, the romantic beauty and wild scenery of which were very remarkable; and, after passing successively a series of portages, rapids, falls, lakes, and rivers, on the 27th Back observed from the summit of a high hill a very large lake, full of deep bays and islands, and which has been named Aylmer Lake, after the Governor-General of Canada at that time. The boat was sent out, with three men, to search for the lake, or outlet of the river; which they discovered on the second day, and Back himself, during their absence, also accidentally discovered its source in the Sand Hill Lake, not far from his encampment. Yielding to that pleasurable emotion which discoverers, in the first bound of their transport, may be pardoned for indulging, Back threw himself down on the bank, and drank a hearty draught of the limpid water.

On the 30th of August they began to move toward the river, but, on reaching Musk-ox Lake, it was found impossible to stand the force of the rapids in their frail canoe, and, as winter was approaching, their return to the rendezvous on Slave Lake was determined on. At Clinton Colden Lake some Indians visited them from the chief Akaitcho, who had been a guide of Sir John Franklin. Two of these Indians remembered Back, one having accompanied him to the Coppermine River on Franklin's first expedition. At the Cat or Artillery Lake they had to abandon their canoe, and perform the rest of the journey on foot over precipitous rocks, through frightful gorges and ravines, heaped with masses of granite, and along narrow ledges, where a false step would have been fatal. At Fort Reliance the party found Mr. McLeod had, during their absence, erected the frame-work of a comfortable residence for them, and all hands set to work to complete it. After many obstacles and difficulties, it was finished. Dr. King joined them on the 16th of September, with two laden batteaux.

On the 5th of November they exchanged their cold tents for the new house, which was fifty feet long by thirty broad, and contained four rooms, besides a spacious hall in the centre, for the reception and accommodation of the Indians, to which a sort of rude kitchen was attached.

An observatory was constructed at a short distance,

wherein certain mysterious and complicated instruments were fixed and erected ; iron in all forms being carefully excluded, and a fence run round it to guard it more effectually from the men, as they walked about with their guns, ice-chisels, and axes. Here Back and Mr. King used to sit in solemn conclave for many an hour during the winter, closely observing the various interesting phenomena of earth and sky ; and awfully mysterious did this building appear to the simple Indians and voyageurs. They would approach as near as they dared, and, with their arms folded, brows knit, and heads down, would stand for hours wondering at the dead silence of its occupants, broken only at long intervals by such exclamations as "now" — "stop" — insomuch that they at last, after very mature and grave deliberation, came to the conclusion that they were "raising the devil!"

As the winter advanced bands of starving Indians continued to arrive, in the hope of obtaining some relief, as little or nothing was to be procured by hunting. They would stand around while the men were taking their meals, watching every mouthful with the most longing, imploring look, but yet never uttering a complaint.

At other times they would, seated round the fire, occupy themselves in roasting and devouring small bits of their reindeer garments, which, even when entire, afforded them a very insufficient protection against a temperature of 102° below freezing point.

The sufferings of the poor Indians at this period are described as frightful. "Famine, with her gaunt and bony arm," says Back, "pursued them at every turn, withered their energies, and strewed them lifeless on the cold bosom of the snow." It was impossible to afford relief out of their scanty store to all, but even small portions of the mouldy pemmican intended for the dogs, unpalatable as it was, were gladly received, and saved many from perishing. "Often," adds Back, "did I share my own plate with the children, whose helpless state and piteous cries were peculiarly distressing. Compassion for the full-grown may or may not be felt, but that heart must be cased in steel which is insensible to the cry of a child for food."

To add to the distress of Back, he received information that his friend Augustus, the affectionate Esquimaux interpreter who had accompanied him on a former journey, hearing of his being again in the country, set out from Hudson's Bay, in company with a Canadian and an Iroquois; they lost their way, were separated, and poor Augustus fell a sacrifice to famine. His remains were found on the barrens not far from the Rivière à Jean. It appeared that the gallant little fellow was retracing his steps to the establishment, when, either exhausted by suffering and privation, or caught in the midst of an open traverse in one of those terrible snow-storms, which may be almost said to blow through the frame, he had sunk to rise no more. "Such," says Back, "was the miserable end of poor Augustus! a faithful, disinterested, kind-hearted creature, who had won the regard, not of myself only, but, I may add, of Sir John Franklin and Dr. Richardson also, by qualities which, wherever found, in the lowest as in the highest forms of social life, are the ornament and charm of humanity."

At this critical juncture, Akaitcho made his appearance with an opportune supply of a little meat, which in some measure enabled Back to relieve the sufferers around him, many of whom, to his great delight, went away with Akaitcho. The stock of meat was soon exhausted, and they had to open their pemmican. The officers contented themselves with the short supply of half a pound a day, but the laboring men could not do with less than a pound and three quarters. The cold now set in with an intensity which Back had never before experienced, — the thermometer, on the 17th of January, being 70° below zero. "Such, indeed," he says, "was the abstraction of heat, that, with eight large logs of dry wood on the fire, I could not get the thermometer higher than 12° below zero. Ink and paint froze. The sextant cases and boxes of seasoned wood, principally fir, all split. The skin of the hands became dry, cracked, and opened into unsightly and smarting gashes, which we were obliged to anoint with grease. On one occasion, after washing my face within three feet of the fire, my hair was actually clotted with ice before I had time to dry it."

The hunters suffered severely from the intensity of the cold, and compared the sensation of handling their guns to that of touching red-hot iron; and so excessive was the pain, that they were obliged to wrap thongs of leather round the triggers, to keep their fingers from coming into contact with the steel.

The sufferings which the party now endured were great, and, had it not been for the exemplary conduct of Akaitcho in procuring them game, it is to be doubted whether any would have survived to tell the misery they had endured. The sentiments of this worthy savage were nobly expressed — "The great chief trusts in us, and it is better that ten Indians perish than that one white man should perish through our negligence and breach of faith."

About the middle of April preparations were begun for their intended journey to the sea-coast; but on the 25th a messenger arrived bringing to Back the welcome intelligence of the safety of Ross and his party. His feelings at this news are thus described: "In the fulness of our hearts, we assembled, and humbly offered up our thanks to that merciful Providence which, in the beautiful language of Scripture, hath said, 'Mine own will I bring again, as I did sometime from the deeps of the sea.'"

On the 7th of June, Back and Mr. King left Fort Reliance for the Polar Sea. Their boat, thirty feet long, was placed on runners, and dragged over the yet unmelted ice of the lakes and swamps. A singular fact in regard to temperature is mentioned. About the end of May, just before they set out, the weather was sultry, the temperature in the sun being 106°! an extraordinary contrast to that of January 17th, when it was 70° below zero. They now experienced some cold and foggy weather. McLeod, with a party of Indians, was sent on ahead to hunt and make *caches* of the meat, to be picked up as the main party behind came up to them.

On the 28th of June they were fairly launched on the head waters of the Thlew-ee-choh. From this time till their approach to the sea, a constant succession of falls, and rapids, and cataracts, more or less obstructed their progress, and, as Back says, "made him hold his breath, expecting to see the boat dashed to shivers against some protruding rocks amid the foam and fury at the foot of a rapid." In passing down one of these, where the river was full of large rocks and bowlders, the boat was obliged to be lightened; and Back says, "I stood on a high rock, with an anxious heart, to see her run it. Away they went with the speed of an arrow, and in a moment the foam and rocks hid them from my view. I heard what sounded in my ear like a wild shriek; I followed with an agitation which may be conceived, and, to my inexpressible joy, found that the shriek was the triumphant whoop of the crew, who had landed safely in a small bay below." In short, strong and heavy rapids, with falls and whirlpools, kept the men, for eighty or ninety miles, in a constant state of exertion and anxiety.

He gives an instance, on one occasion, of the consummate skill of De Charloit, a half-breed canoe-man, who "ran our rickety and shattered canoe down four successive rapids, which, under less able management, would have whirled it, and everybody in it, to certain destruction. Nothing could exceed the self-possession and nicety of judgment with which he guided the frail thing along the narrow line between the high waves of the torrent and the returning eddy. A foot in either direction would have been fatal; but, with the most perfect ease, and, I may add, elegant and graceful action, his keen eyes fixed upon the *run*, he kept her true to her course through all its rapid windings."

On the 13th of July a glimpse of sunshine tempted the captain to halt for the purpose of taking observations; and, while he was thus engaged, the men were permitted to scour the country in pursuit of deer and musk-oxen, which literally swarmed in the barren grounds. The hunters soon returned with four fine bucks, which afforded them an agreeable change from the customary meal of pemmican.

The latitude was 65° 38′ 21″ N., and longitude 106° 35′ 23″ W. At this place the river began to take an easterly bend, which perplexed them much; causing great anxiety as to whether it would ultimately lead them to the Frozen Sea, or terminate in Hudson's Bay. In any case, they had nothing for it but to push on; and their labors were rewarded by their finding that the river trended again in a northerly direction, and their hopes were further increased by the discovery, on the 16th of July, of some old Esquimaux encampments. Once, indeed, they thought they saw tents of the Esquimaux ahead ; but, on a nearer approach, they turned out to be some luxuriant clumps of willows, which were inhabited by thousands of geese, which had selected the spot as convenient for the operation of casting their feathers. Thousands upon thousands of the most excellent quills were found scattered over the sand. A curious feature in this part of the country was the number of huge bowlder-stones, not only in the river, but on the very pinnacles of the highest hills.

On the 28th of July they met the first Esquimaux, who, as usual on their first seeing Europeans, exhibited consternation by shouts, yells, antics, and gesticulations ; under the impression, apparently, that by so doing they would frighten their new visitors away. The boat continued to approach the shore, despite the brandishing of spears and other belligerent demonstrations ; whereupon the whole nation formed in a semicircle round the spot where the boat grounded, and stood on the defensive. Back, however, soon established friendly relations with them, by walking boldly up, unarmed, and alone, at the same time calling out *Tima* — peace — with great emphasis, tossing up his arms in true Esquimaux style, and, finally, shaking hands all round. This quieted them, and they soon mingled with the men, from whom they received a few buttons with great delight.

A portage had to be made at this place, and the Esquimaux here aided them in transporting their boats, to which Back's party were wholly unequal ; so that to the natives he was indebted for getting to the sea at all.

On the 29th of July, while threading their course between some sand-banks, with a strong current, they first caught sight of a majestic headland in the extreme distance to the north, which had a coast-like appearance.

This important promontory Back subsequently named Victoria. "This, then," observes Back, "may be considered as the mouth of the Thlew-ee-choh, which, after a violent and tortuous course of five hundred and thirty geographical miles, running through an iron-ribbed country, without a single tree on the whole line of its banks, expanding into five large lakes, with clear horizon, most embarrassing to the navigator, and broken into falls, cascades, and rapids, to the number of eighty-three in the whole, pours its water into the Polar Sea, in lat. 67° 11′ N., and long. 94° 30′ W., that is to say, about thirty-seven miles more south than the mouth of the Coppermine River, and nineteen miles more south than that of Back's River, at the lower extremity of Bathurst's Inlet."

For several days Back was able to make but slow progress along the eastern shore, in consequence of the solid body of drift-ice. A barren, rocky elevation of eight hundred feet high was named Cape Beaufort. A bluff point on the eastern side of the estuary, which he considered to be the northern extreme, he named Cape Hay. Dease and Simpson, however, in 1839, traced the shore much beyond this. The difficulties met with here began to dispirit the men. They were almost without water, without any means of warmth, or any kind of warm or comforting food, and sinking knee-deep, as they proceeded on land, in the soft slush and snow. So damp was the weather that for ten days, while encamped on Montreal Island, they could not light a spark of fire, or obtain a warm meal.

The low, flat country was the picture of desolation. "It was one irregular plain of sand and stones; and, had it not been for a rill of water, the meandering of which relieved the monotony of the sterile scene, one might have fancied one's self in one of the parched plains of the East, rather than on the shores of the Arctic Sea."

With unflinching ardor did Back push forward, in the hope of reaching a more open sea, and connecting their discoveries with those of Captain Franklin at Point Turnagain. On the 7th of August they reached the extreme point of land which terminates the wide mouth of the river, and whence the coast trends to the westward. This was named Point Ogle, and another cape, seen far to the west, was named Point Richardson. Several portions of the coast of Boothia Felix were also seen in the distance to the northward. Here they were completely baffled in every attempt to advance. Back sent, however, a small party to the westward to trace the coast, which was all that could be done; but they were only able to follow the shore about fifteen miles. The surface was level, and void of vegetation. They found, however, several pieces of drift-wood, one of which was nine feet long and nine inches in diameter, which the men jocularly called "a piece of the north pole."

Back now resolved to retrace his steps. Before doing so, however, the British flag was unfurled, and the land taken possession of, with three enthusiastic cheers, in the name of His Majesty William IV. The latitude of the place was 68° 13′ 57″ N., longitude 94° 58′ 1″ W.

In the middle of August they left the cold precincts of the Arctic Sea. In retracing his route Back ascended the high grounds which divide the northern from the southern streams. The Aylmer, the Artillery, and the Clinton Colden Lakes embellish the landscape, and discharge their waters into the Great Slave Lake. Here he found a splendid cascade, of which he says: "The color of the water varied from a very light to a very dark green; and the spray, which spread a dimness above, was thrown up in clouds of light gray. Niagara, Wilberforce's Falls in Hood's River, the falls of Kakabikka, near Lake Superior, the Swiss or Italian falls, although they may each 'charm the eye with dread,' are not to be compared to this for splendor of effect. It was the most imposing spectacle I had ever witnessed; and, as its berg-like appearance brought to mind associations of another scene, I bestowed upon it the name of our celebrated navigator, Sir Edward Parry, and called it Parry's Falls."

Of the Indians, Back gives, in his narrative, some interesting anecdotes.

Once, speaking with the Camarade de Mandeville, a potent Chipewyan chief, regarding the due observance of certain moral precepts for his future guidance, the chief listened with most profound attention and gravity. When Back had concluded, he raised his head a little, and, with eyes fixed on the floor, said, in a low and solemn tone, "The chief's words have sunk deep into my heart, and I shall often think of them when I am alone. It is true that I am ignorant; but I never lie down at night in my lodge without whispering to the Great Spirit a prayer for forgiveness, if I have done anything wrong that day."

On the 17th of September the return party met Mr. McLeod, according to appointment, at Sandy-Hill Bay. He had long been expecting them, and had spent many an anxious hour in watching the distant objects in the direction of their route. With this gentleman they returned to Fort Reliance, where they arrived on the 27th, "after an absence of nearly four months; tired, indeed, but well in health, and truly grateful for the manifold mercies we had experienced in the course of our long and perilous journey."

Preparations were soon set on foot to spend another winter in the wilderness. Once more the woods resounded with the woodman's axe, and the little rooms glowed with the blazing fires of wood. Again the nets were set and the guns loaded, and the white man and the red ranged the woods in company; while Back and Mr. King found ample and interesting occupation in mapping their discoveries and writing their journals. On the 28th of May, 1835, Back bade adieu to the polar regions, and returned to England, where he arrived on the 8th of September, after an absence of two years and seven months.

This was not the last of Back's labors. In 1836, at the instance of the Geographical Society, the British government equipped an expedition to complete the discovery of the coast-line between Regent's Inlet and Point Turnagain. The ship Terror was set apart for the service; and Captain Back, just returned from his great land journey, was appointed to the command.

The Terror left Chatham on the 14th of June, 1836. On the 29th of July, when a good way across the mouth of Davis's Straits, she came first in view of the ice. The quantity of it was great, and one enormous berg presented a vertical face of not less than three hundred feet in height. Occasional clear and pleasant runs were afterwards made, but, in general, the obstructions were incessant and tremendous. And, so early as from the 1st to the 3d of August, when the ship was near the vexed and foggy shores of Resolution Island, she had to bore and manœuvre her way among dense floes, high packs, and surging whirlpools.

On the 8th of August she was moored to a large iceberg for protection from a gale. But the berg looked dangerous, and was anxiously watched by the officers, lest it should capsize and overwhelm them. Early next morning it was violently struck on the weather-side by a heavy drifting floe, and for some minutes it rocked and oscillated in awful menace of an overturn; but a large piece fell with a splash into the sea from one of its corners, and providentially restored the equilibrium.

On the 14th of August the Terror entered the narrows between Salisbury Island and the north coast. A resolution was now taken to steer for the Frozen Strait. The course for four days continued to be severe, yet afforded considerable promise. But, on the 18th, after the ship had worked for some time in only one hole of water, she was arrested by a dense unbroken pack, of fearful extent and most wildly rugged surface. Yet the ship pushed boldly into it, and very soon, to the surprise and joy of all, the stupendous mass went asunder, and disclosed a path through what seemed an impenetrable barrier.

On the 23d of August they sighted Baffin Island, which flanks the north side of the entrance of the Frozen Strait. But they found not a channel or a water-lane, even of the width of a brook, to invite them on. The scene everywhere around was a tumulated sea of ice, without one break, without one cheering feature, and with a surface so rough, and heaved, and peaked, that no human being could have travelled on it for more than a very brief distance. They all but abandoned expectation of ever getting into the Frozen Strait, and were now glad to attempt to work their way toward Southampton Island. They warped and bored, and spent many an hour in feverish excitement. On the 25th they made some little distance through a slack; but at sunset they were stopped near an extensive floe, where, from the effects of pressure, some ponderous masses, not unlike the blocks of a Titanian ruin, had been heaped up to the height of thirty feet. "The land, blue from distance, and beautifully soft as contrasted with the white cold glare of the interminable ice around, reflecting by the setting sun the tints of the intervening masses thrown into the most picturesque groups and forms, spires, turrets, and pyramids, many in deep shade, presented altogether a scene sufficient for a time to cheat the imagination, and withdraw the mind from the cheerless reality of their situation."

On the 5th of September, when they were firmly fixed about sixteen miles from Southampton Island, and saw some tempting lanes of water at no great distance, they fell to the spirited task of cutting a way through the ice by mechanical force. All the ship's company, officers and men, seized axes, ice-chisels, hand-pikes, and long poles, and vied with one another in driving the blocks asunder, and in driving them away to the nearest pool. They at length succeeded in setting the ship free, and got her into a run of several miles toward the land; but so early as next morning, they were once more "in a fix." High winds and foul weather at the same time came on, and seriously bewildered them, yet, on the whole, did them good service, by driving them slowly toward the shore.

On the 14th of September, within about four miles of the Cape Comfort of Baffin, the ship became severely "nipped." A violent, agitative, landward motion pressed all the surrounding ice into the utmost possible compactness, raised much of it into ponderous pointed heaps of twenty feet and upwards in height, and jammed the ship with perilous tightness between the nearest masses.

The hapless ship was for many days drifted backward and forward along the coast, and away from it, over a range of about thirty miles, just as the wind or the cur-

THE TERROR NIPPED. P. 198.

rent or the tide directed. The black frowning cliffs of Cape Comfort might have seemed to the most sluggish imagination to grin upon her in irony. She lay in the grip of the ice-masses as helplessly as a kid does in the folds of a boa-constrictor; and once, when she slipped from that grip, or was hurtled into a change of position, she left her form as perfectly impressed behind her as if it had been struck in a die. The many old Greenland seamen on board all declared that they had never before seen a ship which could have resisted such a pressure. The perils, too, were increasing; and at length, on the 24th of September, the officers unanimously expressed a conviction, founded on the experience of the preceding thirty-four days, that all hope of making further progress that season toward Repulse Bay was gone.

Captain Back now resolved to cut a dock in the only adjacent floe which seemed sufficiently large and high to afford the ship fair protection. But, on the very next day, by one of those extraordinary convulsions which are the last hope of the ice-bound Arctic voyager, the whole body of ice, for leagues around, got into general commotion, and burst into single masses, and, commencing an impetuous rush to the west, tossed many blocks into heaps, ground others to powder, whirled all into a hurly-burly, and bore away the ship like a feather toward the Frozen Strait. Nothing could be done by the crew but to await the issue; and when the storm subsided, they found themselves midway between Cape Comfort and the entrance of the Frozen Strait, about three miles from the shore, without any prospect of either forcing their way into a harbor, or finding some little shelter in a floe. They were once more firmly beset, with the additional calamity of being so much tilted up, that the stern of the ship lay seven and a half feet above the horizontal, and the bow was jammed downward on the masses ahead. "Thus," says Back, "ended a month of vexation, disappointment, and anxiety, to me personally more distressing and intolerable than the worst pressure of the worst evils which had befallen me in any other expedition."

After a long series of such trying vicissitudes, a time of repose followed. The long calm of winter seemed at last to have set in. Back, remembering the example of Parry, induced the officers to assist him in contriving some amusement for the men. Theatricals were got up, and the farce of Monsieur Tonson went off with hearty laughter and abundant plaudits. An evening school also was instituted, and kept vigorously going. But a startling event was at hand.

The floe, which had been at once cradle, wagon, and bulwark, to the ship, now cracked and split to within about forty paces of it, and gave fearful omen of being ready to go to pieces. It had become a home to the crew, and had been made snug with snow-walls, snow-houses, galleries, and court-yard, which served well some of the best purposes of a deck. It still held together, shattered and crazy, for three or four days, and carried them within sight of Seahorse Point, the south-eastern extremity of Southampton Island. Early on the morning of the 18th of February, there occurred, in rapid succession, first, a terrific crash on the eastern edge of the floe; next, a hoarse rushing sound across it; next, several severe shocks against the ship, and next, a visible rending of the floe right through the centre. The ship now began to strain and quiver; and she then heeled over to port, and relieved herself about six inches from an embankment which had been built against her side. At this time the crashing, grinding, rushing noise beneath the ship, and all over the floe, were appalling. About two hours after, a commotion like an earthquake took place, and made cracks across the snow-houses, galleries, and court-yard, and forced the ship to creak through all her timbers. A semi-circular rampart of ice advanced from the opened sea beyond the floe; and enormous hillocky masses, some round and massy, and others like small packs, had broken loose, and seemed big with woe and ruin. At this awful moment the tumult suddenly ceased. But the ship was in a most perilous position; the ice all around was so splintered and jagged, and so fissured and holed, that it could neither bear a boat nor be made a depository of provisions; and the land was seven or nine miles distant, and probably could not have been reached by even the expertest ice-man, who should have had nothing but his own life to take care of.

On the following day the perils continued and increased, and on the 20th they reached a crisis. All the ice was again in motion, and one of its heaves broke up the floe along the starboard side of the ship, and threw down everything in its way. Some of the galleries now floated away, looking like tunnels; and the ship herself was in open water, subject to the rubs and nips of the ice-masses. A little after, she was violently struck far below the water-line, and creaked hideously from stem to stern, as if she were about to go asunder. All the crew were confounded, and even the poor sick went tottering aft, in an agony of terror. But the ship lifted herself fully eight inches from the pressure of a force which would have crushed a less strengthened vessel to atoms; and the assailing ice-mass either passed in part beneath the bottom, or was wedged against the large masses at the extremities. For upwards of three weeks, similar scenes, and worse, were frequent; and never on the polar seas was there a more marvellous scene of awful dangers without a catastrophe, and of providential deliverances, without any instrumentality of man. The scenery was sometimes magnificently solemn, with such a perspective of moving, frowning, stupendous towers and bulwarks, as few human beings have ever witnessed; and often, on the contrary, was it so enwrapped in fog, that its dreadful perils were much more readily heard than seen.

On several occasions the ship was violently nipped, and lifted herself up vertically to more than twice the former height, and groaned from the severity of the under-pressure. Once the ice-masses near her came impetuously on, and tossed their enormous weight against her, and threw her up and considerably over to starboard. At another time the lateral pressure crushed the contiguous ice into débris, and threw up a huge mass fully nineteen feet above the general level, and rolled the adjacent floe into hummocks, mounds, peaks, splinters, walls, and ramparts. At another time, after some alternations of commotion and quiet, and when all bad symptoms of an uproar had disappeared, the vast contiguous masses suddenly started into tumult, rubbed and tossed one another in furious conflict, flung piece over piece till all was a chaos, made the ship rise up abaft and tremble through hull and rigging, and accompanied the whole with such a whining, and screeching, and howling, as might have been taken for a revelry of demons. Worse scenes than even these followed; and one of the chief of them will be best given in Back's own graphic words.

After describing two remarkable escapes from the tremendous shocks of driving ice, hurled together like mountain masses by an earthquake, he observes: "On the 16th of March another rush drove irresistibly on the larboard quarter and stern, and, forcing the ship ahead, raised her upon the ice. A chaotic ruin followed; our poor and cherished court-yard, its wall and arched doors, gallery, and well-trodden paths, were rent, and in some parts ploughed up like dust. The ship was careened fully four streaks, and sprang a leak as before. Scarcely were ten minutes left us for the expression of our astonishment that anything of human build could outlive such assaults, when another equally violent rush succeeded; and, in its way toward the starboard quarter, threw up a rolling wave thirty feet high, crowned by a blue square mass of many tons, resembling the entire side of a house, which, after hanging for some time in doubtful poise on the ridge, at length fell with a crash into the hollow, in which, as in a cavern, the after-part of the ship seemed imbedded. It was indeed an awful crisis, rendered more frightful from the mistiness of the night and dimness of the moon. The poor ship cracked and trembled violently, and no one could say that the next minute would not be her last; and, indeed, his own too, for with her our means of safety would probably perish."

During all the period of disasters after the disruption of the floe, the ship was carried hither and thither over a range of from twenty-six to forty-eight miles northwest of Seahorse Point, and seldom further than about ten miles from the nearest land. But, after the 16th of March, she set pretty steadily toward the south-east, and kept a good deal nearer the shore. The officers, at a formal consultation, agreed that she now seemed liable to be lost at any moment, and that a light-boat, with provisions, should, if possible, be landed to serve as a last resource, to communicate with the Hudson's Bay Company's factory, in the event of her going down. She still held marvellously firm, and continued to be cradled on a small piece of floe. On the 16th of April apparently by some conflicting action of strong calm currents, she lost the sides of her cradle; yet even then she retained the base of it, and was borne along on this as on a truck.

So late as the 20th of June, the ship still lay immovably fixed in the middle of a large floe, and, though disruptions and openings then became common, at comparatively small distances from her, she continued as firm in her cradle as in the beginning of February. No alternative offered but to cut her out with implements; and this proved an enormous labor, and occupied all the crew till the 11th of July. On that day the men had paused to draw breath, when suddenly the ice-rock burst asunder, barely allowing them time to clamber up, in hot haste, for safety. "Scarcely," says Captain Back, "had I descended to my cabin, when a loud rumbling notified that the ship had broken her ice-bonds, and was sliding gently down into her own element. I ran instantly on deck, and joined in the cheers of the officers and men, who, dispersed on different pieces of ice, took this significant method of expressing their feelings. It was a sight not to be forgotten. Standing on the taffrail, I saw the dark bubbling water below, and enormous masses of ice gently vibrating and springing to the surface: the first lieutenant was just climbing over the stern, while other groups were standing apart, separated by this new gulf; and the spars, together with working implements, were resting half in the water, half on the ice, whilst the saw, the instrument whereby this sudden effect had been produced, was bent double, and in that position forcibly detained by the body it had severed."

A piece of the base of the ship's ice-cradle, however, still clung to her, and continued to do so till the 13th; and when it did break up, it did not set her free. On the contrary, she slowly rose, heeled over to port, and seemed for some moments to be entirely capsizing. Those of her company who were on board felt suddenly as if on the verge of eternity. Yet they evinced no confusion, and cleared off and provisioned the boats with astonishing coolness and promptitude. She went so completely on her beam ends, that no man in her could move without holding on; but she went no further. A submerged ice-mass, whose end was congealed to her bottom, and whose other end projected right out from her, was the cause of her overturn, and it now held her firm in her perilous position. Officers and men beheld it with awe, and set promptly and energetically to the arduous task of sawing it off. They worked from eleven o'clock in the forenoon till two in the following morning, afraid that a squall might arise and ruin them; and when at last they had only ten feet more to saw, but were compelled by fatigue and drowsiness to go in quest of a short repose on the deck, suddenly there was a grating sound of breaking ice, and, before a word could be spoken, the ship sprang free, and entirely righted. The cheering of the crew was vociferous, and their joy unbounded. Four months, all but a day, had the ship been in the grip of the ice; and now, after a romance of perils, and a cycle of providential deliverances, she was again subject to the control of man.

The last scenes we have described took place in the vicinity of Charles Island, about midway between Cape Comfort and the mouth of Hudson's Strait. The query was naturally raised, whether anything could now be done to prosecute the object of the expedition; but the ship was found to be far too shattered to go again in her present state into collision with the ice, and a serious doubt soon arose whether she should be able to cross the sea to a British harbor. There was nothing for it but to run her, with all possible speed, toward home. She was utterly crazy, and broken, and leaky; and not even her perilous tumbling among the ice-masses around the dismal Cape Comfort and the horrid Seahorse Point were more perilous than the struggling, staggering, water-logged voyage which she made across the northern Atlantic. She at last reached the northwest coast of Ireland, gradually sinking by the head, and was run ashore in Lough Swilly on the 3d of September; and, had she been three hours longer at sea, she would certainly have gone to the bottom. Her whole frame proved to be strained and twisted; many of her bolts were either loosened or broken; her forefoot was entirely gone; and upwards of twenty feet of her keel, together with ten feet of her stern-post, had been driven over more than three feet and a half on one side, leaving a frightful opening astern for the free ingress of water. Well, therefore, might her crew, when they afterwards looked on her as she lay dry on the beach at low water, express astonishment that ever they had floated back in her to British shores; and ample occasion had they to cherish adoring gratitude to the all-powerful and all-benevolent Being who had preserved them.

Almost simultaneously with Back's expedition in the Terror, in 1836, the Hudson's Bay Company resolved on completing, if possible, the survey of those portions of the northern coast which Franklin and Back had failed to reach. This service was intrusted to Messrs. Dease and Simpson, two of their employées, with a party of twelve men, who were instructed to descend the Mackenzie River, and, on arriving at the sea, endeavor to follow the coast to the westward, either by land or water, as weather and other circumstances permitted, to the point at which Beechey turned back. They were afterwards to explore to the eastward from Point Turnagain of Franklin; to determine whether Boothia Felix were a peninsula, as Ross supposed, or an island; and then to push on in the same direction to some known point which had been visited by Back.

In July, 1837, they had reached Return Reef, where Franklin was stopped. Beyond this all was new. Two large rivers were discovered, the Garry and Colville, the latter more than a thousand miles in length. Although in the middle of the dog-days, the ground was frozen so hard at four inches beneath the surface, that they could scarcely drive in their tent-pegs. So keen was the north-easterly wind, that "the spray froze on the oars and rigging; and out in the bay the ice lay smooth and solid, as in the depth of a sunless winter." Yet even here a few flowers cheered the eyes of the travellers, and enlivened the stubborn soil. On the 1st of August, further progress by water being impracticable, — they had gained but four miles on the four previous days, — Mr. Simpson, with some of the men, continued the journey on foot, while Mr. Dease and the others remained in charge of the boats. The walking-party, after two or three days' travel, fell in with a number of Esquimaux, from whom they hired an oomiak, or family-canoe, in which to pursue the voyage along the lanes of open water occasionally visible close to the beach. On the 4th, after passing the mouth of a large, deep river, "I saw," says Mr. Simpson, "with indescribable emotions, Point Barrow stretching out to the northward, and enclosing Elson Bay, near the bottom of which we now were." This, it will be remembered, was the furthest point attained by the *Blossom's* barge in 1826, an exploit commemorated by naming the bay after Lieut. Elson, one of the officers in command.

The party returned to the winter station on Great

Bear Lake, and, while there, received instructions to renew their search to the eastward, and were informed of Sir G. Back's expedition, with which they were, if possible, to communicate. They were descending the Coppermine in June, 1838, in pursuance of these instructions, when the stream was swollen by spring floods, and encumbered with floating ice; and, in shooting the numerous rapids, "had to pull for their lives, to keep out of the suction of the precipices, along whose base the breakers raged and foamed, with overwhelming fury. Shortly before noon, we came in sight of Escape Rapid of Franklin; and a glance at the overhanging cliffs told us that there was no alternative but to run down with full cargo. In an instant," continues Mr. Simpson, "we were in the vortex; and, before we were aware, my boat was borne towards an isolated rock, which the boiling surge almost concealed. To clear it on the outside was no longer possible; our only chance of safety was to run between it and the lofty eastern cliff. The word was passed, and every breath was hushed. A stream which dashed down upon us over the brow of the precipice, more than one hundred feet in height, mingled with the spray that whirled upwards from the rapid, forming a terrific shower-bath. The pass was about eight feet wide, and the error of a single foot on either side would have been instant destruction. As, guided by Sinclair's consummate skill, the boat shot safely through those jaws of death, an involuntary cheer arose. Our next impulse was to turn round to view the fate of our comrades behind. They had profited by the peril we incurred, and kept without the treacherous rock in time."

They had navigated but a short distance along the coast when they were stopped by ice, and lingered many days at Boathaven, in a state of utter hopelessness. The time for returning had arrived ere any real work had been accomplished. At length, on the 20th of August, Mr. Simpson started with seven men for a ten days' walk to the eastward, on the first of which they passed Point Turnagain, the limit of Franklin's survey in 1821. By the 23d they had toiled onwards to an elevated cape, rising from a sea beset with ice; and, the land closing all round to the northwards, further progress seemed to be impossible. "With bitter disappointment," writes Mr. Simpson, "I ascended the height, from whence a vast and splendid prospect burst suddenly upon me. The sea, as if transformed by enchantment, rolled its free waves at my feet, and beyond the reach of vision to the eastward. Islands of various shape and size overspread its surface, and the northern land terminated to the eye in a bold and lofty cape, bearing east-north-east, thirty or forty miles distant, while the continental coast trended away south-east. I stood, in fact, on a remarkable headland, at the eastern outlet of an ice-obstructed strait. On the extensive land to the northward I bestowed the name of our most gracious sovereign, Queen Victoria. Its eastern visible extremity I called Cape Pelly, in compliment to the governor of the Hudson's Bay Company."

In 1839 they were more successful, and, favored with mild weather and an open sea, they sailed through the narrow strait that separates Victoria Land from the main. On the 13th of August they doubled Point Ogle, the furthest point of Back's journey in 1834; an event which terminated the long-pursued inquiry concerning the coast-line. They had thus ascertained that the American continent is separated from Boothia to the westward of Back's Estuary. The survey was now complete. A day or two later, the party, with flags flying, crossed to Montreal Island, in Back's Estuary, where they discovered a deposit of provisions which Back had left there five years previously. The pemmican was unfit for use; but out of several pounds of chocolate, half decayed, the men contrived to pick sufficient to make a kettle-full of acceptable drink in honor of the occasion. There were also a tin case and a few fish-hooks, of which, observes Mr. Simpson, "Mr. Dease and I took possession, as memorials of our having breakfasted on the identical spot where the tent of our gallant, though less successful precursor, stood that very day five years before."

They had now obeyed their instructions to the letter; the coast-line was determined, and connected with what was previously known to the eastward. It was time to think of returning, but it still remained a question whether some part of Boothia might not be united to the continent on the *eastern* side of the estuary. Doubling, therefore, its eastern promontory, they passed a point of the continent which they named Cape Britannia, and another called Cape Selkirk, and proceeded toward some islands in the Gulf of Akkolee, so far as to satisfy themselves that they were to the eastward of any part of Boothia. By the 20th of August they had sailed far enough to see the further shore, with its capes, of the Gulf of Boothia, which runs down to within forty miles of Repulse Bay; and they then turned back. On their return, they traced sixty miles of the south coast of Boothia, where at one time they were not more than ninety miles from the site of the magnetic pole, as determined by Sir James Ross. A long extent of Victoria Land was also examined; and, on the 16th of September, they once more happily entered the Coppermine, after a boat voyage of more than sixteen hundred miles, the longest ever performed in the Polar Sea.

CHAPTER XI.

RAE'S LAND EXPEDITION. — SHORES OF HUDSON'S BAY. — ESQUIMAUX CANOES. — REPULSE BAY. — GAME IN PLENTY. — SLEDGE TRAVELLING. — SNOW-HOUSES. — RETURN. — RENEWED INTEREST IN THE DISCOVERY OF A NORTH-WEST PASSAGE. — THE EREBUS AND TERROR. — SIR JOHN FRANKLIN'S LAST VOYAGE. — MYSTERY OF HIS FATE.

THE supposed great bay, extending from the furthest point reached by Messrs. Dease and Simpson, eastward to the Fury and Hecla Strait, now became an object of intense interest. The mystery which overhung the north-east corner of the American mainland seemed, at last, to be almost revealed. Let but the coast-line from the mouth of the Castor and Pollux to the eastern extremity of the Gulf of Akkolee be examined, so as to connect the discoveries of Messrs. Dease and Simpson with those of the second voyage of Parry, and those of the second voyage of John Ross, and all would become plain.

In 1846, accordingly, the Hudson's Bay Company fitted out an expedition to effect this object; and Dr. John Rae was appointed to the command. He was just the man for it: he was surgeon, astronomer, steersman, and leader to the party; had spent several years in the service of the company; and added to his other attainments the not unimportant accomplishments of a first-rate snow-shoe walker and a dead shot.

On the 8th of October, Rae landed at York Factory, after a canoe journey of about two months' duration, through the interior, from Canada. Here he wintered, and, on the 12th of June, set sail in two boats, with six men to each, along the shores of Hudson's Bay, which are here low, flat, and uninteresting. On the 27th they landed at Churchill. They found the people here engaged in killing white whales, which are often seen rolling their bulky forms up the rivers that flow into the bay. Their flesh is used as food for dogs, the house in which it is kept being called the blubber-house ; to find which house, especially in summer, the simple direction, "follow your nose," is sufficient.

Having taken on board Ooligbuck, an Esquimaux interpreter, and the son of Ooligbuck, a sad thief, who had a peculiar fancy for tobacco and buttons, they left Churchill July 5th, 1846. During the day they passed the Pau-a-thau-kis-cow river, where they were overtaken by three Esquimaux, in their kayaks. These little canoes were propelled by their vigorous occupants so swiftly, that they easily kept up with the boats, while sailing at the rate of four miles an hour. The kayak is about twelve feet in length, and two in breadth, tapering off from the centre to the bow and stern, almost to a mere point. The frame is of wood, covered with sealskin, having an aperture in the centre, which barely admits of the stowage of the nether man. They are used solely for hunting, and, by means of the double paddle, are propelled through the water with the velocity of the dolphin. No land animal can possibly escape when seen in the water; the least exertion is sufficient to keep up with the reindeer when swimming at its utmost speed.

The *oomiak*, or women's boat, is much clumsier, slower, and safer, more in the form of a boat than a canoe, and is used to convey the female portion of the community and their families from one part of the coast to another, being propelled by the women, who use small paddles for the purpose.

On the 13th, Chesterfield Inlet was passed. Walruses were here seen. "They were grunting and bellowing," says Rae, "making a noise which I fancy would much resemble a concert of old boars and buffaloes." At the head of Repulse Bay, where they landed on the 25th, they fell in with more Esquimaux, and procured from them some seal-skin boots. When about to put on a pair of these boots, says Rae, "one of our female visitors, noticing that the leather of the foot was rather hard, took them out of my hands, and began chewing them with her strong teeth." By this process they were softened for the wearing.

They quitted the head of Repulse Bay, in latitude 66° 32′ north, and succeeded in conveying one of their boats to the southern extremity of the Gulf of Akkolee, in latitude 67° 13′ north. They found a chain of lakes lying across the isthmus, and derived great aid from it in the conveying of the boat. They proceeded along the coast of the Gulf of Akkolee till the 5th of August, and they observed the tides to be, on the average, far higher than in the Polar Sea, but exceedingly irregular, and varying in rise from four to ten feet; and already they began to entertain a strong presumption that Boothia, after all, is a peninsula of the American mainland. But they were utterly baffled in their progress by ice and fogs and northerly winds, and felt obliged to return at about latitude 67° 30′ north, and spend the winter at Repulse Bay. There they built a house, and procured a stock of provisions by hunting and fishing, principally reindeer and salmon; and, excepting what was used for cooking, they had no fuel throughout the winter. The sporting-book for September showed that they had been diligent: sixty-three deers, five hares, one seal, one hundred and seventy-two partridges, and one hundred and sixteen salmon and trout, having been brought in.

On the 5th of April, 1847, six of the party again started north with sledges, drawn by dogs, and travelled along the west shore of the Gulf of Akkolee ; and, on the 18th, they reached the vicinity of Sir John Ross's most southerly discoveries. The question of the supposed communication with the Polar Sea was here to be set at rest. They decided now to strike off from the coast across the land as nearly north as possible ; and they had a tiresome march through snow, and across three small lakes ; and, at noon, when near the middle of another lake of about four miles in length, they ascertained their latitude to be 69° 26′ 1″ north. They walked three miles more, and came to still another lake ; and, as there was not yet any appearance of the sea, Rae gave orders to the men to prepare their lodgings, and went forth alone to look for the coast. He arrived in twenty minutes at an inlet of not more than a quarter of a mile wide, and traced this westward for upwards of a league, and there found his course once more obstructed by land.

Some rocky hillocks were near, and, thinking he saw from the top of these some rough ice in the desired direction, he inhaled fresh hope, pushed eagerly on to a rising ground in the distance, and there beheld stretched out before him an ice-covered sea, studded with innumerable islands. But it was the sea of Sir John Ross, the Lord Mayor's Bay of the disastrous voyage of the Victory ; and the islands were those which Sir John had named the Sons of the Clergy of the Church of Scotland. Rae, therefore, had simply crossed a peninsula of the Gulf of Akkolee ; and thus did he ascertain that the shores which witnessed the woes of the Victory, the eastern shores of Boothia, are continuous with the mainland of America.

On this expedition, "our usual mode," says Rae, "of preparing lodgings for the night was as follows: As soon as we had selected a spot for our snow-house, our Esquimaux, assisted by one or more of the men, commenced cutting out blocks of snow. When a sufficient number of these had been raised, the builder commenced his work, his assistants supplying him with the material. A good roomy dwelling was thus raised in an hour, if the snow was in a good state for building. Whilst our principal mason was thus occupied, another of the party was busy erecting a kitchen, which, although our cooking was none of the most delicate or extensive, was still a necessary addition to our establishment, had it been only to thaw snow. As soon as the snow-hut was completed, our sledges were unloaded, and everything eatable (including parchment-skin and moose-skin shoes, which had now become favorite articles with the dogs) taken inside. Our bed was next made, and, by the time the snow was thawed or the water boiled, as the case might be, we were all ready for supper. When we used alcohol for fuel (which we usually did in stormy weather), no kitchen was required."

Sir James Clarke Ross, who figured in the voyage of the Victory as Commander Ross, says, "Mr. Rae's description of the inlet he crossed over to in the south-east corner of Lord Mayor's Bay, accords so exactly with what I observed whilst surveying its shores, that I have no doubt of his having reached that inlet on which I found the Esquimaux marks so numerous, but of which no account was published in Sir John Ross's narrative." Rae appropriately named the peninsula Sir John Ross's Peninsula; and the isthmus, connecting it with the mainland, and flanking the inlet, Sir James

Ross's Isthmus. The latter is only one mile broad, and has three small ponds; but it bears evident marks of being an autumnal deer-pass, and, therefore, a favorite resort of the Esquimaux. Rae had thus reached the goal of his wishes.

A progress to the furthest point reached by Messrs. Dease and Simpson was not attempted, for it was now ascertained that this must comprise a journey over land, and either a voyage across a large land-locked estuary, or a coasting along its shores; and for these the explorers had neither time nor resources. They forthwith began to retrace their route to the fort at Repulse Bay. All the *caches* of provisions which had been made during the outward journey were found quite safe, and thus afforded them a plentiful supply of food. On the morning of the 5th of May they reached some Esquimaux dwellings on the shores of Christie's Lake, about fifteen miles from Fort Hope. "At two P. M. on the same day," says Rae, "we were again on the march, and arrived at our home at half-past eight P. M., all well, but so black and scarred on the face, from the combined effects of oil, smoke, and frost-bites, that our friends would not believe but that some serious accident from the explosion of gunpowder had happened to us. Thus successfully terminated a journey little short of six hundred English miles, the longest, I believe, ever made on foot along the Arctic coast."

On the 12th of May, at the head of a similar party, Rae set out to examine the east side of the gulf; and on the 27th, in a bewildering snow-storm, he reached his ultimatum, at a headland which they called Cape Crozier. But, during a blink of the storm, he got a clear view of a headland nearly twelve miles further on, which he called Cape Ellice, and computed to be in latitude 69° 42′ north, and longitude 85° 8′ west, or within about ten miles of the Fury and Hecla Straits. "Our journey," says Dr. Rae, "hitherto had been the most fatiguing I had ever experienced; the severe exercise, with a limited allowance of food, had reduced the whole party very much. However, we marched merrily on, tightening our belts, — mine came in six inches, — the men vowing that when they got on full allowance they would make up for lost time." On the 12th of August the whole original party embarked at Repulse Bay, and on the 31st arrived at Churchill.

The return of Captain Sir James Clarke Ross, in 1844, from his brilliant career in the Antarctic Ocean, gave a sudden stimulus in England to the old craving for the discovery of a north-west passage. The ships Erebus and Terror were now famous for their fitness to brave the dangers of the ice, and could be reëquipped at comparatively small cost. Naval officers and whale-fishermen and hardy seamen were fired with the spirit of adventure. Statesmen panted to send the British flag across all the breadth of the Polar Sea; scientific gentlemen longed for decisions in terrestrial magnetism, which could be obtained only in the regions around the magnetic pole; and, though merchants and other utilitarians could never again regard the old notion of a commercial highway to the Indian seas through Behring's Strait as worthy of consideration, yet multitudes of the curious, among all classes of society, were impatient to have the veil penetrated which had so long hid from the world's wondering gaze the mysteries of the ice-girt archipelago of the north. The very difficulties of the enterprise, together with the disasters or failures of all former expeditions, only roused the general resolution.

Sir John Barrow, Secretary to the Admiralty, had for thirty years been the fervent advocate of every enterprise which could throw light on the Arctic regions, and had incessantly bent in that direction the powerful influence which he wielded; and now again was he at his vocation. Lieut. Col. Sabine, also, whose opinion carried much weight, declared "that a final attempt to make a north-west passage would render the most important service that now remained to be performed toward the completion of the magnetic survey of the globe." The Lords of the Admiralty and the Council of the Royal Society gave a formal assent; and Sir John Franklin, the hero of some most perilous exploits within the Arctic circle, who now stood out to view as the likeliest man to conduct the desired enterprise, had said in 1836, and continued to say still, "that no service was nearer to his heart than the completion of the survey of the north-west coast of America, and the accomplishment of a north-west passage."

The Erebus and the Terror were ordered to be got ready. Both had braved all the perils of the Antarctic expedition under Sir James C. Ross, and the latter was the ship of the terrific ice-voyage of 1836, in Hudson's Bay. They were the best-tested and the best-appurtenanced vessels which had ever faced the frozen regions; and each was now fitted with a small steam-engine and screw-propeller. Sir John Franklin was appointed to the chief command, and hoisted his flag in the Erebus; and Captain Richard Crozier, who had been the distinguished colleague of Sir James C. Ross in the Antarctic voyage, was appointed to the Terror. So many naval officers volunteered their services, that, had all been accepted, they might themselves have completely manned the ships. The total number of persons put on board was one hundred and thirty-eight; and they formed as select, resolute, and experienced a body of adventurers as ever went to sea. The transport Daretto Junior, also, under the command of Lieut. Griffith, was laden with out-stores, to be discharged into the ships in Davis's Strait.

The official instructions to Sir John Franklin were minute, comprehensive, and far-sighted, and made provision for all important contingencies. But only those of them which relate to the main conduct of the expedition possess much public interest; and these, taken in connection with the mournful and exciting mystery into which the ships so soon passed, seem too momentous to allow of much abridgment. "On putting to sea," said they, "you are to proceed, in the first place, by such a route as, from the wind and weather, you may deem to be the most suitable for despatch, to Davis's Strait, taking the transport with you to such a distance up that strait as you may be able to proceed without impediment from ice, being careful not to risk that vessel by allowing her to be beset in the ice, or exposed to any violent contact with it. You will then avail yourself of the earliest opportunity of clearing the transport of the provisions and stores with which she is charged for the use of the expedition; and you are then to send her back to England, giving to the agent or master such directions for his guidance as may appear to you most proper, and reporting by that opportunity your proceedings to our secretary for our information. You will then proceed, in the execution of your orders, into Baffin's Bay, and get, as soon as possible, to the western side of the strait, provided it should appear to you that the ice chiefly prevails on the eastern side or near the middle, the object being to enter Lancaster Sound with as little delay as possible.

"But, as no specific directions can be given, owing to the position of the ice varying from year to year, you will, of course, be guided by your own observations as to the course most eligible to be taken, in order to insure a speedy arrival in the sound above-mentioned. As, however, we have thought fit to cause each ship to be fitted with a small steam-engine and propeller, to be used only in pushing the ships through channels between masses of ice when the wind is adverse, or in a calm, we trust the difficulty usually found in such cases will be much obviated. But, as the supply of fuel to be taken in the ships is necessarily small, you will use it only in cases of difficulty.

"Lancaster Sound and its continuation through Barrow's Strait, having been four times navigated without any impediment by Sir Edward Parry, and since frequently by whaling-ships, will probably be found without any obstacles from ice or islands; and Sir Edward Parry having also proceeded from the latter in a straight course to Melville Island, and returned without experiencing any or very little difficulty, it is hoped that the remaining portion of the passage, about nine hundred miles, to Behring's Strait, may also be found equally free from obstruction; and in proceeding to the westward, therefore, you will not stop to examine any openings either to the northward or southward in that strait, but continue to push to the westward, without loss of time, in the latitude of about 74¼°, till you have reached the longitude of that portion of land on which Cape Walker is situated, or about 98° west. From that point we desire that every effort be used to endeavor to penetrate to the southward and westward, in a course as direct towards Behring's Strait as the position and extent of the ice, or the existence of land, at present unknown, may admit.

"We direct you to this particular part of the Polar Sea as affording the best prospect of accomplishing the passage to the Pacific, in consequence of the unusual magnitude and apparently fixed state of the barrier of ice observed by the Hecla and Griper in the year 1820, off Cape Dundas, the south-western extremity of Melville Island; and we therefore consider that loss of time would be incurred in renewing the attempt in that direction. But, should your progress in the direction before ordered be arrested by ice of a permanent appearance, and should you, when passing the mouth of the strait betwen Devon and Cornwallis's Islands, have observed that it was open and clear of ice, we desire that you will duly consider, with reference to the time already consumed, as well as to the symptoms of a late or early close of the season, whether that channel might not offer a more practicable outlet from the archipelago, and a more ready access to the open sea, where there would be neither islands nor banks to arrest and fix the floating masses of ice.

"And if you should have advanced too far to the south-westward to render it expedient to adopt this new course before the end of the present season, and if, therefore, you should have determined to winter in that neighborhood, it will be a matter for your mature deliberation whether, in the ensuing season, you would proceed by the above-mentioned strait, or whether you should persevere to the south-westward, according to the former directions.

"You are well aware, having yourself been one of the intelligent travellers who have traversed the American shore of the Polar Sea, that the groups of islands that stretch from that shore to the northward, to a distance not yet known, do not extend to the westward further than about the one hundred and twentieth degree of western longitude; and that beyond this, and to Behring's Strait, no land is visible from the American shore of the Polar Sea. In an undertaking of this description, much must be always left to the discretion of the commanding officer; and, as the objects of this expedition have been fully explained to you, and you have already had much experience on service of this nature, we are convinced we cannot do better than leave it to your judgment."

He was instructed, also, in the event of reaching Behring's Strait, to proceed to the Sandwich Islands and Panama, and to put an officer ashore at the latter place with despatches.

The ships sailed from the Thames on the 19th of May, 1845. The Erebus and the Terror received the transport's stores, and dismissed her in Davis's Strait, and then had abundant provisions of every kind for three years, besides five bullocks. They were seen by the whaler Prince of Wales, on the 26th of July, moored to an iceberg, waiting for an opening through the long vast body of ice which extends along the middle of Baffin's Bay. They were then in latitude 74° 48′ north, and longitude 66° 13′ west, not far from the centre of Baffin's Bay, and about two hundred and ten miles from the entrance of Lancaster Sound.

CHAPTER XII.

ANXIETY IN REGARD TO FRANKLIN AND HIS SHIPS. — THREE EXPEDITIONS OF SEARCH SENT OUT. — KELLETT AND MOORE'S EXPEDITION BY BEHRING'S STRAIT. — ITS RETURN. — RICHARDSON'S AND RAE'S LAND EXPLORATIONS. — SIR J. C. ROSS'S EXPEDITION BY LANCASTER SOUND. — THE EXPLORERS RETURN UNSUCCESSFUL. — LIEUT. PULLEN, FROM THE BEHRING STRAIT EXPEDITION, ASCENDS THE MACKENZIE. — RETURN TO THE ARCTIC SEA AND BACK. — THE SEASON OF 1850. — PULLEN'S ARRIVAL IN ENGLAND.

TOWARD the end of the year 1847, anxiety began to be felt in regard to the fate of Franklin and his men. Not a word had been heard from them since they had been seen by the Prince of Wales whaler; and apprehension became general that they had shared a similar fate to the Fury of Sir Edward Parry, or the Victory of Sir John Ross. The government, therefore, promptly determined to send three expeditions in search of them. The first was a marine expedition, by way of Behring's Strait, to be conducted by Captain Henry Kellett, of the ship Herald, of twenty-six guns, then in the Pacific, aided by Commander Thomas E. L. Moore, in the Plover, surveying vessel; and this was designed to relieve Sir John Franklin and his companions in the event of their having gone through the north-west passage, and stuck fast at some advanced point of the Polar Sea. The second was an overland and boat expedition, to be conducted by Sir John Richardson, to descend the Mackenzie River, and to examine the coast eastward to the Coppermine; and this was designed to afford relief in the event of the adventurers having taken to their boats westward of the Northern Archipelago, and forced their way to the American continent. The third was a marine expedition, to be conducted by Sir James Clarke Ross, with the ships Enterprise and Investigator, through Lancaster Sound and Barrow's Strait, to examine all the tracks of the missing ships westward as far as they could penetrate into the archipelago; and this was designed to afford relief in the event of the adventurers having been arrested either in the very throat of the supposed passage, or at some point on this side of it, and of their attempting to retrace their steps. This plan of search seemed comprehensive and noble, and was carried with all possible promptitude into execution. The Plover left Sheerness on the 1st January, 1848; but, being a miserable sailer, did not reach Oahu, in the Sandwich Islands, till the 22d August. She was then too late to attempt, that season, any efficient operations within the Arctic Circle, and she passed on to winter quarters at Noovel, on the coast of Kamtschatka. The Herald, meanwhile, had received instructions from home, and gone northward as far as Cape Krusenstern, in Kotzebue Sound, the appointed rendezvous. But, not being prepared to winter there, nor prepared for explorations among ice, she returned, in autumn, to the Sandwich Islands.

On the 30th June, 1849, the Plover left Noovel, and on the 14th July anchored off Chamisso Island, at the bottom of Kotzebue Sound. Next day she was joined by the Herald and by the Nancy Dawson, the latter a yacht belonging to Robert Shedden, Esq., who, in the course of a voyage of pleasure round the globe, got intelligence in China of the intended expedition through Behring's Strait in search of Sir John Franklin, and nobly resolved to devote his vessel and himself to its aid. On the 18th the three vessels left Chamisso; on the 20th they were off Cape Lisburn ; and on the 25th, after having passed Icy Point, they despatched a boat expedition, under Lieut. Pullen.

This boat expedition was designed to connect the proceedings of the present voyage with those of the overland expedition under Sir John Richardson, and to institute search and provide succor for the missing adventurers on the likeliest part of the coast and mainland west of the Mackenzie River. It consisted of the Herald's pinnace, decked over, and three other boats, and comprised twenty-five men, and had nearly three months' provisions for its own use, besides five cases of pemmican for the use of Sir John Franklin's party. But it was accompanied also by Mr. Shedden in his yacht. It was directed, after proceeding a certain distance along the coast in-shore, to return to a rendezvous with the Plover at Chamisso Island, but at the same time to despatch from its furthest point a detachment in two whale-boats, well provisioned and equipped, to extend the search to the mouth of the Mackenzie River, and then to ascend that river, and proceed homeward by Fort Hope and York Factory, in the summer of 1850.

The Herald and the Plover, in the mean while, bore away to the north, and on the 26th, in latitude 71° 5′ north, reached the heavily-packed ice. They sailed sometimes along the edge of this, and sometimes through streams and among floes, till the 28th, when they could proceed no further, on account of the perfect impenetrableness of the pack. They were then in latitude 72° 51′ north, and longitude 163° 48′ west. The ice, as far as it could be seen from the mast-head, trended away west-south-westward ; yet, while densely compact for leagues distant, seemed to be broken by a water-line in the northern horizon. On the 28th the ships came again to the land, and the Herald bore in to examine Wainwright's Inlet, while Commander Moore went on shore, erected a mark, and buried a bottle containing information about the boats. This place, unhappily, was found too shallow to afford harborage; else it would have proved an excellent retreat, on account, at once, of its high latitude, of its being a resort for reindeer, of the friendliness of the natives, and of there being no nearer harbor to the south than Kotzebue's Sound, while even that place was regarded by the ice-masters as an unsafe wintering quarter.

From the 1st of August till the 17th, Cape Lisburn being appointed for a rendezvous, the ships made active explorations in various directions near shore, and away northward as far as they could penetrate. On the 17th the Herald discovered a new territory. "At forty minutes past nine," on that day, says Captain Kellett, "the exciting report of 'Land ho!' was made from the mast-head: both mast-heads were soon afterwards crowded. In running a course along the pack toward our first discovery, a small group of islands was reported on our port-beam, a considerable distance within the outer margin of the ice. Still more distant than this group (from the deck), a very extensive and high land was reported, which I had been watching for some time, anxiously awaiting a report from some one else. There was a fine clear atmosphere (such a one as can only be seen, in this climate, except in the direction of this extended land), where the clouds rolled in numerous immense masses, occasionally leaving the very lofty peaks uncapped; where could be distinctly seen columns, pillars, all very broken, which is characteristic of the higher headlands in this sea — East Cape and Cape Lisburn, for example. With the exception of the north-east and south-east extremes, none of the lower land could be seen, unless, indeed, what I took, at first, for a small group of islands within the pack edge was a point of this great land. This island, or point, was distant twenty-five miles from the ship's track ; higher parts of the land seemed not less, I consider, than sixty. When we hove to off the first land seen, the northern extreme of the great land showed out to the eastward for a moment, and so clear as to cause some who had doubts before to cry out, 'There, sir, is the land quite plain.'" They afterwards ran up to the island, and landed upon it, and found it a solid and almost inaccessible mass of granite, about four and a half miles long, two and a half miles broad, and fourteen hundred feet high. Its situation is latitude 71° 20′ north, and longitude 175° 16′ west. The distant mountainous land seemed to be extensive, and was supposed by Captain Kellett to be a continuation of the lofty range seen by the natives off Cape Jakan, in Asia, and mentioned by Baron Wrangell, in his Polar Voyages.

In the vicinity of Cape Lisburn, on the 24th August, the Nancy Dawson, and the return boats of Lieut. Pullen's expedition, rejoined the Herald. They had searched the coast as far east as Dease's Inlet, and had there parted with the two whale-boats ; and had, at several points, made deposits of provisions, but had not obtained the slightest intelligence of the missing adventurers. Mr. Shedden had been particularly active and daring, and had many times put his yacht in peril. And, it is painful to add, though this is said in anticipation of the date, that he fell a victim to his excessive exertions during the noble service. He died, eight or ten weeks after, at Mazatlan.

On the 1st of September the two ships and the yacht rendezvoused in Kotzebue Sound. Upwards of a fortnight was now spent in making an interesting exploration up the Buckland River, and in establishing friendly relations with the natives. The whole month of September was remarkably fine, the frost to the latest so light as not to arrest the streams, and strong winds generally blowing from the east. The Plover prepared to winter in Kotzebue Sound, with the view of making further researches, and received from her consort as much provisions as she could stow or take care of. And on the 29th September the Herald and the yacht weighed anchor, and stood away for the south.

On the 10th July, 1850, the Herald again joined the Plover at Chamisso Island; and the two ships then set out together on another exploration. They proceeded northward till they sighted the pack-ice, and then separated — the Herald to return in quest of another and stronger expedition which had sailed from England, and which we shall afterwards have occasion to notice; and the Plover to prosecute the search eastward along the coast. Commander Moore, by means of his boats, made minute examination of all the inlets between Icy Cape and Point Barrow; he and his men suffered severely from exposure to cold; but they were entirely unsuccessful in the object of their search. The two ships again fell in with each other off Cape Lisburn on the 13th August; and Captain Kellett eventually gave full victualling to the Plover, ordered her to winter in Grantley Harbor, and then, toward the close of the open season, returned through Behring's Strait on his way to England. Thus, in October, 1850, ended this first western searching expedition, without having thrown one ray of light on the probable fate of Sir John Franklin.

The second searching expedition was the overland one, under the command of Sir John Richardson. In preparation for it, several boats, seven tons of pemmican, large quantities of other provisions and stores, five seamen, and fifteen sappers and miners, were embarked at Gravesend, on board of ships of the Hudson's Bay Company, on the 4th June, 1847. Sir John Richardson and Mr. Rae left Liverpool on the 25th March, 1848, and succeeded in overtaking Chief-trader Bell, in charge of the boats and the men, at Methy Portage, on the 20th June. The whole party reached the last portage on Slave River on the 15th July, and there they divided into a seaward or exploring party, under Sir John Richardson and Mr. Rae, and a landward or auxiliary party, under Mr. Bell. The seaward party comprised three boats, with full loads of pemmican, and eighteen men, and immediately embarked. The landward party comprised two boats and the stores for winter use, and were directed to make the best of their way to Great Bear Lake, to coast round its western shore, and to establish a fishery at its west end, near the site of Fort Franklin, for the convenience of the seaward party, in the event of its having to return up the Mackenzie; to erect, at its north-eastern extremity, near the influx of the Dease River, suitable dwelling-houses and store-houses for winter quarters; and, in the beginning of September, to despatch a well-tried Cree Indian and a native hunter to the banks of the Coppermine, there to hunt till the 20th of that month, and to keep a diligent outlook for the arrival of the boats.

The seaward party reached the sea on the 4th of August. On their way down, they put ashore, at Fort Good Hope, the lowest of the company's posts on the Mackenzie, three bags of pemmican for the use of any party from the Plover, or from Sir James Ross's ships, who might reach that establishment. At Point Separation, also, which forms the apex of the delta of the Mackenzie, they deposited one case of pemmican and a bottle of memoranda, and letters for the use of Sir John Franklin's party, burying them in the circumference of a circle with a ten-feet radius, from the point of a broad arrow painted on a signal-post; and they afterwards did the same thing, or similar, on Whale Island, at the mouth of the Mackenzie; on Point Toker, in latitude 69° 38′ north, and longitude 132° 15′ west; on Cape Bathurst, the most northerly point between the Mackenzie and the Coppermine; and on Cape Parry, at the east side of the entrance of Franklin Bay.

The explorers encountered head winds throughout most of their progress of eight hundred miles or upwards, from the exit of the Mackenzie to the mouth of the Coppermine; and they always kept near the shore, and landed at least twice a day to cook, occasionally to hunt, often to look out from the high capes, and commonly, at night, to sleep on shore. Immediately off the efflux of the Mackenzie they had an interview with about three hundred Esquimaux; and at many subsequent points they communicated with other parties, who were assembled on headlands to hunt whales, or scattered along the coast in pursuit of reindeer and water-fowl. The Esquimaux were confiding and frank, and all said that no ships had recently appeared on the coast; and those west of Cape Bathurst further said that during the preceding six weeks they never saw any ice.

One fellow alone, in answer to inquiries after white men, said, "A party of men are living on that island," pointing, as he spoke, to Richard's Island. As Richardson had actually landed there on the preceding day, he ordered the interpreter to inform him that he knew that he was lying. He received this retort with a smile, and without the slightest discomposure, but did not repeat his assertion. Neither the Esquimaux nor the Dog-rib or Hare Indians feel the least shame in being detected in falsehood; and they invariably practise it, if they think that they can thereby gain any of their petty ends. Even in their familiar intercourse with each other, the Indians seldom tell the truth in the first instance; and if they succeed in exciting admiration or astonishment, their invention runs on without check. From the manner of the speaker, rather than by his words, is his truth or falsehood inferred; and often a very long interrogation is necessary to elicit the real fact.

"The Esquimaux," says Richardson, "are essentially a littoral people, and inhabit nearly five thousand miles of seaboard, from the Straits of Belleisle to the Peninsula of Alaska; not taking into the measurement the various indentations of the coast-line, nor including West and East Greenland, in which latter locality they make their nearest approach to the western coasts of the Old World. Throughout the great linear range here indicated, there is no material change in their language, nor any variation beyond what would be esteemed in England a mere provincialism. Albert, the interpreter, who was born on the East Main, or western shore of James's Bay, had no great difficulty in understanding and making himself understood by the Esquimaux of the estuary of the Mackenzie, though by the nearest coast-line the distance between the two localities is at least two thousand five hundred miles.

"The habit of associating in numbers for the chase of the whale has sown among them the elements of civilization; and such of them as have been taken into the company's service, at the fur-posts, fall readily into the ways of their white associates, and are more industrious, handy, and intelligent, than the Indians. The few interpreters of the nation that I have been acquainted with (four in all) were strictly honest, and adhered rigidly to the truth; and I have every reason to believe that within their own community the rights of property are held in great respect, even the hunting-grounds of families being kept sacred. Yet their covetousness of the property of strangers, and their dexterity in thieving, are remarkable, and they seem to have most of the vices, as well as the virtues, of the Norwegian Vikings. Their personal bravery is conspicuous, and they are the only native nation on the North American continent who oppose their enemies face to face in open fight. Instead of flying, like the northern Indians, on the sight of a stranger, they did not scruple, in parties of two or three, to come off to our boats and enter into barter; and never, on any occasion, showed the least disposition to yield anything belonging to them through fear."

The Esquimaux winter huts are thus described:

"These buildings are generally placed on points where the water is deep enough for a boat to come to the beach, such a locality being probably selected by the natives to enable them to tow a whale or seal more closely to the place where it is to be cut up. The knowledge of this fact induced us generally to look for the buildings when we wished to land. The houses are constructed of drift-timber, strongly built together, and covered with earth to the thickness of from one to two feet. Light and air are admitted by a low door at one end; and even this entrance is closed by a slab of snow in the winter time, when their lamps supply them with heat as well as light. Ten or twelve people may seat themselves in the area of one of these houses, though not comfortably; and in the winter the imperfect admission of fresh air, and the effluvia arising from the greasy bodies of a whole family, must render them most disagreeable as well as unwholesome abodes. I have been told that when the family alone are present, the several members of it sit partly or even wholly naked."

The explorers met floes of drift-ice for the first time after rounding Cape Parry, but they encountered them more numerously as they approached Dolphin and Union Strait. On the 22d of August they had a strong gale from the west; and on the next morning they found themselves hemmed in by dense packs, extending as far as the eye could reach. The weather had hitherto been genial, but now it passed into perpetual frost, with frequent snow-storms. The expedition henceforth got on with great difficulty; and when they had penetrated well up the west side of Coronation Gulf, they were engirdled by rigorous winter, and felt compelled to abandon their boats. They, therefore, were unable to fulfil a portion of their official instructions, which directed them to examine the western and southern shores of Wollaston Land, lying north-west of Coronation Gulf; and during eleven days, from the 2d till the 13th of September, they travelled by land, up the valley of the Coppermine, to their appointed winter home at Fort Confidence, at the north-eastern extremity of the Great Bear Lake. Next summer Sir John Richardson returned to England.

In his official report to the Secretary of the Admiralty, Sir John says: "In the voyage between the Mackenzie and Coppermine, I carefully executed their lordships' instructions with respect to the examination of the coast-line, and became fully convinced that no ships had passed within view of the mainland. It is, indeed, nearly impossible that they could have done so unobserved by some of the numerous parties of Esquimaux on the look-out for whales. We were, moreover, informed by the Esquimaux of Back's Inlet that the ice had been pressing on their shore nearly the whole summer; and its closely-packed condition when we left it, on the 4th of September, made it highly improbable that it would open for ship navigation later in the season.

"I regretted extremely that the state of the ice prevented me from crossing to Wollaston Land, and thus completing, in one season, the whole scheme of their lordships' instructions. The opening between Wollaston and Victoria Lands has always appeared to me to possess great interest; for through it the flood-tide evidently sets into Coronation Gulf, diverging to the westward by the Dolphin and Union Strait, and to the eastward round Cape Alexander. By the fifth clause of Sir John Franklin's instructions, he is directed to steer south-westward from Cape Walker, which would lead him nearly in the direction of the strait in question. If Sir John found Barrow's Strait as open as when Sir Edward Parry passed it on four previous occasions, I am convinced that (complying as exactly as he could with his instructions, and without looking into Wellington Sound, or other openings either to the south or north of Barrow's Strait) he pushed directly west to Cape Walker, and from thence south-westwards. If so, the ships were probably shut up on some of the passages between Victoria, Banks', and Wollaston Lands.

"Being apprehensive that the boats I left on the coast would be broken up by the Esquimaux, and being, moreover, of opinion that the examination of the opening in question might be safely and efficiently performed in the only remaining boat I had fit for the transport from Bear Lake to the Coppermine, I determined to intrust this important service to Mr. Rae, who volunteered, and whose ability and zeal in the cause I cannot too highly commend. He selected an excellent crew, all of them experienced voyageurs, and capable of finding their way back to Bear Lake without guides, should any unforeseen accident deprive them of their leader.

In the month of March (1849) a sufficient supply of pemmican, and other necessary stores, with the equipments of the boat, were transported over the snow on dog-sledges to a navigable part of the Kendall River, and left there under the charge of two men. As soon as the Dease broke up in June, Mr. Rae would follow, with the boat, the rest of the crew, and a party of Indian hunters, and would descend the Coppermine River about the middle of July, at which time the sea generally begins to break up. He would then, as soon as possible, cross from Cape Krusenstern to Wollaston Land, and endeavor to penetrate to the northward, erecting signal-columns, and making deposits on conspicuous headlands, and especially on the north shore of Banks' Land, should he be fortunate enough to attain that coast. He was further instructed not to hazard the safety of his party by remaining too long on the north side of Dolphin and Union Strait, and to be guided in his movements by the season, the state of the ice, and such intelligence as he might obtain from the Esquimaux. He was also requested to engage one or more families of Indian hunters to pass the summer of 1850 on the banks of the Coppermine River, to be ready to assist any party that may direct their course that way." Mr. Rae repeated his elaborate and perilous mission in the summer of 1850.

The third and most important of the three searching expeditions of 1848 was the marine one conducted by Captain Sir James Clarke Ross. This comprised two superb ships, — the Enterprise, of four hundred and seventy tons and seventy men, and the Investigator, of four hundred and twenty tons and seventy men, both as strong as they could be made, and furnished with every possible appliance. Each was provided with a screw-propelled steam-launch, thirty-one and a half feet long, and capable of an average speed of eleven miles an hour. Captain E. J. Bird was appointed to the command of the Investigator. The ships were instructed to proceed together to the head of Barrow's Strait; and the Enterprise, if possible, to push on to a wintering-place about Winter Harbor or Banks' Land, while the Investigator should try to find harborage somewhere about Garnier Bay or Cape Rennell. Parties were to go from the Enterprise along respectively the eastern and the western shores of Banks' Land, to cross Sir John Richardson's expedition on the mainland; and parties from the Investigator were to explore the coasts of North Somerset and Boothia.

The expedition left the Thames on the 12th of May, 1848, and entered Baffin's Bay early in July. A letter was written by Sir James Clarke Ross, from the Danish settlement of Upernavik, on the 12th of July, stating that if, after passing a second winter at or near Port Leopold, he should get no intelligence of Sir John Franklin and his party, he would send the Investigator home to England, and prosecute a further search in the Enterprise alone. The Lords of the Admiralty took alarm at the possible, or even probable, consequences of this excessive heroism, and ordered the North Star store-ship, under command of Mr. James Saunders, to get ready with all speed to take out instructions and supplies to the expedition. Her prime object was to be the replenishing of the expedition's stock of provisions, and the enjoining of the Investigator not to return to England in the way Sir James C. Ross had indicated, but to remain in company with the Enterprise; and if the North Star should not succeed in promptly fulfilling this object, she was instructed to land the supplies at the furthest prominent point she could readily reach, and by all means to keep herself free from besetment in the ice, and to return before the close of the season. She sailed from the Thames on the 16th of May, 1849, and *did not* return that season; and she also became a subject of much public anxiety.

The Enterprise and the Investigator left Upernavik on the 13th of July, 1848; and, after running through an intricate archipelago near the mainland, they arrived, on the 20th, off Cape Shackleton, and there made fast to a grounded iceberg. They were joined there by the Lord Gambier whaling-ship, whose master informed them that, having run to the southward with the rest of the whalers, and having carefully examined the pack, he had found it all so close, compact, and heavy, as not to afford the slightest hope of any ship being able to find an opening through it that season to the west. He had, therefore, returned to the north, and expected that all the other whalers would soon follow him; and he had a very confident hope that he should get round the north end of the pack by the first week of August. But "the middle ice," as this great barrier along Baffin's Bay is called, has ever put the wits of the whale-fishers to the severest trial. The earliest date at which it has been passed in any year is the 12th of June; the latest at which it has been found impassable is the 9th of September; and the average date of the first ship of the season passing it is about the 13th of July. But in 1848 it could be passed only with extreme difficulty, and only by far rounding to the north; and, as was afterwards ascertained, the first and almost only vessel which then got past it was the Prince of Wales, of Hull, on the 6th of August, about latitude 75°.

Early on the morning of the 21st of July, the expedition cast off from the iceberg, and began to tow their way through loose streams of ice toward some lanes of water in the distance. But both on this day and on the following few days they made slow progress, and were often in difficulty. On the morning of the 20th, when they were off the Three Islands of Baffin, in latitude 74° north, at the clearing away of a fog, they saw the Lord Gambier at some distance, standing under all sail to the southward — the unusually bad state of the ice having overturned her master's hopes, and altered his purpose. They pursued their course northward amid much perplexity; and, though still fully expecting to bore their way through the pack, they were so excessively retarded by calms and barriers, as soon to lose all hope of being able to accomplish any considerable part of their mission before the setting in of winter. They spared no exertions, but forced a progress, and even drove on at the expense of danger.

On the 20th of August, during a strong breeze from the north-east, the ships, under all sail, bored through a moderately thick pack of ice, studded with perilously large masses; and they sustained severe shocks, yet, happily, did not receive any serious damage. They gained the open water on the afternoon of that day, in latitude 75½° north, and longitude 68° west, and then steered direct for Pond's Bay. That, as is well known, is the grand scene of the whale-fishery; and thither the expedition went to inquire of any whaler's crew who might have got across to the west, and also of the Esquimaux who annually visit that locality, whether they had seen anything of the missing adventurers.

On the 22d of August they approached the shore, about ten miles south of Pond's Bay, and saw the main pack so closely pressed home to the land, some three or four miles further south, as to leave no room for ships or boats to pass. They next stood in to the bay, and paused within half a mile of the points on which the Esquimaux are known to have their summer residences;

and they fired guns every half-hour, and closely examined every part of the shore with their glasses, but did not get sight of a single human being. They then went slowly to the northward, and sometimes could not hold their own with the current, and always kept so close to the land that neither boats nor persons could escape their notice, yet still were unsuccessful.

On the 26th they arrived off Possession Bay, at the south side of the entrance of Lancaster Sound. A party there went ashore to search for traces of Sir John Franklin having touched at that general point of rendezvous, but they found nothing except a paper recording the visit of Sir Edward Parry, in 1819. The expedition now sailed along the coast of Lancaster Sound, keeping close in-shore, scrutinizing all the seaboard both from the deck and from the mast-head, and fully expecting every hour to see those of whom they were in search. Every day they threw overboard, from each ship, a cask containing papers of information of all their proceedings; and in every fog they periodically fired guns, in every time of darkness they burned rockets and blue lights, and at all times they kept the ships under such easy sail that any boat seeing the signals might have reached them. The drift of the information in the casks told the missing adventurers that no assistance could be given them at Pond's Bay, or anywhere else on the west coast of Baffin's Bay; that the Enterprise and the Investigator were on their way to form a dépôt of provisions at Port Leopold; and that, if the adventurers would go on to that place, they would either find one of the ships there, or see, along with the provisions, a notice of where she might be found.

On the 1st of September the expedition arrived off Cape York, at the east side of the entrance of Prince Regent's Inlet. A party was there sent ashore, under very difficult circumstances, to seek for Sir John Franklin's company, or for traces of them, and to set up a conspicuous mark, with a paper containing similar information to that in the casks. From Cape York the expedition stood over toward North-East Cape, till they came to the edge of a pack about fourteen miles broad, lying in the way to Leopold Island, and too dense for them to penetrate. They wished to get with all possible speed to Port Leopold, to fulfil the promise made in their notices, and were glad to observe that the pack which now arrested them was still in motion, and might be expected soon to go to pieces under some favorable change. But, that no available time might be spent in inaction, they stood away, in the mean time, to the north shore of Barrow's Strait, to examine its numerous inlets, and to seek for a retreat harbor. They thoroughly explored Maxwell Bay, and several smaller indentations; and they got so near the entrance of Wellington Channel as to see that it was firmly and impenetrably barred from side to side by ice, which had not been broken up that season. Even Barrow's Strait was embarrassed by a greater quantity of ice than had ever before been seen in it at the same period of the year.

They now stood to the south-west to seek for a harbor near Cape Rennell; but they found a heavy body of ice extending from the west of Cornwallis's Island, in a compact mass, to Leopold Island. They coasted along this pack during stormy and foggy weather, and had difficulty during the nights in keeping the ships from being beset. With the thermometer every night at 15°, young ice formed so rapidly, and became so thick, as to defeat all their efforts to pass through some of even the looser streams. Yet, after several days of anxious and arduous toil, though the pack still lingered about Leopold Island and North-East Cape, they succeeded in getting through it, and entered the harbor of Port Leopold on the 11th September; and, had they not got in on that day, they would not have got in at all; for, on the following night, the main pack came close home to the land, and completely sealed the mouth of the harbor.

They were happy in having reached Port Leopold, both for their own sake and for the sake of their mission. They had doubted whether the anchorage would be good; but they found it excellent, and saw at once that there could not be a better wintering place for the Investigator. Nor could there have been a fitter locality for making a grand deposit of provisions, and preparing a temporary retreat for any of Sir John Franklin's company who might be entangled among the intricacies of the archipelago. Port Leopold is situated at the junction of the four great channels of Lancaster Sound, Barrow's Strait, Wellington Channel, and Prince Regent's Inlet, and lies closely adjacent to any route which Sir John Franklin could have been likely to pursue in the event of his having had to retrogress from the vicinity of Cape Walker; so that a lodgment in it by the present expedition could scarcely escape the notice of any of Sir John's company who might happen to be proceeding from any part whatever of the archipelago toward Baffin's Bay.

An effort was made to bring the Enterprise out, with the view of her going westward to some harbor nearer Cape Walker. But she was irretrievably ice-bound. The pack which closed the harbor's mouth never once afforded a chance for the egress of even a boat; and across the isthmus, as far as could be discerned from the neighboring heights, the same extensive mass of heavy hummocky ice, which repelled and limited the expedition's movements before entering, remained immovable, and formed a firm barrier all the way over to the shore of North Somerset. Even if the Enterprise had got out, she could not have proceeded far; and in all probability would either have been perilously beset in the pack, or compelled to sail away from it to England. On the 12th October, therefore, the two ships were laid fast in their wintering position, within two hundred yards of each other.

The earliest days after entering the harbor were devoted to the landing of a good supply of provisions upon Whaler Point. In this service the steam-launch proved of most eminent value, not only carrying a large cargo herself, but towing two deeply-laden cutters at the rate of four or five knots through the sheet of ice which then covered the harbor, and which no boat, unaided by steam, could have penetrated beyond her own length. The crews spent the dead of winter in a similar manner to those of former Arctic expeditions. But they probably felt much depressed by thinking on the fate of those whom they had been unsuccessfully seeking, and they had to contend against a rigorous cold, prolonged unusually far into the spring; so that, though they had more comforts, better appliances, and much richer fruits of experience, than the crews of Sir Edward Parry's and Sir John Ross's ships, they were not by any means so healthy. During the winter a great many white foxes were taken alive in traps, and, as they are well known to travel great distances in search of food, they were fitted with copper collars, containing engraved notices of the position of the ships and dépôts of provisions, and then set at liberty, in the hope that they would be caught by the crews of the Erebus and the Terror.

In April and the early part of May short journeys were made to deposit small stores of provisions westward of Cape Clarence, and southward of Cape Seppings. On the 15th May a party of thirteen, headed by Sir James C. Ross, and taking with them forty days' provision, and a supply of clothes, blankets, and other necessaries, on two sledges, started on an exploratory journey to the south. They were accompanied for five days by a fatigue party of nearly thirty, under Captain Bird. Their object was to penetrate as far as possible in the direction which Sir John Franklin was instructed first to pursue, and to make a close scrutiny of every bay and inlet in which any ships might have found shelter. They got on with difficulty, and did their work with much toil, yet went resolutely forward.

The north shore of North Somerset trends slightly to the northward of west, till it attains its highest latitude, the highest latitude of continental America, a few miles beyond Cape Rennell; it thence trends slightly to the southward of west till it rounds Cape Bunny; and then it suddenly assumes a direction nearly due south. From high land adjacent to Cape Bunny they obtained a very extensive view, and observed that all Wellington Channel on the north, and all the space between Cape Bunny and Cape Walker on the west, were occupied by very heavy hummocky ice; but that the frozen expanse southward, along the west flank of North Somerset, was smoother. They proceeded to the south, tracing all the indentations of the coast, and heroically enduring great exposure and fatigue, but not without the pain and delay of several of their number becoming useless from lameness and debility. They stopped on the 5th of June. They were then too weak to go further, and had consumed more than half of their provisions; and they encamped for a day's rest, preparatory to their return.

Their brave leader and two of the men, however, went onward to a vantage-ground about eight or nine miles distant. This extreme point of the journey is the western extremity of a small high peninsula, situated in latitude 72° 38′ north, and longitude 95° 40′ west. The atmosphere at the time was peculiarly clear, and would have carried the eye to land of any great elevation at the distance of one hundred miles. But the most distant visible cape in the direction toward Boothia and Victoria Land was not further off than fifty miles, and lay nearly due south. Several small bays and inlets intervened, and though, perhaps, not forming a continuous sweep of the sea, they prove Prince Regent's Inlet at Cresswell and Brentford Bays to be separated from the western ocean by a very narrow isthmus — a distinct natural boundary between North Somerset and Boothia.

The party resting at the encampment were not idle. Lieut. McClintock, who headed them, took some magnetic observations, which had great value, on account of the near vicinity of the place to the magnetic pole. Two of the men pierced the ice, and found it to be eight feet thick, and set in a stick for ascertaining the state of the tides; and all the others who could work erected a large cairn, into which was put a copper cylinder, containing all requisite information for the guidance of any of Sir John Franklin's company who might journey along that coast. The time for expecting those missing ones there that season, on the supposition of their having abandoned their ships in the vicinity of Melville Island, had almost or altogether passed. The thaw had commenced, the suitable conditions for travelling were over, and the present explorers had, at least, the satisfaction of knowing that no wanderers from the Erebus and the Terror then lay unheeded or perishing on the coast of North Somerset.

The explorers began their return journey on the 6th

June. They forced their way through various difficulties, and arrived at the ships on the 23d. They were so worn and injured, that every man of them, from some cause or other, went into the doctor's hands for two or three weeks. One of the assistant surgeons, too, had died; several men of both crews were severely ailing; and the general health was far from good.

During the absence of the large exploring party in North Somerset, three small ones were despatched by Captain Bird in other directions. One, under the command of Lieut. Barnard, went to the north shore of Barrow's Strait; another, under the command of Lieut. Browne, went to the east shore of Prince Regent's Inlet; and the third, under the command of Lieut. Robinson, went to the west shore of that inlet. These parties were comparatively a short time away; yet all — especially the last, who penetrated several miles beyond Fury Beach — suffered from snow-blindness, sprained ankles, and debility.

Preparations were now made for leaving Port Leopold. The season was far advanced, and a strong desire was felt to have the ships as soon as possible set free, in order to push them on toward the west. But something further was first done to extend the appliances of the place as a refuge for the missing adventurers. A house was built of the spare spars of the ships, and covered with such of the housing-cloths as could be wanted. The dépôt of provisions and fuel was raised to a sufficient quantity to serve for a twelvemonth. And the Investigator's steam-launch was lengthened seven feet, and made a fine vessel, capable of conveying the whole of Sir John Franklin's party to the whale-ships.

The crews were ill able to work the ships out of the harbor, and to set them once more before the breeze;

but they went with a will to the task. The season was far advanced, and exceedingly unpromising, and seemed clearly to demand the utmost promptitude and strenuousness of exertion. At a time when most other navigable parts of the Arctic seas were open, Port Leopold continued as close as in the middle of winter. Not a foot of water was to be seen on the surface of the surrounding ice, except only along the line of gravel about the harbor's mouth; and small prospect existed that any natural opening would occur. The crews were obliged to cut a way out with saws. All hands that were at all able went to work, and made a canal two miles in length, and sufficiently wide to let the ships pass outward to the adjacent sound. They did not complete this till the 15th of August, and then had the mortification to see that the ice to seaward remained, to all appearance, as firmly fixed as in the winter. But it was wasting away along the shores, and it soon broke up, and gave promise of a navigable channel. The ships got out of the harbor on the 28th of August, exactly one fortnight less than a twelvemonth from the time when they entered it.

They proceeded toward the north shore of Barrow's Strait, with the view of making further examination of Wellington Channel, and of scrutinizing the coasts and inlets westward to Melville Island. But they were arrested about twelve miles from the shore by fixed land-ice, which had remained unbroken since the previous season, and which appeared to extend away to the western horizon in a uniform heavy sheet. They were in a loose pack, struggling with blocks and streams as they best could, and they kept hovering about the spot which afforded the greatest probability of an opening. But, on the 1st of September, the loose pack was suddenly put in commotion by a strong wind, and it came down upon them and beset them. During two or three days the heavy masses at times severely squeezed them, and ridges of hummocks were thrown up all around them, and then the temperature fell nearly to zero, and congealed the whole body of ice into a solid mass. The crew of the Enterprise were unable, for some days, to unship the rudder, and when at last they released it, by means of the laborious operation of sawing away the hummocks which clove to the stern, they found it twisted and damaged ; and, at the same time, the ship was so much strained as to increase the leakage from three inches in a fortnight to fourteen inches in a day.

The ice now remained for some days stationary. The lighter pieces had been so interlaced and imbricated by pressure, as to form one entire sheet across the whole width of Barrow's Strait, and away eastward and westward to the horizon ; and all the blocks and strata below them were so firmly cemented by the extreme severity of the temperature as to seem little likely to break up again that season. The ships appeared fixed for the winter ; and who could tell whether they might not be exposed to a series of as terrific perils as those which so often menaced the Terror with destruction in her awful ice-voyage of 1836 ?

On the wind shifting to the west, the crews, with a mixture of hope and anxiety, beheld the whole body of ice beginning to drive to the eastward, at the rate of eight or ten miles a day. They made all possible efforts to help themselves, but made them in vain, for no human power could have moved either of the ships a single inch. The field of ice which held them fast in its centre was more than fifty miles in circumference. It carried them along the south shore of Lancaster Sound, and then went down the west side of Baffin's

Bay, till they were abreast of Pond's Bay, and there it threatened to precipitate them on a barrier of icebergs. But, just in the very crisis of their alarm, it was rent, as if by some unseen power, into innumerable fragments, and they were set almost miraculously free.

The crews sprang from despair to hope, and from inaction to energy. All sail was set, and warps were run out from each quarter to work the ships past the heavy floes. The Investigator got into open water on the 24th, and the Enterprise on the 25th. "It is impossible," says Ross, "to convey any idea of the sensation we experienced when we found ourselves once more at liberty; many a heart poured forth its praises and thanksgivings to Almighty God for this unlooked for deliverance." The harbors of Baffin's Bay were now all closed by ice, and the course to the west was barred by the pack from which the ships had just been liberated. The expedition, therefore, had no alternative but to return to England, and they arrived off Scarborough on the 3d of November, 1849. Thus ended the third of the government explorations in search of Sir John Franklin.

Lieutenant Pullen, who, it will be remembered, was despatched from the Plover on the western coast, and ordered to extend his search to the mouth of the Mackenzie, ascended that river and reached Fort Simpson on the 13th of October. Here he wintered, and, while on his way to York Factory, the following spring, received instructions by express to attempt a passage in boats across the sea to Melville Island. He immediately hurried back, and, on being supplied with four thousand five hundred pounds of pemmican and jerked venison by Rae, descended the Mackenzie. The season of 1850 proved more severe, however, than that of the previous year. Pullen found the sea, from the Mackenzie to

Cape Bathurst, covered with unbroken ice, a small channel only existing in-shore, through which he threaded his way to the vicinity of the cape. Failing in finding a passage out to sea to the north of Cape Bathurst, he remained in its vicinity, watching the ice for an opening, until the approach of winter compelled him to return to the Mackenzie. He had reached the sea on the 22d of July, and he did not quit it till the 1st of September. As he ascended the Mackenzie, ice was driving rapidly down. "It was one continued drift of ice and heavy snow-storms." He reached Fort Simpson on the 5th of October, and arrived in England to take command of the North Star, and join the expedition under Sir E. Belcher.

CHAPTER XIII.

OPINIONS IN REGARD TO THE FATE OF FRANKLIN. — CLIMATE. — RESOURCES OF GAME. — REWARDS OFFERED. — REPORTS FROM WHALERS. — RENEWED SEARCHES. — COLLINSON AND M'CLURE. — RAE'S INSTRUCTIONS. — OTHER EXPEDITIONS, PUBLIC AND PRIVATE. — GRINNELL'S EXPEDITION. — MEETING IN THE ARCTIC SEAS. — TRACES OF FRANKLIN. — GRAVES. — SLEDGING PARTIES. — RETURN HOME.

It was the opinion of Sir John Richardson, the former companion of Franklin, that his plans were to shape his course, in the first instance, for the neighborhood of Cape Walker, and to push to the westward in that parallel; or, if that could not be accomplished, to make his way southwards, to the channel discovered on the north coast of the continent, and so on to Behring's Strait; failing success in that quarter, he meant to retrace his course to Wellington Sound, and attempt a passage northwards of Parry's Islands; and if foiled there also, to descend Regent's Inlet, and seek the passage along the coast discovered by Messrs. Dease and Simpson.

Captain Fitzjames, the second in command under Sir John Franklin, was much inclined to try the passage northward of Parry's Islands; and he would, no doubt, endeavor to persuade Sir John to pursue this course, if they failed to the southward. In a private letter to Sir John Barrow, dated January, 1845, Fitzjames writes: "It does not appear clear to me what led Parry down Prince Regent Inlet, after having got as far as Melville Island before. The north-west passage is certainly to be gone through by Barrow's Strait, but whether south or north of Parry's Group, remains to be proved. I am for going north, edging north-west till in longitude 140°, if possible."

Captain Sir John Ross records, in February, 1847, his opinion that the expedition was frozen up beyond Melville Island, from the known intentions of Sir John Franklin to put his ships into the drift-ice at the western end of Melville Island; a risk which was deemed in the highest degree imprudent by Lieutenant Parry and the officers of the expedition of 1819–20, with ships of a less draught of water, and in every respect better calculated to sustain the pressure of the ice, and other dangers to which they must be exposed. The expedition certainly did not succeed in passing Behring's Strait; and, if not totally lost, must have been carried by the drift-ice to the southward, on land seen at a great distance in that direction, from which the accumulation of ice behind them would, as in Ross's own case, forever prevent the return of the ships. When we remember with what extreme difficulty Ross's party travelled three hundred miles over much smoother ice after they abandoned their vessel, it appears very doubtful whether Franklin and his men, one hundred and thirty-eight in number, could possibly travel six hundred miles.

In the contingency of the ships having penetrated some considerable distance to the south-west of Cape Walker, and having been hampered and crushed in the narrow channels of the archipelago, which there are reasons for believing occupies the space between Victoria, Wollaston, and Banks's Lands, it is remarked by Sir John Richardson, that such accidents among ice are seldom so sudden but that the boats of one or of both ships, with provisions, can be saved; and, in such an event, the survivors would either return to Lancaster

Strait, or make for the continent, according to their nearness.

Colonel Sabine remarks, in a letter dated Woolwich, 5th of May, 1847: "It was Sir John Franklin's intention, if foiled at one point, to try, in succession, all the probable openings into a more navigable part of the Polar Sea. The range of coast is considerable in which memorials of the ships' progress would have to be sought for, extending from Melville Island, in the west, to the great sound at the head of Baffin's Bay, in the east."

Admiral Sir Francis Beaufort, in his report to the Lords Commissioners of the Admiralty, Nov. 24, 1849, observes: "There are four ways only in which it is likely that the Erebus and Terror would have been lost — by fire, by sunken rocks, by storm, or by being crushed between two fields of ice. Both vessels would scarcely have taken fire together; if one of them had struck on a rock, the other would have avoided the danger. Storms in those narrow seas, encumbered with ice, raise no swell, and could produce no such disaster; and, therefore, by the fourth cause alone could the two vessels have been at once destroyed; and, even in that case, the crews would have escaped upon the ice — as happens every year to the whalers; — they would have saved their loose boats, and reached some part of the American shores. As no traces of any such event have been found on any part of those shores, it may, therefore, be safely affirmed that one ship, at least, and both the crews, are still in existence; and, therefore, the point where they now are is the great matter for consideration.

"Their orders would have carried them towards Melville Island, and then out to the westward, where it is therefore probable that they are entangled amongst islands and ice. For, should they have been arrested at some intermediate place, — for instance, Cape Walker, or at one of the northern chain of islands, — they would, undoubtedly, in the course of the three following years, have contrived some method of sending notices of their position to the shores of North Somerset or to Barrow's Strait.

"If they had reached much to the southward of Banks's Land, they would surely have communicated with the tribes on Mackenzie River ; and if, failing to get to the westward or southward, they had returned with the intention of penetrating through Wellington Channel, they would have detached parties on the ice towards Barrow's Strait, in order to have deposited statements of their intentions. The general conclusion, therefore, remains that they are still locked up in the archipelago to the westward of Melville Island."

Captain Sir George Back, in a letter to the Secretary of the Admiralty, December 1st, 1849, says: "You will be pleased, sir, to impress on my Lords Commissioners that I wholly reject all and every idea of any attempts on the part of Sir John Franklin to send boats or detachments over the ice to any point of the mainland eastward of the Mackenzie River, because I can say, from experience, that no toil-worn and exhausted party could have the least chance of existence by going there. On the other hand, from my knowledge of Sir John Franklin, — having been three times on discovery together, — I much doubt if he would quit his ship at all, except in a boat ; for any attempt to cross the ice a long distance on foot would be tempting death ; and it is too laborious a task to sledge far over such an uneven surface as those regions generally present. That great mortality must have occurred, and that one ship may be lost, are greatly to be feared ; and, as on all former expeditions, if the survivors are paralyzed by the depressing attacks of scurvy, it would then be impossible for them, however desirous they might be, to leave the ship, which must thus become their last most anxious abode.

"If, however, open water should have allowed Sir John Franklin to have resorted to his boats, then I am persuaded he would make for either the Mackenzie River, or, which is far more likely, from the almost certainty he must have felt of finding provision, Cape Clarence and Fury Point. I am aware that the whole chances of life, in this painful case, depend on food; but when I reflect on Sir John Franklin's former extraordinary preservation under miseries and trials of the most severe description, living often on scraps of old leather and other refuse, I cannot despair of his finding the means to prolong existence till aid be happily sent him."

In regard to the advantages of an exploration by the way of Behring's Strait, Sir John Richardson writes:

"The climate of Arctic America improves in a sensible manner with an increase of western longitude. On the Mackenzie, on the 135th meridian, the summer is warmer than in any district of the continent in the same parallel; and it is still finer, and the vegetation more luxuriant, on the banks of the Yucon, on the 150th meridian. This superiority of climate leads me to infer that ships well fortified against drift-ice will find the navigation of the Arctic seas more practicable in its western portion than it has been found to the eastward. This inference is supported by my own personal experience, as far as it goes. I met with no ice in the month of August, on my late voyage, till I attained the 123d meridian, and which I was led, from that circumstance, to suppose coincided with the western limits of Parry's Archipelago.

"The greater facility of navigating from the west has been powerfully advocated by others on former occasions; and the chief, perhaps the only reason why the attempt to penetrate the Polar Sea from that quarter has not been resumed since the time of Cook is, that the length of the previous voyage to Behring's Strait would considerably diminish the store of provisions; but the facilities of obtaining supplies in the Pacific are now so augmented, that this objection has no longer the same force."

It was urged that, though the crews of the Erebus and the Terror had provisions with them for only three years, they could make these serve, by reduced allowance, for a somewhat longer period, and would in all probability obtain large additions to them by means of their guns. The Arctic regions, far from being so destitute of animal life as might be supposed from the bleak and inhospitable character of the climate, are proverbial for the boundless profusion of various species of the animal kingdom, which are to be met with in different localities during a great part of the year.

The air is often darkened by innumerable flocks of Arctic and blue gulls, the ivory gull, or snow-bird, the kittiwake, the fulmar petrel, snow-geese, terns, coons, dovekies, &c. The cetaceous animals comprise the great Greenland whale, the sea-unicorn, or narwhal, the white whale, or beluga, the morse, or walrus, and the seal. There are also plenty of porpoises occasionally to be met with; and, although these animals may not be the best of food, yet they can be eaten. Of the land animals, we may instance the polar bear, the musk-ox, the reindeer, the Arctic fox, and wolves.

Parry obtained nearly four thousand pounds' weight

of animal food during his winter residence at Melville Island; Ross nearly the same quantity from birds alone, when wintering at Port Leopold.

Sir John Richardson, speaking of the amount of food to be obtained in the polar region, says: "Deer migrate over the ice in the spring from the main shore to Victoria and Wollaston Lands in large herds, and return in the autumn. These lands are also the breeding-places of vast flocks of snow-geese; so that, with ordinary skill in hunting, a large supply of food might be procured on their shores, in the months of June, July, and August. Seals are also numerous in those seas, and are easily shot, their curiosity rendering them a ready prey to a boat-party." In these ways, and by fishing, the stock of provisions might be greatly augmented; and we have the recent example of Mr. Rae, who passed a severe winter on the very barren shores of Repulse Bay, with no other fuel than the withered tufts of a herbaceous andromada, and maintained a numerous party on the spoils of the chase alone for a whole year.

With an empty stomach the power of resisting external cold is greatly impaired; but when the process of digestion is going on vigorously, even with comparatively scanty clothing, the heat of the body is preserved. There is, in the winter time, in high latitudes, a craving for fat or oleaginous food; and for such occasions the flesh of seals, walruses, or bears, forms a useful article of diet. Captain Cook says that the walrus is a sweet and wholesome article of food. Whales and seals would also furnish light and fuel. The necessity for increased food in very cold weather is not so great when the people do not work.

In March, 1848, the British Admiralty announced their intention of rewarding the crews of any whaling-ships that brought accurate information of the missing expedition, with the sum of one hundred guineas or more, according to circumstances. Lady Franklin, also, about the same time offered rewards of two thousand and three thousand pounds, to be distributed among the owner, officers, and crew, discovering and affording relief to her husband, or making extraordinary exertions for the above object, and, if required, bringing Sir John Franklin and his party to England.

On the 23d of March, 1849, the British government offered a reward of twenty thousand pounds "to such private ship, or by distribution among such private ships, or to any exploring party or parties, of any country, as might, in the judgment of the Board of Admiralty, have rendered efficient assistance to Sir John Franklin, his ships, or their crews, and might have contributed directly to extricate them from the ice." This, also, was meant mainly for the whalers, but was not promulged till most of them had sailed, and had no adaptation to compensate owners and masters and crews proportionately to their losses on the fishery, and, therefore, did not produce any effect.

In the spring of 1849 Mr. Parker, master of the whaling-ship Truelove, carried out from Lady Franklin a supply of provisions and coals for the possible use of the missing expedition, and landed them on the conspicuous promontory of Cape Hay, on the south side of Lancaster Sound.

In 1849 Dr. Goodsir, brother of the assistant surgeon of the Erebus, embarked in the whaling-ship Advice, of Dundee, on her annual trip to Baffin's Bay, in the hope that he might get early intelligence of the missing expedition. Mr. William Penny, the master of the Advice, was well known for enterprise and energy, and had made strenuous efforts, in 1834, to assist Sir John Ross and his party, and now felt fervid and generous zeal to be useful in the affair of Sir John Franklin. They proceeded in the ordinary manner of a whaling cruise, yet penetrated into Lancaster Sound, and proposed to go as far as Prince Regent's Inlet; but were stopped, on the 4th of August, by a firm, compact barrier, extending quite across, in crescentic outline, from Cape York, on the south, to the vicinity of Burnet's Inlet, on the north. They were only seven days within sight of the shores of Lancaster Sound, and saw few other parts of them than such as had been closely scrutinized by the Enterprise and the Investigator; yet they searched them with a keen eye, and deposited on them several conspicuous notices.

The demand for new researches now became pressing. Three great divisions of search were adopted. These corresponded, in general sphere and character, to the three primary searching expeditions of 1848. One was marine, by way of Behring's Strait; another was overland, to the central northern coasts; and the third was marine, by way of Baffin's Bay.

The ships Enterprise and Investigator were refitted with all possible speed, to go round South America, and up to Behring's Strait. Captain Richard Collinson was put in command of the Enterprise, and Commander M'Clure, who had served as first lieutenant of the Enterprise in the recent expedition under Sir James C. Ross, was put in command of the Investigator. The ships were provisioned for three years, and supplied with balloons, blasting appliances, ice-saws, and many other contrivances for aiding their movements and research. Each, also, was provided with a pointed piece of mechanism, about fourteen pounds in weight, attached by a tackle to the end of the bowsprit, suited to be worked from the deck, and capable, by means of a series of sudden falls, to break ice of any ordinary thickness, and open a passage through a floe or light pack. The ships, though dull sailers, were the only ones fit for the service which could be got promptly ready; and, in order to expedite their progress, steamers were put in requisition to tow them in more than one part of their voyage, and particularly through the Magellan Strait, the Wellington Channel, and on to Valparaiso.

They sailed from Plymouth Sound on the 20th of January, 1850. The captains had minute orders for their guidance on the way to Behring's Strait, and with reference to the previous expeditions of the Herald and the Plover; and were also furnished with memoranda, suggestions, and conditional instructions, for their aid in the polar seas; but, with the exception of two or three general commands, bearing comprehensively on the grand object of their mission, they were left almost entirely to their own discretion, after they should enter the ice. They were told to reap all the advantage they could from the experience of the Herald and the Plover; to form a dépôt, or point of succor, for any party to fall back upon; to retain the Plover, and get her replenished from the Herald, and send her a wintering and cruising on nearly her former ground till the autumn of 1853; to keep the Enterprise and the Investigator steadily in each other's company, and onward as far as safety would permit to the east; to cultivate the friendship of the Esquimaux, and induce them to carry messages to the Hudson's Bay Company's settlements; to throw occasionally overboard tin cylinders containing information, and to use every precaution against getting into any position which might possibly hold them fast till their provisions should become exhausted.

Both ships made a comparatively speedy passage to Behring's Strait. On the 29th of July the Enterprise reached the western end of the Aleutian Chain; on the

11th of August she reached the island of St. Lawrence; and on the 16th of August fell in with the ice. But the weather was then so unfavorable, and the ice so thick, that Captain Collinson abandoned a purpose which he had formed to attempt to penetrate that season to Cape Bathurst. After several encounters with the ice, he reached Grantley Harbor, and there found the Plover preparing for winter quarters, and was next day joined by the Herald. On consulting with Captains Kellett and Moore, he determined, instead of wintering in the north, to proceed to Hong Kong, there to replenish his provisions, and not to set out again for the north till at least the first of April, 1851. The Investigator was later in getting through the Pacific than the Enterprise; and Commander Moore, of the Plover, writing at sea, in latitude 51° 26′ north, and longitude 172° 35′ west, on the 20th of July, gave a sketch of his intended operations, and said that no apprehension need be entertained about his safety till the autumn of 1854, as he had on board full provisions of every kind for three years after the first of September, and intended to issue, in lieu of the usual rations, whatever food could be obtained by hunting parties from the ship.

Dr. Rae, it will be remembered, was left by Sir John Richardson to attempt to overtake, in the summer of 1849, an unaccomplished part of the objects of the overland expedition of 1848. This had special reference to the examination of the coasts of Victoria Land and Wollaston Land; and now that Sir John Franklin's ships were believed to have certainly gone beyond Cape Walker, and to have probably bored their way southwestward to some position between that place and the mainland, this was deemed to be much more important than before. Early in 1850 instructions were despatched to Dr. Rae, by Governor Sir George Simpson, of the

Hudson's Bay Company, requiring him, in the event of his explorations of 1849 having been unsuccessful, to organize another expedition for the summer of 1850. This was to penetrate further, to range more widely, and to examine the coasts of Banks's Island, the coasts around Cape Walker, and the north coast of Victoria Land. Two small parties, at the same time, were to proceed westward on the mainland in the direction of Point Barrow; and one of these was to descend the Mackenzie, and explore the coast to the west of it, while the other was to pass on to the Colville River, and to descend that stream to the sea; and both were to induce the natives, by rewards and otherwise, to prosecute the search, and spread intelligence in all directions. Dr. Rae was particularly instructed to keep an ample supply of provisions, clothing, ammunition, fishing-tackle, and other necessaries, at Fort Good Hope, as that seemed an eminently probable retreat to which parties of the missing adventurers might try to force their way. But in most other matters, and especially in all the details of the expedition, he was left solely to his own discretion.

The expedition equipped by the British government for renewed search by way of Baffin's Bay and Lancaster Sound comprised two strong teak-built ships, — the Resolute and the Assistance, — and two powerful screw-propelled steam-vessels — the Pioneer and the Intrepid. These ships had a tonnage, the former of five hundred, and the latter of four hundred and thirty tons, and were alike strong, commodious, elegant, and admirably appurtenanced. The steam-vessels had strength and adaptation not only for towing the ships in open channels, but for conflicting with the perils of the polar seas, and forcing a passage through small floes and thin packs of ice. Captain H. T. Austin was put in command of the Resolute, Captain E. Ommaney of the Assistance, and Lieut. Sherard Osborne of the Pioneer. Multitudes of officers nobly vied as volunteers to obtain the subordinate appointments; and some of the most experienced whale-fishers were obtained for the forecastle. The instructions given were similar in scope and spirit to those of the Behring's Strait expedition, and differed chiefly in adaptation to the different route. The expedition sailed in the spring of 1850.

An expedition under the command of the veteran Sir John Ross was equipped by a public subscription, toward which the Hudson's Bay Company contributed five hundred pounds. This consisted of a schooner-rigged vessel of one hundred and twenty tons (which Sir John called the Felix, in honor of his late patriotic friend, Sir Felix Booth), and of a small tender, of twelve tons, called the Mary. They were provisioned for eighteen months, and they set sail in the latter part of April. Sir John was in excellent spirits, as full of fire and daring as in his younger years; and he enlisted in his service an old expert Esquimaux interpreter. His plan was to proceed as quickly as he could to Barrow's Strait to commence operations at Cape Hotham, on the west side of the entrance of Wellington Channel; to examine all the headlands thence to Banks's Land, and then, if still unsuccessful, to leave the Mary there as a vessel of retreat, and to push the search in the Felix alone during another year.

An expedition also was equipped at the instance of the devoted Lady Franklin, wholly by her own zeal, and mainly at her own expense. This was put under the command of Mr. Penny, formerly master of the Advice whale-ship, and consisted of a fine ship of two hundred and twenty-five tons, called The Lady Franklin, and a new clipper-brig of one hundred and twenty tons, named the

Sophia. The larger vessel was fitted up at Aberdeen, and the smaller one at Dundee — both with great celerity, and in a style of the best possible adaptation to an Arctic voyage; and they also sailed in the spring of 1850. Their proposed plan of procedure was somewhat coincident with that of the government expedition; yet entirely independent, except in the way of coöperation or mutual aid, and liable to be much controlled or modified by circumstances.

Another expedition, supplementary to the preceding, was equipped at the instance of Lady Franklin. She herself defrayed about two thirds of the cost of it, by means of selling out of the funds all the money which she could legally touch; and her friends defrayed the rest. The only vessel was the Prince Albert, a schooner-rigged craft of ninety tons, but as fine a little structure as ever "walked the waters," and strengthened and fitted in the most artistic way for buffeting the perils of the Arctic seas. She was commanded by Commander Charles C. Forsyth, of the Royal Navy; and was served in a variety of capacities, most laboriously and dexterously, by Mr. W. P. Snow, —both volunteers, who wished no compensation but the honor of the enterprise. The object was to examine the shores of Prince Regent's Inlet and the Gulf of Boothia, and to send out travelling parties to explore the west side of the land of Boothia down to Dease and Simpson's Strait. At the time when Sir John Franklin sailed, a belief was general that Boothia was an island, and that Prince Regent's Inlet communicated with the Polar Sea through Dease and Simpson's Strait; so that, in the event of his being baffled in finding a north-west passage by way of Cape Walker, or up Wellington Channel, he would very probably enter Prince Regent's Inlet, with the view of passing round the south of Boothia.

Hence the present expedition. The Prince Albert sailed from Aberdeen on the 5th of June.

An expedition also was equipped in America. This was got up mainly by the exertions and at the cost of Henry Grinnell, Esq., a merchant of New York, but was put in order and sent forth by the United States Navy department. It consisted of two vessels, the Advance and the Rescue, of respectively one hundred and twenty-five and ninety-five tons; and was put under the command of Lieut. De Haven, who had served in the United States Exploring Expedition, under Commodore Wilkes, in the Antarctic seas. It sailed from New York on the 24th of May, and was accompanied for two days in his yacht by Mr. Grinnell. Its object was to push promptly forward, in any way it could, in the direction of Melville Island and Banks's Land; to winter wherever it might happen to stick fast, in the pack, or out of the pack; and to move on and make search as long as it might be able, in any direction which should offer most promise of success.

The North Star transport, which left England in 1849 to convey stores to the expedition under Sir James C. Ross, may in some sense be regarded likewise as one of the exploring ships of 1850. She became beset in Melville Bay on the 29th of July, 1849, and gradually drifted till the 26th of September; and being then abreast of Wolstenholme Sound, and able to bore a way through the loosened ice, she pressed up to the head of that sound, and there wintered in lat. 76° 33′ N., being the most northerly position in which any vessel, except Dr. Kane's, has been known to be laid up. She lost four of her crew during the dismal seclusion of the Arctic night, but not from causes attributable to the climate; and she found a large proportion of the preserved meats she had brought from England to be of bad quality, and was obliged to put the surviving crew upon two-thirds allowance. She got out of Wolstenholme Sound on the 1st of August, 1850, passed through "the middle ice" in the centre of Ross's Bay, reached Possession Bay on the evening of the 8th, left despatches there, and arrived at Leopold on the 13th. She found that harbor full of ice, and was not able to land stores at it, and with great difficulty communicated with the shore by boat, to leave a notice of her visit. She next went toward Port Bowen, but found that place entirely blocked with ice; and then stretched across out of the inlet, and spoke first the Lady Franklin, and afterwards the Felix, and got intelligence from them of the great searching operations of that season. She next proceeded to Navy Board Inlet, and there, on the mainland, behind Wollaston Island, she put ashore her surplus stores of fuel and provisions. She had suddenly to scud away before a gale; and, running out of the mid-channel of Lancaster Sound, on the 28th of September she arrived in Scotland.

The several expeditions of 1850 up Baffin's Bay encountered enormous difficulties from "the middle ice" and the Melville Bay barrier. Though the ships sailed from widely different points at widely different periods, they nearly all got into view of one another, and most were for some time closely in company. All were at several times arrested or beset; and the best and largest spent five weeks in effecting a northward distance of thirty miles. The perils which they braved were only a degree or two less terrible than those of the Terror in Hudson's Bay in 1836. The crews of the smaller vessels were repeatedly all prepared, with their bundles and loose stores, to leap on the ice from expected shipwreck, and to betake themselves to sledging or foot-travelling for escape to the land. The environment, by massive towering icebergs, was sometimes so complete as to exclude every perceptible outlet, sometimes so close as almost to rub the ships, and sometimes so unsteady or whirling as to threaten overwhelming somersets. Some whaling-ships which got early to the north, though commanded by the most experienced masters, and manned by the most select crews, turned about and sailed back to the south, fully believing the penetration of Melville Bay that season to be either an impossibility or practicable only at fearful hazards.

The expedition ships, however, were little, if at all, daunted, conscious of possessing higher powers, and resolutely determined to get on. The means which they used for forcing their way comprised all the known methods of boring, tracking, and cutting, and were sometimes effected with prodigious labor and indomitable perseverance; and they comprised also, in the case of the British government expedition, the smashing of all thin floes, and sometimes the perilous assault of thick ones, by the impetus of the steamers. The smaller vessels of the private expeditions might have seemed incompetent for such rough work; but, though ill able to attack, they were well able to run and manœuvre; and, on the average of the voyage through the ice, they were found to be fully as safe, and more than fully as manageable, as the large ships.

The little Prince Albert, in particular, did wonders; and on one occasion, disdaining to lie ice-fast, she made a daring attack upon a neck of ice which lay between her and an open piece of water. With a tremendous blow, that for the moment made her rebound and tremble, she struck the ice in the exact point, and rent it into fragments.

The steamers, for a long way, accelerated the progress not only of the government ships, but also of the Felix and the Prince Albert, by towing them through pervious masses of loose ice, and by forcing a passage through impediments. One of the scenes, described by Snow, in this part of the voyage illustrates its arduousness and novelty: "We came to a heavy nip, and all the vessels had to be made fast to a floe until a passage could be cleared. The Pioneer, immediately on casting off the Resolute's tow-rope, was directed to dash at the impediment, under full power. This she did boldly and fearlessly, rushing stem on, and fairly digging her bows into it in a most remarkable manner. Backing instantly astern, and then again going ahead, she performed the same manœuvre, fairly lifting herself up on end, like a prancing war-horse. By this time the nip was too heavy to be so broken, though both the steamers had previously cleared many similar impediments in that manner. It was now, however, necessary to resort to other means; and, accordingly, parties from every ship were sent on the ice to assist in blowing it up, and removing the fragments as they got loosened. The same plan as that, I believe, adopted in blasting rocks, was here pursued. Powder was sunk to a certain depth, a slow match applied, and at a given signal ignited. Due time was allowed, and then the enormous masses would be seen in convulsive movement, as though shaken by a volcanic eruption, until piece upon piece was sent in the air, and the larger bodies were completely rent into innumerable fragments. The steamers then darted forward, and with warps dragged out the immense blocks that had been thus dissevered. Several efforts had to be made by blasting and forcing the ice before a passage could be cleared."

On the 14th of August the Lady Franklin and the Sophia were for a little while in company with the other ships, and then, amidst deafening cheers, stood away, under all sail, to the west. On the following night, when the little fleet were off Cape Dudley Digges, the Intrepid, the Assistance, and the Felix, parted company to make a search in Wolstenholme Sound. On the 15th the Pioneer, the Resolute, and the Prince Albert, were quite into the "North Water," away from the ice ; and on the 16th Captain Austin announced his intention to call at Pond's Bay and Possession Bay. He expressed a wish that the Prince Albert would examine the south shore of Lancaster Sound from Cape Hay onward ; and stated that the Intrepid and the Assistance would examine the north shore, and come to a rendezvous with the Resolute somewhere about the mouth of Wellington Channel.

Early on the 21st of August the Prince Albert arrived off Port Leopold. A landing was effected with great difficulty in a gutta-percha boat, and could not have been effected at all in any ordinary boat. The house constructed by Sir James C. Ross was found much rent in several places on the top and at the sides, but otherwise in excellent order, and quite fit to be a temporary retreat to any forlorn or cast-away Arctic adventurers. The stores were abundant and in prime condition. The steam launch seemed a noble little vessel, in which a brave-hearted party might venture anywhere, and was so placed that she could very easily be run into the sea. But not a trace was found of the visit of any wanderer from the Erebus and the Terror.

The Prince Albert now stood away down Prince Regent's Inlet ; and towards evening, when she was gliding past the ice of Batty Bay, her crew were startled for a moment into a thrill of hope. The men on deck thought they heard a gun fired on shore ; the officers ran to scrutinize the land through their glasses aloft ; the vessel was steered closer to the bay ; the howitzer was cleared away, and fired ; but not the slightest sign of life could be seen ; not the faintest answering sound was heard. The supposed shot had been merely the falling of a piece of rock, or the collision of some heavy masses of ice.

Next morning the vessel was off Fury Beach, and in a thick fog ; and when the fog cleared away, she proved to be in a bight of the ice, within a few yards of a continuous, heavy, hummocky expanse, which contained not, as far as it could be seen from the crow's nest, one pool or crack, or the slightest promise of an opening. The officers examined this long and anxiously, and were forced to conclude that any attempt to penetrate it that season would be impracticable. They gloomily but irresistibly felt the specific object of their voyage, the examination of the shores of Boothia, to be defeated ; and saw at once that they must turn about and lose little time in returning to Britain. But they resolved first to look at some of the most accessible shores and headlands about the throat of Barrow's Strait, and a brief way up Wellington Channel.

During twenty-four hours, Mr. Snow, with a small boat party, made a romantic land search of the coast around Batty Bay, and on to Port Leopold ; and he found the latter place far more blocked up than on the 21st, and did not get away from it without enormous labor and difficulty. When he again reached his vessel they had to stand well away to avoid collision with a heavy stream of ice which filled a large portion of the adjacent sounds. When they got a little way into Barrow's Strait, they saw coming right towards them a schooner, which they first supposed to be the Felix, but afterwards found to be the American brig Advance. On the morning of the 24th, they were standing across to Cape Hurd, under a clear sky and with a moderate breeze, while a heavy pack was visible from the crow's nest, extending all along the coast of North Somerset, from outside of Leopold Island on the east, to the vicinity of Cape Rennell, where it appeared to enlarge, and began to take a curved direction toward Cape Hotham. The Advance was still behind them ; the Lady Franklin and the Sophia were to windward, struggling along shore in the vicinity of Radstock Bay ; and, as the day wore on, three more ships were observed at the mouth of Wellington Channel.

An hour before noon of the 25th, when the Prince Albert was off Cape Spencer, her officers saw that she must stop. An extensive pack was then a short distance ahead, broken only by a few lanes of water, through which the ships in advance had evidently passed ; and the wind was blowing in a direction, happily, quite favorable for carrying these ships rapidly on to the regions of most desirable search, but fitted also to make a prompt closure of the pack against any return that season to the east. If the Prince Albert should now go forward more than a mile or two, she might be suddenly caught by the ice, and helplessly and uselessly shut up for the winter. At noon, therefore, she bore up when about midway between Cape Spencer and Point Innes ; and then Mr. Snow went to the masthead to take a last view of the position and seeming prospects of the several exploring vessels.

Cape Hotham was seen to the west enveloped in a thick haze. The Assistance appeared some distance to the north-east of it, endeavoring to get to it, seemingly either in a hole of water or along a lane. The Lady Franklin was not far from the Assistance, but, probably, about mid-channel, either working toward Cape Hotham, or trying to get right away to the west. The Sophia, also under all sail, was some distance astern of the Lady Franklin, and more to the east. The Rescue was still further to the east, considerably in-shore, and apparently beset. All these vessels were among heavy ice. The Advance could not be seen, but was supposed to be behind one of the points of land ; and she was afterwards spoken in the vicinity of Cape Riley, close in-shore, fast to an iceberg. The Intrepid, too, was not then visible, but had been seen in the morning. All Wellington Channel, as far as the eye could reach, was filled with one solid pack, broken only here and there by a small lane. Some high land, appearing dim and filmy from haze and distance, was seen toward Cape Bowden, trending apparently to the north-west. One heavy pack extended athwart all the south-west, and seemed to be impenetrable. The only clear water visible lay immediately around the Prince Albert, and backward along the way by which she had come.

On the same day, soon after the Prince Albert had turned her bow homeward, a flag-staff, like a signal-post, was observed on Cape Riley. The officers, supposing this to have been set up by a party from some one of the exploration ships, sent a boat ashore to ascertain what it meant. A cylinder was found at the flag-staff, containing a notice that the officers of the Assistance and the Intrepid had landed on Cape Riley on the 23d ; that they had collected there distinct traces of an encampment by some party belonging to the royal navy of Britain ; that they had found traces of the same party on Beechey Island, and that they purposed to proceed thence to Cape Hotham and Cape Walker, in search of further traces.

The little boat-party from the Prince Albert were too zealous to be satisfied with this mere notice. They looked eagerly around, and soon observed five spots on which tents seemed to have been fixed, and also obtained a piece of navy rope, a piece of canvas, a chip of timber, and a number of meat-bones. These, all poor and pitiful though they might seem of themselves, seemed to throw so perceptible a light on at least the commencement of the mystery of the Franklin expedition, that they were esteemed a precious prize.

The Prince Albert arrived at Aberdeen on the 1st of October; and the relics from Cape Riley were speedily sent to the Admiralty, and subjected there to a rigorous scrutiny. The piece of rope was found to be of navy-yard manufacture, not later than 1841; the piece of canvas to have a corresponding character; the chip of timber to have a recent cut, with seemingly an European axe; the meat-bones to bear exactly the marks of a ship's provisions used about five years back; the reported tent-marks to be nearly such as might be expected from a party making a long stay for the purpose of scientific observation; and the entire circumstances of the traces on Cape Riley unaccountable by any known or supposable event, except a prolonged visit, in 1845 or 1846, by a party from the Erebus and the Terror.

The first traces of the missing ships were discovered by Captain Ommaney, in the Assistance, at Cape Riley, on the 23d August, 1850. The cape is a point at the eastern entrance of Wellington Channel; about three miles west of it rises the bold abrupt coast of Beechey Island; and between the shores of this isle and the mainland lies a bay to which extraordinary interest is now attached. On its coast were observed numerous sledge-tracks; and at Cape Spencer, about ten miles from Cape Riley, up Wellington Channel, the party discovered the ground-place of a tent, the floor neatly paved with small smooth stones.

Around the tent a number of birds' bones, as well as remnants of meat-canisters, seemed to indicate that it had been inhabited for some time as a shooting station and a look-out place, for which latter purpose it was admirably chosen, commanding a good view of Barrow's Strait and Wellington Channel.

Some sledge-tracks led northward for about twenty miles, but the trail ceased south of Cape Bowden, and an empty bottle and a piece of newspaper were the last things found. The results of examining Beechey Island must be given in more detail. Lieut. Osborne says: "A long point of land slopes gradually from the southern bluffs of this now deeply interesting island, until it almost connects itself with the land of North Devon, forming on either side of it two good and commodious bays. On this slope a multitude of preserved-meat-tins were strewed about; and near them, and on the ridge of the slope, a carefully-constructed cairn was discovered; it consisted of layers of fitted tins, filled with gravel, and placed to form a firm and solid foundation. Beyond this, and along the northern shore of Beechey Island, the following traces were then quickly discovered: the embankment of a house, with carpenters' and armorers' working-places, washing-tubs, coal-bags, pieces of old clothing, rope, — and, lastly, the graves of three of the crew of the Erebus and Terror, bearing date of the winter of 1845–6. *We, therefore, now had ascertained the first winter quarters of Sir John Franklin.*

"On the eastern slope of the ridge of Beechey Island a remnant of a garden (for remnant it now only was, having been dug up in the search) told an interesting tale; its neatly-shaped, oval outline — the border carefully formed of moss lichen, poppies, and anemones, transplanted from some more genial part of this dreary region — contrived still to show symptoms of vitality; but the seeds which, doubtless, they had sowed in the garden, had decayed away. Nearer to the beach, a heap of cinders and scraps of iron showed the armorers' working-place; and, along an old water-course, now chained up by frost, several tubs, constructed of the ends of salt-meat casks, left no doubt as to the washing-places of the men of Franklin's squadron. Happening to cross a level piece of ground, which as yet no one had lighted upon, I was pleased to see a pair of cashmere gloves laid out to dry, with two small stones on the palms to prevent their blowing away; they had been there since 1846. I took them up carefully, as melancholy mementoes of my missing friends. In another spot a flannel was discovered; and this, together with some things lying about, would, in my ignorance of wintering in the Arctic regions, have led me to suppose that there was considerable haste displayed in the departure of the Erebus and Terror from this spot, had not Captain Austin assured me that there was nothing to ground such a belief upon, and that, from experience, he could vouch for these being nothing more than the ordinary traces of a winter station; and this opinion was fully borne out by those officers who had, in the previous year, wintered in Port Leopold, one of them asserting that people left winter quarters too well pleased to escape, to care much for a handful of shavings, an old coal-bag, or a washing-tub."

The most interesting traces of winter residence were the graves of Franklin's three seamen. Each grave was marked by an oaken head and foot board, and the inscriptions were as follow:

"Sacred to the memory of J. Torrington, who departed this life January 1st, 1846, on board of H. M. S. Terror, aged 20 years."

"Sacred to the memory of J. Hartnell, A.B., of H. M. S. Erebus, died January 4th, 1846, aged 23 years.

Thus saith the Lord of Hosts, Consider your ways.— Haggai 1 : 7."

"Sacred to the memory of Wm. Braine, R.M., of H. M. S. Erebus, died April 3d, 1846, aged 32 years. *Choose ye this day whom ye will serve.*— Josh. 24 : 15."

Lieut. De Haven, of the Advance, landed on Cape Riley on the morning of the 25th August, where he examined the traces of Sir John Franklin, before described, and erected a second signal-post. On the same day the Prince Albert visited the place, and by her, as we have seen, the first intelligence of the discovery was carried to England. Afterwards Captain Penny and his officers examined Beechey Island and the whole neighborhood very carefully and minutely. But the thorough search made by all these parties failed to discover any memorandum or record to indicate Franklin's past efforts or future intentions.

All that can be learned from the traces discovered is, that Franklin's ships wintered, in 1845–6, on the south side of Beechey Island, and that three of his men died at that point. The mortality does not exceed that of previous expeditions ; and we may therefore conclude that the expedition was in highly effective order when it left that anchorage, with only a moderate inroad into its stock of preserved meats, the seven hundred empty tins found on the island forming but a small proportion of the twenty-four thousand canisters with which the ships were supplied.

How long Franklin's ships remained at Beechey Island, when and under what circumstances they left, and what course they pursued, are mere matters of conjecture, as to which various opinions have been formed. Some experienced officers believe that the expedition did not leave its winter anchorage till the end of August or beginning of September, 1846. It is also inferred, from some appearances, that it left suddenly; that probably a great and unexpected disruption of the ice had summoned the crews to resume progress in the ships; but this is contested by other officers of equal experience, who contend that there could have been no hurry in removing from Beechey Island, as everything bore the stamp of order and regularity, utterly forbidding the idea that Franklin had been forced away by the ice.

On the 8th September, 1850, most of the searching vessels got once more free from the ice, and unfurled their sails in open water, along the south side of Cornwallis Island. They bore boldly away, in the hope of penetrating well to the west, but were soon arrested by a vast floe, which extended from the south-west end of Griffith Island, as far as the eye could reach. They kept close to this, and strove with it, from the 10th till the 13th, and then began again to get forward; yet proceeded only a short distance, amid great embarrassment and severe exertion, when they were compelled to stick fast for the winter. The government ships were locked up in the ice between Cornwallis Island and Griffith Island; and all the others were sufficiently near to admit of easy communication among the whole squadron.

Arrangements were early made for performing exploratory journeys with sledges in spring. Captain Austin superintended those for the lands and islands along what may be called Parry's Strait, — the band of sea westward from Barrow's Strait to Melville Island, and the north end of Banks's Land; and Captain Penny undertook to conduct the search of Wellington Channel. Sledges were sent out, before the severest period of the winter, to place provisions in dépôt for the use of the explorers in spring; and exercises of walking and sledge-dragging were afterwards, in all favorable weather, practised near the ships, to keep the men vigorous, and to train them for their journeyings.

On the 12th of April the parties for the westward exploration, amounting to one hundred and four men, with fourteen sledges, were all ready, and proceeded, under the command of Captain Ommaney, to an encampment at the north-west end of Griffith Island. There they underwent a close inspection by Captain Austin, and spent three days in repose, and in waiting for the abatement of a tempestuous wind. On the evening of the 15th they united in a special prayer to the Divine Being for protection and guidance, and then, with enthusiastic determination, started on their arduous enterprise.

Six of the parties were "extended" ones, — to go to the utmost possible distance, — three along the south shore, and three along the north shore. The first sledge on the south shore, the Reliance, under Captain Ommaney, travelled four hundred and eighty miles, discovered two hundred and five miles of previously unknown coast, and was absent sixty days. The second, the True Blue, under Lieut. Osborne, travelled five hundred and six miles, discovered seventy miles of coast, and was absent fifty-eight days. And the third, the Enterprise, under Lieut. Browne, travelled three hundred and seventy-five miles, discovered one hundred and fifty miles of coast, and was absent forty-four days. In this travelling sails were occasionally hoisted on the sledges, and large kites were also attached. When the wind was high, these aids propelled the sledge very rapidly, and the whole of the party then rode; but when the wind fell, the sledges, with their provisions and stores, had to be dragged by main force over the ice by the men harnessed to them. The most western point reached was the extreme one of the True Blue, and is situated in west longitude 103° 25′, almost half way between Leopold Island and Point Turnagain on the American continent.

The first sledge on the north shore, the Lady Franklin, under the command of Lieut. Aldrich, travelled five hundred and fifty miles, discovered seventy miles of coast, and was absent sixty-two days. The second, the Perseverance, under the command of Lieut. M'Clintock, travelled seven hundred and sixty miles, discovered forty miles of coast, and was absent eighty days. And the third, the Resolute, under the command of Surgeon Bradford, travelled six hundred and sixty-nine miles, discovered one hundred and thirty-five miles of coast, and was absent eighty days. Lieut. M'Clintock's party achieved the furthest westing of the three ; and the furthest, indeed, which has ever been attained in the polar seas, — a point in latitude 74° 38′ and west longitude 114° 20′.

He left the ships on the 15th of April, and, taking a course due west, reached Point Griffith, on the eastern shore of Melville Island, on the 11th of May. On the 21st he sighted Winter Harbor ; but, there being neither ships, tents, nor any sign of human habitation, to be seen, he deferred any close scrutiny of it until his return. By the 27th of May he had reached Cape Dundas, at the western extremity of Melville Island ; and on the following day, ascending a high cliff, made out the coast of Banks's Land.

To the north of Banks's Land, at a distance from it of about seventy miles, he discovered a range of land apparently running nearly due west. "This does not present steep cliffs, but a bold and deeply indented coast ; the land rising to the interior, and intersected by valleys rather than ravines." The sea he imagined to continue to the westward. Following the coast of

SLEDGING WITH SAILS.

P. 278.

Melville Island to the north-east, he entered Liddon Gulf, and here saw fragments of coal of good quality. Leaving the shore, he crossed the gulf to gain Bushman Cove, where Parry, in his journey across the island, in 1820, had left the "strong but light cart," in which he had carried his tent and stores. On the 1st of June M'Clintock reached the west point of the cove, and, leaving two men to prepare supper, he commenced a search, with four others, for Parry's encampment of the 11th of June, 1820:

"On reaching the ravine leading into the cove," he says, "we spread across, and walked up, and easily found the encampment, although the pole had fallen down. The very accurate report published of his journey saved us much labor in finding the tin cylinder and ammunition. The crevices between the stones piled over them were filled with ice and snow; the powder completely destroyed, and cylinder eaten through with rust, and filled with ice. From the extreme difficulty of descending into such a ravine with any vehicle, I supposed that the most direct route, where all seemed equally bad, was selected; therefore sent the men directly up the northern bank, in search of the wheels which were left where the cart broke down. They fortunately found them at once; erected a cairn about the remains of the wall built to shelter the tent; placed a record on it, in one tin case within another. We then collected a few relics of our predecessors, and returned with the remains of the cart to our encampment. An excellent fire had been made with willow stems; and upon this a kettle, containing Parry's cylinder, was placed. As soon as the ice was thawed out of it, the record it contained was carefully taken out. I could only just distinguish the date. Had it been in a better state of preservation, I would have restored it to its lonely position."

As the weather was misty, M'Clintock did not explore the head of the gulf, but struck directly across the land for Winter Harbor. It was evident that no one had visited the place since Parry's departure, in 1820.

On the shore, above Winter Harbor, is a large sandstone bowlder, near the site of Parry's observatory, on the flat face of which Mr. Fisher, his surgeon, had cut this inscription :

His Britannic Majesty's
Ships HECLA and GRIPER,
Commanded by
W. E. Parry and Mr. Liddon,
Wintered in the adjacent
Harbor 1819–20.
A. Fisher, Sculpt.

This inscription, M'Clintock says, appeared quite fresh. A hare, discovered at the foot of this rock, was so tame that she entered the tent, and would almost allow the men to touch her. "I have never seen," he says, "any animal, in its natural state, so perfectly fearless of man ; and there cannot be a more convincing proof that our missing countrymen have not been here. A ptarmigan alighted on the rock, and was shot, without in the least disturbing puss as she sat beneath it."

M'Clintock carved the figures 1851 on the rock, and left it and the hare.

On the 6th June he left Winter Harbor, and reached the ships on the 4th of July. The latter part of his journey was fatiguing, from the extensive pools of water in the ice ; but all his men arrived in excellent health and spirits. He was out eighty days, and had travelled seven hundred and seventy miles. Several reindeer, musk-oxen, and bears, were shot, besides numerous birds ; and the food thus obtained was of very material importance to the people. They travelled when the cold was so intense that bottles of water, carried by the men in their breasts, froze after an hour or so; salt pork broke like suet, and rum thickened. This journey made it certain that Franklin had not passed west of the Parry Islands.

The other two parties moved in higher latitudes, and were stopped a little west of Sabine Island, yet they traversed tracts and encountered incidents of high interest.

The parties of less limited range than the "extended" ones deposited provisions, set up marks, made observations, ascertained positions, and effected minor explorations; and were absent during periods of from twelve to thirty-four days. They may seem to have had easier work than the others; yet they suffered more severely, for no fewer than twenty-eight of their men were frost-bitten, and one died from exhaustion and cold. The extended parties got back in good health, and needed only a little rest and comfort to repair the effects of their privation and fatigue. But not one of all the parties, near or remote, obtained the slightest trace of the missing adventurers; and Captain Austin, after receiving and considering well the reports of all, "arrived at the conclusion that the expedition under Sir John Franklin did not prosecute the object of its mission to the southward and westward of Wellington Strait."

The sledge-parties for the exploration of Wellington Channel amounted to six, and comprised forty-one men, and were officered by Captain Stewart, Messrs. Marshall, Reid, and J. Stuart, and Surgeons Sutherland and Goodsir. They started on the 17th of April, under the general superintendence of Captain Penny; but they soon encountered severe weather, and were buffeted and baffled by it for a series of days, and compelled to return; and on the 6th of May, after special prayer to God for support, they again started. Some coursed so far and so curvingly as to make a near approach to the most northerly of Captain Austin's parties; and all figured largely and respectably in the squadron's aggregate of exploits. But their chief feat — the feat, at least, of those on the channel and west of it — was a discovery which put a stop to their progress toward the north, and gave an entirely new complexion to the search in which they were engaged, — the discovery of a wide westward strait of open water, lying along the further side of the lands which flank Barrow's Strait and Parry's Strait.

Captain Penny personally shared in this discovery, and made great exertions to follow it up. The explorers, proceeding up Wellington Channel, arrived in latitude 75° 22′ at Cape Duhorn, and thence ten miles north-westward to Point Decision. Penny, on the 15th of May, went from this point, over the ice, north-west by north, to an island which he called Bailie Hamilton Island. The ice was in a very decayed state; and on the 17th, after travelling round the island, first in a north-easterly and next in a north-north-westerly direction, he arrived at the open strait, saw in it twenty-five miles of clear water, and discovered a headland fifteen miles distant, west by north, over-canopied by a dark sky, which indicated an expanse of open water on the further side. This point was found to be in latitude 76° 2′ and west longitude 95° 55′; and the strait received the name of Victoria Channel.

Penny hastened back to the ships for a boat, and used every exertion to have one promptly mounted on sledges and sent forward; but he did not get it up to the strait without vast effort, and some tantalizing delays. But at length he launched it, loaded it, and pushed off. He had proceeded only ten miles, when he was obliged to seek refuge in a bay from a westerly gale and a strong head sea; and he afterwards contended much and almost constantly with unfavorable winds and rapid tides; yet he succeeded in examining three hundred and ten miles of coast, and did not desist till his stock of provisions began to fail. He put about on the 20th of July, and made his way to the ships amid constant rain and tempest, insomuch that, in the route over the ice, he had to ford rapid streams.

Penny thus ranks high as a discoverer; but as to the immediate object of his adventures, he had all his labor for nothing. He found not a trace of the Erebus and the Terror; yet he confirmed his convictions that they had gone up Wellington Channel and along Victoria Channel.

The American explorers were prevented from taking any part in the searching operations of the spring, by their experiencing the same kind of involuntary ejection from Lancaster Sound which befell Sir James Ross's expedition in the Enterprise and the Investigator. Their vessels were frozen in opposite Wellington Channel, and were carried thence to the east, slowly and rigidly, and in stern defiance of all possible resistance by man, to a point south of Cape Walsingham. They drifted a linear distance of at least one thousand and fifty miles, and suffered much from the commotion of the ice, and were not set free till the 10th of June.

Captain Austin seems to have concurred with Sir John Ross in the opinion that the Erebus and the Terror had gone back to Baffin's Bay. After the failure of searches for further traces of them west and north of the mouth of Wellington Channel, Austin supposed that they probably tried to reach the Polar Sea through Jones's

Sound, which opens off the north side of the upper part of Baffin's Bay. He accordingly went round to that place with his two steamers, and explored it. He found it about sixty miles wide at the entrance, — a width which greatly exceeds that given it in the Admiralty charts; and he sailed about forty-five miles up its southern shore, and was there arrested by a fixed barrier of ice; and he then sailed along the face of that barrier, twenty-five miles, to the northern shore, and traced that shore down to the entrance. But he saw nothing to indicate that the Erebus and the Terror had been there; and he judged, from well-defined appearances to the west, that the sound is closed by land not very far above the point which he reached, and has no communication with the Polar Sea. He then thought all further attempts at exploration either useless or inconsistent with his instructions, and set sail for England, where he arrived in the autumn of 1851.

ESQUIMAUX KAYAK.

CHAPTER XIV.

FURTHER PARTICULARS OF THE SEARCHING EXPEDITIONS. — SIR JOHN ROSS'S VOYAGE. — RESULTS. — CARRIER-PIGEONS. — PENNY'S EXPEDITION. — DR. SUTHERLAND'S SCIENTIFIC OBSERVATIONS. — GLACIERS AND ICEBERGS. — WINTER CLIMATE. — ANECDOTES. — ESQUIMAUX DOGS. — USE OF SNOW. — FIRST GRINNELL EXPEDITION. — ADVENTURES IN THE ICE. — WINTER IN THE ARCTIC OCEAN. — DANGEROUS DRIFTING. — BREAKING UP OF THE ICE. — RETURN.

Having sketched generally in the last chapter the progress of the vessels which coöperated, in 1850, in prosecuting the search for Sir John Franklin from the direction of Baffin's Bay, we shall now take up each expedition separately, and present such further details as may tend to add interest and completeness to our history of their proceedings.

Of the four vessels comprising the squadron of Commodore Austin, and also of the Prince Albert, we have already related all that is important, concluding with their safe return to England.

Sir John Ross, in the Felix discovery yacht, with her tender, the Mary, after obtaining an Esquimaux interpreter at Holsteinborg, and calling at Whale Fish Islands, proceeded northward through Waygat's Straits, and overtook Commodore Austin's squadron on the 11th of August, 1850. Arrangements were made with that officer for a combined examination of every part of the eastern side of a north-west passage, in which it was probable that the missing ships could be found. On the

13th of August, in company with Lieut. Cator in the Intrepid, Ross held communication with a party of Esquimaux near Cape York, who told him a story, the purport of which, according to his interpreter, was that in the winter of 1846 two ships were crushed in the ice in the direction of Cape Dudley Digges, and afterwards burned by a fierce tribe of natives; and that their crews, some of whom were described as wearing epaulets, were subsequently killed by the natives. Although Mr. Petersen, the interpreter attached to the Lady Franklin, which lay a few miles off, wholly discredited this story, and gave a translation of the Esquimaux communication wholly at variance with the other, it was thought of sufficient consequence by Capt. Austin to merit an investigation. Meantime the further information was received that a ship had passed the last winter safely housed in Wolstenholme Sound. A party, taking both interpreters, was accordingly sent to examine Wolstenholme Sound; and by them it was ascertained that the ship which wintered there was no other than the North Star, and that in all probability that circumstance was the whole foundation of the Esquimaux story, whatever it might have been. Nevertheless, Sir John Ross, who was long ago noted for "jumping at conclusions," still seems to have had a lingering belief that in this wild tale he had learned the fate of the Erebus and Terror. It was perhaps this belief which led him soon after to announce his intention of returning to England; and even after his arrival there he is said to have adhered to his theory that Franklin and his companions perished in Baffin's Bay. He pressed on to Cape Riley, however, before leaving the field of discovery, and bore his part in the search there made for traces of the missing navigators.

There is little more to relate concerning his expedition. The only results of which we have any account are stated by himself to be that he was able to make "many important corrections and valuable additions to the charts of the much-frequented eastern side of Baffin's Bay, which," he adds, "has been more closely observed and navigated by this than by any former expedition; and, much to my satisfaction, confirming the latitude and longitude of every headland I had the opportunity of laying down in the year 1818."

One interesting incident, however, is worthy of mention before we take leave of Sir John Ross. When he left England on this expedition, he took with him four carrier-pigeons belonging to a lady in Ayrshire, intending to liberate two of them when the state of the ice rendered it necessary to lay his vessel up for the winter, and the other two when he discovered Sir John Franklin. A pigeon made its appearance at the dove-cot in Ayrshire, on the 13th of October, which the lady recognized by marks and circumstances that left no doubt on her mind of its being one of the younger pair presented by her to Sir John. It carried no billet, but there were indications, in the loss of feathers on the breast, of one having been torn from under the wing. Though it is known that the speed of pigeons is equal to one hundred miles an hour, the distance from Melville Island to Ayrshire, being, in a direct line, about twenty-four hundred miles, is so great, that evidence of the bird having been sent off as early as the 10th of October was required before it could be believed that no mistake was made in the identification of the individual that came to the dove-cot. It was afterwards ascertained that Sir John Ross despatched the youngest pair on the 6th or 7th of October, 1850, in a basket suspended to a balloon, during a W. N. W. gale. By the contrivance of a slow-match, the birds were to be liberated at the end of twenty-four hours. The reader can form his own opinion as to the identity of the pigeon in question.

We have already alluded to Captain Penny's expedition, fitted out by Lady Franklin. His little vessels, the Lady Franklin and the Sophia, entered Davis's Strait on the 26th of April, 1850 ; but they did not get into the open water at the head of Baffin's Bay until the 18th of August. Nearly four months they were squeezed about among the drifting ice in this tedious and terrible passage, sometimes closely wedged on the shore-ice, and sometimes tracking by manual labor through the breaking pack. Some facts of a scientific interest are mentioned by Dr. Sutherland, who accompanied Penny.

The first great difficulty the Arctic voyager has to contend with is the capricious state of the navigation in the grand approach to the Polar Sea. The melting of the ice and snow in the north of Baffin's Bay produces a continuous stream of water, which flows steadily to the south. As soon as this current leaves the projecting points at the head of the bay, a thin film of ice is formed on it. This ice gets thicker and thicker as it moves southwards, by congealing new layers of sea-water on its under surface, and by storing up snow and sleet above, until it becomes what the whaler calls the middle-ice of the bay. In winter it extends from shore to shore ; but in summer it is separated from the Greenland coast by an open lane of water, in consequence of its connection with the fringe of land, ice being dissolved where northerly winds prevail. An open space of water is always left by this southward drift of the ice-pack at the northern extremity of Baffin's Bay ; the extent of the space varies, however, with the season. In winter, it is diminished by the shooting out of the land-ice towards the drift, and the quickened formation of the young ice ; in summer, it is increased by the breaking up of the land-ice, and the arrest of the formation of young ice. The great object of the mariner bound to Lancaster Sound is to push his way through the open lane of water along the Greenland coast, and to get round the northern extremity of the drift-ice. But he finds this to be no easy task: every southerly gale crushes the ice in upon the shores of the bay, and squeezes any unfortunate vessel chancing to be placed therein before it, often wedging it up immovably, or even breaking it to pieces under the violence of the nip. The only resource of the captive voyager, under such circumstances, is to seek a refuge beneath the lee of some huge ice-mountain that has grounded a mile or two off the land, or to take timely warning, and cut docks in the solid land-floe, into which he may retire when the pressure comes. The driving iceberg is, however, a fearful neighbor, if the water prove not shallow enough to arrest its movement; for it will then sometimes plough its onward way through miles and miles of field and pack ice, heaving up the frozen masses before its tremendous impulse, and sweeping everything away that opposes its course.

According to Dr. Sutherland, there is more chance of an easy passage to the open water at the head of Baffin's Bay early in the season, before the shore-ice is much broken, and when the middle-ice moves away from it bodily, without any intervening detritus, than later in the season, when there is a greater quantity of loosened ice to be packed into the channel.

The entire length of the Baffin's Bay coast of Greenland is indented with bays and fiords, towards which glaciers descend from the higher interior land. At Cape Farewell the termination of the glacier-ice is still miles away from the sea; between Cape Farewell and Cape York, the land, devoid of the incursions of glacier-ice, gets narrower and narrower. North of Cape York the ice-stream projects into the sea itself, even beyond the line of prominent headlands. It is from this region that the vast icebergs, drifted out into the open Atlantic by the southward current, are derived; for it is a singular fact that there is no glacier-ice along the shores westward of Lancaster Sound. All the snow which there falls, even so far north as 77° latitude, escapes to the sea in streams of water, carrying with them vast quantities of mud and shingle. The land on both sides of Barrow's Strait is composed of limestone; but Greenland, and the coasts which form Davis's Strait, Baffin's Bay, and Lancaster Sound, where the fallen snow is retained for ages before it slips, as the solid glacier, back to the ocean, are all made of hard crystalline rock. Dr. Sutherland thinks that this difference of mineral constitution may in some way affect the temperature, and so determine the abundance of glaciers in the one position, and their absence in the other.

We may here remark that the ice which obstructs the navigation of the Arctic seas is of two kinds: the one produced by the congelation of fresh, and the other by that of salt water. In those inhospitable tracts, the snow, which annually falls on the islands or continents, being again dissolved by the progress of the summer's heat, pours forth numerous rills and limpid streams, which collect along the indented shores, and in the deep bays enclosed by precipitous rocks. There this clear and gelid water soon freezes, and every successive year supplies an additional investing crust, till, after the lapse, perhaps, of several centuries, the icy mass rises at last to the size and aspect of a mountain, commensurate with the elevation of the adjoining cliffs. The melting of the snow, which is afterwards deposited on such enormous blocks, likewise contributes to their growth;

and, by filling up the accidental holes or crevices, it renders the whole structure compact and uniform. Meanwhile the principle of destruction has already begun its operations. The ceaseless agitation of the sea gradually wears and undermines the base of the icy mountain, till at length, by the action of its own accumulated weight, when it has perhaps attained an altitude of a thousand or even two thousand feet, it is torn from its frozen chains, and precipitated, with a tremendous plunge, into the abyss below. This mighty launch now floats like a lofty island on the ocean; till, driven southwards by winds and currents, it insensibly wastes and dissolves away in the wide Atlantic. Icebergs have been known to drift from Baffin's Bay to the Azores.

Such is believed to be the real origin of the icy mountains or icebergs, entirely similar in their formation to the glaciers which occur on the flanks of the Alps and the Pyrenees. They consist of a clear, compact, and solid ice, having the fine green tint, verging to blue, which ice or water, when very pure and of a sufficient depth, generally assumes. From the cavities of these icebergs the crews of the northern whalers are accustomed, by means of a hose or flexible tube of canvas, to fill their casks easily with the finest and softest water.

The projecting tongues of the glaciers are not dissolved where they extend into the sea, but broken off by a species of "flotation." Heavy spring-tides are driven into the head of the bay, and up the fiords, by strong southerly winds; and the buoyant ice is heaved up by the rising water, and broken off from its parent stream. The floating power of large masses of ice must be enormous. Dr. Sutherland observed upon a small island, at an elevation of forty feet, a block of granite that measured sixteen feet in length, and must have contained at least one hundred and eighty-six tons of solid rock! He calculated that a cube of ice, forty feet across the side, could easily have carried off this burden in water seven fathoms deep. Icebergs thus broken off from the parent glacier were often observed tumbling about in the sea. Some of these were four times bigger than St. Paul's Cathedral, and shrouded themselves in a veil of spray as they rolled over, emitting sounds that could only be compared to terrific thunder-peals, and turning up the blue mud from depths of two and three hundred fathoms. Oscillations in the sea were produced by such disturbances, which, after travelling a dozen miles, pounded into fragments the ice-field on which they ultimately fell.

While icebergs are the slow growth of ages, the fields or shoals of saline ice are annually formed and destroyed. The ice generated from melted snow is hard, pellucid, and often swells to an enormous height and dimensions. But the concretion of salt water wants solidity, clearness, and strength, and never attains to any very considerable thickness. It seldom floats during more than part of the year; though, in some cold seasons, the scattered fragments may be surprised by the early frost, and preserved till the following summer.

Captain Penny's expedition reached the entrance of Wellington Channel on the 25th of August. On the 14th of September young ice formed round the ships; and they were compelled to take up their winter quarters in Assistance Bay, near the south-west point of Wellington Channel. Captain Austin's squadron, of four ships, was fixed on Griffith's Island, a few miles further west. November 7th, the sun was beneath the horizon at noon, the thermometer was seven degrees below zero, and the sea-ice three feet thick. January 13th, mercury froze for the first time. At the end of January the ice was five feet thick. The sun rose

FLOATING ICEBERGS. P. 292.

above the southern horizon for an instant at noon, February 7th. February 24th was the coldest day, the thermometer sinking forty-five degrees below zero. April 3d, the ice was seven feet thick. In the beginning of May it attained its maximum thickness of seven feet nine inches. June 12th, the thermometer rose to 55°, the highest point of the season. Two days after, the first rain fell. At the end of June small streams of water began to flow from the land. At the end of July the sea-ice was diminished to a thickness of four feet by the melting of the upper surface. August 8th, the bay-ice broke up, and set the ships free, after eleven months' close detention. Four days afterwards, the young ice began again to form on the sea at night.

Throughout this winter of intense cold, the temperature of the sea remained nearly uniform. It never sank so low as twenty-nine degrees. A hole was kept open through the ice, near the ships, for the purpose of observing the water, as well as for noticing the rise and fall of the tides. The ice invariably increased its thickness by additions to its lower surface. As the sea-water froze, a considerable portion of its salt was separated from it, and blown along the surface of the ice, mixing with the fresh-fallen snow as it went. On this account snow-wreaths could never be used for melting into water; the snow on the land often contained traces of salt, miles away from the sea. The sea-ice hardly ever contained more than one quarter the quantity of salt found in an equal volume of sea-water.

The interior of the ships was warmed to between forty and fifty degrees. This was found to be the highest limit of safety ; in it, the hoar-frost was never thawed in the beds ; the blankets and night-caps of the sleepers often adhered inconveniently to the ships' planks. With a higher temperature, the vapor of the interior of the ships was deposited in the beds as moisture instead of ice, and then rheumatic attacks were troublesome among the crew. With this range, the difference of heat experienced on going into the open air often amounted to one hundred degrees.

Much less food was consumed during the winter's rest than during the labors of summer. On this account, the provisions were served out without weighing, and considerable weekly savings were effected. The men took instinctively just what nourishment the waste of their bodies required.

A vast abundance of the lower forms of life was found everywhere in the inclement region in which the ships sojourned. Small cavities, from two to six feet deep, studded the under surface of the sea-ice. A greenish, slimy substance, composed of animalcules and microscopic plants, was found in these. The cavities, in fact, had been hollowed out by the higher temperature attendant upon the vital action going on in these minute creatures. The most intense cold seemed to have the power of destroying some kinds of life-germs. Mity cheese, that had been exposed throughout the winter, never again manifested any return of crawling propensity.

The influence of solar light was exceedingly small during the depth of winter. A little trace of daylight was always perceptible at noon; but for seven days before and after the 22d of December, chloride of silver was not blackened by exposure to the south horizon. On the 1st of January it began to assume a slight leaden tinge. Mustard and cresses were reared with great care; but the young plants were composed of ninety-four per cent. of water, and contained only half the quantity of nutritious and antiscorbutic matters that had been present in the seeds.

The men were kept amused during the winter by theatrical representations, balls, and masquerades, after Captain Parry's example; but the schools and libraries were the most valuable auxiliaries in preventing ennui. Geographical studies were especially popular. After the nightly lessons, it was often necessary to settle forecastle disputes as to the insular character of Cape Horn, the Roman Catholic faith of the Chinese, and the identity of the crocodiles of the Nile with the alligators of the Mississippi.

Far from the least interesting members of this Arctic community were a kennel of Esquimaux dogs, that had been established in a snow-hut near the ships. The four oldest had accompanied Mr. Petersen, the Danish interpreter, from Greenland. But these had thriven and multiplied amid the congenial scenes of ice and snow, so that complete teams for two sledges could be furnished out in spring. They were great favorites among the seamen, and flocked eagerly round the first person who emerged from the snow-covered ships in the morning. They were, nevertheless, of highly jealous temperament; for, if one of them chanced to receive more notice than his companions, the lucky fellow was forthwith attacked by the rest of the pack. This so constantly occurred, that some of the cunning young dogs became afraid of the men's caresses, and ran away the moment any marked demonstrations of kindness were directed towards them.

In many points, amusing instances of the adaptation of canine instinct to the necessities of Arctic life were displayed. In fine, sunny weather, the dogs satisfied their thirst by lapping the surface snow; but in colder periods of the season they burrowed some inches down for their supply of frozen water. In extremely severe weather, they constantly coiled themselves closely up, and covered their noses with the shaggy fur of their tails. At these times, they never rose even to shake off the accumulating wreaths of falling snow; if their masters called them, they answered by turning their eyes, but without removing their natural respirators from their nostrils, and no demonstration, short of a determined kick, could make them shift their quarters; but, at other times, they lay stretched out at full length, and were on their legs in obedience to the first tone of a familiar voice.

The young dogs had to learn some painful experiences. The first time they were taken to the open water, they mistook it for ice, coolly walked into it, and were nearly drowned. One poor fellow undertook to lick a tempting morsel of fat from an iron shovel, when, greatly to his surprise, the cold metal stuck fast to his tongue, and he dragged the shovel along for some distance, at last only extricating himself from it by a strong effort, and at the expense of leaving some inches of mucous membrane behind him. When the dogs were employed in sledging-work, it was no uncommon thing for them to start off with their loads in full pursuit of bears. In the spring, two carrier-pigeons were despatched in the car of a small balloon. The balloon fell upon the ice, while still in sight, and dragged along for some distance. An object that was so full of interest to their masters could not, by any means, be slighted by the dogs; in a moment they were all off after it, the men following them pell-mell to save the pigeons. The four-footed animals had by far the best of the race; but the balloon, fortunately for its freight, cleared the edge of the ice just as they came up with it. When the ice around the ships broke up, the dogs understood the indication, and galloped about in mad joy, leaping from piece to piece, and whining restlessly, or swimming round the ship until they were picked up and established upon the decks.

The Esquimaux dog is described as resembling in form the shepherd's dog, rising to the height of the Newfoundland, but broad like the mastiff; having short pricked ears, a furry coat, and a bushy tail. In general they are observed to bear a strong resemblance to the wolf, and the opinion is even prevalent that the former exhibit only the latter in a tamed state; but the avidity with which the wolf devours his supposed brethren does not seem quite consistent with so close an affinity. Frequent beatings are necessary to train these dogs for acting as a regular team. But their greatest sufferings respect the want of food. Captain Parry saw one which ate a large piece of canvas, a cotton handkerchief laid out to dry, and a piece of a linen shirt. When these animals are yoked in the sledge, a whip of twenty feet long enforces obedience; while peculiar cries indicate the right or left, to turn, or to stop.

A singular fact is related in Dr. Sutherland's journal in regard to the use of snow for allaying thirst: "The use of snow when persons are thirsty does not by any means allay the insatiable desire for water; on the contrary, it appears to be increased in proportion to the quantity used, and the frequency with which it is put into the mouth. For example: a person walking along feels intensely thirsty, and he looks to his feet with coveting eyes; but his sense and firm resolutions are not to be overcome so easily, and he withdraws the open hand that was to grasp the delicious morsel and convey it into his parching mouth. He has several miles of a journey to accomplish, and his thirst is every moment increasing; he is perspiring profusely, and feels quite hot and oppressed. At length his good resolutions stagger, and he partakes of the smallest particle, which produces a most exhilarating effect; in less than ten minutes he tastes again and again, always increasing the quantity; and in half an hour he has a gum-stick of condensed snow, which he masticates with avidity, and replaces with assiduity the moment that it has melted away. But his thirst is not allayed in the slightest degree; he is as hot as ever, and still perspires; his mouth is in flames, and he is driven to the necessity of quenching them with snow, which adds fuel to the fire. The melting snow ceases to please the palate, and it feels like red-hot coals, which, like a fire-eater, he shifts about with his tongue, and swallows without the addition of saliva. He is in despair; but habit has taken the place of his reasoning faculties, and he moves on with languid steps, lamenting the severe fate which forces him to persist in a practice which in an unguarded moment he allowed to begin. . . . I believe the true cause of such intense thirst is the extreme dryness of the air when the temperature is low."

The result of Captain Penny's labors, so far as exploration is concerned, is already known. Sledging parties went out in the spring. A large whaling-boat was dragged bodily up Wellington Channel, and launched in the clear water beyond the ice-barrier. Two thousand miles were travelled over, seven hundred and ten of which were in districts seen for the first time by human eyes. No further traces of the missing expedition were, however, found. The Lady Franklin and Sophia left Assistance Bay, homeward bound, on the 12th of August; five weeks afterwards, they were in the Thames.

We have seen that Mr. Grinnell's expedition was undertaken with two small brigs — the Advance and the Rescue. The Advance was intended originally for carrying heavy castings from an iron foundery. Both vessels were strengthened with great skill and at large expense for the Arctic service. The vessels were placed under the command of Lieut. De Haven. His officers consisted of Mr. Murdoch, sailing-master; Dr. E. K. Kane, surgeon and naturalist; and Mr. Lovell, midshipman. The Advance had a crew of twelve men when she sailed; but two of them complaining of sickness, and expressing a desire to return home, were left at the Danish settlement at Disco Island, on the coast of Greenland.

The expedition passed the eastern extremity of Newfoundland, June 3d, 1850, ten days after leaving Sandy Hook, and then sailed east-north-east, directly for Cape Comfort, on the coast of Greenland. The weather was generally fine; and only a single accident occurred on the voyage to that country of frost and snow. Off the coast of Labrador they met an iceberg making its way toward the tropics. The night was very dark; and the Advance, going at the rate of seven or eight knots an hour, ran against the huge voyager, and lost her jib-boom.

The voyagers did not land at Cape Comfort, but, turning northward, sailed along the south-west coast of Greenland, sometimes in an open sea, and sometimes in the midst of broad acres of broken ice (particularly in Davis's Straits), as far as Whale Island. From this place a boat, with two officers and four seamen, was sent to Disco Island, a distance of about twenty-six miles, to a Danish settlement there, to procure skin clothing and other articles necessary for use during the rigors of a polar winter. The officers were entertained at the government house, while the seamen were comfortably lodged with the Esquimaux, sleeping in fur bags at night. They returned to the ship the following day, and the expedition proceeded on its voyage. When passing the little Danish settlement of Upernavik, they were boarded by natives for the first time. They were out in government whale-boats, hunting for ducks and seals. These hardy children of the Arctic Circle were not shy, for through the Danes, the English whalers, and government expeditions, they had become acquainted with men of other latitudes.

When the expedition reached Melville Bay, which, on account of its fearful character, is also called the Devil's Nip, the voyagers began to witness more of the grandeur and perils of Arctic scenes. Icebergs of all dimensions came bearing down from the polar seas like vast squadrons, and the roar of their rending came over the waters like the booming of the heavy broadsides of contending navies. They also encountered immense floes, with only narrow channels between; and at times their situation was exceedingly perilous.

On one occasion, after heaving through fields of ice for five consecutive weeks, two immense floes, between which they were making their way, gradually approached each other; and for several hours they expected their tiny vessels — tiny when compared with the mighty objects around them — would be crushed. An immense *calf* of ice, six or eight feet thick, slid under the Rescue, lifting her almost "high and dry," and careening her partially upon her beam ends. By means of ice-anchors (large iron hooks) they kept her from capsizing. In this position they remained about sixty hours, when, with saws and axes, they succeeded in relieving her. The ice now opened a little, and they finally warped through into clear water. While they were thus confined, polar bears came around them in abundance, greedy for prey, and the seamen indulged a little in the perilous sports of the chase.

The open sea continued but a short time, when they again became entangled among bergs, floes, and hummocks, and encountered the most fearful perils. Sometimes they anchored their vessels to icebergs, and sometimes to floes and to masses of hummock. On one of these occasions, while the cook, an active Frenchman, was upon a berg, making a place for an anchor, the mass of ice split beneath him, and he was dropped through the yawning fissure into the water, a distance of almost thirty feet. Fortunately, the masses, as is often the case, did not close up again, but floated apart, and the poor cook was hauled on board more dead than alive, from excessive fright. It was in this fearful region that they first encountered pack-ice, and there they were locked in from the 7th to the 23d of July.

While in this situation they were joined by the British yacht Prince Albert, under Captain Forsyth, and together the three vessels were anchored, for a while, to an immense field of ice, in sight of the Devil's Thumb, a high, rocky peak, situated in latitude 74° 22′. It was now about thirty miles distant, and, with the dark hills adjacent, presented a strange aspect where all was white and glittering. The peak and the hills are masses of rock, with occasionally a lichen or a moss growing upon their otherwise naked surfaces. In the midst of the vast ice-field loomed up many lofty *bergs*, all of them in slow and majestic motion.

From the Devil's Thumb the American vessels passed onward through the pack toward Sabine's Islands, while the Prince Albert essayed to make a more westerly course. They reached Cape York at the beginning of August. Far across the ice, landward, they discovered, through their glasses, several men, apparently making signals; and for a while they rejoiced in the belief that they saw a portion of Sir John Franklin's companions. Four men were despatched, with a whaleboat, to reconnoitre. They soon discovered the men to be Esquimaux, who, by signs, professed great friendship, and endeavored to get the voyagers to accompany them to their homes beyond the hills. They declined; and, as soon as they returned to the vessel, the expedition again pushed forward, and made its way to Cape Dudley Digges, which they reached on the 7th of August.

At Cape Dudley Digges they sighted the Crimson Cliffs, a name suggested by the patches of red snow, which in the distance impart a rose-hue color to the acclivities. These lofty cliffs are of dark brown stone. It was a magnificent sight, in that cold region, to see such an apparently warm object standing out in bold relief against the dark blue back-ground of a polar sky. This was the most northern point to which the expedition penetrated. The whole coast which they had passed from Disco to this cape is high, rugged, and barren, only some of the low points, stretching into the sea, bearing a species of dwarf fir. North-east from the cape rise the Arctic Highlands, to an unknown altitude; and, stretching away northward, was the then unexplored Smith's Sound, filled with impenetrable ice.

From Cape Dudley Digges, the Advance and Rescue, beating against wind and tide in the midst of the ice-fields, made Wolstenholme Sound, and then, changing their course to the south-west, emerged from the fields into the open waters of Lancaster Sound. Here, on the 18th of August, 1850, they encountered a tremendous gale, which lasted about twenty-four hours. The two vessels parted company during the storm, and remained separate several days. Across Lancaster Sound, the Advance made her way to Barrow's Straits, and on the 22d discovered the Prince Albert on the southern shore of the straits, near Leopold Island, a mass of lofty, precipitous rocks, dark and barren, and hooded and draped with snow. The weather was fine, and soon the officers and crews of the two vessels met in friendly greeting. Those of the Prince Albert were much astonished at the encounter. They had left the Americans in Melville Bay on the 6th, pressing northward through the pack; and could not conceive how they so soon and safely penetrated it, when the Prince, though towed by a steamer, had made such poor progress. Captain Forsyth had attempted to reach a particular point, where he intended to remain through the winter; but, finding the passage thereto completely blocked up with ice, he had resolved, on the very day when the Americans appeared, to return home.

The two vessels remained together a day or two, when they parted company, the Prince Albert to return to England, and the Advance to make further explorations. Off Leopold Island, on the 23d of August, the Advance took the lead through the vast masses of floating ice. "The way was before them," says Mr. Snow, of the Prince Albert, who stood upon the deck of the Advance; "the stream of ice had to be either gone through boldly, or a long *detour* made; and, despite the heaviness of the stream, they pushed the vessel through in her proper course. Two or three shocks, as she came in contact with some large pieces, were unheeded; and the moment the last block was past the bow, the officer sang out, 'So! steady as she goes on her course;' and came aft as if nothing more than ordinary sailing had been going on. I observed our own little bark nobly following in the American's wake; and, as I afterward learned, she got through it pretty well, though not without much doubt of the propriety of keeping on in such procedure after the 'mad Yankee,' as he was called by our mate."

From Leopold Island the Advance proceeded to the

north-west, and on the 25th reached Cape Riley, another amorphous mass, not so regular and precipitate as Leopold Island, but more lofty. Here a strong tide, setting in to the shore, drifted the Advance toward the beach, where she stranded. Around her were small bergs and large masses of floating ice, all under the influence of the strong current. It was about two o'clock in the afternoon when she struck. By diligent labor in removing everything from her deck to a small floe, she was so lightened, that at four o'clock the next morning she floated, and soon everything was properly replaced.

Near Cape Riley the Americans fell in with a portion of an English expedition; and there also the Rescue, left behind in the gale in Lancaster Sound, overtook the Advance. There was Captain Penny, with the Sophia and Lady Franklin; the veteran Sir John Ross, with the Felix, and Commodore Austin, with his flag-ship the Resolute. Together the navigators of both nations explored the coast at and near Cape Riley, and on the 27th they saw in a cove on the shore of Beechey Island, or Beechey Cape, on the east side of the entrance to Wellington Channel, unmistakable evidence that Sir John Franklin and his companions were there in April, 1846. There they found the articles known to belong to Franklin's ships, as described in the preceding chapter. They also visited the graves, the inscriptions on which we have already given.

How much later than April 3d (the date upon one of the head-boards) Franklin remained at Beechey, cannot be determined. There were evidences of his having gone northward, for sledge-tracks in that direction were visible. It was the opinion of Dr. Kane that, on the breaking up of the ice in the spring, Sir John Franklin passed northward with his ships through Wellington

Channel into the great polar basin, and that he did not return. This, too, was the opinion of Captain Penny, who zealously urged the British government to send a powerful screw steamer to pass through that channel and explore the coasts beyond.

Leaving Beechey Cape, the American expedition forced its way through the ice to Barlow's Inlet, where they narrowly escaped being frozen in for the winter. They endeavored to enter the inlet, for the purpose of

ADVANCE AND RESCUE IN BARLOW'S INLET.

making it their winter quarters, but were prevented by the mass of pack-ice at its entrance.

It was on the 4th of September, 1850, when the Advance and Rescue arrived at Barlow's Inlet; but, after remaining seven or eight days, they abandoned the attempt to enter. On the right and left of the entrance were dark rocks, in the centre the frozen waters, and beyond, a range of hills. There was much smooth ice within the inlet, and, while the vessels lay anchored to the "field," officers and crew exercised and amused themselves by skating. On the left of the inlet they discovered a cairn (a heap of stones with a cavity), eight or ten feet in height, which was erected by Capt. Ommaney, of the English expedition then in the polar waters. Within it he had placed two letters, for "whom it might concern." Commander De Haven also deposited a letter there. It is believed to be the only post-office in the world free for the use of all nations. The rocks here presented vast fissures made by the frost; and at the foot of the cliff on the right that powerful agent had cast down vast heaps of *débris*.

From Barlow's Inlet the American expedition moved slowly westward, battling with the ice every rood of the way, until they reached Griffin's Island, at about 96° west longitude from Greenwich. This was attained on the 11th of September, and was the extreme westing made by the expedition. All beyond seemed impenetrable ice; and, despairing of making any further discoveries before the winter should set in, they resolved to return home. Turning eastward, they hoped to reach Davis's Straits by the southern route, before the cold and darkness came on; but they were doomed to disappointment. Near the entrance to Wellington Channel they became completely locked in by hummock-ice, and soon found themselves drifting with an irresistible tide up that channel toward the pole.

Now began the most perilous adventures of the navigators. The summer day was drawing to a close; the diurnal visits of the pale sun were rapidly shortening, and soon the long polar night, with all its darkness and horrors, would fall upon them. Slowly they drifted in those vast fields of ice, whither, or to what result, they knew not. Locked in the moving yet compact mass; liable every moment to be crushed; far away from land; the mercury sinking daily lower and lower from the zero figure, toward the point where that metal freezes, they felt small hope of ever reaching home again. Yet they prepared for winter comforts and winter sports, as cheerfully as if lying safe in Barlow's Inlet. As the winter advanced, the crews of both vessels went on board the larger one. They unshipped the rudders of each to prevent their being injured by the ice, covered the deck of the Advance with felt, prepared their stores, and made arrangements for enduring the long winter, now upon them. Physical and mental activity being necessary for the preservation of health, they daily exercised in the open air for several hours. They built ice huts, hunted the huge white bears and the little polar foxes, and, during the darkness of the winter night, they arranged in-door amusements and employments.

Before the end of October, the sun made its appearance for the last time, and the awful polar night closed in. Early in November they wholly abandoned the Rescue, and both crews made the Advance their permanent winter home. The cold soon became intense; the mercury congealed, and the spirit thermometer indicated 46° below zero. Its average range was 30° to 35°. They had drifted helplessly up Wellington Channel almost to the latitude from whence Captain Penny saw an open sea, supposed to be the great polar basin, where there is a more genial clime than that which intervenes between the Arctic Circle and the 75th degree. Here, when almost in sight of the open ocean, that mighty polar tide, with its vast masses of ice, suddenly ebbed, and our little vessels were carried back, as resistlessly as before, through Barrow's Straits, into Lancaster Sound. All this while the immense fields of hummock-ice were moving, and the vessels were in hourly danger of being crushed and destroyed. At length, while drifting through Barrow's Straits, the congealed mass, as if crushed together by the opposite shores, became more compact, and the Advance was elevated almost seven feet by the stern, and keeled two feet eight inches, starboard. In this position she remained, with very little alteration, for five consecutive months; for, soon after entering Baffin's Bay in the midst of the winter, the ice became frozen in one immense tract, covering millions of acres.

Thus frozen in, sometimes more than a hundred miles from land, they drifted slowly along the south-west coast of Baffin's Bay, a distance of more than a thousand miles from Wellington Channel. For eleven weeks that dreary night continued, and during that time the disc of the sun was never seen above the horizon. Yet nature was not wholly forbidding in aspect. Sometimes the aurora borealis would flash up still further northward; and sometimes mock suns and mock moons would appear, in varied beauty, in the starry sky. Brilliant, too, were the northern constellations; and when the real moon was at its full, it made its stately circuit in the heavens without descending below the horizon, and lighted up the vast piles of ice with a pale lustre, almost as vivid as the morning twilights of more genial skies.

Around the vessels the crews built a wall of ice; and in ice huts they stowed away their cordage and stores, to make room for exercise on the decks. They organized a theatrical company, and amused themselves and the officers with comedy well performed. Behind the pieces of hummock each actor learned his part; and by means of calico they transformed themselves into female characters, as occasion required. These dramas were acted upon the deck of the Advance, sometimes while the thermometer indicated 30° below zero ; and actors and audience highly enjoyed the fun. They also went out in parties during that long night, fully armed, to hunt the polar bear, the grim monarch of the frozen north, on which occasions they often encountered perilous adventures. They played at foot-ball, and exercised themselves in drawing sledges heavily laden with provisions. Five hours of each twenty-four they thus exercised in the open air, and once a week each man washed his whole body in cold snow-water. Serious sickness was consequently avoided ; and the scurvy, which attacked them, soon yielded to remedies.

Often, during that fearful night, they expected the disaster of having their vessels crushed. All through November and December, before the ice became fast, they slept in their clothes, with knapsacks on their backs, and sledges upon the ice, laden with stores, not knowing at what moment the vessels might be demolished, and themselves forced to leave them, and make their way toward land. On the 8th of December, and the 23d of January, they actually lowered their boats and stood upon the ice, for the crushing masses were making the timbers of the gallant vessel creak, and its decks to rise in the centre. They were then ninety miles from land, and hope hardly whispered an encouraging idea of life being sustained. On the latter occasion, when officers and crew stood upon the ice, with the ropes of their provision-sledges in their hands, a terrible snow-drift came from the north-east, and intense darkness shrouded them. Had the vessel then been crushed, all must have perished.

A strange picture might have been seen on Christmas

day, 1850, by a spirit who could have roamed from end to end of the icy continent, and taken it in at a glance. No less than ten Arctic discovery-ships were wintering within a few hundred miles of each other. Under Griffith's Island lay her majesty's ships the Resolute, Assistance, Pioneer, and Intrepid; in a small bay in North Devon were securely sheltered Captain Penny's two brigs; the Investigator lay in Prince of Wales Strait; and at the mouth of Lancaster Sound, drifting helplessly in the pack which had borne them already twelve degrees to the eastward, were the two unfortunate ships of the Grinnell expedition. But this was not all. Only three to four hundred miles from the Investigator's winter quarters, Mr. Rae was waiting on the border of Great Bear Lake for weather that would allow him to start on his land journey. And, in all human probability, on that same Christmas day, Sir John Franklin and his men, the objects of so many expeditions and so much anxious hope, were miserably subsisting on short allowance somewhere in King William's Land, or on the bank of Peel Sound.

Dr. Kane, who wrote a deeply interesting account of the first Grinnell expedition, says, under date of February 28th, 1851, when, for some days, the average temperature was 53 degrees below zero: "Cold as it was, our mid-day exercise was never interrupted unless by wind and drift-storms. We felt the necessity of active exercise; and, although the effort was accompanied with pains in the joints, sometimes hardly bearable, we managed, both officers and crew, to obtain at least three hours a day. The exercise consisted of foot-ball and sliding, followed by regular games of romps, leap-frog, and tumbling in the snow. By shovelling away near the vessel, we obtained a fine bare surface of fresh ice, extremely glib and durable. On this we constructed a skating-ground and admirable slides. I walked regularly over the floes, although the snows were nearly impassable. With all this, aided by hosts of hygienic resources, feeble, certainly, but still the best at my command, scurvy advanced steadily."

On the 21st April Dr. Kane encountered a bear on the ice, on which he remarks: "We are at least eighty miles from the nearest land, Cape Kater; and channels innumerable must intervene between us and terra firma. Yet this majestic animal, dependent upon his own predatory resources alone, and, defying cold as well as hunger, guided by a superb instinct, confides himself to these solitary, unstable ice-fields.

"Parry, in his adventurous polar effort, found these animals at the most northern limit of recorded observation. Wrangell had them as companions on his first Asiatic journey over the Polar Ocean. Navigators have also found them floating upon berg and floe far out in open sea; and here we have them in a region some seventy miles from the nearest stable ice. They have seldom or never — if we except Parry's Spitzbergen experience — been seen so far from land. In the great majority of cases, they seem to have been accidentally caught and carried adrift on disengaged ice-floes. In this way they travel to Iceland; and it may have been so, perhaps, with the Spitzbergen instances.

"There is something very grand about this tawny savage: never leaving this utter destitution, this frigid inhospitableness; coupling in May, and bringing forth in Christmas time; a gestation carried on all of it below zero, more than half of it in Arctic darkness; living in perpetual snow, and dependent for life upon a never-ending activity; using the frozen water as a raft to traverse the open seas, that the water *unfrozen* may yield him the means of life. No time for hibernation has this polar tiger; his life is one great winter."

Early in February the northern horizon began to be streaked with gorgeous twilight, the herald of the approaching sun; and on the 18th his disc first appeared above the horizon. As the golden rim rose above the glittering snow-drifts and piles of ice, three hearty cheers went up from those hardy mariners, and they enthusiastically welcomed their deliverer from the chains of frost. Day after day the sun rose higher and higher, and vast masses of ice began to yield to his fervid influences. The scurvy disappeared, and from that time, until their arrival home, not a man suffered from sickness. As they slowly drifted through Davis's Straits, and the ice gave indications of breaking up, the voyagers made preparations for sailing. The Rescue was reöccupied (May 12th, 1851), and her stern-post, which had been broken by the ice in Barrow's Straits, was repaired. To accomplish this, they were obliged to dig away the ice, which was from twelve to fourteen feet thick around her. They re-shipped their rudders; removed the felt covering; placed their stores on deck, and then patiently awaited the disruption of the ice. This event was very sudden and appalling. It began to give way on the 5th of June, and in the space of twenty minutes the whole mass, as far as the eye could reach, became one vast field of moving floes.

On the 10th of June, 1851, they emerged into open water a little south of the Arctic Circle, in latitude 65° 30′. They immediately repaired to Godhaven, on the coast of Greenland, where they re-fitted, and, unappalled by the perils through which they had just passed, they once more turned their prows northward, to encounter anew the ice squadrons of Baffin's Bay. Again they traversed the coast of Greenland to about the 73d degree, when they bore to the westward, and on the 7th and 8th of July passed the English whaling-fleet near the Dutch

Islands. Onward they pressed through the accumulating ice to Baffin's Island, where, on the 11th, they were joined by the Prince Albert, then out upon another cruise They continued in company until the 3d of August, when the Albert departed for the westward, determined to try the more southern passage. Here again the Americans encountered vast fields of hummock-ice, and were subjected to the most imminent perils. The floating ice, as if moved by adverse currents, tumbled in huge masses, and reared upon the sides of the sturdy little vessels like monsters of the deep intent upon destruction These masses broke in the bulwarks, and sometimes fell over upon the decks with terrible force, like rocks rolled over a plain by mountain torrents. The noise was fearful — so deafening that the mariners could scarcely hear each other's voices. The sounds of these rolling masses, together with the rending of the icebergs floating near, and the vast floes, produced a din like the discharge of a thousand pieces of ordnance upon a field of battle.

Finding the north and west closed against further progress, by impenetrable ice, De Haven was balked; and, turning his vessels homeward, they came out into an open sea somewhat crippled, but not a plank seriously started. During a storm off the banks of Newfoundland, a thousand miles from New York, the vessels parted company. The Advance arrived safely at the Navy Yard, at Brooklyn, on the 30th of September, 1851; and the Rescue joined her there a few days afterward. Toward the close of October the government resigned the vessels into the hands of Mr. Grinnell, to be used in other service, but with the stipulation that they were to be subject to the order of the Secretary of the Navy in the spring, if required for another expedition in search of Sir John Franklin.

CHAPTER XV.

THE PRINCE ALBERT REFITTED BY LADY FRANKLIN. — MR. KENNEDY THE COMMANDER. — DEPARTURE OF THE VESSEL. — UPERNAVIK. — TRIAL OF CARRIER-PIGEONS. — DISASTROUS SEPARATION. — RELIEF AND REÜNION. — PREPARATIONS FOR WINTERING. — WINTER JOURNEYS. — VISIT TO FURY BEACH. — THE GRAND JOURNEY. — SEVERE GALE. — THE FURY'S STORES. — DOGS. — CAIRNS NOT ALWAYS SEEN. — CAPE WALKER. — RETURN TO BATTY BAY. — HOMEWARD BOUND. — BELLOT. — RAE'S LAND JOURNEY IN 1851.

The discovery of the traces of Franklin's visit to Point Riley, the account of which was brought home by the Prince Albert, gave encouragement for a renewal of the search. On the 3d of June, 1851, the Prince Albert, which had been refitted by Lady Franklin for the purpose of exploring the shores of Prince Regent's Inlet, set sail from Stromness. She was under the command of Mr. William Kennedy, formerly in the service of the Hudson's Bay Company, and who has published an interesting narrative of his adventures.

The Prince Albert had been well strengthened for encounters with ponderous masses of ice. Along her sides, from the keel to about two feet above the water-line, there was a doubling of elm planking of fully two and a half inches thick, intended not only to fortify the hull of the little vessel, but to preserve her sides from the tear and wear of sailing through, and rubbing against, sharp, rasping pieces of ice. The bow and stern-post were sheathed with wrought iron a quarter of an inch thick, and a broad strip of thick sheet-iron ran along the water-line as far aft as the main-mast. Her hold was a perfect labyrinth of cross-beams and massive fastenings, to enable her to withstand the evil consequences of a "nip;" and the arrangements generally were conducted in a manner which, while it indicated the dangerous nature of the service, also served to assure her crew that nothing had been left undone which could in any way conduce to their comfort and safety.

She was supplied with several boats. One was made of gutta-percha, and another of mahogany; the third being a small *dingy*, of the ordinary kind. She had also one of Halkett's Mackintosh boats, and a tin kayak, made in imitation of those used by the Esquimaux. Dressed moose-skins and parchment, to be converted during the voyage into moccasins, snow-shoes, dog-sledge-traces, &c., were abundantly supplied. Provision for two years was put on board, and part of this consisted of a ton and a half of pemmican.

The ship's company consisted of eighteen in all, including Mr. Kennedy, the commander, Lieutenant J. Bellot, the second in command, and Mr. Cowie, the surgeon. Bellot was a spirited young officer from the French navy, whose romantic love of adventure led him to offer his services to Lady Franklin in the search which had now been going on for some years. He soon proved himself to be in every way a most useful auxiliary, and an honor to the nation to which he belonged.

Among the crew, who were all picked men, there was John Hepburn, who will be remembered by every reader of Arctic travel as the faithful attendant of Sir John Franklin during his first adventurous, and in some respects tragic journey, through North America. Hepburn's spirit was fired with an irresistible desire to assist in searching for the hero with whom, in his youth, he had shared the perils of the wilderness ; and now, in his old age, he was going to face a wilder form of perils on the ice-laden waters of the Polar Sea. Another of the men had travelled with Dr. Rae, on his first expedition to Repulse Bay ; and another had accompanied Sir John Richardson in his boat journey through the interior of America. Lady Franklin herself was present to see the vessel off. She took an affectionate leave of officers and crew ; and the Prince Albert bounded from the shore and stretched out into the wide Atlantic, the Union-Jack at her peak, and the French flag, in honor of Lieutenant Bellot, flying at the fore.

On Sunday, the 24th of June, they descried the coast of Greenland on the distant horizon. In Baffin's Bay they were visited by the captains of two whaling-vessels, who created great excitement by telling them of the discovery of Franklin's winter quarters in 1845, with the details of which the reader is already acquainted. This information induced Kennedy to direct his course to Upernavik, the Danish colony on the west coast of Greenland, partly for the purpose of taking in additional supplies for the use of the winter travelling parties, but chiefly with the hope of gaining further information of the recent discoveries, from the American searching vessels which had wintered in the pack. In this, however, he was disappointed.

Of Upernavik, which he reached June 10th, 1851, Kennedy says : "It is one of that interesting group of little colonies with which the enterprise of the Danes has dotted the west coast of Greenland. Here, considerably within the Arctic Circle, we found a Christian community, not only living, but, after a fashion, thriving. We were informed by the governor that there were, even at this early period of the season, one thousand

Danish tons of oil and blubber stored, from the produce of the summer fishery. There was likewise visible evidence in every direction of an abundance of venison, water-fowl, and eggs, as well as seals. The houses were built of wood, very small, and had a singularly amphibious look about them, from being covered with tar from top to bottom, — appearing, for all the world, like so many upturned herring-boats, ready, on any emergency, to take to the water.

"A party of the Esquimaux, attached to the settlement, had come in with the produce of some hunting excursion in which they had been engaged; and I was much struck with their intelligence, and their well-clad, comfortable, and healthy appearance. This, I learned, was in a great measure due to the benevolent interest of the Danish government in their behalf. There is not a station, I was given to understand, along the whole coast of Greenland, which has not its missionary and its schoolmaster for the instruction of the natives; and, judging from what we saw and learned at Upernavik, the Danish exchequer is not without material and substantial proofs of the gratitude of the poor '*Innuit.*' Thus instructed, cared for, and their energies disciplined and directed, the Esquimaux of Greenland give employment to six ships annually, in carrying the produce of their hunts and fisheries to Denmark."

At this place six large Esquimaux dogs, for dragging sledges, were purchased. A few pairs of seal-skin boots, shoes, and trousers, *à la Esquimaux*, were also procured, and the Prince Albert proceeded on her voyage. The much-dreaded "middle ice" was reached soon after leaving, and four days were spent in passing through it to the western side of the bay, during which time the men were constantly employed in sailing, boring, pushing, thumping, and warping — not unfrequently exposed to the perilous nips, which are sometimes productive of such dire consequences. At this point in the voyage it was deemed advisable to test the powers of some carrier-pigeons with which they had been provided ; but the poor birds refused to take the long flight to England, and resolutely persisted in returning to the ship again, after a short survey of the icy region in which they were let loose.

During the passage of the middle-ice, a large quantity of provisions had been got up on deck, to be ready in case an unfortunate crush should sink the vessel. This was now re-stowed in the hold, on getting into the comparatively clear western waters of Baffin's Bay.

One evening about this time, while they were sailing quietly among beautiful and fantastically formed fragments of ice, which obliged them frequently to deviate a little from their course, a shout was heard ringing through the calm, still atmosphere, and very soon four Esquimaux paddled out to them in their seal-skin kayaks. They speedily clambered on board, and one of the crew happening to have some slight knowledge of English, a vigorous flow of query and reply commenced, in the course of which much useful information as to the nature of the coast and inlets was obtained. One, especially, proved to be an expert draftsman, and by means of a bit of chalk drew on the deck the outlines of various parts of the coast, which were of some service.

The progress of the vessel was now much interrupted by ice and contrary gales. All attempts to reach Cape Riley, and, subsequently, to enter Leopold Harbor, were completely frustrated. Far as the eye could reach down the west side of Prince Regent's Inlet, — which was to be the scene of their searching operations, — huge barriers of ice met the view. The voyagers pushed boldly in amongst it, however, and succeeded, after a tortuous course, in reaching Elwin Bay, which they found quite closed up. Batty Bay and Fury Beach were next visited, where they met with similar disappointment, and where they also perceived that the ice — between which and the shore they had been sailing — was setting down upon them ; so they were obliged to beat a hasty retreat, in order to escape being crushed to pieces. It was now obviously fruitless to attempt the western side of the inlet under present circumstances ; so they put about and ran for Port Bowen, on the eastern shore, which was comparatively free from ice. Here they found traces of the party which wintered at this spot with Sir Edward Parry, in 1825.

To winter here, while all their intended work lay on the other shore of the inlet, was quite out of the question ; so it was resolved at all hazards to attempt a landing again. Accordingly, on the 9th of September, they recrossed the strait, and succeeded in approaching close enough to the shore to render an attempt to land somewhat feasible. The gutta-percha boat was therefore got out, and Kennedy, with four of his men, jumped into her and rowed for the beach. This they reached without difficulty, by means of a narrow lane of open water which was opportunely discovered. On ascending the cliffs of Cape Seppings, Kennedy found, to his joy, that the harbor of Port Leopold was quite free from ice, and, if the ship could maintain her position for a few hours longer, he had no doubt of being able to effect an entrance. On descending to the beach, however, he found, to his consternation, that the passage by which they had entered was blocked up. The boat had not been fastened to the beach, but to a large piece of ice, which, with the whole body of the pack, was drifting down the inlet, carrying boat, ship, and men, along with it. To make matters worse, night was coming on, and nothing could be seen or heard around but huge masses of ice grinding, tossing, and rearing furiously on every side. To return to the ship under these circumstances was out of the question ; so they made for the shore as fast as possible, dragging the boat along with them. On reaching it, they pulled the boat up and turned it over so as to form a kind of shelter from the night-air, and then prepared to pass the night under it, although little sleep was anticipated ; for, besides the anxiety occasioned by their strange position, their clothes were almost covered with ice, and they had no blankets or coverings of any kind. From his former experience in Arctic scenes, Kennedy knew the danger of falling *asleep* under such circumstances ; and, notwithstanding the strong desire that he and his men felt to indulge in repose, he only allowed them to *rest* for an hour at a time, obliging them during the remainder of the night to keep in active motion.

With the dawn of the following morning the shivering party scrambled to the top of the highest cliff of Cape Seppings, but not a vestige of the vessel was to be seen ! The consternation of the poor men, who were thus cast away on this bleak shore, may be imagined. Without provisions, scantily clad, no vessel, and an approaching hyperborean winter, their condition seemed forlorn indeed. One fortunate circumstance, however, cheered them not a little ; and this was the fact that, two years before, Sir James Ross had left a deposit of provisions at Whaler Point, on the other side of the harbor. Should this be found in good condition, there was every reason to hope that they might manage to pass the winter in at least some degree of comfort. Thither, therefore, Kennedy and his four men now directed their steps. A short walk brought them to the spot, where, to their great joy, they found the provisions just as they had been left, and quite good, with the exception of a cask of tallow, a case of chocolate, and a barrel of biscuit, which had been destroyed, and their contents demolished, by the bears and foxes. A house erected by Sir James Ross was also found in pretty good condition, being only a little damaged in the roof. Near to this there was a flag-staff, to which a cylinder was attached, containing a notice of the deposit of provisions, and of the future intentions of the party by whom they had been left.

"It was now," says Kennedy, "the 10th of September. Winter was evidently fast setting in, and, from the distance the ship had been carried during that disastrous night, — whether out to sea or down the inlet we could not conjecture, — there was no hope of our being able to rejoin her, at least during the present season. There remained, therefore, no alternative but to make up our minds to pass the winter, if necessary, where we were. The first object to be attended to was the erecting of some sort of shelter against the daily increasing inclemency of the weather; and for this purpose the launch, left by Sir James Ross, was selected. Her mainmast was laid on supports at the bow and stern, about nine feet in height, and by spreading two of her sails over this a very tolerable roof was obtained. A stove was set up in the body of the boat, with the pipes running through the roof; and we were soon sitting by a comfortable fire, which, after our long exposure to the wet and cold, we stood very much in need of."

Kennedy now arranged his plans for the future. To undertake a long winter journey over the country on foot had been his original intention; but, under the present circumstances, this was impossible. He therefore determined first to send out travelling parties, as soon as the state of the ice should permit, to institute a strict search for the ship in every direction in which it was likely that she could have been carried; and, secondly, in the event of being unsuccessful in this, it was determined to make a journey early in spring to Cape Walker, to search in that direction for traces of Captain Franklin and his crews; and so accomplish at least part of the object for which this expedition had been fitted out.

There were difficulties in the way, however. Shoes were wanted. Without shoes nothing could be done at all; so it behoved them to exert their ingenuity. There was nothing in the dépôt of provisions that could be turned to this use; but, fortunately, a good deal of the canvas covering of the old house was left, and out of this several pairs of shoes were made. They answered pretty well, although, indeed, they lasted not much longer than a few days; so two of the party were set to work to devote their whole time to the making of a supply of canvas shoes, which should last them during the whole winter.

In contriving and constructing such clothing and implements as were absolutely necessary, and in preparing for their intended journeys, they now spent much of their time. The Sabbaths were always days of rest, and devoted to the worship of God, whose tender care had thus provided them with all the necessaries, and not a few of the comforts, of life.

On the 17th of October, while they were engaged in the usual routine of daily duty, a shot was heard to reverberate among the cliffs of Cape Seppings. So unwonted a sound caused them to rush tumultuously from their occupations, when they found, with emotions of inexpressible thankfulness and joy, that it proceeded from a party of seven of the Prince Albert's men, headed by Bellot, who had dragged the jolly-boat all the way from Batty Bay, in the hope of finding and succoring their long-lost comrades.

"I cannot refrain," writes Kennedy, "from recording here my warmest thanks to Mr. Bellot, not only for this, but two other attempts which he had made to communicate to us the intelligence of the Prince Albert's position, and to bring us a supply of clothing. He had set out with two men to come by land to Port Leopold, the third day after getting into Batty Bay; but, after three days' march, over the wild and rugged hills, wading through deep snow, and walking against continual drift, they were obliged to return to the ship, after much suffering from cold and wet. He next made a gallant attempt along shore by means of dogs and sledges; but, getting on weak ice, fell through, and had again to return, with the loss of the sledge and part of its contents. The third (the present) attempt was more successful. The little boat, as already stated, had been dragged all the way, in case of any occasion arising for its use where the ice had not formed. They found the ice, however, formed all the way to this point, and in many places so rough that they had often to drag their boats over points of land."

From those who had thus opportunely arrived to succor them they learned that the Prince Albert was securely moored in Batty Bay; and, as there was nothing now to prevent their setting out to rejoin the vessel, preparations were commenced immediately. The activity and reäctionary flow of spirits among the men was very high, at thus meeting with their long-lost comrades. Five weeks had elapsed since their disastrous separation; and that evening a truly joyous party assembled under the covering of the old launch, and caused her timbers to quake with the sound of rough old sea-songs, and tough yarns, while they quaffed brimming bowls of hot, strong chocolate to the success of their expedition.

On Wednesday, the 22d of October, their preparations being completed, a paper was deposited in the cylinder, containing an account of their proceedings, and they commenced their journey to Batty Bay.

A strong sledge had been made, on which the boat was placed; then all their goods and provisions, etc., had been securely stowed away in the latter, and hauled down to the ice on Leopold Harbor, which stretched out a smooth and level plain before them. The mast was then erected, the sails set, and, the whole party jumping in, away they went over the bay before a spanking breeze, at a rate that was quite marvellous. But, just as they got about half-way across the bay, the sledge broke down, leaving them to repair damages for the remainder of the day. Night overtook them ere they could gain the land; and, as it was not desirable to sleep on the frozen sea, they were obliged to make their way on in the dark, which was rendered, if possible, still more palpable by a heavy fall of snow. After much stumbling into crevices and cracks, frequent wanderings about they knew not where, and occasional dashings of the shins upon sharp pieces of projecting ice, a small bit of solid land was found in the shape of a flat limestone rock, surrounded by large masses of stranded ice. Here they erected a tent, and with some coals which had been brought from Whaler Point boiled a large kettle of tea, and enjoyed themselves exceedingly after the fatiguing and protracted march of the day.

But they experienced some embarrassment in disposing themselves to rest. The tent was small, and the party numbered thirteen. Six sat down on one side, and six on the other, by which they managed to have about three feet of space for stretching their legs.

Bellot — whose good-humored aptitude to accommodate himself to all varieties of circumstances was always conspicuous — undertook to squeeze in under the twelve pairs of legs, a small space at one end being left clear for his head. But the arrangement was not propitious to sleep; and it was resolved to "make a night of it." They had a candle, but no candlestick; so each man held the candle for a quarter of an hour, and then passed it to his neighbor. Songs were sung, and there was some hilarious merriment. But the candle went out, and then there was a renewal of the abortive attempts to sleep. These were accompanied with nods, groans, and sighs, — especially from poor Bellot, on whom the weight of twenty-four heavy legs began to tell with the effect of a hydraulic press. At length the gray dawn warned them to rise and resume their journey.

Their discomforts had been such that they determined in future to adopt the Esquimaux plan of building a snow hut each night, in which to sleep. Kennedy's description of these primitive dwellings is interesting: "The process of constructing a snow-house goes on something in this way, varied, of course, by circumstances of time, place, and materials. First, a number of square blocks are cut out of any hard-drifted bank of snow you can meet with, adapted for the purpose; which, when cut, have precisely the appearance of blocks of salt sold in the donkey-carts in the streets of London. The dimensions we generally selected were two feet in length by fourteen inches in height, and nine inches in breadth. A layer of these blocks is laid on the ground nearly in the form of a square; and then another layer on this, cut so as to incline slightly inwards, and the corner blocks laid diagonally over those underneath, so as to cut off the angles. Other layers follow in the same way, until you have gradually a dome-shaped structure rising before you, out of which you have only to cut a small hole for a door, to find yourself within a very light, comfortable-looking bee-hive on a large scale, in which you can bid defiance to wind and weather. Any chinks between the blocks are filled up with loose snow with the hand from outside; as these are best detected from within, a man is usually sent in to drive a thin rod through the spot where he discovers a chink, which is immediately plastered over by some one from without, till the whole house is as air-tight as an egg."

In these snowy dwellings they afterwards passed many nights in considerable comfort, and on the present occasion certainly found them a great improvement on the small tent. In a few days they reached the ship, where a hearty welcome from their comrades greeted them.

Preparations were now vigorously begun for passing the next eight months of the winter of 1851–2 in the ice, and for getting ready for the land journeys which it was intended to make during that season. Portions of the stores were removed from the vessel's hold to the shore, where snow-houses were built to receive them. A wash-house, a carpenter's shop, a forge, and a powder-magazine, were also built of the same material. The decks of the Prince Albert were covered with a housing, and an embankment of snow as high as the gunwale built around her.

In all the excursions of the adventurers, Bellot, the young Frenchman, seems to have been ever foremost. He headed travelling parties, so soon as the ice permitted, to make deposits of provisions, etc., for the grand travelling expeditions in prospect; and, besides lending very efficient assistance in all departments on board, made daily pilgrimages to a hill in the neighborhood, where he occasionally succeeded in obtaining a meridian observation of the sun, and *always* succeeded in getting his fingers frozen in the operation.

Kennedy, being almost the only man on board who had ever seen a snow-shoe or a dog-sledge before, was constantly engaged in constructing these indispensable implements for winter travelling, and in teaching his crew the use of them. Thus occupied, the time passed cheerfully by. The nights were long and dark, and grew rapidly longer and darker. The cold winds howled over them from off the chilly regions around the pole, bearing in their course blinding clouds of snow, circling and screaming madly round the solitary ship, and whistling among the rigging as if impatient for its destruction, and then roaring away over the frozen sea, to spend their fury at last on the black waves of Hudson's Bay. Sometimes the sun shone brightly out in a clear, cloudless sky, glittering on the icy particles which floated in the still, cold atmosphere, and blazing on the tops of the neighboring hills, whose white outlines were clearly and sharply defined against the blue heavens ; and, as if Nature desired to make some compensation for the lengthened period of darkness to which she doomed the land, one, and sometimes two mock-suns, or, as the sailors sometimes call them, "sun-dogs," shone in the firmament, vieing in splendor with the glorious orb of day himself.

About the 5th of January, 1852, all was ready for the commencement of the long-talked-of winter journeys, and the morning of that day was ushered in with the clattering of snow-shoes and sledges, the cracking of whips, the shouts of men, and the howling and yelping of dogs. Although all the men of the Prince Albert were out upon the ice, only five of them were appointed to undertake the first exploratory journey. These were Kennedy, Bellot, and three of the hardiest among the crew. "The first object of the journey," says Kennedy, "was, of course, to ascertain whether Fury Beach had been a retreating point to any of Sir John Franklin's party since it was visited by Lieut. Robinson, of the Enterprise, in 1849. A secondary object, should our expectations in this respect not be realized, was to form a first dépôt of provisions here, with the view of carrying out a more extended search as soon as circumstances would permit. It was desirable at the same time to ascertain the state of the *roads*, by which, of course, I mean the yet untrodden surface of the snow or ice, in the direction in which we meant to go, before commencing any transport, on a large scale, between the ship and Fury Beach; and it was thought advisable, therefore, to go comparatively light. A small supply of pemmican was all we took with us in addition to our travelling requirements, consisting of a tent and poles, blanketing and provisions for a week, some guns and ammunition, fuel, and a cooking apparatus, in all weighing from two hundred to two hundred and fifty pounds."

Troubles and difficulties, not, however, of a very serious kind, assailed them at the very commencement. The "roads" were so bad as to be almost impassable, owing to the ice being detached from the shore, and so leaving as their only pathway the beach at the base of stupendous cliffs. Huge fragments of ice and large bowlder stones met them at every turn, often rendering it a work of extreme difficulty for the united efforts of dogs and men to drag the sledge along. Occasionally they met with what is termed a "pressure," or a set of ice upon the shore, which blocked up the path altogether, and compelled them to have recourse to axes to cut their way through; and sometimes they came to banks of hard-drifted snow sloping down the face of the cliffs, and leaving only an inclined plane to drag the sledge over. On one occasion Bellot was pitched head foremost into one of these huge snow-drifts, leaving only six inches of his protruding legs to tell of his whereabouts.

The first night, not having time to erect a snow-hut, owing to the lateness of the hour, they slept in the tent, but found it very small and uncomfortable; so that, on the following evening, they stopped for the night, after eight hours' walking, and built their snow-hut at the foot of a high precipice, with a perpendicular mass of stranded ice at the bottom, which served for a gable. The ice, which was undergoing a "pressure," groaned, ground, and crashed around them all night, and finally left them in the morning with a pile at least thirty feet high, within a few yards of the encampment.

On the 8th, being within a short distance of Fury Beach, it was resolved to leave the sledge and two of the men, while Kennedy and Bellot, with one man, should proceed forward unencumbered. Accordingly they started, and got over the ground much more rapidly than before. That night they reached Fury Beach, and stood upon the spot around which, for several days past, their anxious hopes had been circling; but all was still and desolate as the grave. "Every object distinguished by the moonlight in the distance," says Kennedy, "became animated, to our imaginations, into the forms of our long-absent countrymen; for, had they been imprisoned anywhere in the Arctic seas, within a reasonable distance of Fury Beach, here, we felt assured, some of them, at least, would have been now. But, alas for these fond hopes!"

It was with sad feelings and slow steps that Kennedy and Bellot entered the ruined walls of "Somerset House," and prepared to take a few hours' repose. A fire was lighted in the stove, which had heated the end of the building occupied by Sir John Ross's crew during the dreary winter of 1832–33. Around this they sat and supped; and, after reposing, set out, about eleven P. M., on their return to the encampment where the sledge had been left. They reached it about two A. M. of the following morning. From this point they retraced their steps again to the ship, where they arrived on the 10th, at five o'clock in the afternoon, without having encountered anything worth recording.

During the winter, travelling parties were occasionally sent out for the purpose of placing provisions *en cache*, for the benefit of those who should afterwards undertake a journey along shore to the southward, and across the country in various directions. These parties were often arrested by violent gales and snow-storms, which seem to have prevailed very much during the whole winter; so much so, indeed, that the veteran Hepburn observed, "that he had known but one gale since entering Batty Bay, and that was the gale which began when they came, and ended when they went away!"

They had a good library on board, and spent much of their time in reading. The doctor kept school, and the crew would often sit in groups, listening to his discourses, or employed in making flannel socks, canvas jackets, and other useful articles.

Spring now drew on apace. This was indicated by the increasing power of the sun and length of the day, though the country retained its wintry aspect for months afterwards. About the middle of February, 1852, everything being in a proper state of advancement for the commencement of the "grand journey," preparations for an immediate start were made ; and, on the 25th of that month, equipped with snow-shoes, sledges, and dogs, they left the vessel.

The party which now set out were a detachment of five men, under the command of Kennedy. These were to be followed in a few days by another detachment, under Bellot, who was to be waited for at Fury Beach, whence the whole, amounting to fourteen men, were to start upon hitherto untrodden ground. They were escorted as far as the south point of Batty Bay by part of the ship's company, who were to remain behind. At this point they separated with many kind farewells and three hearty cheers, after which they were soon lost to each other in the mist.

During the first part of the journey, the equinoctial gales blew with great violence. They were frequently detained for whole days at a time in their encampment by these fierce winds, from whose bitter fury they were, however, well protected by the snow-houses which they built. "The gale," says Kennedy, "of Saturday (28th February) continuing during three days, we were of necessity compelled to remain in camp. During a short interval, about the 2d of March, the weather appearing to get more moderate, we were enabled to return for what cargo had been left behind during our former trip. It was taken onward as far as we dared, and we returned to the camp against a wind so keen, that no face escaped being frost-bitten — the strong wind, in this instance, being the cause rather than the degree of temperature, for this was comparatively moderate. On the morning of the 3d a lull of an hour or so enticed us to bundle up and lash our sleigh. No sooner had we done this, and proceeded a short distance, than the gale came on with redoubled fury, in consequence of which we had to hasten back to our snow retreat, and were glad enough to have been still so near a shelter when caught by it, as we had much difficulty in keeping on our feet, from the violence of the whirling eddies that came sweeping along an exposed headland near us. Such was the force of the wind, that column after column of whirling spray was raised by it out of a continuous lane of water, more than a mile broad, which the present gale had opened out along the coast, at the distance of only a few yards from our present encampment. As these successive columns were lifted out of the water, they were borne onward with a speed scarcely less rapid than the 'wings of the wind' itself. Whilst detained here, we narrowly escaped being buried by an infant avalanche; a hardened mass of snow of several tons' weight having been disengaged from the summit of the cliff above us."

So severe did this part of the road prove, that the sledges, moccasins, and snow-shoes, were severely damaged. On the whole party being collected at Fury Beach, it was found necessary to send back to the ship for additional supplies. They were much indebted here to the old stores of the Fury, which were found to be in excellent preservation, although they had lain for thirty years exposed to the weather on the shores of these icy seas.

The journey on which they had now entered would occupy, it was supposed, about three months, during which time they hoped to survey upwards of a thousand miles. It was found, upon calculation, that six men could not carry a sufficient quantity of provisions to sustain them for so long a period; so the plan was adopted of taking fourteen men as far as Brentford Bay, from which point eight of the travellers were to return to the ship, while the remaining six would proceed onwards with as much as they could possibly drag or carry of the necessaries of life.

Among their provisions and equipments, procured from the old deposit at Fury Beach, were seven hundred and fifty pounds of pemmican, one small sack of flour, five gallons of spirits of wine, a hundred and twenty pounds of coal, four bags of biscuits, and various knives, saws, astronomical instruments, &c.

Of these old stores of the Fury, Kennedy says, he found the provisions "not only in the best preservation, but much superior in quality, after thirty years of exposure to the weather, to some of our own stores, and those supplied to the other Arctic expeditions. This high state of preservation I cannot help attributing in some measure to the strength and thickness of the tins, in which the preserved meats, vegetables, and soups, had been placed. The flour had all caked in solid lumps, which had to be reground and passed through a sieve before it was fit for the cook's hands. In other respects it was fresh and sweet as ever, and supplied us with a stock of excellent biscuit."

These articles, with the tackling and sledges, made altogether a total dead weight of about two thousand tons; the whole being lashed down, to the smallest possible compass, on four flat-bottomed Indian sledges, two of which were drawn by the five dogs, assisted by two of the men, the other two being dragged by the rest of the party.

It was a fine, clear, mild day when they started, and they found the travelling very good at first, the beach being flat, and the ice sufficiently smooth to admit of proceeding with facility. Fortune, however, seldom favors Arctic travellers long. They soon found their bright sky overcast, and the mild breeze changed into a cold, bitter, frosty gale. Under these circumstances they travelled from day to day, enduring it as stoically as possible, and making up to some extent for their discomfort while travelling by enjoying themselves beneath their snow-burrows during the few hours allotted to repose. The frost-biting of their faces, however, became at last so intolerable, that they fell upon the expedient of protecting the parts most vulnerable by means of sundry curious and original kinds of coverings. "For the eyes," says Kennedy, "we had goggles of glass, of wire-gauze, of crape, or of plain wood with a slit in the centre, in the manner of the Esquimaux. For the face, some had cloth-masks, with neat little crevices for the mouth, nose, and eyes; others were muffled up in the ordinary chin-cloth, and, for that most troublesome of the facial members, the nose, a strong party, with our always original carpenter at their head, had gutta-percha noses, lined with delicate soft flannel." These contrivances, though admirable in theory, proved complete failures in practice. They were ultimately discarded, with the exception of the chin-cloths and goggles.

The daily routine of operations was as follows: They rose at six, but did not *dress* — having slept in their clothes, that operation was unnecessary; then they breakfasted; after which came the bundling up and lashing of the sledges, and the harnessing of the dogs — the latter operation always being accomplished amidst considerable uproar. Then came the start; Kennedy leading the way, Bellot following, and the party in a string bringing up the rear. So on they went, over hill and dale and along shore, from morn till night, stopping every hour for five minutes to rest the men and breathe the dogs, and halting, when opportunity offered, to find their latitude and longitude. The construction of a snow-hut, and the consumption of the evening meal, concluded the labors of the day, which were seldom over before nine or ten at night.

On the 6th of April they arrived at Brentford Bay, and the fatigue-party began their retrograde journey to the ship.

At this point Kennedy discovered a strait running westward, which was found to separate North Somerset from Boothia Felix, and was named Bellot Strait, in honor of the gallant young Frenchman, who had secured the affectionate regard not only of the leader of the party, but also of all the men. Thence Kennedy crossed over Victoria Strait to Prince of Wales Land, naming the most prominent headlands, bays, and islands. Numerous tracks of deer, wolves, bears, and musk-oxen, were seen ; but none of the animals themselves, except one bear, which came incautiously close to the snow-hut, and was chased away by the dogs.

On the 17th April the thermometer indicated +22 ; "a temperature," says Kennedy, "which, to our sensations, was absolutely oppressive. One of our dogs, through over-exertion, combined with the unusual heat, fainted in his traces, and lay gasping for breath for a quarter of an hour ; but, after recovering, went on as merrily as ever. These faithful creatures were perfect treasures to us throughout the journey. They were all suffering, like ourselves, from snow-blindness, but did not in the least relax their exertions on this account. The Esquimaux dog is, in fact, the camel of these northern deserts ; the faithful attendant of man, and the sharer of his labors and privations."

During a great portion of the journey the men were much annoyed by snow-blindness, caused by the fierce glare of the sun upon the snow ; and this was rendered all the more unbearable by the sharp winds which prevailed so much, and dashed the drift into their eyes.

The country over which they travelled was generally very flat, rendering it a matter of no small difficulty to keep their westerly course, the compasses being of little use in such close proximity to the magnetic pole. Their great hope in travelling westward was, that they should meet with a sea which would conduct them northward to Cape Walker, and so enable them to ascertain whether or not there was any promising western channel or strait through which Franklin might have penetrated. After thirteen days' marching, however, they reached the hundredth degree of west longitude without meeting with the wished-for ocean; so it was resolved to turn their steps northward.

"Being now satisfied," says Kennedy, "that Sir James Ross had, in his land journey along the western shore of North Somerset, in 1849, mistaken the very low and level land over which we had been travelling for a western sea, I felt no longer justified in continuing a western course. Whatever passage might exist to the south-west of Cape Walker, I felt assured must now be on our north. I determined, therefore, from this time forward, to direct our course northward, until we should fall upon some channel which we knew must exist not far from us, in this direction, by which Franklin might have passed to the south-west."

The weather still continued boisterous and changeable. The channel of which they were in search was nowhere to be found. Scurvy, too, began to show itself among the men; so it was resolved to turn eastward again, and proceed towards the channel laid down to the east of Cape Bunny, which they resolved to follow up to Cape Walker.

During the march they met several herds of deer, and succeeded in shooting a few brace of ptarmigan. As they had no means of cooking them, however, they adopted the practice, common among Indians, of *freezing* them, and, while in this state, eating them raw; and we are assured that a "frozen ptarmigan, after a hard day's march, is by no means an unwelcome addition to an Arctic traveller's bill of fare!"

At last they arrived at Cape Walker. Its bold and conspicuous headland first met their gaze on the 4th of May; but here, as at Fury Beach, they were doomed to disappointment. Not a sign of Franklin's expedition having visited the spot was to be met with. Bellot carefully followed the windings of the rough ice outside the beach, in order to have a commanding view of the cliffs, while Kennedy searched along shore; but all without success. Ignorant that he had been preceded by Captain Austin's parties, Kennedy mistook the large cairn they had erected for a part of the cliff, and actually *walked over a smaller one* deeply covered with snow, without for a moment suspecting that the spot had been previously visited. If the large cairns, formed by the parties of Ommaney and Osborne the previous spring, could thus be overlooked, might not signals erected by Franklin have been equally undistinguishable amid the deep snow which enveloped this bleak and rugged coast?

Their stock of provisions now getting very low, Kennedy's party were obliged to go on short allowance; and, to make it last longer, they fed the dogs, from this time forward, on "old leather shoes, and fag-ends of buffalo robes"—on which, we are told, "they thrived wonderfully." It is added that one old snarling brute, who had received the name of Boatswain from the men on account of his ill-nature, "never seemed thoroughly to enjoy his meals till put upon a course of old shoes."

From this time the men grew worse and worse with scurvy; but were much revived by lighting upon a

29

small dépôt of provisions, which had been left near Cape McClintock by Sir James Ross, in 1849. This enabled them to start again with vigor for Whaler Point, which they reached on the 15th, and at which place they remained until the 27th, making free use of the lime-juice, cranberries, etc., which were deposited there. After being sufficiently restored, they started on their return to the ship, which they finally reached on the 30th of May, having been absent ninety-seven days, during which time six men with five dogs had travelled about eleven hundred miles, dragging, for most of the way, two thousand pounds' weight, sleeping in snow-houses, encamping at times on frozen seas, and rarely having fire when they halted to recruit.

The travellers found that all had gone on well at Batty Bay, in their absence. Nothing now remained but to get the ship clear of ice and return home. But there was little as yet in the appearance of ice or land to indicate that June had returned, except the falling in of some of the snow-houses. Gradually, however, the fierce glare of the sun began to make itself felt; and, on the 6th of August, after some sawing and blasting, the imprisoned vessel was liberated. On the 19th Kennedy reached Beechey Island, where he found the dépôt-ship North Star, attached to Sir E. Belcher's expedition, engaged in sawing into winter quarters. On the 7th of October, 1853, the Prince Albert arrived in England.

In concluding his narrative, Kennedy remarks of the young Frenchman who was associated with him, and whose subsequent fate, in connection with the history of Arctic discovery, is interesting: "To Mr. Bellot, my constant companion, not only do I owe the most valuable assistance from his scientific attainments, but his amiable qualities have cemented a deep personal regard, which can only end with my life."

Meanwhile researches from the North American coast were renewed by Mr. Rae. He left Fort Confidence, on the Coppermine, April 25th, 1851, with four men and three sledges drawn by dogs. Reaching the coast May 1st, he found the ice favorable for travel. On the 5th he landed at Douglas Island, and on the 7th gained the opposite shore. Traversing it to the east, until he reached 110° W. longitude, where his survey met that of Dease and Simpson, he retraced his steps, and advanced west until he turned Cape Baring, past latitude 70°, and longitude 117° W. From some elevated ground in this neighborhood high land could be seen to the north, but none was visible to the west. He got back to his provision station on the Kendall River upon the 10th of June, having travelled eight hundred and twenty-four geographical, or nine hundred and forty-two English miles, in forty days. In this lengthened journey his arrangements were much the same as during his survey of Committee Bay. He slept in snow houses, and, as he advanced, buried provisions to serve for his return. In the months of July and August he explored the coast of Victoria Land, east and north, in boats; marking every indentation, from the 101st to the 117th degree of latitude — an achievement, under the circumstances, of which any officer might be proud. On this newly-discovered coast he met many parties of Esquimaux; but his inquiries as to the grand subject were all fruitless. The American coast had now been diligently examined, from the entrance of Behring's Strait to the head of Hudson's Bay; and the conclusion was, that Franklin never reached so low a latitude.

CHAPTER XVI.

SIR EDWARD BELCHER'S EXPEDITION. — ARRIVAL IN BAFFIN'S BAY. — THE AMERICAN WHALER. — ARRIVAL AT BEECHEY ISLAND. — SEARCH COMMENCED. — INGLEFIELD'S VOYAGE. — THREE MORE EXPEDITIONS. — INGLEFIELD'S RETURN. — NEWS FROM M'CLURE. — PARRY AND FRANKLIN. — M'CLURE'S EXPLORATIONS. — ADVENTURES WITH ESQUIMAUX. — PERILOUS NAVIGATION. — DISCOVERY OF THE NORTH-WEST PASSAGE. — PERSONAL PERILS. — ABUNDANCE OF GAME. — WINTER QUARTERS. — SLEDGE-PARTIES. — STILL FROZEN UP. — PLAN OF ESCAPE.

THE unexpected and somewhat premature return of the squadrons under command of Captains Austin and Penny, in the autumn of 1851, increased the universal desire that the mysterious fate of Sir John Franklin's expedition should be thoroughly investigated. The interesting details brought back of the discovery of Franklin's winter quarters on Beechey Island, in 1845–46, revived the hopes that had begun to fade rapidly away. The opinion of those engaged in the sledging operations of 1851, that the missing ships had proceeded up Wellington Channel, and entered the open sea discovered by Captain Penny, and believed by him to be the great polar basin, — and the supposition that the lost ones might still be imprisoned, and alive, in its gloomy solitude of ice, — all tended to influence the public mind in favor of a continuance of the search.

Accordingly, in the spring of 1852, another expedition — the most extensive that had yet sailed for the polar regions — was fitted out, and placed under the command of Sir Edward Belcher. This squadron consisted of five vessels — the Assistance, the Resolute, the North Star, and two steamers, the Pioneer and Intrepid. These set sail in April for Baffin's Bay, purposing to make Beechey Island their head-quarters, whence the various vessels were to set out, separately or together, as might be thought best, to search the neighboring coasts. The Assistance and Pioneer were directed to sail up Wellington Channel, under the command of Sir Edward Belcher. The other two were to proceed, under Captain Kellett, to Melville Island, there to deposit provisions for the use of Captain Collinson and Commander M'Clure, should these gentlemen be successful in making the passage from Behring's Strait, for which they had set sail, it will be remembered, in January, 1850. The North Star was to remain at Beechey Island, as a dépôt store-ship.

The squadron sailed from England on the 28th April, 1852. On the 6th of July it was making its way through the ice in Baffin's Bay, in company with a fleet of whalers, which were there beset. Caught at the head of a bight in the ice, with the Assistance and the Pioneer, the Resolute was, for the emergency, docked there; and, by the ice closing behind her, was for a while detained. Meanwhile the rest of the fleet, whalers and discovery ships, passed on by a little lane of water, the American whaler McLellan leading.

The North Star, of the English squadron, followed the McLellan. A long train stretched out behind, — whalers and government ships, as they happened to fall into line, — a long three quarters of a mile. It was lovely weather, and, though the long lane closed up so that they could neither go back nor forward, nobody apprehended injury, till it was announced, on the morning of the 7th, that the McLellan was nipped in the ice, and her crew were deserting her. Sir Edward Belcher sent his carpenters to examine her, put a few charges of powder in the ice to relieve the pressure upon her, and by the end of the day it was agreed that her injuries could be repaired, and her crew went on board again. But the next morning there was a fresh wind, the McLellan was caught again, and the water poured into her, a steady stream. She drifted about, unmanageable, now into one ship, now into another; and the English whalemen began to pour on board, to help themselves to such plunder as they chose. At the captain's request, Sir Edward Belcher, to put an end to this, sent sentries on board; and he also sent working parties, to clear her as far as might be, and keep account of her stores. In a day or two more she sank to the water's edge, and a charge or two of powder put her out of the way of harming the rest of the fleet. After such a week spent together, it will easily be understood that the New London whalemen did not feel strangers on board one of Sir Edward's vessels, when, as we shall see, they found her "ready for occupation," three years and more afterwards.

On the 10th August the squadron reached its appointed head-quarters at Beechey Island. The season was remarkably open; Wellington Channel and Barrow's Straits were equally clear of ice. On the 14th Sir E. Belcher, with the Assistance and Pioneer, stood up the channel; and the following day Capt. Kellett, with the Resolute and Intrepid, sailed in open water for Melville Island. In this position we leave the expedition for the present, and proceed to give an account of the next that entered the field.

In consequence of the report, set afloat by Sir John Ross, on the authority of his Esquimaux interpreter, that Franklin and his crews had been murdered, by the natives, at Wolstenholme Sound, Lady Franklin refitted the Isabel screw-steamer, and sent her out, under Commander Inglefield, to ascertain the truth of the story. Inglefield sailed from England on the 6th July, 1852; coasted the northern shores of Baffin's Bay; advanced much further up Whale Sound than any previous navigator, — finding, as he proceeded, an immense expanse of open water; and pushed through Smith's Sound as far as latitude 78° 28′ 21″ north, without discovering any opposing land. Instead of the narrow strait which Smith's Sound has usually been thought, Captain Inglefield found it about thirty-six miles across, expanding considerably as it extended northward. The sea was open — that is, free from islands, except one looming in the extreme distance, to which the discoverer gave the name of Louis Napoleon.* From appearances, the leader of the expedition inferred that he had reached a more genial climate than that of Baffin's Bay; instead of the eternal snow which he had left behind, the rocks appeared of their natural color. There was ice, indeed, and in pretty large quantities; some of the mariners conceived they saw an ice-blink to the north; but the captain thought he could steam through. A gale, however, arose, which, increasing in violence, fairly blew them back — perhaps providentially, for they were not well fitted to winter in those high latitudes, with the probability of being held fast for an indefinite time.

"It was deemed, by every one on board, madness to attempt a landing; and thus," says Inglefield, "I was forced to relinquish those desires ere we bore up, which,

* "An island similar in position to that designated by Capt. Inglefield as Louis Napoleon does not exist. The land sighted in that direction may have been the top of a high mountain on the north side of Franklin Pierce Bay, though this supposition requires us to assume an error in the bearing; for, as given in the chart, no land could be within the range of sight. In deference to Capt. Inglefield, I have continued for this promontory the name which he had impressed upon it as an island." — *Kane's Narrative of the Second Grinnell Expedition*, vol. I., page 323.

with the heavy gale that now blew, was the most prudent step I could take. The rest of the 27th and the following day were spent in reaching, under snug sail, on either tack, whilst the pitiless northerly gale drove the sleet and snow into our faces, and rendered it painful work to watch for the icebergs, that we were continually passing. On this account, I could not heave the ship to, as the difficulty of discerning objects rendered it imperative that she should be kept continually under full command of the helm. The temperature, 25°, and the continual freezing of the spray, as it broke over the vessel, combined with the slippery state of the decks from the sleet that fell and the ice which formed from the salt water, made all working of ropes and sails not only disagreeable, but almost impracticable ; so that I was not sorry when the wind moderated.

"By four A. M., of the 29th, it fell almost to a calm ; but a heavy swell, the thick fog and mist remaining, precluded our seeing any distance before us ; and thus we imperceptibly drew too near the land-pack off the western shore, so that, a little after Mr. Abernethy had come on deck, in the morning watch, I was called up, as he said that the ship was drifting rapidly into the ice. Soon on deck, I found that there was no question on that score ; for even now the loose pieces were all round us, and the swell was rapidly lifting the ship further into the pack, whilst the roar of waters, surging on the vast floe-pieces, gave us no very pleasant idea of what would be our fate if we were fairly entrapped in this frightful chaos. The whale-boat was lowered, and a feeble effort made to get her head off shore ; but still in we went, plunging and surging amongst the crushing masses.

"While I was anxiously watching the screw, upon which all our hopes were now centred, I ordered the boiler, which had been under repair, and was partly disconnected, to be rapidly secured, the fires to be lighted, and to get up the steam ; in the mean time the tackles were got up for hoisting out our long-boat, and every preparation was made for the worst. Each man on board knew he was working for his life, and each toiled with his utmost might ; ice-anchors were laid out, and hawsers got upon either bow and quarter, to keep the ship from driving further in ; but two hours must elapse before we could expect the use of the engine. Eager were the inquiries when *will* the steam be up ? and wood and blubber were heaped in the furnace to get up the greatest heat we could command.

"At last the engineer reported all was ready ; and then, warping the ship's head round to seaward, we screwed ahead with great caution ; and at last found ourselves, through God's providence and mercy, relieved from our difficulties. It was a time of the deepest suspense to me ; the lives of my men and the success of our expedition depended entirely on the safety of the screw ; and thus I watched, with intense anxiety, the pieces of ice, as we drifted slowly past them ; and, passing the word to the engineer, 'Ease her,' 'Stop her,' till the huge masses dropped into the wake, we succeeded, with much difficulty, in saving the screw from any serious damage, though the edges of the fan were burnished bright from abrasion against the ice."

Besides penetrating one hundred and forty miles further than previous navigators, and finding an open sea stretching northwards, from Baffin's Bay, to at least the latitude of 80°, Captain Inglefield discovered a strait, in about 77½°, which he named Murchison Strait, and which he supposed to form a northern boundary to Greenland. In addition to the shores of the polar basin, he more accurately surveyed the eastern side of Baffin's Bay, from Carey's Islands to Cape Alexander, often remaining on deck the four-and-twenty hours round — for night there was none. He entered Jones's Sound, but was stopped by the ice, and came to the conclusion that there is no available channel from the sound into the polar basin, though there is possibly some narrow frozen strait. Inglefield then made for Beechey Island, where he arrived on the 7th September, and where he met the North Star, the dépôt ship of the Admiralty expedition. Thence, after a short delay, he shaped his course homeward. In spite of the advancing season, he examined a considerable part of the western coast of Baffin's Bay; and, though sorely beset on more than one occasion, managed to get through, and reached Stromness on the 4th of November — exactly four months from the date of his departure from Woolwich.

It is hardly necessary to add that Inglefield's investigations established the utter falsity of the story told by Sir John Ross's interpreter.

In the beginning of the year 1853 three expeditions were fitted out, partly to continue the search for Franklin, and partly to reinforce the vessels already in the field of action. The Rattlesnake, under Commander Trollope, and the Isabel screw-steamer — again refitted by Lady Franklin, and placed under the command of Mr. Kennedy — sailed for Behring's Strait, in order to carry supplies to Captains Collinson and M'Clure. Mr. Rae was again despatched to the Isthmus of Boothia, to make a further examination of the coast in that quarter; and Commander Inglefield was sent to Barrow's Straits, with the Phœnix and the Lady Franklin, to reinforce the squadron under Sir E. Belcher. Mr. Grinnell, of New York, aided by Mr. Peabody, of London, also fitted out an expedition, under the command of Dr. E. K. Kane, and sent it to explore the passages leading out of Baffin's Bay into the unknown ocean around the pole.

In the autumn of 1853 the deep interest of the British nation was aroused by the return of Captain Inglefield, in the Phœnix, with despatches conveying the intelligence that the north-west passage had at length been discovered by Captain M'Clure, of the Investigator, who had passed through Behring's Strait, and sailed to within a few miles of the most westerly discoveries made from the eastern side of America, at which point he had been frozen up for more than two years, and where his ship still lay, unable to advance or to retreat. No vessel had yet made the entire passage ; but, from the two extreme points of discovery, on either side, parties from the Investigator had walked over the frozen ocean ; and one gentleman — namely, Lieut. Cresswell, the bearer of despatches from Captain M'Clure — had sailed from England, entered Behring's Strait, and returned again to England by the Atlantic Ocean, having thus passed through the long-sought north-west passage.

This interesting intelligence, coupled with the announcement of M'Clure's safety, concerning which much anxiety had begun to be felt, was joyfully received ; and Lieut. Cresswell, the bearer of the good news, was treated with marked attention in England. At a public dinner, given him in his native town of Lynn, Sir Edward Parry, who was present, made some remarks on the probable fate of Sir John Franklin, which will be read with interest in this connection :

"While we are rejoicing over the return of our friend, and the probable return of his shipmates, we cannot but turn to that which is not a matter of rejoicing, but rather a matter of sorrow and regret — that there has not been found a single token of our dear long-lost Franklin and his companions. Not only has that been the case in the expedition in which Lieut. Gurney Cresswell has been engaged, but I understand it to be the case with Sir Edward Belcher, who has gone up the Wellington Inlet, where I certainly thought traces must be found, because at Beechey Island we knew Franklin passed the first winter when he went out. There we found three graves of his men, — and that is, up to the present moment, the only token whatever we have received of him. I do consider it a most mysterious thing, and I have thought of it as much as anybody. I can form but a single idea of the probable fate of Franklin. I do not agree with our friend Gurney Cresswell about the probability of both ships having gone down, and nothing been seen of them, because, although it is true that nothing might have been seen of the ships themselves, I do not believe the crews would have all perished at one moment. I think there is that stuff and stamina in one hundred and thirty Englishmen, that, somehow or other, they would have maintained themselves as well as a parcel of Esquimaux would. They would have found the Esquimaux, and there would have been something like a trace of them, if they had been on earth. The only thing which I can suggest is this: Wellington Strait was discovered by myself, on the expedition I spoke of. It is a large opening from Lancaster Sound.

"When I was going up westward from Melville Island, we saw Wellington Strait perfectly free from ice, and so I marked it on my chart. It was not my business to go north as long as I could get west, and, therefore, we ran past and did not examine it; but it has always been a favorite idea of those who imagined that the north-west passage was to be easily made by going north. That, we know, was the favorite idea of

Franklin; and we know he did intend, if he could not get westward, to go up Wellington Channel. We have it from his own lips. My belief is still that, after the first winter, he did go up that channel; and that, having steam-power (which I had not in my time), it is possible he may have gone up in a favorable season; for you cannot imagine anything more different than a favorable and an unfavorable season in those regions. You cannot imagine the changes that take place in the ice there. I have been myself sometimes beset for two or three days together by the ice, in such a way that from the mast-head I could not see sufficient water to float that bottle in; and in twenty-four hours there was not a bit of ice to be seen — nobody could tell why — I cannot tell why; and you might have sailed about as you may in your own river, as far as ice is concerned.

"Therefore, in a favorable season he may have gone up that inlet, and may, by the power of steam and favorable circumstances, have got so far to the north-east that, in an ordinary season, he could not get back again. And those who knew Franklin know this — that he would push on, year after year, so long as his provisions lasted. Nothing could stop him. He was not the man to look back, if he believed the thing was still possible. He may have got beyond the reach of our searching parties; for Sir Edward Belcher has not been able to get far up, and we have not been able to get the investigation completed. In speaking of Franklin, every one will feel sorrow for his probable fate. My dear friend Franklin was sixty years old when he left this country; and I shall never forget the zeal, the almost youthful enthusiasm, with which that man entered upon that expedition. Lord Haddington, who was then first lord of the Admiralty, sent for me, and said, 'I see, by looking at the navy-list, that Franklin is sixty years old: do you think we ought to let him go?' I said, 'He is a fitter man to go than any I know; and if you don't let him go, the man will die of disappointment.' He did go, and has been gone eight years; and, therefore, I leave to yourselves to consider what is the probability of the life of that excellent and valuable man. In the whole course of my experience I have never known a man like Franklin. I do not say it because he is dead — upon the principle *de mortuis nil nisi bonum;* but I never knew a man in whom different qualities were so remarkably combined. In my dear friend Franklin, with all the tenderness of heart of a simple child, there was all the greatness and magnanimity of a hero."

To this touching tribute, from the lips of a fellow-navigator, we append the following beautiful lines, quoted by a writer in one of the British quarterly reviews:

"Where is he? — where? Silence and darkness dwell
About him; as a soul cut off from men:
Shall we behold him yet a citizen
Of mortal life? Will he return to tell
(Prisoner from Winter's very citadel
Broken forth) what he before has told, again
How to the hearts and hands of resolute men,
God aiding, nothing is impossible?
Alas! the enclosure of the stony wave
Is strong, and dark the depths of polar night;
Yet One there is omnipotent to save,
And this we know, if comfort still we crave,
Into that dark he took with him a light —
The lamp that can illuminate the grave."

It will be remembered that Captains Collinson and M'Clure sailed for Behring's Strait in 1850, through which, in connection with the Plover and Herald, they endeavored to pass, but without success, except in the case of the Investigator (Captain M'Clure), which was seen on the 4th August, 1850, bearing gallantly into the heart of the "polar pack." The Enterprise (Captain Collinson), finding it impossible to follow, sailed to Hong-Kong, and wintered there; but in May, 1851, returned to Behring's Strait, and succeeded in entering the ice. The Plover remained at Port Clarence, as a reserve for these two vessels to fall back upon, while the Herald returned to England. From that date nothing was heard of these two vessels, until the arrival of the Phœnix, with the despatches of Captain M'Clure, bringing assurance of the safety of the Investigator.

On parting company with the Herald in Behring's Strait, in July, 1850, Captain M'Clure stood to the north-north-west, with a fresh breeze, with the intention of making the ice, which was accomplished on the 2d of August. During several days the Investigator battled with the foe — now boring through densely-packed masses, and then winding among the lanes which opened here and there as the currents or winds acted upon the pack. Occasionally they struck with considerable violence, but succeeded, at length, in rounding Point Barrow, and discovered clear water on the afternoon of the 7th — so far ahead, however, that it could only be seen from the "crow's nest."

Hundreds of walruses were seen huddled together on the ice, like sheep in a fold. M'Clure seems to have been rather favorably impressed in regard to these animals, on account of the affection shown by the mothers for their young. He would not allow them to be shot.

The most remarkable feature of the walrus consists in two teeth, or tusks, which project in a curved line from the upper jaw, and are nearly two feet in length. They are of beautiful white bone, almost equal to ivory, and much used in the fabrication of artificial teeth. The front face, when seen at a little distance, bears a striking resemblance to the human ; and its appearance is suspected to have sometimes given rise to the fanciful reports of mermaids in the northern seas. The walrus is monogamous, and the mother brings forth her young only one at a birth, either on the shore or on the ice. Like all the cetaceous tribes, to which the walrus is allied, he is disposed to be peaceful and harmless. Parry describes the supine security with which a number of them lay on the ice, piled over each other, without discomposing themselves at the approach of a party armed for their destruction. In Spitzbergen, however, where they have been long the object of chase to the Russian hunters, they are reported to keep very strict watch ; it being said that one stands guard while the others sleep. Even when sensible of danger, they are not forward to face it, but rather shun the attack by rushing beneath the ice, while those behind, with their tusks, urge forward their companions. Yet, when they are compelled to combat, they give battle with the utmost coolness and courage ; they then stand firm by each other, rush in one united body against the boats (as in the attack on the Trent's boat, page 71), and, striking with their tusks, endeavor to overset them. When repulsed, too, they repeatedly rally, and in the end yield only to the fire-arms of Europeans, or to the stratagems of the Esquimaux. Maternal tenderness, and the determination with which the female defends her young, are equally conspicuous in them as in the whale species. The walrus must live near open water.

"The wind," writes McClure, "almost immediately failing, the boats were all manned, and towing commenced amid songs and cheers, which continued, with unabated good-humor, for six hours. Being in perfectly clear water in Smith's Bay, a light air springing up, we worked to the eastward. At two A. M. of the 8th, being off Point Drew, I sent Mr. Court (second master) on shore to erect a cairn, and bury a notice of our having passed. Upon landing, we were met by three natives, who at first were very timid; but, upon exchanging signs of friendship, which consisted of raising the arms three times over the head, they approached the boat, and, after the pleasant salutation of rubbing noses, became very communicative; when, by the assistance of our valuable interpreter, Mr. Miertsching, we found the tribe consisted of ten tents (this being the only approach to their numbers he could obtain); that they had arrived only three days previously, and that they hold communication with a party inland, who trade with the Russian Fur Company." They had observed us the evening before, and had thought our masts were trees in motion, and wondered at the sight.

The natives seen here had spent their lives between the Coppermine River and Point Barrow; and, from the circumstances of their not having met with any of Franklin's party, M'Clure concludes that the latter could not have been lost on these shores. "The coast," says he, "is inhabited throughout, and the natives are, to all appearance, a kind and merry race; and, when we gave them presents, through the medium of the interpreter, we told them that we were looking for our lost brothers, and if they saw any white men in distress they were to be very kind; to which they assented by saying that they would, and would give them 'plenty of deer's flesh.'"

So narrow was the passage of open water between the ice and the shore, along which the Investigator had to pass, that she had great difficulty sometimes in tacking, — requiring to do so, in some places, nearly every ten minutes; and, on one occasion, they actually took the ground while "in stays." Fortunately the bottom was soft clay, and they hove off again immediately. Gradually, however, the lane widened, the reaches became longer and longer, and all apprehension of being forced on shore was soon over. On the 10th of August, 1850, they passed the mouth of the Colville River, the influence of which stream was found to extend twelve or fourteen miles out to sea; the surface, at that distance from shore, being of a dirty mud-color, and scarcely salt.

At this part of the coast they again fell in with natives, who came off in two *baidars*, to the number of thirty. A very animated and curious scene ensued. A vigorous barter was immediately commenced, after the curiosity of the wondering Esquimaux with regard to the ship was satisfied. Their imitative propensity was rather oddly brought into play during the traffic. Seeing the sailors cut the tobacco into pieces, to give in exchange for salmon-trout, they at once began to do the same with the fish! but were soon checked in this, and were obliged to succumb to the white men.

During the afternoon, while standing along a low flat island, a pair of seal-skin inexpressibles were observed fluttering from the top of a pole, held up by a number of natives, who took this method of intimating their desire to receive a visit. In obedience to the signal, the boats were lowered, and pulled in to the shore. The Esquimaux appeared to regret their temerity, however; for, on the near approach of the sailors, the inexpressibles were dropped, and the whole tribe fled. As usual, however, they regained courage on observing the friendly gesticulations of the white men, and soon approached them, tossing up their arms, and making other signs of friendship; ending, at last, by rubbing noses with, and affectionately embracing, the gallant tars.

These poor people had never seen white men before: they had no article of European manufacture about their persons, and spent their lives in hunting walruses and seals on these low islands during the summer months, retiring to their warm residences on the mainland during winter. After holding some communication with them, through the medium of the interpreter, Captain M'Clure left them, having first made them a few presents, and, among other things, a boat's ensign, in commemoration of the first man-of-war whose flag has floated over these sterile regions. The magnificence of this latter gift quite astounded them, and caused them to rush tumultuously to their canoes to carry it off to their women, who were encamped on another island close at hand.

Some of these primitive people were apparently addicted to stealing. While M'Clure was placing some presents in the right hand of a chief, in token of good will, he felt the fellow's left hand in his pocket. The Esquimaux, however, laughed heartily when they were caught in their thefts; and so the Englishmen thought best to do the same, and not allow peccadilloes to mar the harmony of their intercourse.

Coasting along, as they found opportunity, the voyagers advanced slowly—sometimes with much and sometimes with little water—till the morning of the 13th, when the ice closed round, and hemmed them in completely. In this dilemma, the boats were sent to sound, and shortly returned, reporting a practicable passage in three fathoms water. Unfortunately, they hit on a spot with only two and a half fathoms, and so were soon fast aground. As it turned out, however, the bottom was sandy, so that no damage was done to the ship; but one of the whale-boats, which contained part of the cargo taken out to lighten the vessel, upset, and eleven casks of salt beef were lost. This was a serious loss at such a time. After five hours' hard work, they got once more into deep water.

In this way they continued to coast along the margin of the pack for about four or five hundred miles, when it became somewhat more open. It was now resolved to shape a course to the north-north-west for Banks's Land. In doing this, however, they were frequently obliged to alter, and often to retrace their course, owing to the deceptive nature of the lanes of water, and the perplexing fogs that constantly prevailed, obliging them to proceed chiefly by soundings.

On the 21st of August they passed the mouth of the Mackenzie River, and made the Pelly Islands. Soon after, they reached Warren Point, where natives were seen on the shore; and as M'Clure wished to forward despatches by them, if possible, to the Hudson's Bay Company's posts on the Mackenzie, the boats were ordered out. M'Clure believed the natives to have been in connection with these posts, and expected a friendly reception from them. "Great, therefore," says he, "was my surprise, upon approaching the beach, to find, instead of being greeted by the usual friendly signs, that two savages, with gesticulations the most menacing, having bended bows, with arrows on their strings, and one with a large knife, which he brandished most significantly, waved us off. Taking no heed of these hostile demonstrations, we pulled in; they retreated, yelling furiously. Upon our reaching the beach, we made the same signs of friendship which we had used with the Esquimaux further west, but without any effect, until joined by the interpreter, who was in full native costume. This gave them confidence, and, upon his explaining our friendly intentions, they approached; but when within about thirty yards, remarking some muskets which the boat's crew had, their fury revived. To pacify them, they were laid upon the ground, where they became the object of a cautious examination. Still unsatisfied, they beckoned to take them to the boat. Seeing that nothing short of this would allow of any communication, I sent them away, when they approached, and permitted us to examine their bows and arrows."

It was found that these Esquimaux had no communication with the Mackenzie, in consequence of their being at war with the neighboring tribes, and having had several skirmishes with the Indians of that quarter. This may in some measure account for their fierce dispositions, so very different from those previously met with. A flat brass button was observed suspended from the ear of one of the chiefs of this tribe; and, on being questioned as to where he got it, he replied that "it had been taken from a white man who had been killed by one of his tribe. The white man belonged to a party which had landed at Point Warren, and there built a house; nobody knew how they came, as they had no boat; but they went inland. The man killed had strayed from the party, and he (the chief) and his son had buried him upon a hill at a little distance."

No satisfactory or intelligible reply could be got as to when this event occurred. M'Clure remained at this place for a short time to investigate the matter, but only found two huts, which, from the rottenness of the wood of which they were built, appeared to be of a very old date indeed. The grave of the white man was not found.

All along this coast they met with parties of natives, who almost invariably showed a hostile front on their first appearance, and as invariably became amicable after a little coquetting. In these interviews they had frequently curious scenes, especially in the distribution of presents to some natives near Cape Bathurst, who could scarcely be restrained when the gaudy gifts were presented to their longing eyes. Mr. Miertsching, the interpreter, was always of the greatest use on these occasions, and won so much the esteem of one old chief, that, in the fulness of his heart, he prayed him to stay with the tribe forever; and, by way of inducement to do so, presented him with his daughter, a pretty girl of about fifteen, to be his wife, assuring him, at the same time, that a tent, and all the etceteras of an Esquimaux establishment, should be given to him along with her! They were frequently invited to partake of native hospitality in the shape of roasted whale and venison, besides salmon, blubber, and other Arctic delicacies.

Great numbers of whales were seen about this time; also a polar bear on a fragment of ice. On the 5th of September, the hopes of the navigators were suddenly raised, and as speedily cast down again. "The weather," says M'Clure, "which had been squally, accompanied by a thick fog during the early part of the day, cleared towards noon, when a large volume of smoke was observed about twelve miles south-west. . . . As divers opinions were in circulation respecting its probable cause, and the ice-mate having positively reported that from the crow's nest he could distinguish several persons moving about, dressed in white shirts, and observed some white tents in the hollow of the cliff, I certainly had every reason to imagine they were a party of Europeans in distress; for I was convinced that no travellers would remain for so long a period as we had remarked the smoke, for their pleasure; therefore, to satisfy myself, equally as others, I determined to send a boat on shore, as it was now calm. The first whale-boat, under Lieut. Cresswell, with Dr. Armstrong and Mr. Miertsching, was despatched to examine into the cause, who, on their return, reported that the smoke emanated from fifteen small mounds of volcanic appearance, occupying a space of about fifty yards, the place strongly impregnated with sulphur, the lower mounds being about thirty feet above the sea-level, the highest about fifty feet. The land in its vicinity was blue clay, much intersected with ravines and deep water-courses, varying in elevation from three hundred to five hundred feet; the mark of a reindeer was traced to a small pond of water immediately above the mounds. Notice of our having landed was left, which would not long remain, as the cliff is evidently rapidly crumbling away. Thus the mystery of the white shirts and tents was most satisfactorily explained."

At four A. M. of the 6th they were off the small islands, near Cape Parry, bearing north-east-by-north, with a fine westerly breeze. The same day, high land was observed on the port-bow, on the western shore of which the main body of the ice rested. This was the first sight obtained of *terra incognita*. Hitherto they had been sailing along a shore which had in former years been surveyed, on foot and in boats, by Franklin, Back, Dease, Simpson, and others; although, indeed, theirs was the first *ship* that had sailed in these waters; but the land which now appeared to them on the left bow was quite new. Accordingly, they hove to, and landed and took possession in the name of her majesty, calling it "Baring's Island," in honor of the first lord of the Admiralty. The south cape of this land, a fine, bold headland, rising almost perpendicularly to the height of about a thousand feet, was named "Lord Nelson's Head." The latitude was found to be 71° 6′ north, longitude 123° 0′ west. A note of their progress being deposited here, they returned to the ship and sailed along the eastern coast, as being freer from ice than that on the west. It was afterwards found that the land taken possession of, instead of being an island, was the southernmost point of the shore which had been named "Banks's Land," by Parry, in 1820. The name Baring Island was accordingly changed to Baring Land.

"We observed," writes M'Clure, "numerous traces of reindeer, hare, and wild-fowl. Moss, and divers species of wild-flowers, were also found in great abundance; many specimens of them, equally as of other subjects of interest to the naturalist, were selected, with much care, by Dr. Armstrong. From an elevation obtained of about five hundred feet, we had a fine view towards the interior, which was well clothed with moss, giving a verdant appearance to the ranges of hills that rose gradually to between two thousand and three thousand feet, intersected with ravines, which must convey a copious supply of water to a large lake situated in the centre of a wide plain, about fifteen miles distant. The sight to seaward was favorable in the extreme; open water, with a very small quantity of ice, for the distance of full forty miles toward the east, insured good progress in that direction."

At noon, September 9th, 1850, observations placed the Investigator only *sixty* miles from Barrow's Strait. "I cannot," writes M'Clure, "describe my anxious feelings. Can it be possible that this water communicates with Barrow's Strait, and shall prove to be the long-sought north-west passage? Can it be that so humble a creature as I am will be permitted to perform what has baffled the talented and wise for hundreds of years? But all praise be ascribed unto Him who hath conducted us so far in safety. His ways are not our ways: nor the means that He uses to accomplish his ends within our comprehension. The wisdom of the world is foolishness with Him." Land was observed to the eastward, to which M'Clure gave the name of Prince Albert's Land. Several remarkable peaks appeared to be of volcanic origin.

On the 16th the Investigator was making slow progress toward Barrow's Strait; and on the 17th of September, 1850, they reached their most advanced position, in latitude 73° 10′ north, and longitude 117° 10′ west, *about thirty miles* from the waters of that series of straits, which, under the names of Melville, Barrow, and Lancaster, communicate with Baffin's Bay. At this tantalizing distance the ship ceased to drift, and the ice appeared to have reached a point beyond which some unknown cause would not allow it to proceed. The heavy pack of Melville Strait, lying across the head of the channel, was supposed to be the reason of the ice of Prince of Wales Strait ceasing to move on to the north-east; and the impassable nature of the pack in the same direction, in the following year, confirmed this hypothesis.

On the 9th of September M'Clure tells us he had debated in his mind whether to abandon all hope of reaching Barrow's Strait that year, and retrace his course southward in search of a wintering place, or to hold on, so far as he might, and run the risk of wintering in the pack. "I decided," he says, "on the latter of these two courses;" and the consideration which influenced him in this difficult choice was, "that to relinquish the ground obtained through so much labor and anxiety, for the remote chance of finding safe winter quarters, would be injudicious, thoroughly impressed as I was with the absolute importance of retaining every mile to insure any favorable results while navigating these seas." Besides this, it was desirable to hold as advanced a position as possible, in order that the spring sledge-

31

parties in 1851 might be at once set to work upon new and unsearched coast-lines.

The smallest pools of water now became rapidly covered with ice ; the eider-duck, the hardiest of Arctic birds, was last seen on the 23d of September. On the 27th, the temperature being then at zero, preparations were begun for housing over the ship. These preparations were made under circumstances that might well shake the nerves of a strong man. As the ice surged, the ship was thrown violently from side to side, now lifted out of water, now plunged into a hole. "The crushing, creaking, and straining," says Captain M'Clure, in his log, "is beyond description ; the officer of the watch, when speaking to me, is obliged to put his mouth close to my ear, on account of the deafening noise."

The officers had just time to congratulate themselves upon the escape from past dangers, and to express gratitude at having lost only thirty miles of latitude by the drifting of the pack, when a change of wind set it all again in motion. The 28th was spent in breathless anxiety, as, helpless in their icy trammels, they swept northward again toward the cliffs of Princess Royal Island.

These cliffs rose perpendicularly from the sea at the part against which the ship appeared to be setting, and, as the crew eyed them for a hope of safety, if the good craft should be crushed against their face, they could see no ledge upon which even a goat could have established a footing, and an elevation of four hundred feet precluded a chance of scaling them. To launch the boats over the moving pack was their sole chance, — and that a poor one, rolling and upheaving, as it was, under the influence of wind, tide, and pressure.

"It looks a bad job, this time," inquiringly remarked one of the sailors, as he assisted another in coiling down neatly a frozen hawser. "Yes!" was the rejoinder, as the other shaded his eyes from the driving snow, and cast a glance at the dark cliff looming through the storm, "the old craft will double up like an old basket when she gets alongside of them rocks!"

The Investigator's hour was not yet come, however; and, when within five hundred yards of the rocks, the ice *coach-wheeled* her along them, and finally swept her past the islands upon the eastern side.

No water was in sight from the mast-head; yet onwards they drifted slowly, and on the 30th became again stationary, in latitude 72° 50′ N., and longitude 117° 55′ W., very nearly as far north as they had sailed a fortnight before.

"On the 8th of October," says M'Clure, "our perplexities terminated with a nip that lifted the vessel a foot, and heeled her four degrees to port, in consequence of a large tongue getting beneath her, in which position we quietly remained." Here the Investigator passed the winter of 1850–51.

From the 10th to the 21st of October, preparations were made to despatch a sledge-party to the northward to reach Barrow's Strait, and get assurance of the fact of the discovery of a north-west passage. A remarkable rise of temperature to 24° *plus* of Fahrenheit, from 2° *minus*, with the wind blowing fresh from *north-east*, would seem to indicate that the winter of this region is modified by the warm air from the open water of Barrow's Strait. This sudden change was far from pleasant to the crew; and the old hands warned the novices against "being fools enough to pull their clothes off on account of such a bit of sunshine; for, perhaps, in an hour's time *Zero* would be about again."

On the 21st October, 1850, M'Clure started for Barrow's Strait, with a sledge manned with six men; but it broke down before they had proceeded far, and they had to send to the ship for another. It did not reach them till the next day. After some difficulty in crossing ridges of broken ice, they reached vast fields of smooth ice of the present season's formation; and here a new obstacle awaited them. The autumnal snow had accumulated upon the surface of these young ice-fields, and, weighing them down, caused the sea-water to flow through sufficiently to render the under part of the snow almost as tenacious as clay. The fatigue of hauling two hundred pounds apiece over such a road was excessive. Unfortunately, no water could be had, and the crew suffered much from thirst; for every handful of snow which they thrust into their parched mouths augmented rather than assuaged their sufferings, as it contained more or less of the salts of the sea-water.

On the 24th a cape was seen at what appeared a distance of twelve miles, and every man now dragged with a will, in the hope of reaching that night the end of his journey; but, after seven hours' labor, the cape still retained its original position, and they seemed not a mile nearer to it. M'Clure then saw that he had been much deceived in its apparent distance, owing to the clearness of the atmosphere, and that thirty miles was a nearer estimate than twelve of the probable length of their march. After a night's rest, and another hard day's work, they were still two miles off the cape, when night closed in, obliging them to halt and encamp. Though disappointed in not sighting Barrow's Strait on the 25th, they were all much cheered by the multiplying proofs around them of its close proximity. Away to the north-east they already saw that wonderful oceanic ice described by Sir Edward Parry in his voyage to Melville Island, in 1819. The latitude was now 73° 25′ N.

The morning of the 26th October, 1850, was fine and

cloudless. It was with no ordinary feelings of joy and gratitude that M'Clure and his party started before sunrise to obtain from the adjacent hill a view of that sea which connected their discoveries with those of Sir Edward Parry. Ascending a hill six hundred feet above the sea-level, they patiently awaited the increase of light to reveal *the long-sought-for north-west passage from the Atlantic to the Pacific Ocean.*

As the sun rose, the panorama slowly unveiled itself. First the land called after Prince Albert showed out on an easterly bearing; and, from a point since named after Sir Robert Peel, it evidently turned away to the east, and formed the northern entrance of the channel upon that side.

The coast of Banks's Land terminated about twelve miles further on than where the party stood; and thence it turned away to the north-west, forming the northern coast of that land, the loom of which had been so correctly reported by Parry more than thirty years before. Away to the north, and across the entrance of Prince of Wales Strait, lay the frozen waters of Barrow's, or, as it is now called, Melville Strait; and, raised as they were at an altitude of six hundred feet above its level, the eye-sight embraced a distance which precluded the possibility of any land lying in that direction between them and Melville Island.

The north-west passage was discovered! All doubt as to the water communication between the two great oceans was removed; and it now alone remained for M'Clure, his officers and men, to perfect the work by traversing the few thousand miles of known ground between them and their homes.

The position of Mount Observation, from which the important discovery had been made, was ascertained to be in latitude 73° 30′ 39″ N., longitude 114° 39′ W.

The travellers encamped that night on Cape Lord John Russell, and cheered lustily as they reached the shores of Barrow's Strait. A mimic bonfire, of a broken sledge and dwarf willow, was lighted by the seamen in celebration of the event.

The question of a north-west passage was now placed beyond all doubt. From the point in Barrow's Strait upon which they were looking — a point opposite to Cape Hay, in Melville Island — Parry had sailed into Baffin's Bay and home. The existence, therefore, of a water communication round the north coast of America was finally demonstrated. They had not found any trace of Franklin; but they had done the next best thing, and enough for M'Clure's fame.

The rapid fall of temperature now warned M'Clure that he should return without delay to the ship. From Point Lord John Russell, the coast of Banks's Land was seen to trend away to the westward, and increase in boldness of outline and altitude. Much vegetation, for this latitude, was observed, and numerous traces of animals, such as the deer, hare, and ptarmigan, as well as of the fox and wolf; but no animal was seen. A large cairn was constructed, a due record of the visit of the party placed therein, and then, in the teeth of a south-east gale, they commenced their return to the Investigator.

M'Clure came near perishing in trying to get back. On the 30th of October, at two P. M., having seen the Princess Royal Isles, and knowing the position of the ship from them, he left his sledge, with the intention of pushing for the ship, and having a warm meal ready for his men on their arrival. When still six miles from the ship the night overtook him; and with it came a dense mist, accompanied with snow-drift, which rolled down the strait, and obscured every object. Unable to see his road, but endeavoring to preserve a course by the wind, M'Clure continued to hasten on, until repeated and heavy falls amongst the broken ice warned him to desist, or incur the additional peril of broken limbs.

"I now," he says, "climbed on a mass of squeezed-up ice, in the hope of seeing my party, should they pass near, or of attracting the attention of some one on board the vessel by firing my fowling-piece. Unfortunately, I had no other ammunition than what it was loaded with; for I had fancied, when I left the sledge, that the two charges in the gun would be all I should be likely to require. After waiting for an hour patiently, I was rejoiced to see through the mist the glare of a blue light, evidently burnt in the direction in which I had left the sledge. I immediately fired to denote my position; but my fire was unobserved, and, both barrels being discharged, I was unable to repeat the signal. My only hope now rested upon the ship's answering; but nothing was to be seen; and, although I once more saw, at a greater distance, the glare of another blue light from the sledge, there seemed no probability of my having any other shelter for the night than what the floe afforded. Two hours elapsed; I endeavored to see the face of my pocket-compass by the light of a solitary lucifer match, which happened to be in my pocket; but in this hope I was cruelly disappointed, for it fizzed and went out, leaving me in total darkness.

"It was now half-past eight; there were eleven hours of night before me, a temperature 15° below zero, bears prowling about, and I with an unloaded gun in my hands. The sledge-party might, however, reach the ship, and, finding I had not arrived, search would be made, and help be sent; so I walked to and fro upon my hummock until, I suppose, it must have been eleven o'clock, when that hope fled likewise. Descending from the top of the slab of ice upon which I had clambered, I found under its lee a famous bed of soft, dry snow; and, thoroughly tired out, I threw myself upon it

RESTING IN THE SNOW.

and slept for perhaps three hours, when, upon opening my eyes, I fancied I saw the flash of a rocket. Jumping upon my feet, I found that the mist had cleared off, and that the stars and aurora borealis were shining in all the splendor of an Arctic night. Although unable to see the islands or the ship, I wandered about the ice in different directions until daylight, when, to my great mortification, I found I had passed the ship fully the distance of four miles."

Retracing his steps, M'Clure reached the Investigator on the 31st October, very tired, but otherwise none the worse for his rough and dangerous exposure to a winter's night in 73° north latitude. A few hours afterwards the sledge arrived, and great was the rejoicing on board at the news confirming the discovery of a north-west passage.

During the absence of the captain and his party, the officers of the Investigator had not been idle. Upon the adjacent shores of Prince of Wales Strait they succeeded in killing a fine herd of musk-oxen, consisting of three bulls, a cow, and a calf, and yielding a supply of twelve hundred and ninety-six pounds of solid meat.

During the first fortnight in December the temperature of the external air ranged from 23° to 37° below zero, whilst between decks from +40° to +50° was the average. From the 9th January, 1851, to the 16th, was the coldest period on board the Investigator — the thermometer showing 40° to 50° below zero.

Early one dark and icy morning in January, a man named John Eames was walking out upon the floe, when he saw a small herd of reindeer trot by. "It is pretty evident," says M'Clure, "that, during the whole winter, animals may be found in these straits, and that the want of sufficient light alone prevents our larder being stored with fresh food." "Subsequent observation," says Commander Osborne, "has completely overthrown the idea that the reindeer, musk-ox, or other animals inhabiting the archipelago of islands north of America, migrate southward to avoid an Arctic winter. Throughout Banks's Land, Melville Island, Bathurst, and Cornwallis Land, there have been found indubitable proofs of the reindeer, bear, musk-ox, marmot, wolf, hare, and ptarmigan, — in short, all the Fauna of these climes, — wintering in the latitudes in which they are found during the summer." A raven, which had haunted the ship during the period of cold and darkness, left it before the sun reäppeared, and his departure was sensibly felt by every one on board.

Early in March, 1851, a whale-boat was carried on sledges, with much labor, to the Princess Royal Island, and a dépôt established of three months' victualling for the entire crew. In April three sledges were laden with provisions for six weeks, and, with six men to each sledge, were sent on different courses. One sledge, commanded by Lieut. Haswell, was directed to proceed to the south-east, following the coast of Prince Albert's Land, toward the land seen north of Dolphin and Union Strait, and named by its discoverer Wollaston Land; another sledge, under Lieut. Cresswell, was to follow the coast of Banks's Land to the north-west; whilst the remaining party, with Mr. Wynniatt, was charged with the duty of examining the coast of Albert Land to the north-east, toward Cape Walker. On the 18th April the several parties, with their sledges, left the ship to search for traces of Sir John Franklin and his men.

They returned, after intervals of from three to seven weeks, but without having found any traces of the missing navigators, or gained any contributions of moment for geographical science. The most important incident seems to have been Lieut. Haswell's encounter with some Esquimaux, who said they had never before cast eyes on a white man. Copper of the purest description seemed to be plentiful with them, for all their implements were of that metal; their arrows were tipped with it, and some of the sailors saw a quantity of it in a rough state in one of the tents. M'Clure afterwards had some friendly interviews with these people, in whose decaying prospects he became quite interested.

As spring advanced, signs of a change began to multiply. First came a seal at the hole in the floe kept open near the ship in case of fire; then a large polar bear; and, lastly, hares and ptarmigan. Among the startling narratives of Arctic escapes, few exceed that of Whitfield, one of the hunters, who lost his way in a snow-drift, and was found within a yard of the tent, stiff and rigid as a corpse, his head thrown back, his eyes fixed, his mouth open and filled with snow, his gun slung over his shoulder, and his body being fast buried in a snow-wreath. When happily brought to himself, he related that whilst struggling with the snow-storm he felt a chill, and then a fit came on, during which he imagined people came close to him ; he had partially recovered, and, discovering a track, had nearly reached the tent-door, when he was overtaken by another fit, and had sunk down, a yard from the tent-door, in the attitude of supplication in which he was found. Had not one of the hunters looked out of the door by chance, he must have been frozen to death in that position, within a yard of a place of refuge!

There was great joy on board the Investigator from the 10th to the 14th of July, 1851. The floe had commenced breaking up, and on the 17th the good ship cast off, — only, however, to be caught in the pack-ice, and once more drifted with the crushing floes against the cliffs of Princess Royal Island. Finally she drifted to the tantalizing distance of twenty-five miles from the waters of Barrow's Strait. Further than that, no effort could advance the ship ; the young ice at nights had already begun to form again, the sun once more set at night, the pack-ice closed up the exit, and M'Clure was obliged to give the passage up as a hopeless thing, and to retrace his steps, in order that, by going round by the south of Banks's Land, he might try and reach Melville Island from that direction.

It was a truly grievous position to be placed in, to be within some thirty miles of a clear sea, which, had they once been able to pass into, they could have reached England the same summer, — and to have to turn back with the prospect of another winter in the polar regions. But the ice was as inexorable as if the Isthmus of Panama had stood between them and the Atlantic ; and there was no help for it. At first matters went on well, in their southerly progress ; not a particle of ice was met with. Floes, hummocks, and the huge piles of ice that fringed the coast, had alike disappeared.

On the 24th of July they had nearly reached Point Armstrong, upon which the ice was resting. Here their course was checked. There was much drift-wood on the beach, of large dimensions, mostly American pine. The cutter was consequently despatched for a load, and some of the pieces appeared so fresh that the carpenter was of opinion that two years was the extreme of their quitting the forest. "The wind, veering to the westward during the night," says M'Clure, "set large bodies of ice into the water we occupied, which was rapidly filling. To prevent being forced on shore, we were obliged, at eight A. M. of the 25th, to run into the pack, where we drifted, according to the tide, about a mile and a half from the beach; but, during the twenty-four hours, made about two miles and a half to the north-east, from which, when taken with the quantity of drift-wood that is thickly strewed along the beach, I am of opinion that on this side of the strait there is a slight current to the north-east, while upon the opposite one it sets to the southward, upon which there is scarcely any wood, and our progress, while similarly situated, was in a southern direction. We continued drifting in the pack, without meeting any obstruction, until ten A. M. of the 1st of August, when a sudden and most unexpected motion of the ice swept us with much velocity to the north-east, toward a low point, off which were several shoals, having many heavy pieces of grounded ice upon them, toward which we were directly setting, decreasing the soundings from twenty-four to nine and a half fathoms. Destruction was apparently not far distant, when, most opportunely, the ice eased a little, and, a fresh wind coming from the land, sail was immediately made, which, assisted by warps, enabled the ship to be forced ahead about two hundred yards, which shot us clear of the ice and the point into sixteen and a half fathoms, in which water we rounded the shoals; the ice then again closed, and the ship became fixed until the 14th of August, when the fog, which since the previous day had been very dense, cleared, and disclosed open water about half a mile from the vessel, with the ice loose about her."

The difficulty of clearing away large masses of ice was, to some extent, obviated by blasting. "Previously to quitting the floe," says M'Clure, "I was desirous of trying what effect blasting would have upon such a mass. A jar containing thirty-six pounds of powder was let down twelve feet into the water near the centre; the average thickness was eleven feet, and its diameter four hundred yards. The result was most satisfactory, rending it in every direction, so that with ease we could effect a passage through any part of it."

Cape Kellett was rounded with some little difficulty, the ship passing between the edge of grounded ice and the coast. The land was now so low that the hand lead-line became for a while their best guide; the soundings happily were regular, and, aided by it and a fair wind, they advanced apace to the northward. Throughout the 19th of August, 1851, the ship sometimes ran as much as seven knots per hour, the width of the lane of water in which they were sailing varying from three to five miles. Noon that day found them in 73° 55′ north latitude, and 123° 52′ 30″ west longitude; and already did M'Clure count upon extending his voyage to the north of Melville Island, and then striking for some strait or sound leading into Baffin's Bay.

That night, however, a sudden and remarkable change took place. They had just crossed Burnet Bay, within Norway and Robilliard Island, when the coast suddenly became as abrupt and precipitous as a wall; the water was very deep, — sixty fathoms by the lead-line within four hundred yards of the face of the cliffs, and fifteen fathoms water when actually touching them. The lane of water had diminished to two hundred yards in width where broadest; and even that space was much hampered by loose pieces of ice aground or adrift. In some places the channel was so narrow that the quarter-boats had to be topped up to prevent their touching the cliffs upon the one hand, or the lofty ice upon the other; and so perfectly were they running the gauntlet, that on many occasions the ship could not "round to," for want of space.

Their position was full of peril; yet they could but push on, for retreat was now as dangerous as progress. The pack was of the same fearful description as one they had fallen in with in the offing of the Mackenzie River, during the previous autumn; it drew forty and fifty feet of water, and rose in rolling hills upon the surface, some of them a hundred feet from base to summit. Any attempt to force the frail ship against such ice was of course mere folly; all they could do was to watch for every opening, trust in the mercy of God, and push ahead in the execution of their duty. If the ice at such a time had set in with its vast force against the sheer cliff, nothing, they all felt, could have saved them.

Enough has been said to give a correct idea of the peril incurred at this stage of the voyage, without entering into minute details of the hair-breadth escapes hourly taking place; but one instance may be given as a sample of the rest. After the 20th of August the Investigator lay helplessly fixed off the north-west of Banks's Land; the wind had pressed in the ice, and for a while all hopes of further progress were at an end. On the 29th of August, however, a sudden move took place, and a moving floe struck a huge mass to which the ship had been secured, and, to the horror of those on board, such was the enormous power exerted that the mass slowly reared itself on its edge close to the ship's bows, until the upper part was higher than the fore-yard; and every moment appeared likely to be the Investigator's last, for the ice had but to topple over to sink her and her crew under its weight. At the critical moment there was a shout of joy; for the mass, after oscillating fearfully, broke up, rolled back in its original position, and they were saved.

Hardly, however, was this danger past than a fresh one threatened; for the berg to which the ship was secured was impelled forward by the whole weight of the driving pack toward a low point of land, on which with frightful pressure the great floes were breaking up, and piling themselves tier upon tier. The Investigator had no power of escape; but every hawser was put in requisition, and hands stationed by them. An attempt to blow up a grounded berg, upon which the ship was driving, only partially succeeded; the nip came on, the poor ship groaned, and every plank and timber quivered from stem to stern, in this trial of strength between her and the ice. "Our fate seemed sealed," says M'Clure; and he made up his mind to let go all hawsers. The order was given, and with it the wreck of the Investigator seemed certain: all the leader hoped for was — to use his own words — "that we might have the ship thrown up sufficiently to serve as an asylum for the winter." If she should sink between the two contending bergs, the destruction of every soul was inevitable.

But, at the very moment when the order to "let go all hawsers" was given, and even before it could be obeyed, a merciful Providence caused the berg, which most threatened, to break up, and the Investigator was once more saved; though still so tightly was she beset, that there was not room to drop a lead-line down round the vessel, and the copper upon her bottom was hanging in shreds, or rolled up like brown paper. By midnight the ice was stationary, and everything quiet.

They were now upon the north-west extreme of Banks's Land, and here officers and men rambled into the interior, which they did not find so sterile as the view from the sea had led them to expect. Traces of musk-oxen and deer abounded, and both were seen; but perhaps the most extraordinary discovery of all was a great accumulation of fossil trees, as well as fragments not fossilized, lying over the whole extent of the land, from an elevation of three hundred feet above the sea to its immediate level. Writing on the 27th of August, M'Clure says: "I walked to-day a short distance into the interior; the snow that had fallen last night lay unthawed upon the high grounds, rendering the prospect most cheerless. The hills are very remarkable, many of them peaked, and standing isolated from each other by precipitous gorges. The summits of these hills are about three hundred feet high, and nothing can be more wildly picturesque than the gorges which lie between them. From the summit of these singularly-formed hills to their base, abundance of wood is to be found; and in many places layers of trees are visible, some protruding twelve or fourteen feet, and so firm that several people may jump on them without their breaking: the largest trunk yet found measured one foot seven inches in diameter."

Again, on September 5th, some miles from the hills just alluded to, M'Clure says: "I entered a ravine some miles inland, and found the north side of it, for a depth of forty feet from the surface, composed of one mass of wood similar to what I had before seen. The whole depth of the ravine was about two hundred feet. The ground around the wood or trees was formed of sand and shingle ; some of the wood was petrified, the remainder very rotten, and worthless even for burning."

At a subsequent period, Lieutenant Mecham met with a similar kind of fossil forest in Prince Patrick Island, nearly one hundred and twenty miles further north.

This phenomenon gives rise to speculation as to some period in the world's history when the absence of ice and a milder climate allowed forest-trees to grow in a region where now the ground willow and dwarf birch have to struggle for existence.

On the 1st of September, 1851, winter appeared to have overtaken the Investigator in her forlorn position ; but on the 18th the wind veered, and the ice went off from the coast, carrying the ship with it, drifting her to the northward. On the 19th, having got free of the ice which clung to her sides, the ship got into a lane of water stretching eastward; and, on the 22d, rounding Cape Austin, fairly entered into Melville Strait. At length, on the 24th, they found themselves in a large bay at the western extremity of Banks's Land, and, seeing that it was impossible to round its north-eastern horn, M'Clure made up his mind to winter where he was ; and, in token of his gratitude for his many providential escapes, he appropriately called the place "The Bay of Mercy." That night they were firmly frozen in.

It was now certain that they would have to spend another winter in the ice. With slight exceptions, the arrangements made were much the same as those of the previous winter. The allowance of food was reduced, to meet the contingency of an escape from the ice not being effected the following year ; but this inconvenience was, to some extent, obviated by its being discovered that the land teemed with deer and hares. "As there appeared much game in the vicinity," writes Captain M'Clure, "and the weather continued mild, shooting parties were established in different directions between the 9th and 23d of October; so that, with what was killed from the ship, our supply of fresh provisions at the commencement of the winter consisted of nine deer, fifty-three hares, and forty-four ptarmigan, all in fine condition, the former having from two to three inches of fat."

The herds of deer and troops of hares that congregated on the broad plains of dwarf willow, reindeer-moss, and coarse grasses in the interior, are described as perfectly marvellous. Wolves and foxes also abounded, and, as cold and darkness increased, the former, pressed by hunger, used to haunt the ship to a disagreeable extent; and the sad prolonged howl of these gaunt creatures in the long nights added, if possible, to the dismal character of the scene. Two ravens also established themselves as friends of the family in Mercy Bay, and used to trick the ship's dog out of his meals by enticing him away, flying a few yards at a time, he running at them till they had got him some distance away, when they would make a direct flight back, and have done good execution before the mortified dog detected the imposition practised upon him, and rushed back again.

"In consequence of our favored position," says M'Clure, "the crew were enabled to ramble over the hills almost daily in quest of game, and their exertions happily supplied a fresh meal of venison three times a fortnight, with the exception of about three weeks in January, when it was too dark for shooting. The small game, such as ptarmigan and hares, being scarce, were allowed to be retained by the sportsmen as private property. This healthy and exhilarating exercise kept us all well and in excellent spirits during another tedious winter, so that on the 1st of April we had upwards of a thousand pounds of venison hanging at the yard-arms."

Musk-oxen were very numerous. They were found to be very ferocious, and great danger sometimes attended the attacks. They were easily approached, but when wounded they ran headlong at their assailant. On one occasion, Sergeant Woon, of the marines, while in pursuit of a wounded deer, unexpectedly met a couple of musk-bulls, which he succeeded in wounding. Having expended his shot, as one of the wounded and infuriated monsters rushed towards him, he fired his "worm" when at a few yards, but without much effect. The animal continued his advances, evidently, however, weak from loss of blood, till he had reached within six feet, when he put his head to the ground, as if for a final rush. As his last resource, the sergeant fired his iron ramrod, which, entering behind the animal's left shoulder, passed through the heart and out at the right flank, dropping him lifeless.

December found the crew of the Investigator passing their time cheerfully in their far-distant home in Mercy Bay. The month came in with a succession of those tremendous snow-storms, which are, perhaps, the most frightful visitations of the polar regions. But, after the new year (1852) began, the weather was fine, with a keen and steady cold of from seventy to eighty degrees below the freezing-point of water — a temperature which severely tests the vital energies of man. Yet, what with cheerfulness, exercise, and regular habits, the crew were in good health.

One of the hunting parties had well-nigh proved fatal to a colored man serving on board the ship. He had wounded a deer, and chased it till a fog came on, and he lost his way. It was in January, and the weather was bitterly cold; the poor fellow began to fancy himself frozen to death, and lost his wits entirely. While in this state, Sergeant Woon met him, and offered to lead him to the ship. The negro, beside himself with terror, could not be made to understand anything, and stood crying and shuddering till he fell down in a fit. The sergeant waited till he was restored, and then either carried him on his back or rolled him down hills and hummocks for ten long hours, till he got him within a mile of the ship. But the sergeant was by this time exhausted. He exerted all his powers of eloquence upon the negro to induce him to walk. The poor creature only begged to be "let alone to die." Finding all his arguments unavailing, the sergeant laid him in a bed of deep snow, and, with all his remaining strength, ran alone to the ship. He procured assistance directly, and, returning to the place where he had left the negro, found him with his arms stiff and raised above his head, his eyes open, and his mouth so firmly frozen that it required great force to open it to pour down restoratives. He was alive, however, and eventually recovered, though his hands, feet, and face, were much frostbitten. This case, and a similar one already related, illustrate, in a striking manner, not only the effect of intense cold on the body and mind, but also how much the safety of the former depends on the exercise of the latter.

On the 5th of February the sun was seen above the horizon, and the sportsmen became more successful, scarcely a day passing without a deer or hare being shot; and keen must have been the hunger of those sportsmen, for more than one of them, when, after a long and weary walk, he shot a deer or hare, refreshed himself with a draught of the animal's hot blood, or by eating a mouthful or two of the raw meat. The wolves had also become exceedingly bold, and tales are told of the sportsman pulling at one end of a slain deer, and the wolves at the other!

On the 11th of April, 1852, a sledge excursion was made to Winter Harbor, Melville Island, — the old winter quarters of Sir Edward Parry, — and notice found of Lieutenant M'Clintock's having been there from the west, the previous summer. M'Clure here deposited a notice of his own visit, under the same cairn that had protected the notice left by his predecessor.

It is remarkable that, shortly after M'Clure's visit to this spot, a sledge-party from the Enterprise, which had wintered at the south end of Prince of Wales Strait, after having been up to near its northern extremity, and having been foiled, like the Investigator, in getting into Melville Strait, actually visited the same spot, without either party knowing that the other was so close, so great is the difficulty of meeting one another in regions like those of the Arctic archipelago.

Although the sportsmen continued to meet with great success, and at one period no less than twenty head of deer were hanging up round the ship, yielding a thousand pounds of meat, scurvy began to show itself, and to make marked progress among the crew. On the 1st of July there were six men in their beds, and sixteen had evident symptoms of debility, with incipient scurvy. On the 16th open water was seen in the straits, but the ice in the bay prevented their getting to it, and on the 24th the *lead of water had closed!* It became too obvious that the winter was again setting in. All hope of deliverance for another season was cut off!

"On the 20th of August, 1852," says M'Clure, "the temperature fell to 27°, when the entire bay was completely frozen over; and, on the 27th, the temperature fell to 19°, so that the whole aspect was cheerless in the extreme. The young ice was two and a half inches thick, so that the whole bay might be safely perambulated. Indeed, the summer was fairly gone, for the uplands were all snow-covered, the wild-fowl all departed, and the flowers, which gave cheerful variety to this bleak land, were all withered. The very season might be considered as one long, sunless day, as since the latter part of May the great luminary had been scarcely visible, or his influence scarcely felt upon those icy masses which block Barrow's Strait entirely across; nor do I imagine that the Polar Sea had broken up that season, as not a drop of water had been seen in that direction.

"During July, and the early part of August, the crew were daily employed gathering sorrel, of which there was a great quantity upon the hills in this vicinity. Eaten as a salad, with vinegar, or boiled, when it resembled spinach, it was found a most admirable antiscorbutic, and a great benefit to all, being exceedingly relished; but this hardy and miserable herbage could not withstand the rigorous summer beyond the 15th of the month.

"For several days the ice had been perfectly stationary, and no water visible in any direction, that along the cliffs of Banks's Land being frozen; so that I felt assured that the winter had fairly set in, and all hopes of any release this year were totally annihilated, the young ice being five inches thick. Having previously determined what course I should adopt under circumstances thus unfavorable, upon the 8th of September I announced my intentions to the crew of sending half of them to England next April, with all the officers not in charge of stores, *viâ* Baffin's Bay (taking the boat from Cape Spencer) and the Mackenzie, detaining the remainder with the hope of extricating the vessel during the summer of 1853; or, failing that, to proceed with sledges in 1854 by Port Leopold, our provisions admitting of no other arrangement.

"Although we had already been twelve months upon two thirds allowance, it was necessary to make preparations for meeting eighteen months more; a very severe deprivation and constitutional test, but one which the service we were employed upon called for, the vessel being as sound as the day she entered the ice; it would, therefore, be discreditable to desert her in 1853, when a favorable season would run her through the straits and admit of reaching England in safety, where the successful achievement of the long-sought-for and almost hopeless discovery of the north-west passage would be received with a satisfaction that would amply compensate for the sacrifices made and hardships endured in its most trying and tedious accomplishment. This statement was well received, and its execution will, I hope, be carried out without difficulty."

It is due to Captain M'Clure to reproduce one passage in the dispatch which he had prepared to send home with the land parties he was about to forward in the spring of 1853.

"Should any of her majesty's ships be sent for our relief, and we have quitted Port Leopold, a notice, containing information of our route, will be left on the door of the house at Whalers' Point, or on some conspicuous position. If, however, no intimation should be found of our having been there, it may at once be surmised that some fatal catastrophe has happened, either from our being carried into the Polar Sea, or smashed in Barrow's Strait, and no survivors left. If such be the case, — which, however, I will not anticipate, — it will then be quite unnecessary to penetrate further to the westward for our relief, as, by the period that any vessel could reach that port, we must, from want of provisions, all have perished. In such a case, I would submit that the officers may be directed to return, and by no means incur the danger of losing other lives in quest of those who will then be no more."

The ship was banked up with snow and housed over on the 18th of November, and every preparation made for spending a third winter in this region of icy desolation. The spirits of the crew, however, did not flag. Resort was again had to the hunting expeditions which had occupied and cheered them so much in previous years, and their larder was kept well stocked with provisions. The wolves so harassed the deer, that the latter poor creatures actually fled to the ship for protection.

"The hares and ptarmigan," writes M'Clure, "have descended from the high ground to the sea ridges, so that a supply of game has been kept up during the winter, which has enabled a fresh meal to be issued twice weekly, and the usual Christmas festivities to pass off with the greatest cheerfulness. As it was to be our last, the crew were determined to make it memorable, and their exertions were completely successful; each mess was gayly illuminated and decorated with original paintings by our lower-deck artists, exhibiting the ship in her perilous positions during the transit of the Polar Sea, and divers other subjects; but the grand features of the day were the enormous plum-puddings (some weighing twenty-six pounds), haunches of venison, hares roasted, and soup made of the same, with ptarmigan and sea pies. Such dainties in such profusion I should imagine never before graced a ship's lower-deck; any stranger, to have witnessed this scene, could but faintly imagine that he saw a crew which had passed upwards of two years in these dreary regions, and three entirely upon their own resources, enjoying such excellent health — so joyful, so happy: indeed, such a mirthful assemblage, under any circumstances, would be most gratifying to any officer; but, in this lonely situation, I could not but feel deeply impressed, as I contemplated the gay and plenteous sight, with the many and great mercies which a kind and beneficent Providence had extended toward us, to whom alone is due the heartfelt praises and thanksgivings of all for the great blessings which we have hitherto experienced in positions the most desolate which can be conceived."

So another winter passed. The spring again returned, and the season rapidly approached when the crew was to divide, and the travelling parties were to set out on their long and perilous journeys: the one to return home by the way of the Mackenzie River and Canada; the other to proceed to Cape Spencer (where a boat and provisions had been deposited), and thence by Barrow's Strait to make their way to the nearest inhabited coast. That these journeys would prove long and dangerous in the extreme, could not be doubted; for the return parties were composed of the most weakly hands, thirty of the healthiest men being retained to stand by the ship with the captain, and brave the rigors of another Arctic winter.

But, while M'Clure and his gallant comrades were thus about to resort to their last desperate expedient for communicating with the civilized world, relief was at hand of which they had little expectation. Providential circumstances interposed to do away with the necessity of committing their forlorn hopes to the snow and ice deserts of the polar regions. These extraordinary circumstances will be narrated in another chapter.

CHAPTER XVII.

VOYAGE OF THE RESOLUTE AND INTREPID. — ARRIVAL AT DEALY ISLAND. — SLEDGE-PARTIES. — PARRY'S SANDSTONE AGAIN. — NEWS FROM THE INVESTIGATOR. — PIM'S JOURNEY. — MEETING WITH M'CLURE. — RETURN TO THE RESOLUTE. — MORE DEATHS REPORTED. — ABANDONMENT OF THE INVESTIGATOR. — A WEARY SUMMER. — CRESSWELL SENT WITH DISPATCHES. — INCIDENTS IN THE VOYAGE OF THE PHŒNIX. — LOSS OF THE BREDALBANE TRANSPORT. — DEATH OF BELLOT. — HIS AMIABLE CHARACTER. — THE PHŒNIX AND TALBOT SENT OUT.

A PARENT'S solicitude for his son saved the crew of the Investigator. We must now again take up the story of Sir Edward Belcher's expedition, which we left at Beechey Island on the 15th of August, 1852, just separating into two divisions, — one to proceed north, the other west. It is the westward division with which we have now to do. It was suggested to the British Admiralty by Mr. Cresswell, who had a son with M'Clure, that that part of Belcher's expedition which was destined for Wellington Channel should be directed upon Melville Island, as it was the opinion of General Sabine and Captain Kellett that if Captains Collinson and M'Clure were unable to reach that island with their ships, still they would push in there with their sledges. The senior lord of the Admiralty saw the soundness of Mr. Cresswell's views; and the Resolute and Intrepid, under Captains Kellett and M'Clintock, were ordered to proceed to Melville Island.

In nearing Assistance Bay, only thirty miles from Beechey Island, at which point Captain Kellett was to leave a dépôt, the Resolute grounded, was left with but seven feet of water, thrown over on her starboard bilge, and almost lost. At midnight, however, she was got off, leaving sixty feet of her false keel behind.

Kellett forged on in her, leaving dépôts here and there as he proceeded; and at the end of the summer had reached Melville Island, the westernmost point attained by Parry in 1820. Kellett's associate, Capt. M'Clintock, of the Intrepid, had commanded the only party which had been here since Parry, having come over with sledges from Austin's squadron, in 1851, as the reader will remember.

The Resolute and Intrepid came to anchor off Dealy Island, the place selected for their winter quarters; and then Capt. Kellett and his officers, with great spirit, began to prepare for the extended searching parties of the next spring. Officers were already assigned to the proposed lines of search; and in order to extend the searches as much as possible, and to prepare the men for the work when it should come, sledge-parties were sent forward to make advanced dépôts, in the autumn, under the charge of the gentlemen who would have to use them in the spring.

One of these parties — the "South line of Melville Island" party — was under a spirited young officer, Mr. Mecham, who had seen service in the last expedition. He had two sledges, the Discovery and the Fearless, a dépôt of twenty days' provision to be used in the spring, and enough for twenty-five days' present use. All the sledges had little flags, made by some young lady friends of Sir Edward Belcher's. Mr. Mecham's bore an armed hand and sword on a white ground, with the motto, "*Per mare, per terram, per glaciem.*" Over mud, land, snow, and ice, they carried their burden; and were nearly back, when, on the 12th of October, 1852, Mr. Mecham visited "Parry's Sandstone," near Winter Harbor, where he had been bidden to leave a record. He went on in advance of his party, meaning to cut the date, 1852, on the stone. On top of it was a small cairn, built by M'Clintock the year before. Mecham examined this, and, to his surprise, a copper cylinder rolled out. "On opening it," he says, "I drew out a roll folded in a bladder, which, being frozen, broke and crumbled. From its dilapidated appearance, I thought, at the moment, it must be some record of Sir Edward Parry; and, fearing I might damage it, laid it down with the intention of lighting the fire to thaw it. My curiosity, however, overcame my prudence, and, on opening it carefully with my knife, I came to a roll of cartridge-paper with the impression fresh upon the seals. My astonishment may be conceived on finding it contained an account of the proceedings of her majesty's ship Investigator since parting company with the Herald (Capt. Kellett's old ship), in August, 1850, in Behring's Strait: also a chart which disclosed to view not only the long-sought north-west passage, but the completion of the survey of Banks's and Wollaston Lands. I opened and endorsed Commander M'Clintock's dispatch, and found it contained the following additions:

'Opened and copied by his old friend and messmate, upon this date, April 28, 1852. ROBERT M'CLURE.

'Party all well, and return to Investigator to-day.'"

A great discovery, indeed, to flash across one in a minute! The Investigator had not been heard from for more than two years. Here was news of her not yet six months old! The north-west passage had been dreamed of for three centuries and more. Here was news of its discovery, — news that had been known to M'Clure for two years! M'Clure and M'Clintock were lieutenants together in the Enterprise when she was sent after Sir John Franklin, in 1848, and wintered together in her at Port Leopold. Now, from different hemispheres, they had come so near meeting at this old block of sandstone! Mr. Mecham bade his mate build a new cairn, to put the record of the story in, and hurried on to the Resolute with his great news.

It thus became known to Kellett and his companions that the Investigator had been frozen up in the Bay of Mercy, only one hundred and seventy miles from their own position. It must have been a sore trial, to all parties, to wait the winter through, and not even get a message across. But, until winter made it too cold and dark to travel, the ice in the strait was so broken up that it was impossible to attempt to traverse it, even with a light boat for the lanes of water. So, the different autumn parties came in, and the officers and men entered on their winter's work and play, to push off the winter days as quickly as they could.

The system of travelling in the fall and spring abridges materially the length of the Arctic winter as Ross, Parry, and Back, used to experience it; and it was only from the 1st of November to the 10th of March that Kellett's party were left to their own resources. Late in October one of the Resolute's men died, and in December one of the Intrepid's; but, excepting these cases, they had little sickness — for weeks no one on the sick-list; — indeed, Capt. Kellett says that a sufficiency of good provisions, with plenty of work in the open air, will insure good health in the Arctic climate.

As early in the spring as he dared risk a travelling party, namely, on the 10th of March, 1853, he sent what they all called a forlorn hope across to the Bay of Mercy, to find traces of the Investigator; for they scarcely ventured to hope that she was still there. This start was earlier by thirty-five days than the early parties had started on the preceding expedition. But it was every way essential that, if M'Clure had wintered in the Bay of Mercy, the messenger should reach him before he sent off any or all his men, in travelling parties, in the spring. The little forlorn hope consisted of ten men, under the command of Lieut. Pim, an officer who had been with Kellett in the Herald on the Pacific side, had spent a winter in the Plover up Behring's Strait, and had been one of the last men whom M'Clure and his crew had seen before they sailed into the Arctic Ocean, to discover, as it proved, the north-west passage.

Lieut. Pim started with a sledge and seven men under his own immediate command, and a dog-sledge with two men under Dr. Domville, the surgeon, who was to bring back the earliest news to Captain Kellett. There was also a relief-sledge to accompany the party a portion of the way. Pim's orders were to go at once to the Bay of Mercy in search of the Investigator; if she was gone, to follow any traces of her, and if possible to communicate with her or her consort, the Enterprise.

One of the sledges broke down soon after the party started, and they had to send back for another. Bad weather came on, and compelled them to encamp on the ice. "Fortunately," says the lieutenant, "the temperature arose from fifty-one degrees below zero to thirty-six below, and there remained;" while the drifts accumulated to such a degree around the tents, that within them the thermometer was only twenty below, and when they cooked rose to zero. There they lay three days, smoking and sleeping in their bags. On the fourth day a new sledge arrived from the ship, and they got under way again. Thus far they were running along the shore; but they soon sent back the relief-party which had brought the new sledge, and a few days after set out to cross a strait, some thirty miles wide, which, when it is open (as no man has yet seen it), is one avenue of the north-west passage discovered by these expeditions.

They got on slowly, and with great difficulty. Only three miles the first day, four miles the second day, two and a half the third, and half a mile the fourth; this was all they gained by most laborious hauling over the broken ice, dragging one sledge at a time, and sometimes carrying forward the stores separately, and going back for the sledges. Two days more gave them another eight miles, but on the seventh day of their passage across this narrow strait the great sledge slipped off a smooth hummock, broke one runner, and brought the party to a stand-still.

Having now nothing but the little dog-sledge to carry them on, — with the ship a hundred miles off, and the thermometer at eighteen below zero, — the two officers had some discussion as to their future proceedings. Dr. Domville, whose sledge, the James Fitzjames, was still sound, thought they had best leave the stores and go back; but Lieut. Pim, who had the chief command, thought otherwise; so he took the James Fitzjames, with the two men belonging to it, and pushed on, leaving the doctor in the floe, but giving him directions to take the broken sledge back to land, and there wait for him to return.

On went the lieutenant and his two men, over ice, over hummock, — feeding their dogs on preserved meats for want of game, — until they left the strait behind, and came to Banks's Land. Still they found no game. Pim was taken sick, and for a whole day was obliged to remain shut up in the tent. A few hours' sleep refreshed him, and the party started on again. At last, after many weary days' travel, they got upon the Bay of Mercy. No ship was in sight. Right across the bay went the lieutenant to search for records, when, at two o'clock P. M., one of the men saw something black in the distance. Pim looked through his glass, and made it out to be a ship. Forthwith the whole party proceeded as fast as possible toward it. Pim, hurrying along, soon got in advance of the sledge, and walked on alone.

On the 6th of April, 1853, the little crew of the Investigator was in low spirits: one of their comrades had just poisoned himself. All hands were preparing for the separation which was to take place in the following week, and were looking forward with gloomy forebodings to their slender chances of escape, when an event occurred, which we give in M'Clure's own words:

"While walking near the ship, in conversation with the first lieutenant upon the subject of digging a grave for the man who died yesterday, and discussing how we could cut a grave in the ground whilst it was so hardly frozen (a subject naturally sad and depressing), we perceived a figure walking rapidly towards us from the rough ice at the entrance of the bay. From his pace and gestures we both naturally supposed, at first, that he was some one of our party pursued by a bear; but, as we approached him, doubts arose as to who it could be. He was certainly unlike any of our men; but, recollecting that it was possible some one might be trying a new travelling-dress preparatory to the departure of our sledges, and certain that no one else was near, we continued to advance.

"When within about two hundred yards of us, the strange figure threw up his arms, and made gesticulations resembling those used by Esquimaux, besides shouting at the top of his voice words which, from the wind and intense excitement of the moment, sounded like a wild screech : and this brought us both fairly to a standstill. The stranger came quietly on, and we saw that his face was as black* as ebony ; and really, at the moment, we might be pardoned for wondering whether he was a denizen of this or the other world ; as it was, we gallantly stood our ground, and, had the skies fallen upon us, we could hardly have been more astonished than when the dark-faced stranger called out, 'I'm Lieutenant Pim, late of the Herald, and now in the Resolute. Captain Kellett is in her, at Dealy Island.'

"To rush at and seize him by the hand was the first impulse, for the heart was too full for the tongue to speak. The announcement of relief being close at hand, when none was supposed to be even within the Arctic Circle, was too sudden, unexpected, and joyous, for our minds to comprehend it at once. The news flew with lightning rapidity ; the ship was all in commotion ; the sick, forgetful of their maladies, leaped from their hammocks ; the artificers dropped their tools, and the lower deck was cleared of men ; for they all rushed for the hatchway, to be assured that a stranger was actually among them, and that his tale was true. Despondency fled the ship, and Lieut. Pim received a welcome — pure, hearty, and grateful — that he will surely remember and cherish to the end of his days."

On the 8th of April, Pim and his men, accompanied by M'Clure with a sledge-party, set out on their return. Dr. Domville, who had improved his time by mending the broken sledge and killing five musk-oxen, joined them on the way ; and on the 19th they all arrived at the quarters of the Resolute and Intrepid. Capt. Kellett

* Rendered black by the lamp-smoke in his tent.

was at first inclined to favor M'Clure's plan of endeavoring to save the Investigator; but on the 2d May Lieut. Cresswell arrived from her with the report of two more deaths. Then it was arranged that Dr. Domville should go back with M'Clure and hold a survey on the health of the crew; that those who were unfitted to stand another winter should be ordered home, and that the healthy should have their option of going or remaining. The result was that only four men were willing to remain, though the officers all gallantly volunteered to stand by the vessel. Boats, stores, &c., were accordingly landed to form a dépôt for the use of Collinson, Franklin, or any other person who might happen along, and on the 3d June, 1853, the colors were hoisted to the mast-head, and officers and crew bade a last farewell to the Investigator. They arrived at Dealy Island on the 17th, and were accommodated on board the Resolute and Intrepid.

Kellett's plan was to send them down to Beechey Island in the Intrepid at the first breaking up of the ice. More than half his crews were out on searching expeditions when the Investigator's men arrived. Parties under M'Clintock, Mecham, and Hamilton, were searching every foot of land to the north and north-west of Melville Island. They all came in at last, having found no traces of Sir John Franklin. Finding that nothing more could be done in a north-west direction, Kellett determined to take both vessels to Beechey Island as soon as the ice would admit. All his arrangements were made for starting at any moment. He built a store-house on the island, stocked it well with provisions, and left in it this record:

"This is a house which I have named the 'Sailor's Home,' under the especial patronage of my Lords Commissioners of the Admiralty.

"*Here* royal sailors and marines are fed, clothed, and receive double pay for inhabiting it."

All the other usual expedients were resorted to to while away the time; but after the excitement of the searching parties was over the summer passed drearily. The ice showed no sign of breaking up. Mr. Roche, mate of the Resolute, who had been sent down to the North Star for provisions, returned unexpectedly, having been to Beechey Island and back, a distance of six hundred miles, in six weeks. Capt. Richards arrived from Northumberland Sound, bringing news from Belcher's division. Little else occurred to break the monotony.

Meanwhile Lieut. Cresswell had been sent down to Beechey Island with dispatches for the Admiralty. There he had the good fortune to be taken on board of the Phœnix, in which, as we have seen, he returned to England, bringing the first news of the safety of the Investigator, and the discovery of the north-west passage.

Before we proceed further with the adventures of the companions whom he left at Dealy Island, there are some other matters of interest connected with this voyage of the Phœnix, which it will be well to relate in this place. One of these is the loss of the Bredalbane transport, by one of those terrible "nips" which are so often encountered in the polar seas. This occurred near Cape Riley, on the 21st August, 1853, and was witnessed by the crew of the Phœnix, in which vessel the Bredalbane's crew took refuge. It shows how very easily a vessel may be destroyed in the Arctic regions, without a vestige being left behind to tell the tale. We give the incident in the words of Mr. Fowckner, the agent for the ship, who was on board at the time:

"About ten minutes past four the ice passing the ship awoke me, and the door of my cabin, from the pressure, opened. I hurriedly put on my clothes, and, on getting up, found some hands on the ice endeavoring to save the boats, but these were instantly crushed to pieces. I went forward to hail the Phœnix, for men to save the boats; and whilst doing so the ropes by which we were secured parted, and a heavy nip took the ship, making her tremble all over, and every timber in her creak. I looked in the main hold, and saw the beams giving way; I hailed those on the ice, and told them of our critical situation. I then rushed to my cabin, and called to those in their beds to save their lives. On reaching the deck, those on the ice called out to me to jump over the side — that the ship was going over. I jumped on the loose ice, and, with difficulty, and the assistance of those on the ice, succeeded in getting on the unbroken part. After being on the ice about five minutes, the timbers in the ship cracking up as matches would in the hand, the nip eased for a short time, and I, with some others, returned to the ship, with the view of saving some of our effects. Captain Inglefield now came running toward the ship. He ordered me to see if the ice was through the ship; and, on looking down in the hold, I found all the beams, &c., falling about in a manner that would have been certain death to me had I ventured down there. It was too evident that the ship could not last many minutes. I then sounded the well, and found five feet in the hold; and whilst in the act of sounding, a heavier nip than before pressed out the starboard-bow, and the ice was forced right into the forecastle. Every one then abandoned the ship, with what few clothes he could save — some with only what they had on. The ship now began to sink fast, and from the time her bowsprit touched the ice until her mast-heads were out of sight it was not above one minute and a half. From the time the first nip took her until her disappearance, it was not more than fifteen minutes."

But the saddest episode in Arctic history that Inglefield had to report was the death of Lieut. Bellot, the gallant young Frenchman who acted so prominent a part in the voyage of the Prince Albert, under Kennedy. Bellot's zeal and enthusiasm had led him again into the regions of ice and snow, under Inglefield. While there, he volunteered to lead a party over the ice, in August, 1853, to Sir Edward Belcher's squadron, which was at that time near Cape Beecher, in Wellington Channel. This party consisted of four men — namely, Harvey, Johnson, Madden, and Hook.

On Friday, the 12th of August, he started, with his little band, from Beechey Island (at which place the North Star was lying), in charge of dispatches from Captain Pullen. At this season of the year travelling on ice is always considered dangerous, both on account of its decayed condition, and its liability to separate from the shore and break up. Accordingly, Pullen cautioned Bellot to keep as close to the eastern shore of Wellington Channel as possible, and provided the party with one of the light India-rubber boats, which could be easily dragged on their sledge, and without which, at such a season, it would have been very unsafe to travel.

That evening they encamped about three miles from Cape Innes. Next day they made considerable progress, and when night approached made their bed upon the broken ice over which they had been plodding during the day. This was near Cape Bodwen. On the following day, which was Sunday, they passed a crack about four feet wide, running across the channel. During all this time no doubts were entertained as to the safe condition of the ice; and Bellot, in his usual encouraging way, cheered on the men, and put his shoulder to the tracking-lines, saying that he wished to get to a cape which was seen a good way ahead, and which he called

34

Cape Grinnell. Near this it was desirable to encamp in-shore, if possible.

On arriving at the cape, it was found that there was a broad belt of water between the ice and the shore. This would have been a matter of little moment, had there been no wind, as they could have easily crossed it in the boat; but there was unfortunately a strong breeze blowing from the south-east, which curled up the surface of the cold black waves in a very ominous way. There was no help, however; so the boat was launched, and Bellot endeavored to reach the shore in it alone, intending to convey a line by which the remainder of the party and the provisions might be dragged over. In this attempt he failed, the violence of the gale being too much for him; he therefore returned to the ice, and ordered Harvey and Madden to get in and attempt the passage together. This they did, and were successful in landing; after which they began the operation of passing and repassing the boat between the ice and the shore, by means of lines. In this way three loads were landed from the sledge, and the party on the ice were hauling the boat off for a fourth, when Madden, who had hold of the shore-line, and was up to his middle in the water, called out suddenly that the ice was on the move, and driving off shore. It was evident that he could not hold the line longer without being dragged into deep water; so Bellot called out to him to let go, which he did.

Bellot and his two men then hauled the boat on to the sledge, and ran it up to the windward side of the ice, intending to launch it there and make for the shore. Ere this could be accomplished, however, the ice, whose motion was rapidly increasing, had drifted so far from the shore as to render all idea of reaching it hopeless. It may be imagined with what feelings Madden and

Harvey now hastened to an eminence, and watched their comrades drifting out to sea on a floe of ice, with a bitter breeze urging them further and further from hope of escape, and deeper among the drifting ice. During two hours they sat thus watching them, until at last they were lost to view amid the driving snow. When last seen, the two men were standing by the sledge, and Bellot on the top of a hummock.

Madden and Harvey now descended to the shore, and instantly began their return-journey to the ship. They walked round Griffin Bay, with very little provisions, and reached Cape Bowden, where they remained to take some rest. While there, two men were seen hastening toward them. To their great surprise and joy, these proved to be Johnson and Hook, who had almost miraculously escaped from their perilous position on the ice; but their sad countenances too truly told that their companion, the brave young Frenchman, was gone.

After getting a little refreshment, the whole party now returned to their ship, which they reached in safety, though not without much difficulty and severe privation. The melancholy fate of poor Bellot cannot be better told than by giving it in the words of Johnson, who was with him on the ice at the time of his death. "We got the provisions on shore," says he, "on Wednesday, the 17th. After we had done that, there remained on the ice Hook, Lieut. Bellot, and myself, having with us the sledge, Mackintosh-awning, and little boat. Commenced trying to draw the boat and sledge to the southward, but found the ice driving so fast that we left the sledge and took the boat only; but the wind was so strong at the time that it blew the boat over and over. We then took the boat with us, under shelter of a piece of ice, and Mr. Bellot and ourselves commenced cutting an ice-house with our knives for shelter. Mr. Bellot sat for half an hour in conversation with us, talking on the danger of our position. I told him I was not afraid, and that the American expedition was driven up and down this channel by the ice. He replied, 'I know they were; and when the Lord protects us, not a hair of our heads shall be touched.'

"I then asked Mr. Bellot what time it was. He said, 'About quarter past eight A. M.' (Thursday, the 18th), and then lashed up his books, and said he would go and see how the ice was driving. He had only been gone about four minutes, when I went round the same hummock under which we were sheltered to look for him, but could not see him; and, on returning to our shelter, saw his stick on the opposite side of a crack, about five fathoms wide, and the ice all breaking up. I then called out 'Mr. Bellot!' but no answer — (at this time blowing very heavy). After this, I again searched round, but could see nothing of him.

"I believe that when he got from the shelter the wind blew him into the crack, and, his south-wester being tied down, he could not rise. Finding there was no hope of again seeing Lieut. Bellot, I said to Hook, 'I 'm not afraid: I know the Lord will always sustain us.' We commenced travelling, to try to get to Cape De Haven, or Port Phillips; and, when we got within two miles of Cape De Haven, could not get on shore; and returned for this side, endeavoring to get to the southward, as the ice was driving to the northward. We were that night and the following day in coming across, and came into the land on the eastern shore a long way to the northward of the place where we were driven off. We got into the land at what Lieut. Bellot told us was Point Hogarth.

"In drifting up the straits towards the Polar Sea, we

saw an iceberg lying close to the shore, and found it on the ground. We succeeded in getting on it, and remained for six hours. I said to David Hook, 'Don't be afraid; we must make a boat of a piece of ice.' Accordingly, we got on to a piece passing, and I had a paddle belonging to the India-rubber boat. By this piece of drift-ice we managed to reach the shore, and then proceeded to where the accident happened. Reached it on Friday. Could not find our shipmates, or any provisions. Went on for Cape Bowden, and reached it on Friday night."

When the Esquimaux heard of Bellot's death, they shed tears, and cried "Poor Bellot! poor Bellot!" Two years before, he had seen an Esquimaux dragging himself painfully over the ice, with a broken leg. To call the carpenter, give him directions to make a wooden leg for the poor fellow, and to teach him to walk with it, were matters of course for the generous young Frenchman; but they were unusual kindnesses for a white man to show to an Esquimaux, and the simple-hearted people remembered it when they cried "Poor Bellot!"

Poor Bellot! — his was a brave, a generous, and a kindly heart. His talents and energy were deeply appreciated by the nation to which he had volunteered his services; and his affectionate, manly disposition had endeared him to the comrades with whom he had spent so many stormy days and nights in the regions of ice and snow. The howling blast of the north, and the dark waters of the polar seas, are sweeping over his mortal frame; but an imperishable wreath — a tribute of gratitude and affection, twined by the hands of France and England — shall rest upon his brow forever.

Mr. Bellot is another added to the list of those brave, enthusiastic spirits, that have been thus prematurely snatched away, and wrapt in the cold embrace of the Arctic seas. The English have expressed their sense of his services and his virtues by a subscription for his family, and for a monument to be erected to his memory in Greenwich Hospital.

Capt. Inglefield, in his steamer the Phœnix, accompanied by the sailing-vessel Talbot, was sent to the Arctic regions again in 1854, with dispatches and supplies for Sir E. Belcher. There we shall hear of him again in the course of our narrative.

CHAPTER XVIII.

THE RESOLUTE AND INTREPID. — BESET AGAIN. — WINTER IN THE PACK. — BOTH VESSELS ABANDONED. — BELCHER'S EXPLORATIONS. — REMAINS OF STRUCTURES. — ATTEMPT TO REACH BEECHEY ISLAND. — ABANDONMENT OF THE ASSISTANCE AND PIONEER. — ALL PARTIES ASSEMBLE AT BEECHEY ISLAND. — ARRIVAL OF THE PHŒNIX AND TALBOT. — RETURN TO ENGLAND. — OUTWARD VOYAGE OF THE PHŒNIX. — COLLINSON'S VOYAGE. — RAE'S EXPEDITION. — RELICS OF FRANKLIN. — ANDERSON'S JOURNEY.

THE Resolute and Intrepid, with their inmates, including the sixty men from the Investigator, remained icebound at Dealy Island during the best part of the summer of 1853. At last, on the 18th of August, a strong gale blowing off shore broke up the ice. The vessels at once got under way; by night they were at sea, and the navigators congratulated themselves that they were now fairly making progress towards home. But within twenty-four hours they were brought up by the pack of Byam Martin Channel; and there they lay watching for an opening to dash across to Bathurst Land, and run for Beechey Island under its lee.

Day after day passed. The drifting pack presented no available opening. Winter was fast advancing. The prospect of escape before another season began to look gloomy. Still, the navigators did not abandon the hope; but they occupied themselves in securing game, as a provision against the coming winter. This they found in abundance, especially musk-oxen; and some ten thousand pounds were obtained and frozen. An attempt was finally made to force through the pack;

but on the 9th of September the vessels became firmly imbedded in the newly-formed ice, and, a north-west gale forcing the pack upon them, they were fairly beset, and obliged to go whither it and Providence listed.

Two months they were drifting helplessly, amidst great perils. Right pleased was Kellett to find that after the 12th of November the ships were at rest, having reached a point about due east of Winter Harbor, Melville Island, in longitude 101° west, — an admirable position for an early escape in the ensuing season. Here they passed the winter of 1853–4, — long months of darkness and weariness, but with no worse mishap than the loss of one officer, who died on the 14th of November.

The log-book of that winter is a curious record; the ingenuity of the officer in charge was well tasked to make one day differ from another. Each day has the first entry for "ship's position" thus: "In the floe off Cape Cockburn;" and the blank for the second entry thus: "in the same position." Lectures, theatricals, schools, etc., whiled away the time.

The spring of 1854 arrived. M'Clure and his crew started with sledges on the 14th of April for Beechey Island, to find a resting-place on board the North Star and at the dépôt. Kellett made arrangements to continue the search. While thus engaged, he received a letter from Sir Edward Belcher, suggesting that, rather than risk the detention of another season, he should abandon his ships and meet him (Belcher) at Beechey Island before the 26th of August. Kellett remonstrated, stating that the vessels were in a favorable position for escape; that they had abundance of provisions, and that parties concerned in deserting ships under such circumstances "would deserve to have the jackets taken off their backs." Then came a positive order from Belcher. Both vessels were to be abandoned.

Two distant travelling parties were already out on searching expeditions. Word was left at a proper point for their guidance. Then, having fitted the Intrepid's engines so that she could be got under steam in two hours, having stored both ships with provisions, and made them in every respect "ready for occupation," Kellett ordered the hatches to be calked down, all hands looked their last on the Resolute and Intrepid, and on the 15th of May, 1854, they started, with sledges, for Beechey Island, where their unexpected arrival caused much surprise to the officers and crew of the Investigator, who had preceded them.

All this time the other division of the squadron, consisting of the Assistance and Pioneer, under Sir Edward Belcher, which, as we have seen, sailed north on the day before Kellett sailed west, namely, on the 14th of August, 1852, had been engaged in exploring Wellington Channel. Having reached latitude 76° 52′, and longitude 37° west, the vessels came to anchor in a locality near Cape Beecher, which was chosen for their winter quarters. Boat and sledge explorations to the northward were commenced on the 23d of August. On the 25th, when rounding a point where the coast suddenly turns to the eastward, the remains of several well-built Esquimaux houses were discovered. "They were," says Belcher, "not simply circles of small stones, but two lines of well-laid wall in excavated ground, filled in between by about two feet of fine gravel, well paved, and, withal, presenting the appearance of great care — more, indeed, than I am willing to attribute to the rude inhabitants or migratory Esquimaux. Bones of deer, wolves, seals, etc., were numerous, and coal was found." There is no mention of any search having been made for a record, though in all probability this was not neglected; yet the absence of any cairn would seem to render it unlikely that such a document existed.

The explorations led to the discovery of various lands, to the most extensive of which the name of North Cornwall was given, and of several islands washed by a sea open to the north, which Belcher regarded as the polar basin. The name of Victoria Archipelago was given to a group of islands in 78° 10′; and the easternmost, forming the channel which communicates with the Polar Sea, was named North Kent.

On the 2d of May, 1853, the north-east division of the sledging-parties left the ship, and soon reached the limit of their discoveries of the previous year.

During this journey Belcher pushed toward North Cornwall and Jones's Strait; but was unexpectedly stopped beyond Cape Disraeli, about the end of the month on which he set out, by the early disruption of the ice.

"The sight which I obtained from this cape," says he, "elevated six hundred and eighty feet above the sea, led me to hope for better success due east. On that course we proceeded three days on a smooth floe, making thirty-six miles, when we reached, on the 18th, the entrance of a splendid channel. Fog had for some time worried us with indistinct glimpses of the approaches; but, as it now cleared off, and the sun enlivened the scene, we were regaled with such a magnificent view of successive beetling headlands on either side of the channel, and extending for about twenty miles, that it really became a puzzling matter to find names for them. Of one thing I felt quite convinced — namely, that we were now really in Jones's Channel. The latitude, the direction, the limit in longitude to which we could see, only required an extension of sixty miles to lead to the cairn erected by Captain Austin's party. The roughness of the frozen pack now compelled us to take to the land, and we advanced easily five or six miles, when a further stop to our progress was opposed in the shape of an abrupt glacier, and the mortifying discovery that its base was washed by the sea, while the off-lying pack was rotten and tumbling asunder.

"Not easily daunted, it was determined to try an overland route, and avoid this unfortunate hole, as we then thought it. Provisions, etc., were strapped on, and we soon started to view what we had to contend with before deciding on our ultimate mode of action. The hills continued increasing in height as we advanced, until they reached fifteen hundred feet. We then descended and took up another position at nearly the same height as the last bluff, when we encamped for the night. All our hopes were crushed! Between us and the distant bluff the open sea prevailed on the 20th of May! The horizon was streaked with open 'sailing-ice,' and all communication cut off for sledges. The bluff, distant sixteen miles, was clearly the turning-point into Jones's Channel; no land was visible beyond it."

More than once their hopes were raised, during the return-journey, by the discovery of the remains of structures that had evidently been made by human hands, yet not, apparently, by those of Esquimaux. "Our progress was tantalizing, and attended with deep interest and excitement. In the first place, I discovered, on the brow of a mountain about eight hundred feet above the sea, what appeared to be a recent and a very workmanlike structure. This was a dome, — or rather a double cone, or ice-house, — built of very heavy and tabular slabs, which no single person could carry It consisted of about forty courses, eight feet in diameter, and eight feet in depth, when cleared, but only five in height from the base of the upper cone as we opened it.

"Most carefully was every stone removed, every atom of moss or earth scrutinized; the stones at the bottom also taken up; but without finding a trace of any record, or of the structure having been used by any human being. It was filled by drift snow, but did not in any respect bear the appearance of having been built more than a season. This was named 'Mount Discovery.'"

A short time afterwards he writes: "Leaving our crew, pretty well fatigued, to pitch the tent and prepare the customary pemmican meal, I ascended the mountain above us, and discovered that we really were not far from our old position of last year, on Cape Hogarth, and had Cape Majendie and Hamilton Island to the west, about twenty miles.

"My surprise, however, was checked suddenly by two structures rather in European form, and apparently graves; each was similarly constructed, and, like the dome, of large selected slabs, having at each end three separate stones, laid as we should place head and foot stones. So thoroughly satisfied was I that there was no delusion, I desisted from disturbing a stone until it should be formally done by the party assembled.

"The evening following — for where the sun is so oppressive to the eyes by day we travel by night — we ascended the hill, and removed the stones. Not a trace of human beings!"

Thus Belcher and his men travelled about during the whole season, exploring the coasts around Wellington Channel, now on foot, and then in boats, as circumstances permitted, but without discovering any clue to the fate of Sir John Franklin. Belcher differs from M'Clure and other explorers in regard to the abundance of animal life in Arctic climes. "By extraordinary good fortune," he says, "bears might fall in the way of the traveller; but, having killed and eaten his proportion, I much doubt if his strength would enable him to drag the remains until another piece of similar good fortune befell him. The assertion, therefore, of any 'teeming or abundance of animal life' in this north-eastern district, is utterly untenable."

On his return from this journey, Belcher first learned of the safety of Captain M'Clure and his crew in the Bay of Mercy.

The ships were liberated from the ice on the 14th of July. Belcher did not persevere in his attempts to push further north, notwithstanding his belief in an open Polar Sea, but shaped his course for Beechey Island. Cape Majendie was reached at an early day. Some time was then spent in surveying the Bays of Baring and Prince Edward, when the further advance of the ships was stopped by a solid floe of ice. After much warping and blasting to no purpose, in which many serious risks were encountered, the vessels were beset for a second winter (1853–4) at the southern horn of Baring's Bay.

When the spring came, Sir Edward's whole thoughts seem to have been turned towards getting himself and crews safe back to England. He determined, at all events, that they should not remain another winter in the ice. With this view, he sent the order to Captain Kellett, which we have related, and proceeded to manage his own vessels in a similar spirit.

On the 6th of August, 1854, the Assistance and Pioneer broke out of their winter quarters, and advanced slowly down the channel. The ice in Barrow's Strait broke up at the same time, and by the 22d the floe of Wellington Channel was open for fifteen miles north of the strait. A belt of ice, only twenty miles in extent, and that much cracked, was all that remained between the ships and the waters communicating with the Atlantic ; yet it was determined to abandon the vessels, and, on the 26th of August, 1854, both the Assistance and Pioneer were deserted, and the crews made their way to Beechey Island.

Kellett and M'Clure, with the men under their command, were there awaiting them. The searching parties had come in during the summer, and, on the 12th of June, Lieutenant Mecham had brought from Princess Royal Island news of the Enterprise, the first that had been heard from her since 1851. He had found records left by Collinson, as late as August, 1852, in which the latter announced his intention to follow the channel between Wollaston and Prince Albert's Land. Kellett was in favor of remaining and sending parties to his relief; but Belcher was bent on going home. All the officers and men of the Assistance, Pioneer, Resolute, Intrepid, and Investigator, accordingly got on board the North Star, and had just made sail when the Phœnix and Talbot, under Inglefield, hove in sight, rounding Cape Riley. A distribution of the crews was made among the three vessels. On the 6th of September they reached Disco, and on the 28th of September, 1854, were all safely landed in England.

The outward voyage of Inglefield on this occasion seems to have had its full share of dangers. After safely crossing the Atlantic in his steamer, the Phœnix, accompanied by the sailing vessel Talbot, he proceeded up Baffin's Bay, speaking some whalers by the way, and touching at Lievely for coal, which is abundant in these regions. Ice soon began to retard them, but they were enabled to break through it much more easily than were the navigators of former years, in consequence of the power of steam, which has greatly altered the mode of progression even in the regions of the north, not only by enabling the vessels to wend their way among loose ice in calm weather, but by giving them the power of *charging* the opposing masses under full steam, and so smashing a passage in places where, formerly, the unwieldy sailing-ship would have been detained for weeks, and perhaps set fast for the winter.

"For ten days," says Inglefield, "we pushed on through heavy ice, blasting, boring, charging the nips, and making but slow advance, the bay-ice, forming strong every night, much retarding our progress; and, on the 17th of August, we were closely beset at the edge of a large floe some miles in extent. Luckily, a strong gale from the westward broke up the edges of this floe, and, on the weather moderating, slacked the ice sufficiently to admit of our pushing through, and on the 19th we were fortunate enough to get into the west water."

After this he proceeded to Wollaston Island, where he found that a dépôt of provisions had been discovered by the Esquimaux, and almost entirely broken up. "Deeming it beneficial for the service upon which I was employed, and acting under the discretionary orders with which their lordships have been pleased to supply me, I determined upon examining the dépôt near Wollaston Island, deposited by the North Star, in 1850. For that purpose I made the south shore of Lancaster Sound, and, on the 21st, about 8.30 P. M., we passed near enough to Cape Hay to observe the coals deposited there, in 1849, by Captain Parker, of the Truelove. Observing that the staff and two casks containing letters and provisions were missing, I landed, and found that no trace remained of these but a portion of the head of one of them, and some broken preserved meat-tins. The coals, too, had been either carried away by the Esquimaux or the ice, there being only twenty-one bags. A little after ten we rounded Cape Castlereagh, and soon found the remains of the North Star's dépôt. Anchoring in five fathoms, we lashed the Talbot alongside, and on landing I found that this spot had also been visited by the Esquimaux. They had not only plundered it of all that was useful to them, but had showed a reckless wantonness in the destruction of every remaining article.

"Of the six hundred and eight casks and cases that were landed by Mr. Saunders, only one hundred and fourteen remained; and each had been stove for the examination of their contents, which consisted of flour, peas, Scotch barley, oat-meal, and tobacco. Finding the flour only partially destroyed in each cask, I determined on embarking all that still remained; and the whole was shipped off to the Phœnix, with ten tons of patent fuel, which latter I did not hesitate to embark, as Sir Edward Belcher had sent a vessel two years before to examine this dépôt, and directed her commander to take the whole of the coal from the neighboring point."

From this point, the Phœnix and Talbot sailed to Cape Warrender, at which place they were very nearly lost. Captain Inglefield went ashore to examine a cairn that he had erected there the previous year. Returning on board, he found a strong westerly breeze with ebb-tide, which prevented much headway being made; so they returned to seek anchorage for the night in Dundas Harbor. "Unfortunately," says Inglefield, "when picking up a berth, we struck soundings in fifteen fathoms, and, immediately after three, both ships grounded on a mud bank, and, the tide falling, every exertion to get the Phœnix afloat proved useless, though the Talbot was warped off into deep water, where, both her bower anchors being let go, the chain of the small one was passed into the Phœnix's quarter hawse-hole, and a heavy strain brought upon it. At three the following morning the strong breeze broke the ice away from the head of the bay, and, driving out, took the Phœnix on her starboard broadside, and laid her over on her beam ends, forcing her still further on shore, and tearing off the whole of the false keel. The Talbot, though pushed again on the bank, escaped any damage from the ice, being sheltered by this vessel, which was to windward of her. The day flood proving only a half-tide, we remained immovably fixed until the evening, by which time all the boats of both vessels had been laden with heavy stores to lighten this vessel: and I am happy to say that, about 11 P. M., both ships floated off into deep water, with no other damage than I have stated."

Having now disposed of all the searching expeditions on the Baffin's Bay side of the continent, excepting only that of Dr. Kane, to which we shall devote a separate chapter, it remains for us to complete the history of the other expeditions that proceeded by way of Behring's Strait. To connect the thread of our narrative, we must remind the reader that we left her majesty's ship Enterprise, Captain Collinson, consort of the Investigator, in the Pacific Ocean. She reached the latitude of Icy Cape, September 22d, 1850; when, meeting the pack-ice, she went south for a warmer climate, so as to be ready to resume operations in the season of 1851. All that Collinson knew of the position of M'Clure was a report from the Plover that the Investigator had been seen, under a press of canvas, steering northward, off Wainwright Inlet. Unfortunately, one of the rumors connected with this report induced Collinson to allow an enterprising young officer, Lieutenant Barnard, to be landed in the Russian north-west American settlements, in order to inquire into the truth. In carrying out this service, Barnard was brutally murdered, in February, 1851, by Indians, in a surprise of one of the Russian posts, called Darabin redoubt, not far from Norton Sound. The sad catastrophe is briefly told in the handwriting of poor Barnard, in the annexed note to Dr. Adams:

"DEAR ADAMS: I am dreadfully wounded in the abdomen; my entrails are hanging out. I do not suppose I shall live long enough to see you. The Cu-u-chuc Indians made the attack while we were in our beds. Boskey is badly wounded, and Darabin is dead.

"I think my wound would have been trifling had I had medical advice. I am in great pain. Nearly all the natives of the village are murdered. Set out for this place in all haste. JOHN BARNARD."

The hand-writing of this note betrayed the anguish which the gallant writer was suffering, and parts of it were nearly illegible.

On the 29th of July, 1851, Collinson, in the Enterprise, rounded Point Barrow, steered up Prince of Wales Strait, and here, on Princess Royal Island, discovered the Investigator's dépôt, and a cairn containing information up to June 15th, 1851. Passing on, the Enterprise, on the 30th of August, reached the north end of the strait, but only to be foiled in any attempt to pass beyond it. Collinson now decided on taking a course exactly similar to that of his more fortunate predecessor, M'Clure; but, on the 3d of September, little thinking that the Investigator had preceded him in his intended course, he found, to his surprise, on Cape Kellett, a record placed there on August 18th. The ice was now too close for him to push on; and, no harbor fit for winter quarters offering itself as high as latitude

72° 54′ north, Collinson bore up, and eventually wintered his ship on the eastern side of the entrance of Prince of Wales Strait. Thence he pursued his explorations in the neighborhood of Banks's Land, Albert Land, Wollaston Land, and Victoria Land, concerning the geography of which he obtained much valuable information. At Cambridge Bay, in Wollaston Land, where the Enterprise passed the winter of 1852–3, he saw in the possession of the Esquimaux a piece of iron and fragment of a doorway, or hatch-frame, which it is thought must have belonged to the Erebus or Terror; but this trace led to no further discoveries, nor was anything ascertained in regard to the fate of Sir John Franklin.

The Enterprise was absent longer than any of the other searching expeditions, and was equally distinguished by the ability, heroism, and endurance, displayed by her officers and crew; but, as their adventures are similar to those already related, we do not think it necessary to give them in more detail. Long after the people of England were assured of the safety of M'Clure, they continued to feel anxiety regarding the fate of Collinson. But the latter had the good fortune to retrace his steps by the way he came, and brought his ship and crew safely back to England. In the mean time, the Plover, the other vessel of the Pacific squadron, had also reached home in safety. Mr. Kennedy, in the Isabel, who sailed in 1853 to carry assistance to Collinson, was shipwrecked on the coast of South America, where his crew having mutinied and deserted, his voyage was abandoned.

Shortly after the return of Belcher and M'Clure, with the crews of their deserted ships, another note of information was sounded from the Arctic regions, but its tone was very sad. The *Montreal Herald* of October 21st, 1854, published a letter from Dr. Rae to the governor of the Hudson's Bay Company, giving an account of the exploration from which he had just returned. From this letter, which was dated York Factory, 4th August, 1854, it appeared that Rae reached his old quarters, at Repulse Bay, on the 15th of August, 1853, and there passed the ensuing winter. On the 31st of March, 1854, his spring journey commenced. On the 17th he reached Pelly Bay, where he met Esquimaux, from whom he obtained several articles which were identified as belonging to various members of Sir John Franklin's party.

The possession of these articles by the Esquimaux was accounted for by a story which is related in the following extract from Dr. Rae's journal, published soon after his arrival in England: "On the morning of the 20th we were met by a very intelligent Esquimaux, driving a dog-sledge laden with musk-ox beef. This man at once consented to accompany us two days' journey, and in a few minutes had deposited his load on the snow, and was ready to join us. Having explained to him my object, he said that the road by which he had come was the best for us; and, having lightened the men's sledges, we travelled with more facility. We were now joined by another of the natives, who had been absent seal-hunting yesterday, but, being anxious to see us, had visited our snow-house early this morning, and then followed up our track. This man was very communicative, and, on putting to him the usual questions as to his having seen 'white man' before, or any ships or boats, he replied in the negative; but said that a party of 'Kabloomans' had died of starvation a long distance to the west of where we then were, and beyond a large river. He stated that he did not know the exact place, that he never had been there, and that he could not accompany us so far. The substance of the information then and subsequently obtained from various sources was to the following effect:

"In the spring, four winters past (1850), while some Esquimaux families were killing seals near the north shore of a large island, named in Arrowsmith's charts King William's Land, about forty white men were seen travelling in company southward over the ice, and dragging a boat and sledges with them. They were passing along the west shore of the above-named island. None of the party could speak the Esquimaux language so well as to be understood, but by signs the natives were led to believe that the ship or ships had been crushed by ice, and that they were now going to where they expected to find deer to shoot. From the appearance of the men — all of whom, with the exception of an officer, were hauling on the drag-ropes of the sledge, and looked thin — they were then supposed to be getting short of provisions; and they purchased a small seal, or piece of seal, from the natives. The officer was described as being a tall, stout, middle-aged man. When their day's journey terminated, they pitched tents to rest in.

"At a later date the same season, but previous to the disruption of the ice, the corpses of some thirty persons and some graves were discovered on the continent, and five dead bodies on an island near it, about a long day's journey to the north-west of the mouth of a large stream, which can be no other than Back's Great Fish River (named by the Esquimaux Oot-koo-hi-ca-lik), as its description and that of the low shore in the neighborhood of Point Ogle and Montreal Island agree exactly with that of Sir George Back. Some of the bodies were in a tent, or tents; others were under the boat, which had been turned over to form a shelter; and some lay scattered about in different directions. Of those seen on the island, it was supposed that one was that of an officer (chief), as he had a telescope strapped over his shoulders, and a double-barrelled gun lay underneath him.

"From the mutilated state of many of the bodies, and the contents of the kettles, it is evident that our wretched countrymen had been driven to the dread alternative of cannibalism as a means of sustaining life. A few of the unfortunate men must have survived until the arrival of the wild-fowl (say until the end of May), as shots were heard, and fresh bones and feathers of geese were noticed near the scene of the sad event.

"There appears to have been an abundant store of ammunition, as the gunpowder was emptied by the natives in a heap on the ground out of the kegs or cases containing it, and a quantity of shot and ball was found below high-water mark, having probably been left on the ice close to the beach before the spring commenced. There must have been a number of telescopes, guns (several of them double-barrelled), watches, compasses, &c., all of which seem to have been broken up, as I saw pieces of these different articles with the natives, and I purchased as many as possible, together with some silver spoons and forks, an Order of Merit in the form of a star, and a small silver plate engraved 'Sir John Franklin, K.C.B.'"

Dr. Rae concludes by expressing the opinion that no violence had been offered to the sufferers by the natives, but that they were starved to death. The following is a list of the articles obtained from the Esquimaux: One silver table-fork — crest, an animal's head with wings extended above; three silver table-forks — crest, a bird with wings extended; one silver table-spoon — crest, with initials "F. R. M. C." (Captain Crozier, Terror); one silver table-spoon and one fork — crest, bird with laurel-branch in mouth, motto, "*Spero meliora*;" one silver table-spoon, one tea-spoon, and one dessert-fork — crest, a fish's head looking upwards, with laurel-branches on each side; one silver table-fork — initials, "H. D. S. G." (Harry D. S. Goodsir, assistant-surgeon, Erebus); one silver table-fork — initials, "A. M'D." (Alexander M'Donald, assistant-surgeon, Terror); one silver table-fork — initials, "G. A. M." (Gillies A. Macbean, second master, Terror); one silver table-fork — initials, "J. T.;" one silver dessert-spoon — initials, "J. S. P." (John S. Peddie, surgeon, Erebus); a round silver plate, engraved, "Sir John Franklin, K.C.B.;" a star or order, with motto, "*Nec aspera terrent*, G. R. III. MDCCCXV."

On obtaining the above information, Dr. Rae instantly hastened to England, for the purpose of preventing any further expeditions being despatched in search of the lost navigators. His report, as might have been expected, was subjected on all hands to criticism and comment. Many were of opinion that the information obtained did not warrant the conclusion that the whole party was lost. Some of the criticisms made on his report induced Dr. Rae to take up the pen in self-defence; and in a letter which he addressed to the editor of the *London Times* we find the following remarks, which come with great weight from one who, of all others, is most competent to speak authoritatively. They were written in reply to an attack made upon him by a gentleman who had a relative with the lost expedition, and serve to show how difficult it is to form a correct judgment on subjects of which we have not had personal experience.

"It is asked by your correspondent," says Dr. Rae, "'where Esquimaux can live, where Dr. Rae's party could find abundant means, what should prevent Sir John Franklin and his party from subsisting too?'

"No man but one perfectly unacquainted with the

subject could ask such a question. At the season when Sir John Franklin's party was seen travelling over the ice, the seal-holes are covered by snow, and can only be discovered by the acute sense of smell of the native dogs; and, after the seal-hole is discovered, much patience, experience, and care, are requisite to kill the seal. As soon as the snow thaws (say in June) the seals show themselves on the ice; but they are then so difficult of approach that not one of my men (Ouligbuck, the interpreter, excepted), although they often made the attempt, could approach near enough to shoot any of these animals.

"I wintered at a part of the Arctic coast remarkable by its geographical formation for the abundance of deer during the autumn migrations, but only then; and it was at that time that we laid up our winter stock of food; but it was hard work even for us (all practised sportsmen, picked men, and in full strength and training) to collect a sufficiency.

"That portion of country near to and on which a portion of Sir John Franklin's party was seen is, in the spring, notoriously the most barren of animal life of any of the Arctic shores; and the few deer that may be seen are generally very shy, from having been hunted during the winter by Indians, on the borders of the woodlands. To prove this scarcity of game, I may add, that during my spring journey of fifty-six days' duration, one deer only and a few partridges were shot by us.

"It is asked by your correspondent, 'Why the unfortunate men should have encumbered themselves with silver forks and spoons and silver plates?' &c. The total weight of the silver forks and spoons could not be more than four or five pounds at the utmost, and would not appear much when divided among forty persons; and any officer who has ever had the misfortune to abandon his ship or boat anywhere, but more particularly in the Arctic sea, knows how apt men are to encumber themselves with articles far more useless and bulky than a few forks and spoons. I suppose, by 'silver plates,' your correspondent alludes to the silver plate with Sir John Franklin's name engraved thereon, and which may possibly weigh half an ounce, — no great addition to a man's load.

"Again, your correspondent says, 'that the ships have been abandoned, and pillaged by the Esquimaux.' In this opinion I perfectly agree so far as regards the abandonment of the ships, but not that these ships were pillaged by the natives. Had this been the case, wood would have been abundant among these poor people. It was not so, and they were reduced to the necessity of making their sledges of musk-ox skins folded up and frozen together, — an alternative to which the want of wood alone could have reduced them. Another proof that the natives had very little wood among them may be adduced. Before leaving Repulse Bay, I collected together some of the most respectable of the old Esquimaux, and distributed among them all the wood we could spare, amounting to two or three oars and some broken poles. When these things were delivered to them, I bade the Esquimaux interpreter, who speaks both his own and the English language fluently, to ask whether they or their acquaintances near Pelly Bay had now most wood. They all immediately shouted out, holding up their hands, that they themselves had most. I need scarcely add that, had the ships been found by the Esquimaux, a stock of wood sufficient for many years for all the natives within an extent of several hundred miles would have been obtained."

From all this it will be seen that the evidence of Dr. Rae went to show that the fate of thirty-five men of the expedition had been but too surely ascertained; but there were yet one hundred and three to be accounted for. No one, familiar with the history of Arctic discovery, could entertain much hope of ever seeing the gallant crews of the Erebus and Terror *alive;* but there was every reason to believe that the *trail* had been at last struck, and that in a short time we should have the melancholy satisfaction of at least knowing how, when, and where, they perished. For the purpose of ascertaining this, of obtaining the papers of the lost ships, and of burying the remains of their crews, if they should be found, the British government resolved to send out a land expedition to follow up the search of Dr. Rae.

A party was accordingly organized in the summer of 1855, and placed under the command of Mr. James Anderson, chief factor of the Hudson's Bay Company; Dr. Rae, to whom the command was first offered, having declined it, on account of ill-health. Anderson's expedition started from Fort Resolution on the 22d of June, 1855, and commenced the descent of the Great Fish River in three canoes. They were unaccompanied by any interpreter. On the 30th of July, at the rapids below Lake Franklin, three Esquimaux lodges were seen, and numerous articles, belonging to a boat-equipage, were there found — such as tent-poles, paddles, copper and sheet-iron boilers, tin soup-tureens, chisels, and tools of various kinds. The occupants of the lodges, all but one of whom were women, said (by words and signs) that these things were obtained from a boat, and that the white men belonging to it had died of starvation.

Pushing on again, the party reached Point Beaufort, and at last Montreal Island. There they found some chain-hooks, tools, rope, bunting, and a number of sticks strung together on one of which was cut the name of "Mr. Stanley" (surgeon of the Erebus); also chips, shavings, ends of plank, etc., apparently sawed by unskilful hands. On one the word "Terror" was carved. It was evident to Mr. Anderson that this was the spot where the boat was cut up by the Esquimaux; but not a vestige of human remains could be discovered, or a scrap of paper. Point Ogle was next examined, and small articles of a similar character were also found there; but with no other result.

On the 8th of August, 1855, the party began to retrace their steps, having seen no Esquimaux, except the few at the rapids before mentioned, and having been unable to reach King William's Land.

This information was received in England early in 1856, and is confirmatory of Rae's supposition that the Great Fish was the river on which the party he heard of had retreated; but, so far as the particulars of their fate is concerned, it leaves the whole matter as much involved in mystery as ever.

CHAPTER XIX.

SECOND GRINNELL EXPEDITION. — DR. KANE'S PLAN. — DEPARTURE. — IN THE ICE. — SEARCH FOR A HARBOR. — FROZEN IN. — TEMPERATURE. — INCIDENTS. — LOSS OF DOGS. — DISASTROUS SLEDGING-PARTY. — THE RESCUE. — MEETING WITH ESQUIMAUX. — DISCOVERIES. — ATTEMPT TO REACH BELCHER'S SQUADRON. — ANOTHER WINTER. — PRIVATION AND PERIL. — ABANDONMENT OF THE VESSEL. — FAREWELL TO THE ESQUIMAUX. — IN SAFETY. — REPORT TO NAVY DEPARTMENT. — THE OPEN POLAR SEA. — CHARACTER OF DR. KANE'S ADVENTURES. — HIS PUBLISHED NARRATIVE.

THE expedition under the command of Dr. Kane sailed from New York on the 30th of May, 1853. It consisted of eighteen chosen men, besides the commander, embarked in a small brig of one hundred and forty-four tons burden, named the Advance, which was furnished by Mr. Grinnell, other expenses being contributed by Mr. Peabody and several generous individuals and societies. Dr. Kane's predetermined course was to enter the strait discovered the previous year by Captain Inglefield, at the top of Baffin's Bay, and to push as far northward through it as practicable. He engaged the services of a native Esquimaux, of the name of Hans Christensen, at Fiskernaes, in Greenland, and then crossed Melville Bay in the wake of the vast icebergs with which the sea is there strewn. These huge frozen masses are often driven one way by a deep current, while the floes are drifted in another by winds and surface-streams, disruptions being thus necessarily caused in the vast ice-fields. The doctor's tactics were to dodge about in the rear of these floating ice-mountains, holding upon them whenever adverse winds were troublesome, and pressing forward whenever an opportunity occurred.

· Dr. Kane's plan was based upon the probable extension of the land-masses of Greenland to the far north — a fact at that time not verified by travel, but sustained by the analogies of physical geography. Greenland, though looked upon as a congeries of islands connected by interior glaciers, was still regarded as a peninsula, whose formation recognized the same laws as other peninsulas having a southern trend.

Believing in the extension of this peninsula nearer to the pole than any other known land, and feeling that the search for Sir John Franklin would be best promoted by a course that might lead most directly to the supposed northerly open sea, Dr. Kane advanced, as inducements in favor of his scheme: Terra Firma as the basis of his operations; a due northern line which would lead soonest to the open sea; the benefit of northern land to check the southern drift of ice; the presumed existence of animal life; and the coöperation of Esquimaux, whose settlements were supposed to extend far up the coast.

The good ship Advance entered the harbor of Fiskernaes, on the 1st of July, "amid the clamor of its entire population assembled on the rocks to greet us." On the 16th of July she passed the promontory of Swartehuk, or Blackhead; and, on the 27th, Wilcox Point; icebergs showing themselves on all sides, and rendering the navigation of Melville Bay full of danger. On the 2d of August they were fairly in the ice, and beset by fogs. It was only at times that the floes opened sufficiently to allow the ship to make her way through them. At midnight of the 3d, however, they got clear of the bay and of its difficulties, Dr. Kane taking credit to himself for having effected this by an outside passage.

The North Water, the highway to Smith's Sound, was now fairly before them. On the 5th they passed Sir John Ross's "Crimson Cliffs," and the patches of red snow could be seen clearly at the distance of ten miles from the coast; and on the 7th they doubled Cape Alexander — the Arctic pillars of Hercules — and passed into Smith's Sound. Arriving at Littleton Island, they deposited there a boat with a supply of stores, not far from the vestiges of an old Esquimaux settlement.

On the 8th they again closed with the ice, and were forced into a land-locked cove. The dogs, of which they had more than fifty on board, began to be very troublesome; they would devour almost everything that came in their way, from an Esquimaux cranium to a whole feather-bed! The men tried to shoot some walruses, but the rifle-balls rebounded from their hides like pebbles; and it was only by accident that they found the carcass of a narwhal, with which to appease the poor dogs for a time.

All attempts to work the vessel seaward through the floes proving unsuccessful, it was resolved to try for a further northing by following the coast-line. But, although even warping was had recourse to, this also was followed by but very trifling success. On midnight of the 14th they reached the lee side of a rocky island, which, from the shelter it afforded, was designated "Godsend Ledge." It was, however, destined to be so but a short time. On the 20th it came on to blow a hurricane; the hawsers parted one after the other, and the ship was left at the mercy of the winds, waves, and ice, combined. It was a most trying time, and the party underwent many perils ere they found temporary shelter beyond a lofty cape, and under an iceberg that anchored itself between them and the gale.

The point to which they were thus unceremoniously driven was ten miles nearer the pole than Godsend Ledge; and on the 22d, the storm having abated, the men were harnessed to the tow-lines, and they began to track along the ice-belt off the coast, warping also at

TRACKING ALONG THE ICE-BELT.

times, but with so little effect that, on the 29th, Dr. Kane rushed on ahead with a small boating-party for a personal inspection of the coast. After twenty-four hours' toil, the boat had to be exchanged for a sledge, with which they also got on but slowly, passing Glacier Bay, Mary Minturn River, — the largest known in North Greenland, being about three fourths of a mile wide at its mouth — Capes Thackeray and Francis Hawkes, to Cape George Russell, from whence could be seen the great glacier of Humboldt, Cape Jackson on the one side, and Cape Barrow on the other, and between them a solid sea of ice.

The gallant captain returned satisfied that he had seen no place combining so many of the requisites of a good winter harbor as the bay in which he had left the Advance. So he gave the orders to warp in between two islands. They found seven fathom soundings, and a perfect shelter from the outside ice; and thus the little brig was laid up in Van Rensselaer Harbor, near a group of rocky islets, in the south-eastern curve of a bay, where she was frozen in on September 10th.

An observatory was erected adjacent to the ship, and a thermal register was kept hourly. The mean annual temperature at this spot appears to be two degrees lower than that of Melville Island, according to Parry. The lowest temperature was observed in February, when the mean of eight instruments gave seventy degrees Fahrenheit. Chloroform froze, essential oils became partly solid and liquid, and, on February 24th, chloric ether was congealed for the first time by natural temperature. For astronomical observations, a transit and theodolite were mounted on stone pedestals, cemented by ice. The longitude was based on moon culminations, corroborated by occultations of planets, and the solar eclipse of May, 1855. The position of the observatory was found to be in lat. 78° 37′, and long. 70° 40′ 6″. Magnetic observations, both absolute and relative, were also kept up.

An excursion was made ninety miles into the interior, when its further progress was arrested by a glacier four hundred feet high, and extending north and west as far as the eye could reach. As to the sledging outfit, they kept on reducing it, until at last they came to the Esquimaux ultimatum of simplicity — raw meat and a fur bag. For the time being, a man thus becomes a mere animal, only with another animal's skin for a cover.

Parties were organized for establishing provision dépôts to facilitate researches in the spring, and more than eight hundred miles were traversed. The Greenland coast was traced for one hundred and twenty-five miles to the north and east, and the largest of the three dépôts along the coast was formed on an island in lat.

70° 12′ 6″, and long. 65° 25′. Darkness arrested these proceedings on November 20th, and the sun continued one hundred and twenty days below the horizon.

One of the first incidents that occurred was setting the ship on fire in an attempt to exterminate the rats with carbonic-acid gas. It ended in nearly asphyxiating the commander and two or three others. The next incident was one of the dogs going rabid — a phenomenon usually supposed to be associated with the heats of summer. Great inconvenience was experienced in the sledge-excursions, and in making "caches" of provisions in this region, from the frequent ice-cracks, or crevasses, as the Swiss would call them, and into which dogs, sledges, and travellers, were sometimes tumbled, at the imminent risk of being carried below the ice by the current — not to mention the danger to health of an immersion with the thermometer many degrees below zero.

The point at which the party were wintering, it is to be observed, was in a higher latitude than the wintering-stations in the Arctic archipelago ; and, except on Spitzbergen, no Christians are known to have passed a winter so near to the pole. The darkness was so intense that it necessarily entailed inaction ; and it was in vain that they sought to create topics of thought, and, by a forced excitement, to ward off the encroachments of disease. The thermometer fell to ninety-nine degrees below freezing point. Human beings could only breathe in such a temperature guardedly, and with compressed lips.

The influence of such severe cold and long intense darkness was most depressing. Most of the dogs died of affections of the brain, which began, as in the instance of some of the men of the Investigator, with fits, followed by lunacy, and sometimes by lock-jaw. Their disease, Dr. Kane remarks, was as clearly mental as in the case of any human being. Fifty-seven died with these symptoms. The loss of his dogs seriously affected Dr. Kane's plans; new arrangements had to be formed, which, owing to the smallness of the party, deprived

DOG-SLEDGE.

of the dogs, were necessarily restricted. The addition of four dogs, contributed by Esquimaux, permitted the operations to be considerably extended. Out of nearly three thousand miles traversed, no less than eleven hundred were made with the dog-sledge; and during the following year Dr. Kane himself travelled fourteen hundred miles with a single team.

The month of March brought back perpetual day. The sunshine had reached the ship on the last day of February; they needed it to cheer them. The scurvy spots that mottled the faces of almost all gave sore proof of the trials they had undergone. The crew were now (March, 1854) almost unfitted by debility for arduous work, and only six dogs remained of nine splendid Newfoundlanders and thirty-five Esquimaux dogs. "An Arctic night and an Arctic day," Dr. Kane emphatically remarks, "age a man more rapidly and harshly than a year anywhere else in all this weary world." Sometimes, in their excursions over the ice, the men had to drag the sledge, and flounder through snow-drifts in which they sank at every step nearly over their legs.

SLEDGE-PARTY.

In order to ascertain whether it were practicable to force a way over the crowded bergs and mountainous ice of the frozen area toward the north, Dr. Kane now organized a party of the strongest men, who volunteered their services for the labor, placing himself at their head; and, on the 19th of March, sent out an advanced corps to place a relief cargo of provisions at a suitable distance from the brig. On the ninth day of their absence the latter encountered a heavy gale from the north-east; the thermometer fell to fifty-seven degrees below zero, and the ice-ridges became so obstructed by snow as to prevent their depositing their stores beyond fifty miles from the brig.

By the 31st three of the members of this advance party returned to the brig, swollen, haggard, and hardly able to speak. They had left four of their number in a tent on the ice, frozen and disabled. On being informed of the disaster, Dr. Kane started for the rescue with nine men, under the direction of Mr. Ohlsen, one of the returned party, whose previous exposure, however, had rendered his services as a guide almost useless. We will here quote the commander's own graphic words:

"We had been nearly eighteen hours out without

water or food, when a new hope cheered us. I think it was Hans, our Esquimaux hunter, who thought he saw a broad sledge-track. The drift had nearly effaced it, and we were some of us doubtful at first whether it was not one of those accidental rifts which the gales make in the surface-snow. But, as we traced it on to the deep snow among the hummocks, we were led to footsteps; and, following these with religious care, we at last came in sight of a small American flag fluttering from a hummock, and lower down a little Masonic banner hanging from a tent-pole hardly above the drift. It was the camp of our disabled comrades: we reached it after an unbroken march of twenty-one hours.

"The little tent was nearly covered. I was not among the first to come up; but, when I reached the tent-curtain, the men were standing in silent file on each side of it. With more kindness and delicacy of feeling than is often supposed to belong to sailors, but which is almost characteristic, they intimated their wish that I should go in alone. As I crawled in, and, coming upon the darkness, heard before me the burst of welcome gladness that came from the four poor fellows stretched on their backs, and then for the first time the cheer outside, my weakness and my gratitude together almost overcame me. 'They had expected me; they were sure I would come!'"

We copy entire Dr. Kane's spirited account of the retreat of the party, now consisting of fifteen souls:

"It was fortunate indeed that we were not inexperienced in sledging over the ice. A great part of our track lay among a succession of hummocks; some of them extended in long lines fifteen and twenty feet high, and so uniformly steep that we had to turn them by a considerable deviation from our direct course: others that we forced our way through, far above our heads in height, lying in parallel ridges, with the space between too narrow for the sledge to be lowered into it safely, and yet not wide enough for the runners to cross without the aid of ropes to stay them. These spaces too were generally choked with light snow, hiding the openings between the ice-fragments. They were fearful traps to disengage a limb from; for every man knew that a fracture, or a sprain even, would cost him his life. Besides all this, the sledge was top-heavy with its load: the maimed men could not bear to be lashed down tight enough to secure them against falling off. Notwithstanding our caution in rejecting every superfluous burden, the weight, including bags and tent, was eleven hundred pounds.

"And yet our march for the first six hours was very cheering. We made, by vigorous pulls and lifts, nearly a mile an hour, and reached the new floes before we were absolutely weary. Our sledge sustained the trial admirably. Ohlsen, restored by hope, walked steadily at the leading-belt of the sledge-lines; and I began to feel certain of reaching our half-way station of the day before, where we had left our tent. But we were still nine miles from it, when, almost without premonition, we all became aware of an alarming failure of our energies.

"I was of course familiar with the benumbed and almost lethargic sensation of extreme cold: and once, when exposed for some hours in the midwinter of Baffin's Bay, I had experienced symptoms which I compared to the diffused paralysis of the electro-galvanic shock. But I had treated the *sleepy comfort* of freezing as something like the embellishment of romance. I had evidence now to the contrary.

"Bonsall and Morton, two of our stoutest men, came to me, begging permission to sleep; 'they were not cold: the wind did not enter them now: a little sleep was all they wanted.' Presently Hans was found nearly stiff under a drift; and Thomas, bolt upright, had his eyes closed, and could hardly articulate. At last, John Blake threw himself on the snow, and refused to rise. They did not complain of feeling cold; but it was in vain that I wrestled, boxed, ran, argued, jeered, or reprimanded: an immediate halt could not be avoided.

"We pitched our tent with much difficulty. Our hands were too powerless to strike a fire: we were obliged to do without water or food. Even the spirits (whiskey) had frozen at the men's feet, under all the coverings. We put Bonsall, Ohlsen, Thomas, and Hans, with the other sick men, well inside the tent, and crowded in as many others as we could. Then, leaving the party in charge of Mr. McGary, with orders to come on after four hours' rest, I pushed ahead with William Godfrey, who volunteered to be my companion. My aim was to reach the half-way tent, and thaw some ice and pemmican before the others arrived.

"The floe was level ice, and the walking excellent. I cannot tell how long it took us to make the nine miles; for we were in a strange sort of stupor, and had little apprehension of time. It was probably about four hours. We kept ourselves awake by imposing on each other a continued articulation of words; they must have been incoherent enough. I recall these hours as among the most wretched I have ever gone through: we were neither of us in our right senses, and retained a very confused recollection of what preceded our arrival at the tent. We both of us, however, remember a bear, who walked leisurely before us, and tore up as he went a jumper that Mr. McGary had improvidently thrown off the day before. He tore it into shreds and rolled it into a ball, but never offered to interfere with our progress. I remember this, and with it a confused sentiment that our tent and buffalo-robes might probably share the same fate. Godfrey, with whom the memory of this day's work may atone for many faults of a later time, had a better eye than myself; and, looking some miles ahead, he could see that our tent was undergoing the same unceremonious treatment. I thought I saw it too; but we were so drunken with cold that we strode on steadily, and, for aught I know, without quickening our pace.

"Probably our approach saved the contents of the tent; for when we reached it the tent was uninjured, though the bear had overturned it, tossing the buffalo-robes and pemmican into the snow; we missed only a couple of blanket-bags. What we recollect, however, and perhaps all we recollect, is, that we had great difficulty in raising it. We crawled into our reindeer sleeping-bags, without speaking, and for the next three hours slept on in a dreamy but intense slumber. When I awoke, my long beard was a mass of ice, frozen fast to the buffalo-skin: Godfrey had to cut me out with his jack-knife. Four days after our escape, I found my woollen comfortable with a goodly share of my beard still adhering to it.

"We were able to melt water and get some soup cooked before the rest of our party arrived: it took them but five hours to walk the nine miles. They were doing well, and, considering the circumstances, in wonderful spirits. The day was most providentially windless, with a clear sun. All enjoyed the refreshment we had got ready: the crippled were repacked in their robes; and we sped briskly toward the hummock-ridges which lay between us and the Pinnacly Berg.

"The hummocks we had now to meet came properly under the designation of squeezed ice. A great chain of bergs stretching from north-west to south-east, moving with the tides, had compressed the surface-floes; and, rearing them up on their edges, produced an area more like the volcanic pedragal of the basin of Mexico than anything else I can compare it to.

"It required desperate efforts to work our way over it — literally desperate, for our strength failed us anew, and we began to lose our self-control. We could not abstain any longer from eating snow; our mouths swelled, and some of us became speechless. Happily, the day was warmed by a clear sunshine, and the thermometer rose to —4° in the shade; otherwise we must have frozen.

"Our halts multiplied, and we fell half-sleeping on the snow. I could not prevent it. Strange to say, it refreshed us. I ventured upon the experiment myself, making Riley wake me at the end of three minutes; and I felt so much benefited by it that I timed the men in the same way. They sat on the runners of the sledge, fell asleep instantly, and were forced to wakefulness when their three minutes were out.

"By eight in the evening we emerged from the floes. The sight of the Pinnacly Berg revived us. Brandy, an invaluable resource in emergency, had already been served out in table-spoonful doses. We now took a longer rest, and a last but stouter dram, and reached the brig at one P. M., we believe, without a halt.

"I say *we believe;* and here, perhaps, is the most decided proof of our sufferings; we were quite delirious, and had ceased to entertain a sane apprehension of the circumstances about us. We moved on like men in a dream. Our foot-marks, seen afterward, showed that we had steered a bee-line for the brig. It must have been by a sort of instinct, for it left no impress on the memory. Bonsall was sent staggering ahead, and reached the brig, God knows how, for he had fallen repeatedly at the track-lines; but he delivered, with punctilious accuracy, the messages I had sent by him to Dr. Hayes. I thought myself the soundest of all; for I went through all the formula of sanity, and can recall the muttering delirium of my comrades when we got back into the cabin of our brig. Yet I have been told since of some speeches, and some orders, too, of mine, which I should have remembered for their absurdity, if my mind had retained its balance.

"Petersen and Whipple came out to meet us about two miles from the brig. They brought my dog-team, with the restoratives I had sent for by Bonsall. I do not remember their coming. Dr. Hayes entered with judicious energy upon the treatment our condition called for; administering morphine freely, after the usual frictions. He reported none of our brain-symptoms as serious, referring them properly to the class of those indications of exhausted power which yield to a generous diet and rest. Mr. Ohlsen suffered some time from strabismus and blindness; two others underwent amputation of parts of the foot, without unpleasant consequences; and two died, in spite of all our efforts. This rescue-party had been out for seventy-two hours. We had halted in all eight hours, half of our number sleeping at a time. We travelled between eighty and ninety miles, most of the way dragging a heavy sledge. The mean temperature of the whole time, including the warmest hours of three days, was at *minus* 41°.2. We had no water except at our two halts, and were at no time able to intermit vigorous exercise without freezing.

"*April* 4, *Tuesday.* — Four days have passed, and I am again at my record of failures, sound, but aching still in every joint. The rescued men are not out of danger, but their gratitude is very touching. Pray God that they may live!"

The first appearance of the Esquimaux is thus described:

"We were watching, in the morning, at Baker's death-bed, when one of our deck-watch, who had been cutting ice for the melter, came hurrying down to the cabin with the report, 'People hollaing ashore!' I went up, followed by as many as could mount the gangway; and there they were, on all sides of our rocky harbor, dotting the snow-shores, and emerging from the blackness of the cliffs — wild and uncouth, but evidently human beings.

"As we gathered on the deck, they rose upon the more elevated fragments of the land-ice, standing singly and conspicuously, like the figures in a tableau of the opera, and distributing themselves around almost in a half-circle. They were vociferating as if to attract our attention, or, perhaps, only to give vent to their surprise; but I could make nothing out of their cries, except 'Hoah, ha, ha!' and 'Ka, kaah! ka, kaah!' repeated over and over again.

"There was light enough for me to see that they brandished no weapons, and were only tossing their heads and arms about in violent gesticulations. A more unexcited inspection showed us, too, that their numbers were not as great, nor their size as Patagonian, as some of us had been disposed to fancy at first. In a word, I was satisfied that they were natives of the country; and, calling Petersen from his bunk to be my interpreter, I proceeded, unarmed, and waving my open hands, toward a stout figure, who made himself conspicuous, and seemed to have a greater number near him than the rest. He evidently understood the movement; for he at once, like a brave fellow, leaped down upon the floe, and advanced to meet me fully half-way.

"He was nearly a head taller than myself, extremely powerful and well-built, with swarthy complexion, and black eyes. His dress was a hooded *capote* or jumper, of mixed white and blue fox-pelts, arranged with something of fancy; and booted trousers of white bear-skin, which, at the end of the foot, were made to terminate with the claws of the animal.

"I soon came to an understanding with this gallant diplomatist. Almost as soon as we commenced our parley, his companions, probably receiving signals from him, flocked in and surrounded us; but we had no difficulty in making them know, positively, that they must remain where they were, while Metek went with me on board the ship. This gave me the advantage of negotiating with an important hostage.

"Although this was the first time he had ever seen a white man, he went with me fearlessly, his companions staying behind on the ice. Hickey took them out what he esteemed our greatest delicacies — slices of good wheat bread, and corned pork, with exorbitant lumps of white sugar; but they refused to touch them. They had evidently no apprehension of open violence from us. I found, afterward, that several among them were singly a match for the white bear and the walrus, and that they thought us a very pale-faced crew.

"Being satisfied with my interview in the cabin, I sent out word that the rest might be admitted to the ship; and, although they, of course, could not know how their chief had been dealt with, some nine or ten of them followed, with boisterous readiness, upon the bidding. Others, in the mean time, as if disposed to give us their company for the full time of a visit, brought up from behind the land-ice as many as fifty-six fine dogs, with their sledges, and secured them within two hundred feet of the brig, driving their lances into the ice, and picketing the dogs to them by the seal-skin traces. The animals understood the operation perfectly, and lay down as soon as it commenced. The sledges were made up of small fragments of porous bone, admirably knit together by thongs of hide ; the runners, which glistened like burnished steel, were of highly-polished ivory, obtained from the tusks of the walrus.

"The only arms they carried were knives, concealed in their boots ; but their lances, which were lashed to the sledges, were quite a formidable weapon. The staff was of the horn of the narwhal, or else of the thigh-bones of the bear, two lashed together ; or sometimes the mirabilis of the walrus, three or four of them united. This last was a favorite material, also, for the cross-bars of their sledges. They had no wood. A single rusty hoop from a current-drifted cask might have furnished all the knives of the party ; but the fleam-shaped tips of their lances were of unmistakable steel, and were riveted to the tapering, bony point, with no mean skill. I learned afterward that the metal was obtained in traffic from the more southern tribes.

"They were clad much as I have described Metek, in jumpers, boots, and white bear-skin breeches, with their feet decorated like his, *en griffe*. A strip of knotted leather worn round the neck, very greasy and dirty-looking, which no one could be persuaded to part with for an instant, was mistaken, at first, for an ornament by the crew ; it was not until mutual hardships had made us better acquainted that we learned its mysterious uses.

"When they were first allowed to come on board, they were very rude and difficult to manage. They spoke three or four at a time, to each other and to us, laughing heartily at our ignorance in not understanding them, and then talking away, as before. They were incessantly in motion, — going everywhere, trying doors, and squeezing themselves through dark passages, round casks and boxes, and out into the light again, anxious to touch and handle everything they saw, and asking for, or else endeavoring to steal, everything they touched. It was the more difficult to restrain them, as I did not wish them to suppose that we were at all intimidated. But there were some signs of our disabled condition, which it was important they should not see ; it was especially necessary to keep them out of the forecastle, where the dead body of poor Baker was lying ; and, as it was in vain to reason or persuade, we had, at last, to employ the 'gentle laying-on of hands,' which, I believe, the laws of all countries tolerate, to keep them in order.

"Our whole force was mustered, and kept constantly on the alert ; but, though there may have been something of discourtesy in the occasional shoulderings and hustlings that enforced the police of the ship, things went on good-humoredly. Our guests continued running in and out and about the vessel, bringing in provisions, and carrying them out again to their dogs on the ice ; in fact, stealing all the time, until the afternoon, when, like tired children, they threw themselves down to sleep. I ordered them to be made comfortable in the hold ; and Morton spread a large buffalo-robe for them not far from a coal-fire in the galley-stove.

"They were lost in barbarous amaze at the new fuel, — too hard for blubber, too soft for fire-stone, — but they were content to believe it might cook as well as seal's fat. They borrowed from us an iron pot, and some melted water, and parboiled a couple of pieces of walrus-meat ; but, the real *pièce de résistance*, some five pounds of head, they preferred to eat raw. Yet there was something of the *gourmet* in their mode of assorting their mouthfuls of beef and blubber. Slices of each, or rather strips, passed between the lips, either together or in strict alternation, and with a regularity of sequence that kept the molars well to their work.

"They did not eat all at once, but each man when and as often as the impulse prompted. Each slept after eating, his raw chunk lying beside him on the buffalo-skin ; and, as he woke, the first act was to eat, and the next to sleep again. They did not lie down, but slumbered away in a sitting posture, with the head declined upon the breast, some of them snoring famously.

"In the morning they were anxious to go ; but I had given orders to detain them for a parting interview with myself. It resulted in a treaty, brief in its terms, that it might be certainly remembered ; and mutually beneficial, that it might possibly be kept. I tried to make them understand what a powerful Prospero they had had for a host, and how beneficent he would prove himself so long as they did his bidding. And, as an earnest of my favor, I bought all the walrus-meat they had to spare, and four of their dogs ; enriching them, in return, with needles and beads, and a treasure of old cask-staves."

The flesh of the seal is eaten universally by the Danes of Greenland, and is, at certain seasons, almost the staple diet of the Esquimaux. These animals are shot lying by their *atluk* or breathing-holes. Their eyes are so congested by the glare of the sun in midsummer as to render them more readily approachable.

"On one occasion," says Dr. Kane, "while working my way toward the Esquimaux huts, I saw a large *Usuk* basking asleep upon the ice. Taking off my shoes, I commenced a somewhat refrigerating process of stalking, lying upon my belly, and crawling along, step by step, behind the little knobs of floe. At last, when I was within long rifle-shot, the animal gave a sluggish roll to one side, and suddenly lifted his head. The movement was evidently independent of me, for he strained his neck in nearly the opposite direction. Then, for the first time, I found that I had a rival seal-hunter in a large bear, who was, on his belly like myself, waiting with commendable patience and cold feet for a chance of nearer approach.

"What should I do? — the bear was doubtless worth more to me than the seal; but the seal was now within shot, and the bear 'a bird in the bush.' Besides, my bullet once invested in the seal would leave me defenceless. I might be giving a dinner to a bear, and saving myself for his dessert. These meditations were soon brought to a close; for a second movement of the seal so aroused my hunter's instincts that I pulled the trigger. My cap alone exploded. Instantly, with a floundering splash, the seal descended into the deep, and the bear, with three or four rapid leaps, stood disconsolately by the place of his descent. For a single moment we stared each other in the face, and then, with that discretion which is the better part of valor, the bear ran off in one direction, and I followed his example in the other."

The month of April was about to close, and the short season available for Arctic search was already advanced, when Dr. Kane started on his grand sledge expedition to the north. "It was," says the enterprising commander, "to be the crowning expedition of the campaign to attain the *ultima thule* of the Greenland shore, measure the waste that lay between it and the unknown west, and seek round the furthest circle of the ice for an outlet to the mysterious channels beyond." The rigor of the climate, the difficulties of the country, the failure of the *caches* which had been broken into by the bears, the enfeebled state of the party, and the inadequacy of means and equipments, all, however, combined to cause failure. By the 5th of May, Dr. Kane had become delirious, and fainted every time that he was taken from the tent to the sledge ; so all idea of further progress had to be given up. He was taken into the brig on the 14th, and lay fluctuating between life and death till the 20th.

Some interesting discoveries were, however, made on this unfortunate trip, more especially of two remarkable freaks of nature, one of which was called the "Three Brother Turrets," the other, "Tennyson's Monument." The latter was a solitary column, or "minaret tower" of greenstone, the length of whose shaft was four hundred and eighty feet, and it rose on a plinth, or pedestal, itself two hundred and eighty feet high, as sharply finished as if it had been cast for the Place Vendôme. But by far the most remarkable feature in the inland Greenland sea is the so-called "Great Glacier of Humboldt."

"I will not attempt" (writes Dr. Kane, speaking of the impossibility of giving an idea of this great glacier by sketches) "to do better by florid description. Men only rhapsodize about Niagara and the ocean. My notes speak simply of the 'long, ever-shining line of cliff diminished to a well-pointed wedge in the perspective ;' and again, of 'the face of glistening ice, sweeping in a long curve from the low interior, the facets in front intensely illuminated by the sun.' But this line of cliff rose in solid glassy wall three hundred feet above the water level, with an unknown, unfathomable depth below it ; and its curved face, sixty miles in length, from Cape Agassiz to Cape Forbes, vanished into unknown space at not more than a single day's railroad-travel from the pole. The interior with which it communicated, and from which it issued, was an unsurveyed *mer de glace,* an ice-ocean, to the eye of boundless dimensions.

"It was in full sight — the mighty crystal bridge which connects the two continents of America and Greenland. I say continents, for Greenland, however insulated it may ultimately prove to be, is in mass strictly continental. Its least possible axis, measured from Cape Farewell to the line of this glacier, in the neighborhood of the eightieth parallel, gives a length of more than twelve hundred miles, — not materially less than that of Australia from its northern to its southern cape.

"Imagine now the centre of such a continent, occupied through nearly its whole extent by a deep unbroken sea of ice, that gathers perennial increase from the water-shed of vast snow-covered mountains, and all the precipitations of the atmosphere upon its own surface. Imagine this moving onward like a great glacial river, seeking outlets at every fiord and valley, rolling icy cataracts into the Atlantic and Greenland seas; and, having at last reached the northern limit of the land that has borne it up, pouring out a mighty frozen torrent into unknown Arctic space.

"It is thus, and only thus, that we must form a just conception of a phenomenon like this Great Glacier. I had looked in my own mind for such an appearance, should I ever be fortunate enough to reach the northern coast of Greenland. But, now that it was before me, I could hardly realize it. I had recognized, in my quiet library at home, the beautiful analogies which Forbes and Studer have developed between the glacier and the river. But I could not comprehend at first this complete substitution of ice for water.

"It was slowly that the conviction dawned on me that I was looking upon the counterpart of the great river system of Arctic Asia and America. Yet here were no water-feeders from the south. Every particle of moisture had its origin within the Polar Circle, and had been converted into ice. There were no vast alluvions, no forest or animal traces borne down by liquid torrents. Here was a plastic, moving, semi-solid mass, obliterating life, swallowing rocks and islands, and ploughing its way with irresistible march through the crust of an investing sea."

"Humboldt Glacier" and "Tennyson's Monument" will deservedly occupy a place in all future editions of those interesting little books called "Wonders of the World." As soon as Dr. Kane had recovered enough to become aware of his failure, he began to devise means for remedying it. Of the ship's company, the only one remaining, qualified to conduct a survey, was Dr. Hayes. He accordingly started with a dog-team, in company with William Godfrey, across Smith's Straits, on the 20th of May, and succeeded in reaching 79° 45′ north latitude, in longitude 69° 12′. The coast was sighted for thirty miles to the northward and eastward, and two large headlands, called Capes Joseph Leidy and John Frazer, were named upon it. The doctor returned to the brig, after a very arduous and fatiguing journey, on the 1st of June, worn out and snow-blind. In many places he could not have advanced but for the dogs. Deep cavities filled with snow intervened between lines of ice-barricades, making the travel slow and tedious. For some time he was not able, from snow-blindness, to use the sextant. The rude harness of the dogs would get tangled and cause delay. It was only after appropriating an undue share of his seal-skin breeches that Dr. Hayes succeeded in patching up his mutilated dog-lines. His pemmican became so reduced that to return was a thing of necessity. The land-ice was travelled for a while at the rate of five or six miles an hour; but after crossing Dobbin Bay, the snows were an unexpected impediment.

Notwithstanding the perils, privations, and sufferings, that had attended all the sledge-parties, Dr. Kane determined to organize another before the brief season for such had gone by. This last, under Messrs. M'Gary and Bonsall, left the brig on the 3d of June, and reached Humboldt Glacier on the 15th. They were provided with apparatus for climbing ice, but failed in all their efforts to scale this stupendous glacial mass. The bears were so bold as actually to poke their heads in at the tent-door, to the great inconvenience of the sleepers within. Four of the party returned to the brig on the 27th, one of them entirely blind.

Hans and Morton remained out, pushing northwards, and keeping parallel to the glacier at a distance of from five to seven miles. They saw rectangular pieces of ice, apparently detached from the glacier, more than a mile long! On the 21st of June they sighted open water. This was afterwards called Kennedy Channel. After turning Cape Andrew Jackson they made better way along the ice-foot; and they pursued their course as far as Cape Constitution, on "Washington Land," in 82° 27′. The highest point on the opposite coast of "Grinnell Land" was a lofty mountain, estimated to be in latitude 82° 30′, and longitude 66° west, which Dr. Kane called Mount Edward Parry: who, he says, "as he has carried his name to the most northern latitude yet reached, should have in this, the highest known northern land, a recognition of his preëminent position among Arctic explorers." This open channel was found to abound in seals; bears were numerous — one with its cub they succeeded in killing; and birds, among which were brent geese, eider-ducks, king-ducks, dovekies, gulls, sea-swallows, and Arctic petrels, were in exceeding plenty. This was the crowning excursion of the expedition, and the results present rich matter for speculation to those who believe in an open polar sea beyond the region of embayed and strangulated ice-floes.

Instead of the Bay of Baffin forming a *cul de sac*, as the old tradition of the whalers conceived, it leads to a strait (Smith's Strait), which passes on into a channel (Kennedy Channel), that apparently expands into an open polar sea, abounding with life, some three hundred miles further to the north than the head of Baffin's Bay. The shores of this channel, terminating in the Cape Constitution of Mr. Morton, in latitude 81° 22′, on the eastern side, and in Sir Edward Parry's peak, about latitude 82° 17′, on the western side, had now been delineated and mapped through an extent of nine hundred and sixty miles, at a cost of two thousand miles of travel on foot and in sledges. Mr. Morton commenced his return on the 25th of June, and reached the ship on the 10th of July, staggering by the side of the limping dogs, one of which was riding as a passenger upon the sledge.

The summer of 1854 was now wearing on, and yet no prospects presented themselves of the ice breaking up, so as to liberate the brig. Under these circumstances, Dr. Kane determined upon making an attempt to communicate with Sir Edward Belcher's squadron at Beechey Island. For this purpose a boat was fitted out, called the *Forlorn Hope*, and was carried across the heavy ice-floe to be launched in open water. On their way to the southward they fell in with an island, upon which they killed a number of eider-ducks, and procured a large supply of eggs. On the 19th of July they made Cape Alexander, and were enabled to determine that the narrowest part of Smith's Strait is not, as has been considered, between Cape Isabella and Cape Alexander, but upon the parallel of 78° 24′, where Cape Isabella bears due west of Littleton Island, and the diameter of

THE FORLORN HOPE EQUIPPED.

the channel is reduced to thirty-seven miles. Hence, they passed from the straits into the open seaway. At this time a gale broke upon them from the north, and they were exposed to all its fury in the open whale-boat. They were glad to drive before the wind into the in-shore floes. The pack, so much feared before, was now looked to as a refuge.

Working their way through the broken pack, they reached Hakluyt Island on the 23d of July, where they rested a while and dried their buffalo-robes. The next morning they renewed their labors, but were arrested by the pack off Northumberland Island. For four days they made strenuous efforts to work through the half-open leads, but in vain; they had reached the dividing pack of the two great open waters of Baffin's Bay, and which Dr. Kane considered to be made up of the ices which Jones's Sound on the west, and Murchison's on the east, had discharged and driven together. Under these circumstances, they were obliged to return to Northumberland Island, which they found to be one enormous homestead of auks, dovekies, and gulls, and where they procured sorrel and cochlearia. Foxes were also very numerous. By the time they got back to the brig, the commander says he and his little party had got quite fat and strong upon the auks, eiders, and scurvy-grass.

On board of the Advance, however, which had now been imprisoned by closely-cementing ice for eleven months, as the season travelled on and the young ice grew thicker, faces began, also, to grow longer every day. It was the only face with which they could look upon another winter. "It is *horrible*," writes Dr. Kane, — "yes, that is the word, — to look forward to another year of disease and darkness, to be met without fresh food and without fuel."

Under these circumstances, Dr. Kane called the officers and crew together, and left to every man his own choice to remain by the ship or to attempt an escape to the Danish settlements to the southward. Eight out of the seventeen survivors resolved to stand by the brig and their commander. The remainder started off, on the 28th, "with the elastic step of men confident in their purpose;" but one returned a few days afterwards, and all ultimately either found their way back, or were brought back by the humane Esquimaux, after hard trials, and almost unparalleled sufferings.

Those that remained with the ship set to work at once gathering moss for eking out the winter fuel, and willow-stems and sorrel as antiscorbutics. The "mossing," although it had a pleasant sound, was in reality a frightfully wintry operation. The mixed turf, of willows, heaths, grasses, and moss, was frozen solid. It had to be quarried with crowbars, and carried to the ship like so much stone. With this they banked up the ship's sides, and below they enclosed a space some eighteen feet square, and packed it with the same material from floor to ceiling. The entrance was also by a low, moss-lined tunnel, and in this apartment the men stowed away for the winter. The closer they lay, the warmer. Dr. Kane was once more nearly lost, however, before darkness came on. In an attempt to kill a seal he got upon thin ice, and was, with dogs and sledge, thrown into open water. He owed his extrication, when nearly gone, to a newly-broken team-dog, who was still fast to the sledge, and drew it and the doctor up on to the floe.

An occasional intercourse had always been kept up with the Esquimaux. We have seen that they came to pilfer, and Dr. Kane retorted by making some of them prisoners. A treaty of friendship was then made, and never broken by the natives. The nearest Esquimaux settlement was distant, by dog-journey, about seventy-five miles; and with this rude but friendly people our adventurers established a communication, and procured from them supplies of bear-meat, seal, walrus, fox, and ptarmigan, which were eaten raw, — the custom in this region. But these supplies became scanty with the approach of the dark months. Attempts to reach the Esquimaux were rendered impracticable by the ruggedness of the ice; and this unfortunate people were themselves reduced to the lowest stages of misery and emaciation by famine, attended with various frightful forms of disease.

On the 14th of January Dr. Kane congratulated himself that *in five more days* the mid-day sun would be only "*eight degrees below the horizon.*" On the 9th of February he wrote in his journal: "It is enough to solemnize men of more joyous temperament than ours has been for some months. We are contending at odds with angry forces close around us, without one agent or influence within eighteen hundred miles whose sympathy is on our side." There were no star observations this winter; the observatory had become the mausoleum of the two of the party who had succumbed after the excursion in the snow-drift. In the beginning of March every man on board was tainted with scurvy; and often not more than three were able to make exertion in behalf of the rest. On the 4th of the month the last remnant of fresh meat was doled out, and the invalids began to sink rapidly. Their lives were only saved by the success of a forlorn-hope excursion of Hans to the remote Esquimaux hunting-station Etah, seventy-five miles away, whither he went in search of walrus.

On one occasion the adventurers killed a bear that had come with its cub, pressed by extreme hunger, close to the brig. It is painful to read the details of the struggle, from the wonderful attachment shown by the mother to its cub, and by the latter to its parent, to whom it always clung, even in death. But the men's lives were valuable; and it was thought excusable to kill two bears when the glaucous gulls were seen gobbling up young eider-ducks in the face of their distracted mothers by mouthfuls. Dr. Kane was the only person who would eat rats. He attributes his comparative immunity from scurvy to "rat-soup." Among the Arctic dainties which seem most to have excited his gastronomic enthusiasm was frozen walrus-liver, eaten raw.

Having no fuel, they were now reduced to the Esquimaux system of relying on lamps for heat; beds and bedding hence became black with soot, and their faces were begrimed with fatty carbon. The journal is now little more than a chronicle of privations and sufferings, interspersed with extraordinary efforts to keep up communications with the Esquimaux. It is, without comparison, the most painfully interesting record of experience in wintering in the far north that has ever yet been published. In the midst of their troubles two of the men tried to desert, but only one — Godfrey — succeeded. He returned, strange to say, on the 2d of April, with food, in a sledge, but would not himself quit the Esquimaux. Under a misapprehension that he had robbed Hans, one of the hunters, of his sledge and dogs, his life was near being sacrificed by the commander from whom he had deserted.

The abandonment of the brig was now resolved on. Before spring could be welcomed, preparations had been going on for some time for a sledge and boat escape from their long imprisonment. The employment thus given to the men exerted a wholesome influence on their moral tone, and assisted their convalescence. They had three boats, and they all required to be strengthened. There was clothing, bedding, and provision-bags, to make. The sledges had to be prepared. The 17th of May was appointed for the start. The farewell to the ship was most impressive. Prayers were read, and then a chapter of the Bible. The flags were then hoisted and hauled down again, and she was left alone in the ice. Godfrey had, by this time, it is to be observed, rejoined the ship ; so the party consisted altogether of seventeen, of whom four were unable to move.

The collections of natural history the party were reluctantly compelled to leave behind, and part of the apparatus for observations, as well as the library of the commander, and the books furnished by the government and Mr. Grinnell for the use of the vessel. Nothing was retained but the documents of the expedition.

At Etah the Esquimaux settlement were found "out on the bare rocks," enjoying the plenty which spring had brought. "Rudest of gypsies, how they squalled, and laughed, and snored, and rolled about! Some were sucking bird-skins; others were boiling incredible numbers of auks in huge soapstone pots; and two youngsters, crying, at the top of their voices, 'Oopegsoak! oopegsoak!' were fighting for an owl.

ESQUIMAUX BOY CATCHING AUKS.

"There was enough to make them improvident. The little auks were breeding in the low cones of rubbish under the cliffs in such numbers that it cost them no more to get food than it does a cook to gather vegetables. A boy, ordered to climb the rocks with one of their purse-nets of seal-skin at the end of a narwhal's tusk, would return in a few minutes with as many as he could carry."

Up to the 23d the progress of Dr. Kane's party was little more than a mile a day. The housed boats luckily afforded tolerably good sleeping-berths at night. On the 5th of June, Ohlsen injured himself so in an attempt to rescue a sledge from falling into a tide-hole, that he died three days afterwards.

"Still passing slowly on, day after day, — I am reluctant," writes Dr. Kane, "to borrow from my journal the details of anxiety and embarrassment with which it abounds throughout this period, — we came at last to the unmistakable neighborhood of open water." This was off Pekintlek, the largest of the Littleton Island group.

On Tuesday, the 19th of June, after a long farewell given to their long-tried friends, the Esquimaux of Etah, who had brought them frequent supplies of birds, and aided them in carrying their provisions and stores, they put to sea, and, the very first day's navigation, one of the boats swamped. They spent the first night in an inlet in the ice, and on the 22d reached Northumberland Island in a snow-storm. Here they got fresh provisions. They crossed Murchison Channel on the 23d, and encamped for the night on the land-floe at the base of Cape Parry — a hard day's travel, partly by tracking over ice, partly through tortuous and zig-zag leads. So it was for many successive days. One day favorable, with open leads of water; another, slow and wearisome, through alternate ice and water. Then the floe would break up and carry them resistlessly against the rocks. Three long days they passed in a cavern of rock and ice, in which, however, they found plenty of birds' eggs.

On the 11th they had doubled Cape Dudley Digges,

and plants, and birds, and birds' eggs, became more common. They spent a week to regain strength at so productive a spot, which they designated as "Providence Halt." At the Crimson Cliffs they again got a plentiful supply of birds. On the 21st of July they reached Cape York, and made immediate preparations for crossing Melville Bay, which was accomplished with great labor and suffering. Once more they were nearly starving, when a great seal came providentially to their succor. Their feet were so swollen that they were obliged to cut open their canvas boots. The most unpleasant symptom was that they could not sleep. On the 1st of August they sighted the Devil's Thumb. Hence they fetched the Duck Islands, and, passing to the south of Cape Shackleton, landed on *terra firma*. Two or three days more, and they were under the shadow of Karkamoot.

"Just then a familiar sound came to us over the water. We had often listened to the screeching of the gulls, or the bark of the fox, and mistaken it for the 'Huk' of the Esquimaux ; but this had about it an inflection not to be mistaken, for it died away in the familiar cadence of a 'halloo.'

"'Listen, Petersen! Oars — men? What is it?' and he listened quietly at first, and then, trembling, said, in a half-whisper, 'Dannemarkers!'"

It was the Upernavik oil-boat, and the next day they were at Upernavik itself, after being eighty-four days in the open air. They could not remain within the four walls of a house without a distressing sense of suffocation.

From Dr. Kane's report to the Navy Department we quote the summing up of the results of the expedition. They embrace :

"1. The survey and delineation of the north coast of Greenland to its termination by a great glacier.

"2. The survey of this glacial mass, and its extension northward into the new land named Washington.

"3. The discovery of a large channel to the north-west, free from ice, and leading into an open and expanding area, equally free. The whole embraces an iceless area of four thousand two hundred miles.

"4. The discovery and delineation of a large tract of land, forming the extension northward of the American continent.

"5. The completed survey of the American coast to the south and west, as far as Cape Sabine; thus connecting our survey with the last determined position of Captain Inglefield, and completing the circuit of the straits and bay heretofore known at their southernmost opening as Smith's Sound."

The view of the open sea referred to was obtained by William Morton, from a precipitous headland, — the furthest point attained by the party, in latitude 81° 22′ N., and longitude 65° 35′ W., at an altitude of five hundred feet above the sea. The reasons assigned by our author for regarding it an iceless open sea are the following:

"1. It was approached by a channel entirely free from ice, having a length of fifty-two and a mean width of thirty-six geographical miles.

"2. The coast-ice along the water-line of this channel had been completely destroyed by thaw and water-action; while an unbroken belt of solid ice, one hundred and twenty-five miles in diameter, extended to the south.

"3. A gale from the north-east, of fifty-four hours' duration, brought a heavy sea from that quarter, without disclosing any drift or other ice.

"4. Dark *nimbus* clouds and water-sky invested the north-eastern horizon.

"5. Crowds of migratory birds were observed thronging its waters."

There is much in Dr. Kane's wonderful narrative to remind the reader of the story of old William Barentz, who, two hundred and fifty-nine years ago, wintered on the coast of Nova Zembla. His men, seventeen in number, broke down during the trials of winter, and three died, just as of the eighteen under Dr. Kane three had gone. Barentz abandoned his vessel, as the Americans abandoned theirs, took to his boats, and escaped along the Lapland coast to lands of Norwegian civilization. The Americans embarked with sledges and boats to attempt the same thing. They had the longer journey, and the more difficult one, before them. Barentz lost, as they did, a cherished comrade by the wayside. But one resemblance luckily does not exist: Barentz himself perished — Dr Kane lived to write an account of all that he suffered in a noble cause. No mere abstract of his narrative can give an idea of its absorbing interest.

His book is above all common praise, on account of the simple, manly, unaffected style in which the narrative of arduous enterprise and firm endurance is told. It is obviously a faithful record of occurrences, made by a man who was quite aware that what he had to tell needed no extraneous embellishment. There is, however, so much of artistic order in the mind of the narrator, that the unvarnished record has naturally shaped itself into a work of distinguished excellence upon literary grounds. The scenes which it describes are so vividly and vigorously brought before the reader, that there are few who sit down to the perusal of the narrative but will fancy, before they rise from the engrossing occupation, their own flesh paralyzed by the cold one hundred degrees greater than frost, and their blood scurvy-filled by the four months' sunlessness.

It is only just also to remark, that there is unmistakable evidence, in the pages of this interesting book, that the doctor was no less eminently gifted for the duties of his command than he has been happy in his relation of its history. Every step in his arduous path seems to have been taken only after the exercise of deliberately matured forethought. A few illustrations must be gleaned, from the many that are scattered through the pages of his journal, to direct attention to this honorable characteristic. When the doctor had formed his own resolution to remain by the brig through the second winter, he made the following entry, under the date of August 22 : "I shall call the officers and crew together, and make known to them, very fully, how things look, and what hazards must attend such an effort as has been proposed among them. They shall have my views unequivocally expressed. I will then give them twenty-four hours to deliberate ; and, at the end of that time, all who determine to go shall say so in writing, with a full exposition of the circumstances of the case. They shall have the best outfit I can give, an abundant share of our remnant stores, and my good-by blessing."

On the 6th of April the Esquimaux auxiliary, Hans, was gone to Etah, with a sledge, to seek a supply of walrus-meat, when, as we have already stated, William Godfrey deserted from the ship ; and, the commander suspected, with some sinister design upon Hans and the sledge. Dr. Kane then wrote : "Clearly, duty to this poor boy calls me to seek him ; and, clearly, duty to these dependent men calls me to stay. Long and uncomfortably have I pondered over these opposing calls, but at last have come to a determination. Hans was faithful to me ; the danger to him is imminent, the danger to those left behind only contingent upon my failure to return. With earnest trust in that same Supervising Agency which has so often before, in graver straits, interfered to protect and carry me through, I have resolved to go after Hans."

The Esquimaux lad was proof both against the violence and the seduction of the deserter. The commander found him invalided, but safe, at Etah. Hans, however, did not return to Fiskernaes with the expedition. His fate is involved in romance. Venus Victrix has a representative even in frost-land. The reader must go to the pages of Dr. Kane to know what became of Hans.

When the preparations for the final escape were under consideration, the following record was made in the doctor's journal: "Whatever of executive ability I have picked up during this brain-and-body-wearying cruise warns me against immature preparation or vacillating purposes. I must have an exact discipline, a rigid routine, and a perfectly thought-out organization. For the past six weeks I have, in the intervals between my duties to the sick and the ship, arranged the schedule of our future course ; much of it is already under way. My journal shows what I have done, but what there is to do is appalling." Appalling as it was, the heroic man who had to look the necessity in the face was equal to the position. There can be no doubt that it was "*the exact discipline, the rigid routine, and the perfectly thought-out organization*," which restored the sixteen survivors of the expedition to civilization and their homes.

CHAPTER XX.

ACTION OF CONGRESS. — RELIEF EXPEDITION IN SEARCH OF DR. KANE. — HARTSTEIN THE COMMANDER. — ICE ENCOUNTERS. — SEARCHES. — THE LOST FOUND. — NARRATIVE BY JOHN K. KANE. — ICEBERGS. — BIRDS. — ESQUIMAUX. — THE MEETING. — THE RESOLUTE. — FOUND BY AMERICAN WHALERS. — INTERNATIONAL COURTESIES. — DEMAND FOR NEW EXPEDITIONS. — SPECULATIONS.

THE apprehensions caused at home, by the detention of Dr. Kane and his party, produced a resolution of Congress, approved February 3d, 1855, authorizing the Secretary of the Navy to despatch a suitable steamer and tender for the relief of the absent voyagers. The bark Release and the steamer Arctic were accordingly procured and equipped, Lieut. Hartstein having been appointed to the command. He was accompanied by a brother of Dr. Kane. They reached Lievely, Isle of Disco, Greenland, July 5th, 1855, having encountered the first iceberg in latitude 51° 30′ north, longitude 51° 40′ west. With seaman-like generosity, Hartstein, in his letter from this place to the Secretary of the Navy, says : "To avoid further risk of human life, in a search so extremely hazardous, I would suggest the impropriety of making any efforts to relieve us if we should not return ; feeling confident that we shall be able to accomplish all necessary for our own release, under the most extraordinary circumstances."

Entering the closely-packed floe of Melville Bay, the

relief vessels forced a passage into the North Water on the morning of the 13th of August. Passing in good view of the coast from Cape York to Wolstenholme Island, Hartstein, in the steamer, examined Cape Alexander and Sutherland Island. Passing on to the most north-western point in sight (Point Pelham), he noticed a few stones heaped together, which, on examination, gave assurance of Kane's having been there; but no clue was afforded. Pushing on to latitude 78° 32′ north, the steamer was opposed by a solid, hummocky field of very heavy ice, to which no limit was visible, interspersed as it was with bergs, all drifting to the southward. Taking now a retrograde course, they examined Cape Hatherton and Littleton Island, and finally took refuge under a projecting point, some fifteen miles northwest of Cape Alexander. Here they were startled by the hail of human voices. Going on shore, they found a party of Esquimaux, and among them various articles that must have belonged to Dr. Kane and his men. An examination of the most intelligent of the natives led to the understanding that Dr. Kane, having lost his vessel somewhere to the north, had been at that spot, with his interpreter (Carl Petersen), and seventeen others, in two boats and a sled, and, after remaining ten days, had gone south to Upernavik.

After some more reconnoitring of the coast, Hartstein, in the Arctic, found himself firmly beset by the ice, and thought, for a time, he was in winter quarters; but, after twenty-four hours' heavy battering, he got out. After having made nearly the whole circuit of the northern part of Baffin's Bay, with the exception of a deep ice-locked indentation between Capes Cowbermere and Isabella, he returned, and, in company with the Release, examined Possession Bay and Pond's Bay, firing guns, burning blue-lights, and throwing up rockets. He now determined to proceed to Upernavik, and, if he did not there find the missing party, to proceed north again, and winter in the ice. This was soon found to be unnecessary. At Lievely the missing party were received with many welcomes on board the vessels sent for their relief. We will leave it to Mr. John K. Kane, the brother of the doctor, to narrate, in his animated account of the relief expedition, the manner and the incidents of the encounter. The article, portions of which we quote, was originally contributed to *Putnam's Magazine;* and conveys, in a novel and spirited style, much interesting description and information in regard to the latitudes visited.

At Etah the relief expedition came in contact with the Esquimaux who had befriended Dr. Kane; and Mr. J. K. Kane selected one of the most forward and intelligent of the natives, a boy named Mayouk, and endeavored by signs to get some information from him. We present the following in Mr. Kane's own words:

"Mayouk was very quick in understanding us, and equally ready in inventing modes of conveying intelligence. Lead-pencil and paper were called into requisition. I took out my note-book, drew a rough sketch of a brig, and showed it to him. He, at once, said 'Dokto Kayen,' and pointed to the north. I then drew a reversed sketch, and pointed south. But Mayouk, shaking his head, began to sway his body backward and forward, to imitate rowing; then said Dokto Kayen again, and pointed south. On this, I drew a whole fleet of boats, and invited him to point out how many of these he referred to. He took the pencil from my hand, and altered the sterns of two into sharp-pointed ones, and then held up two fingers, to indicate that there were two of such. I now drew carefully two whale-boats; he made signs of approval, as much as to say that was *the* thing; and, incontinently squatting down, imitated the voice and gestures of a dog-driver, cracking an imaginary whip, and crying hup-hup-hup, at the top of his voice. After which performance, he laughed immoderately, and, again pointing south, said Dokto Kayen.

"I was not certain as to his meaning; but, on my drawing a picture of a dog-team, he went through the whole performance afresh, and showed the most extravagant signs of delight at being understood. We found out how many dog-sledges and how many men there were of the doctor's party, in the same manner. We examined several other natives separately, and they all told the same story; nor could we confuse them as to the number of men and boats; they were all clear on that head. Nineteen, they made it, neither more nor less. We tried our best to make them say that the boats had gone north, and the vessel south; but without success. Mayouk, on one occasion, being hard pressed, stopped his ears, so as, at least, to secure himself from being supposed to assent to what he had not learning or language enough to controvert.

"At length, a bright thought struck him. He ran down to the beach, and got two white stones; laid them on the ground, and, pointing to the floating masses of ice in the bay, signified to us that these represented the ice. Next, he took a common clay pipe of Mr. Lovell's, and, pointing to the north, said, vomiak sooak, or big ship, 'vomiak sooak, Dokto Kayen.' He next pushed the pipe up between the pebbles, and then pressed them together till the pipe was crushed. Lastly, he pointed to the south, and began imitating the rowing of a boat, the cracking of whips, and the hup-hupping of a dog-driver, vociferating, at intervals, 'Dokto Kayen, he! he! he!' We tried our best to find out how long it had been since the Dokto Kayens had left them, for it was evident that this was their name for the whole party; but we could not make them understand. They would only tell us that their guests had been with them for some time. This they did by pointing to the south, and then following the track of the sun till it reached the north; then, after stretching themselves out on the ground, and closing their eyes, as if in sleep, would again point to the south, rise up, go down to the lake and pretend to wash their faces. The gesture lay in pretence only, however, for they seemed to regard the washing of the Dokto Kayens as a remarkable religious observance. It certainly was not one which had been practically ingrafted into their own formulary of good works. These unsophisticated children of the frost-land never wash off dirt, for the simple reason that of dirt, as such, they have no conception or idea.

"Improvidence is another trait of these 'fresh children of impulse.' We were at their village as late as the 19th of August. Yet, although the auks were flying round them in such quantities that one man could have been able to catch a thousand an hour, they had not enough prepared for winter to last two days. They were all disgustingly fat, and always eating, — perhaps an average ration of eighteen pounds per diem, — yet they had lost seven by starvation during the last winter, though relieved, as far as we could make it out, by the Dokto Kayens.

"They suffer dreadfully from cold, too; yet there is an abundance of excellent peat, which they might dig during the summer. They know its value as fuel, and are simply too lazy to stack it. The little auk, which forms their principal food, may be said also to be their only fuel. Indeed, it quite fills the place which the seal holds among the more southern Esquimaux. Their clothes are lined with its skins, they burn the fat, and, setting aside the livers and hearts, to be dried, and consumed as *bonbons* during the winter, they eat the meat and intestines cooked and raw, both cold and at blood heat.

"They are very hospitable ; the minute we arrived, all hands began to catch birds and prepare them for us. Tearing off the skins with their teeth, they stripped the breasts to be cooked, and presented us with the juicy entrails and remaining portions to eat raw, and stay our appetites. The viands did not look inviting to us, who had witnessed their preparation ; but they appeared so hurt at our refusing to eat, that we had to explain that it was not cooked but raw birds we wanted. This was satisfactory. They set out at once to catch some for us ; and in a few moments three of them were on their way down to our boat loaded with birds.

"Though all the natives had told us that Dr. Kane's party had gone southwards after leaving their settlement, still we were far from certain that they had continued their progress in that direction, and Captain Hartstein was for some time in doubt as to the course which we ought to pursue ; whether we should return at once to Upernavik by our old track, or run across the bay and examine its western coast. He finally determined on the latter, believing that, if Dr. Kane and his party had gone down the eastern coast, they would by this time either have been lost in Melville Bay, or safely arrived at Upernavik ; while, on the contrary, if they had tried to reach the English fleet in Lancaster Sound, being ignorant of its desertion, they might be there now in a starving condition.

"We reached Cape Alexander without any incident worthy of note, and, after searching its barren rocks to no purpose, built a cairn, and in it deposited the record of our want of success. We next ran down to Sutherland Island, took up our now useless flag-staff, and tore down the cairn we had placed there on our way up. There was a poor little white fox watching us from the rocks above, while we were at work, evidently wondering what it all meant. He came so close that we could have knocked him down with a boat-hook, but we let him alone; we were not short of provisions, and had no time to convert him into a specimen.

"We pushed on through rain and fog to Hakluyt Island, where we found our comrades of the Release, and spent a few hurried hours in their company.

"The *red snow*, that Dr. Kane has described in his narrative, was abundant here; and wherever between the ledges of the rock there was a chance for soil, a tiny little horseradish sprang up ambitiously through the frost, with leaves no bigger than your thumb-nail. The miniature plant, flower, root, and all, might have filled a very moderate tea-cup.

"It is hardly worth while to tell of our efforts to find Captain Inglefield's Esquimaux settlement in Whale Sound. It was the old story of fog and drizzle, ice and sleet. We gave it up, and, taking the Release in tow, bent our course for Lancaster Sound.

"But the ice, the everlasting ice! We were more than two hundred miles off when it caught us. It was heavier than any we had seen even in Melville Bay. For some days it held us like flies in amber, in spite of sails, with now and then a puff to fill them, and all the steam that Newell could raise in his boiler. It was, indeed, a mercy that a gale caught us at last, or we might have been there still. We drove before it, the ice keeping us company, as if loth to lose us, and, finding that we could not reach Cape Isabella, made a détour to Possession Bay.

"Pond's Bay, as it is called, seemed to all of us nothing else but an extension of Admiralty Inlet. We kept along its north coast for thirty-five miles, and could see, perhaps, forty miles further, but without finding its westernmost shore. A visit to an Esquimaux village, some twenty miles up the bay, was the only incident. The men, with a single exception, were out on their hunting-parties; but the women were there, as communicative in their unknown dialect as any we had met of the grosser sex. They were certainly no beauties, and their costume was a little extravagant even for the Esquimaux fashions, as we had seen them. They had their faces tattooed with lampblack, in a set of dotted lines, radiating from the corners of the mouth; and their very long wide boots were hitched, awkwardly enough, by a loop to the waistband of their seal-skin trousers.

"They appeared to be of a superior race to the Greenland natives. They were larger and stronger, their kayaks were better built, and they had much more roomy tents.

"The whole of Pond's Bay showed one dreary, inhospitable coast-line. We were all of us glad when our commander gave the order to make for the eastern coast of Baffin's Bay.

"We had an eight-knot breeze, and were not more than two hundred miles from Upernavik. There was every chance of the wind continuing, so that we confidently expected to reach that port in the course of the week. We thought we were to the southward of the pack; and the heavy sea, which made us all sea-sick after our long exemption from rough water, strengthened this conviction. But we were mistaken. The very next day it was before us, an impenetrable barrier. There was no help for it; we had to run further to the south — how much further it was hardly worth while to guess. It was no very difficult matter, you would think, to run along the edge of the ice till we came to the end of it, and then run across. But this ice had all the irregularities of a coast: large inlets and bays running into it, and capes projecting just where you do not expect to meet them; and, over and over again, after running for a whole day, just as we were sure we had reached its southern boundary, we would find ourselves in a cul-de-sac, with the ice on both sides of us. At last we came to a dead halt. We were fairly in the pack — it was before us, behind us, and on both sides of us.

"Day after day passed, and we found we were drifting to the south, fairly glued in. There are only two incidents that I speak of in or about this pleasant little travel. One was just as it began. It was a meeting with an ancient whaler, the Eclipse, of Peterhead, with a jolly old Captain Gray, who insisted on all hands making a trial of a regular Scotchman's hospitality, and tossed half a dozen hams after us into the boat, when we refused to take the half of his cabin stores. The other was the gale that ended it. It was less pleasant at the time; but, like some other things that I have met with in this world, its effects were better than its promise. What a night it was! The bark ran into an iceberg, and came very near being lost. She fired thirteen guns for assistance, but the crashing and grinding was so tremendous that, though we were not three quarters of a mile off, and the wind was blowing directly towards us, we did not hear one of them. I never shall forget the melancholy figure she presented on joining us next morning. We felt quite a glow of sympathy for the poor Release, till Captain Hartstein's hailing our steamer with the information that our cutwater looked like a prize-fighter's nose. We then remembered that we, too, had a night of it.

"After this gale we had little or no more trouble with the ice; one or two trifling detentions of a few days brought us to the open water. We had drifted so far to the south that Lievely was nearer than Upernavik, and Captain Hartstein determined to put in there. We had a heavy gale the night after we left the ice; but so glad were we all to get clear of it, that I heard no complaints about rough weather. It cleared away beautifully towards morning, and we were all on the deck, admiring the clear water, and the fantastic shapes of the water-washed icebergs. All hands were in high spirits; the gale had blown in the right direction, and in a few hours we should be in Lievely. The rocks of its land-locked harbor were already in sight. We were discussing our news by anticipation, when the man in the crow's nest cried out, 'A brig in the harbor!' and the next minute, before we had time to congratulate each other on the chance of sending letters home, that she had hoisted American colors — a delicate compliment, we thought, on the part of our friends, the Danes.

"I believe our captain was about to return it, when, to our surprise, she hoisted another flag, the veritable one which had gone out with the Advance, bearing the name of Mr. Henry Grinnell. At the same moment, two boats were seen rounding the point, and pulling towards us. Did they contain our lost friends? Yes; the sailors had settled that. 'Those are Yankees, sir; no Danes ever feathered their oars that way,' said an old whaler to me.

"For those who had friends among the missing party, the few minutes that followed were of bitter anxiety; for the men in the boats were long-bearded and weather-beaten; they had strange, wild costumes; there was no possibility of recognition. Dr. Kane, standing upright in the stern of the first float, with his spy-glass slung round his neck, was the first identified; then the big form of Mr. Brooks; in another moment all hands of them were on board of us.

"It was curious to watch the effects of the excitement in different people, — the intense quietude of some, the boisterous delight of others; how one man would become intensely loquacious, another would do nothing but laugh, and a third would creep away to some out-of-the-way corner, as if he were afraid of showing how he felt. How hungry they all were for news, and how eagerly they tore open the home letters; most of them, poor fellows, had pleasant tidings, and all were prepared to make the best of bad ones. We were in the harbor, with a fleet of kayaks dancing in welcome around and behind us, before the greetings were half ended, for they repeated themselves over and over again.

"Our old friend, Mr. Olrik, was with the new comers, and as happy as the rest. His hospitality, when we reached the shore, was absolutely boundless; and his house and table were always at our service. Altogether, I never passed three more delightful days than those last days at Lievely. Balls every night; feasts and junketings every day; and, pleasantest of all, those dear home-like tea-tables, with shining tea-urn and clear, white sugar, round which we sat, waiting for the water to boil, and talking of Russia and the Czar, and the world outside the Circle; while Mrs. Olrik would look up from her worsted-work, and the children pressed round me to see the horses and dogs I was drawing for them. It was enough to make one forget his red flannel shirt and rough Arctic rig; Melville Bay and the pack seemed fables. The Danish doctor, too, arrived from Fiskernaes, a very intelligent gentleman, and we talked away bravely to him in bad Latin. He brought us a present of reindeer-meat, — a new dish for some of us, tasting like a cross between Virginia mountain mutton and our Pennsylvania red deer.

But our stay in Lievely ended. The propeller got up steam, and, taking our bark and the Danish brig Marianne in tow, steamed out of the harbor. All the inhabitants of the town were on the shore to see the last of us. Our visit had been as memorable an incident to them as to ourselves. Where ten dollars is a large marriage dower, Jack's liberality of expenditure seemed absolutely royal. There were moistened eyes among them, for they are essentially kind-hearted ; and even the roar of our cannon, in answer to the Danish salute, though it resounded splendidly among the hills, was scarcely heeded, as they stood, with folded arms, watching us disappear in the distance. We carried Mr. Olrik quite out to sea before we bade him good-by ; and it was not until the next morning that the Marianne cast loose.

"We reached home without any incident worthy of note, except that the Esquimaux dogs we had on board did nothing but howl during the whole voyage, — an amiable peculiarity, which still characterizes the single specimen of which I am at present the happy possessor. There he goes — I hear him now."

The return of Hartstein with the survivors of Kane's expedition closes the record of the search for Sir John Franklin.

Never was there such a disastrous state of things in the Arctic regions : six ships left in the ice ! The Investigator at Mercy Bay, the Resolute and Intrepid at Melville Island, the Assistance and Pioneer in Wellington Channel, and the Advance in Smith's Sound, to be added to the Erebus and Terror, which we have reason to believe had been left years before somewhere in the strait of James Ross. The Arctic archipelago was studded with abandoned ships!

None could have imagined that any of these gallant ships would ever carry sail again; or that we might not truly say of each of them, in the words of Dr. Kane, "The ice is round her still."

But of one of these vessels there is a further story to tell; and, as it recounts a kindly interchange of courtesies between the two nations which vied with each other in heroic, though fruitless efforts, to rescue the missing navigators, it will form a pleasant finale to our narrative.

In the month of September, 1855, the whaler George Henry, Captain Buddington, of New London, Connecticut, was drifting along, beset by the ice, in Baffin's Bay, when one morning the captain, looking through his glass, saw a large ship some fifteen or twenty miles distant, apparently working her way towards him. Day after day, while helplessly imprisoned in the pack, he watched her coming nearer and nearer. On the seventh day, the mate, Mr. Quail, and three men, were sent to find out what she was.

After a hard day's journey over the ice,—jumping from piece to piece, and pushing themselves along on isolated cakes,—they were near enough to see that she was lying on her larboard side, firmly imbedded in the ice. They shouted lustily, as soon as they got within hailing distance; but there was no answer. Not a soul was to be seen. For one moment, as they came alongside, the men faltered, with a superstitious feeling, and hesitated to go on board. A moment after, they had climbed over the broken ice, and stood on deck. Everything was stowed away in order — spars hauled up and lashed to one side, boats piled together, hatches calked down. Over the helm, in letters of brass, was inscribed the motto "England expects every man to do his duty." But there was no man to heed the warning.

The whalemen broke open the companion-way, and descended into the cabin. All was silence and darkness. Groping their way to the table, they found matches and candles, and struck a light. There were decanters and glasses on the table, chairs and lounges standing around, books scattered about — everything just as it had been last used. Looking curiously from one thing to another, wondering what this deserted ship might be, at last they came upon the log-book. It was endorsed, "Bark Resolute, 1st September, 1853, to April, 1854." One entry was as follows: "H. M. S. Resolute, 17th January, 1854, nine A. M. — Mustered by divisions. People taking exercise on deck. Five P. M. — Mercury frozen."

This told the story. It was Captain Kellett's ship, the Resolute, which had broken away from her icy prison, and had thus fallen into the hands of our Yankee whalemen.

While the men were making these discoveries, night came on, and a gale arose. So hard did it blow that they were compelled to remain on board, and for two days these four were the whole crew of the Resolute. It was not till 19th September that they returned to their own ship, and made their report.

All these ten days, since Captain Buddington had first seen her, the vessels had been nearing each other. On the 19th he boarded her himself, and found that in her hold, on the larboard side, was a good deal of ice. Her tanks had burst, from the extreme cold; and she was full of water, nearly to her lower deck. Everything that could move from its place had moved. Everything between decks was wet; everything that would mould was mouldy. "A sort of perspiration" had settled on the beams and ceilings. The whalemen made a fire in Kellett's stove, and soon started a sort of shower from the vapor with which it filled the air. The Resolute had, however, four fine force-pumps. For three days the captain and six men worked fourteen hours a day on one of these, and had the pleasure of finding that they freed her of water, — that she was tight still. They cut away upon the masses of ice; and on the 23d of September, in the evening, she freed herself from her encumbrances, and took an even keel. This was off the west shore of Baffin's Bay, in latitude 67°. On the shortest tack, she was twelve hundred miles from where Kellett left her.

There was work enough still to be done. The rudder was to be shipped, the rigging to be made taut, sail to be set; — and it proved, by the way, that the sail on the yards was much of it still serviceable, while a suit of new linen sails below were greatly injured by moisture. In a week more, she was ready to make sail. The pack of ice still drifted with both ships; but, on the 21st October, after a long north-west gale, the Resolute was free.

Capt. Buddington had resolved to bring her home. He had picked ten men from the George Henry, and with a rough tracing of the American coast, drawn on a sheet of foolscap, with his lever watch and a quadrant for his instruments, he squared off for New London. A rough, hard passage they had of it. The ship's ballast was gone, by the bursting of the tanks; she was top-heavy and undermanned. He spoke a British whaling-bark, and by her sent to Captain Kellett his epaulets, and to his own owners news that he was coming. They had heavy gales and head winds, and were driven as far down as the Bermudas. The water left in the ship's tanks was brackish, and it needed all the seasoning which the ship's chocolate would give to make it drinkable. "For sixty hours at a time," says the captain, "I frequently had no sleep ;" but his perseverance was crowned with success, at last, and, on the night of the 23d of December, he made the light off the harbor from which he sailed, and on Sunday morning, the 24th, dropped anchor in the Thames, opposite New London, and ran up the British ensign on the shorn masts of the Resolute.

Her subsequent history is fresh in the minds of our readers. The British government generously released all their claim in favor of the sailors. Thereupon, Congress resolved that the vessel should be purchased and restored as a present to her majesty from the American people. This design was fully carried out. The Resolute was taken to the dry-dock in Brooklyn, and there put in complete order. Everything on board — even the smallest article — was replaced as nearly as possible in its original position ; and, at length, having been manned and officered from the United States navy, and placed under the command of Captain Hartstein, the Resolute, stanch and sound again, from stem to stern, "with sails all set and streamers all afloat," once more shaped her course for England.

On the 12th of December, 1856, after a boisterous passage, she anchored at Spithead, with the United States and British ensigns flying at the peak. "Notwithstanding the furious gale which was then raging," says Captain Hartstein, in his official report, "we were immediately boarded by Captain Peal, of her Britannic Majesty's frigate Shannon, who cordially offered to us every civility and attention. In a few moments afterwards, a steamer arrived from Vice-Admiral Sir George

Seymour (commanding officer of the station), with a tender of services, and congratulations upon our safe arrival. Proceeding to Portsmouth next morning (which I did in a government steamer provided me for that purpose), I visited the United States Consulate, and was there waited upon by Sir Thomas Maitland, who had become commanding officer of the naval station in the absence of the admiral, Sir George Seymour, and received from him a most cordial welcome, with proffers of every possible service, by express instruction from the Admiralty. Accommodations were prepared for us at the first hotel, and orders for a bountiful supply of provisions to be sent on board the Resolute ; also a *carte blanche* for the railroad to London for myself and the officers of the Resolute. In fact, nothing could exceed the kindness and courtesy with which we were treated by Captain Sir Thomas Maitland, who seemed unwilling that any means of adding to his hearty expressions of welcome should pass unexhausted. That morning's post brought me a communication from Sir Charles Wood, first lord of the Admiralty (which I herewith enclose), whose expressions of kindly feeling I beg may be particularly noticed. At noon of the day after our arrival, a royal salute was fired from the Victory (flag-ship), from the fortifications, and from the Shannon, at Spithead."

The Queen having expressed a wish to visit the Resolute, and a desire that the vessel might be taken to Cowes, near her majesty's private palace, the ship was towed thither by the government steamer, escorted by two other steamers, and the steam-frigate Retribution.

Meanwhile, the necessary diplomatic formalities had been exchanged between the American minister and Lord Clarendon.

Of the Queen's visit to the Resolute, which took

place on the 16th of December, we quote the following description from the *London Times:*

"The Queen, accompanied by Prince Albert, the Prince of Wales, the Princess Royal, and the Princess Alice, left Osborne at a quarter past ten o'clock, and drove to the ship in an open carriage, drawn by four gray ponies. Her majesty was attended by a distinguished suite. The Resolute, dressed in her colors, was lashed alongside of the royal embarkation place at Trinity Wharf. The English and American flags were flying at the peak; and, as soon as the Queen set her foot on the deck, the royal standard was hoisted at the main. The Retribution fired a salute, the boats' crews 'tossed' their oars, and the ship's company, standing on the rail, received her majesty with three rounds of cheers. Captain Hartstein received the royal party at the gangway, and the officers, in full uniform, were grouped on either side. All were presented to the Queen by Captain Hartstein, who then addressed her majesty in the following words:

"'Allow me to welcome your majesty on board the Resolute, and, in obedience to the will of my countrymen and the President of the United States, to restore her to you, not only as an evidence of a friendly feeling to your sovereignty, but as a token of love, admiration, and respect, to your majesty personally.'

"The Queen seemed touched by the manly simplicity of this frank and sailor-like address, and replied, with a gracious smile, 'I thank you, sir.' The royal family then went over the ship, and examined her with manifest interest."

After the withdrawal of the royal party, there was an elegant *déjeuner* in the ward-room, at which, among other toasts, was given, "The future success of the Resolute, and may she be again employed in prosecuting the search for Sir John Franklin and his comrades." This sentiment evoked cordial applause.

On the afternoon of the same day, "I received," says Captain Hartstein, "a note, enclosing a check for one hundred pounds, with a request from her majesty that it should be distributed among the crew; which I accepted in their behalf.

"On the morning of December 17th, the Resolute was towed up to the harbor of Portsmouth, escorted by the steam-frigate Retribution; and, on arriving at her anchorage, was received by another royal salute, and with such an outburst of popular feeling as was never known before."

The British government and people were unremitting in their attentions to Captain Hartstein and his officers, during their stay in England. Three splendid Christmas cakes were forwarded by Lady Franklin to Portsmouth, to be presented to the American officers and crew. A passage to the United States, in the British steamer Retribution, was tendered them. This, however, it was thought best to decline. On the 30th of December, 1856, the American flag was hauled down on board the Resolute, when it was saluted by the Victory with twenty-one guns. The union-jack was then hoisted, and the ship was given up to the authorities. The next day the American officers and crew left England, on their return to the United States.

By late English papers, we learn that the Queen has commissioned Mr. William Simpson, the artist of the Crimean war, to paint for her private gallery a picture of the "Reception" on board the Resolute — a very graceful memorial of a most interesting act of international courtesy.

While we write, the expediency of sending out still other expeditions is discussed in England. "There is now little or no doubt," says the *United Service Journal,* "as to the intention of the government to despatch final expeditions in search of further traces of Sir John Franklin. They will probably consist of three parties: one overland, another by the way of Behring's Strait, and a third by the way of Davis's Strait and Baffin's Bay."

Here terminates our history of Arctic adventure and exploration. The results hitherto obtained are altogether different from those of a pecuniary nature. Through their means, the astronomer, the geographer, the physicist, the naturalist, the chemist, and science at large, have acquired facts which could have been gained in no other way. The cost has been great; the cost of the expeditions alone in search of Franklin is estimated at upwards of four millions of dollars: but the consequences will be permanent; and the record of enterprising hardihood, physical endurance, and steady perseverance, displayed in overcoming elements the most adverse, will long remain among the worthiest memorials of human effort.

www.ingramcontent.com/pod-product-compliance
Lightning Source LLC
LaVergne TN
LVHW020912110826
845150LV00004B/653